Th   g study succ   nges the traditional
tend   gard Charlotte Bro   aving existed in a
historica vacu m, by setting her work firmly within the context
of Victorian psychological debate. Based on extensive local
research, using texts ranging from local newspaper copy to the
medical tomes in the Reverend Patrick Brontë's library, Sally
Shuttleworth explores the interpenetration of economic, social
and psychological discourse in the early and mid nineteenth
century, and traces the ways in which Charlotte Brontë's texts
operate in relation to this complex, often contradictory, discursive
framework. Shuttleworth offers a detailed analysis of Brontë's
fiction, informed by a new understanding of Victorian constructions of sexuality and insanity, and the operations of medical and
psychological surveillance.

CAMBRIDGE STUDIES IN NINETEENTH-CENTURY
LITERATURE AND CULTURE 7

CHARLOTTE BRONTË
AND VICTORIAN
PSYCHOLOGY

CAMBRIDGE STUDIES IN NINETEENTH-CENTURY
LITERATURE AND CULTURE

General editors
Gillian Beer, *University of Cambridge*
Catherine Gallagher, *University of California, Berkeley*

Editorial board
Isobel Armstrong, *Birkbeck College, London*
Terry Eagleton, *University of Oxford*
Leonore Davidoff, *University of Essex*
D. A. Miller, *Harvard University*
J. Hillis Miller, *University of California, Irvine*
Mary Poovey, *The Johns Hopkins University*
Elaine Showalter, *Princeton University*

Nineteenth-century British literature and culture have been rich fields for interdisciplinary studies. Since the turn of the twentieth century, scholars and critics have tracked the intersections and tensions between Victorian literature and the visual arts, politics, social organization, economic life, technical innovations, scientific thought – in short, culture in its broadest sense. In recent years, theoretical challenges and historiographical shifts have unsettled the assumptions of previous scholarly syntheses and called into question the terms of older debates. Whereas the tendency in much past literary critical interpretation was to use the metaphor of culture as 'background', feminist, Foucauldian, and other analyses have employed more dynamic models that raise questions of power and of circulation. Such developments have re-animated the field.

This new series aims to accomodate and promote the most interesting work being undertaken on the frontiers of the fields of nineteenth-century literary studies: work which intersects fruitfully with other fields of study such as history, or literary theory, or the history of science. Comparative as well as interdisciplinary approaches are welcomed.

A complete list of titles published will be found at the end of the book.

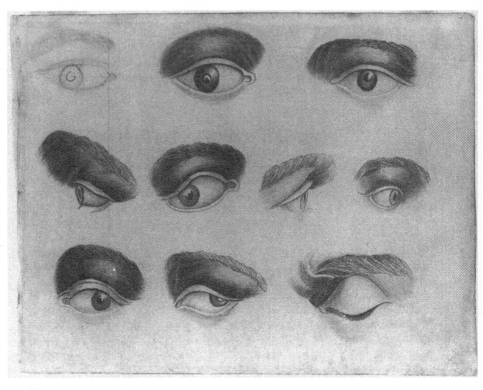

Charlotte Brontë, Study of eyes, 1831. Reproduced from *The art of the Brontës*, edited by Christine Alexander and Jane Sellars (Cambridge University Press, 1995), catalogue no. 42.

CHARLOTTE BRONTË AND VICTORIAN PSYCHOLOGY

SALLY SHUTTLEWORTH

Professor of Modern Literature,
University of Sheffield

CAMBRIDGE
UNIVERSITY PRESS

PUBLISHED BY THE PRESS SYNDICATE OF THE UNIVERSITY OF CAMBRIDGE
The Pitt Building, Trumpington Street, Cambridge, United Kingdom

CAMBRIDGE UNIVERSITY PRESS
The Edinburgh Building, Cambridge CB2 2RU, UK
40 West 20th Street, New York NY 10011–4211, USA
477 Williamstown Road, Port Melbourne, VIC 3207, Australia
Ruiz de Alarcón 13, 28014 Madrid, Spain
Dock House, The Waterfront, Cape Town 8001, South Africa

http://www.cambridge.org

First published 1996
First paperback edition 2004

A catalogue record for this book is available from the British Library

Library of Congress cataloguing in publication data
Shuttleworth, Sally, 1952–
Charlotte Bronte and Victorian psychology / Sally Shuttleworth.
p.   cm. – (Cambridge studies in nineteenth-century literature and culture: 7)
Includes bibliographical references and index.
ISBN 0 521 55149 8 (hardback)
1. Brontë, Charlotte, 1816–1855 – Knowledge – Psychology. 2. Psychology – Great Britain –
History – 19th century. 3. English fiction – Psychological aspects. 4. Psychology in literature.
5. Self in literature. 6. Sex in literature. I. Title. II. Series.
PR4169.S48 1996
823'.8 – dc20
95-4681
CIP

ISBN 0 521 55149 8 hardback
ISBN 0 521 61717 0 paperback

Transferred to digital printing 2004

For John,
Becky and Kate

Contents

Acknowledgements

The first draft of this book was completed during the year I spent as a fellow of the Society for the Humanities, Cornell University. I am grateful to Jonathan Culler and his administrative assistants, Mary Ahl and Aggie Sirrine, for all they did to create such an intellectually stimulating and supportive environment in which to work. The book was subsequently completed with the help of research leave from the School of English, University of Leeds; I would like to thank my colleagues there for all their support.

I am grateful to the staff of all the libraries I have worked in whilst pursuing this research; in particular the library staff of the Brontë Parsonage Museum, the Keighley Public Library, and the Leeds Library. Philip Worsley of Leeds University gave me invaluable computer help when it looked as if my computer discs would never make the transition to the modern world. I am also indebted to my editor, Josie Dixon, for her firm guidance, and to Linda Bree and Polly Richards for their editorial advice and aid.

My work on this project has benefited immeasurably from discussions with friends and colleagues, and from the excellent critical guidance I have received on earlier drafts. I would particularly like to mention here: Gillian Beer, Kate Flint, Mary Jacobus, Vivien Jones, Evelyn Fox Keller, George Levine, Roy Porter, Rick Rylance, Shirley Samuels, Mark Seltzer, Helen Small.

This book would not have been possible without all the levels of support offered over the years by my parents. I am also indebted to my daughters, Rebecca and Katherine, whose arrival undoubtedly helped to delay the appearance of the book, but whose gleeful, demanding presences have helped to place the whole process in due proportion. Finally, my deep gratitude is owed to John Christie for his unerring combination of intellectual rigour and emotional support.

Parts of this book, in earlier versions, have appeared in the following collections: George Levine, ed. *One Culture: Essays in Science and Literature* (Madison: The University of Wisconsin Press, 1987), reprinted with the permission of the publisher; John Christie and Sally Shuttleworth, eds. *Nature Transfigured: Science and Literature, 1700–1900* (Manchester University Press, 1989); Mary Jacobus, Evelyn Fox Keller and Sally Shuttleworth eds. *Body/Politics: Women and the Discourses of Science* (New York and London: Routledge, 1990), reprinted with the permission of the publisher.

Introduction

The language and categories used to articulate the self within each historical era offer a definitive key to cultural interpretation. From the ways a society draws the boundaries of selfhood, one can trace the dominant assumptions governing understanding of both social and psychological order. In each era there are significant shifts in these boundaries, altering, for example, the perceived relationship between visible form and inner quality, social formation and individual subjectivity, or the lines demarcating the normal from the pathological. Changes in the conventions governing the representation of character in the novel highlight, and contribute to, these transformations. Thus generalized references to physical appearance in the eighteenth-century novel are supplanted in the nineteenth by detailed delineations of external features; and the abstract qualities of mind attributed to earlier characters – the 'true elegance of mind' possessed by Austen's heroines – give way to descriptions of physiological surges of energy within the Victorian protagonist. Critics working on the modernist novel have been quick to point out the very direct relationship which exists between formal innovation, and early twentieth-century theories of psychology. With reference to the Victorian novel, however, there has been, correspondingly, comparative silence – an eloquent testimony, perhaps, to the power of the realist illusion.

Nowhere has this tendency to consider novels in isolation from contemporary psychological discourse been more evident than in the domain of Brontë scholarship. The traditional critical image of Charlotte Brontë is that of an intuitive genius who seems to belong more to the Freudian than to the Victorian era.[1] In this double displacement of history, both Brontë and Freud are placed in a vacuum: Brontë is given powers of prophecy, and Freud is endowed with supreme originating authority – the preceding Victorian debates on female hysteria, the unconscious, and psychological drives are miraculously erased. Recent innovative feminist scholarship has done little to remedy this situation, overturning accepted interpretations of Brontë's novels but keeping their component elements in place. Sandra Gilbert and Susan Gubar's celebration of Brontë's 'madwoman', for example, remains resolutely ahistorical, failing to take into account the ways in which Victorian psychiatric discussions of female sexuality had defined the framework both of normality and rebellion.[2] The aim of this study is to place Brontë's work firmly within the context of Victorian psychological discourse. Far from being a throwback to the Romantic era, or an anticipation of the modern, Brontë's fiction actively encodes the language and preoccupations of mid-nineteenth-century social, psychological and economic thought.

The term 'psychological discourse' is here being used in its widest sense: it includes not only the texts of medical psychiatry, and domestic manuals, but also the diverse range of formulations of individual subjectivity and agency to be found in contemporary social and economic discussion, from newspaper copy to popular self-help books. None of these domains of discourse can be considered in isolation: similar language and assumptions occur in very different arenas. Discussions of the bodily economy, for example, employ the same terms as economic debates on the circulation of energy in the body politic. In the more complex realm of metaphoric and metonymic transference, associative nexi of ideas shift between subject areas: descriptions of the city draw on the rhetoric of the female body, and analyses of political revolution mobilize the psychiatric language of insanity. Conversely, images of the industrial city and of disruptive political rebellion inform medical discussions of female physiological and psychological health. Causal links, or explicit connections are rarely drawn; meaning tends to inhere rather in the subtle processes of association operating on the margins of discourse.

For the Victorian novel which functioned metonymically to domesticate the social, using individual figures to explore wider social processes, this mechanism of associative transference is crucial. Brontë's novels prove no exception. Critical tradition, in ignoring this linguistic dimension, has tended to create a very depoliticized Brontë. While older studies applauded her grasp of the invariant principles of human psychology, more recent interpretations have lamented the fact that her focus on individual interaction obscures the workings of class and gender power.[3] Jane Eyre's comparison between herself and revolutionary workers thus becomes an isolated outburst, and the structure of *Shirley* an unwieldy aberration. If attention is focused on the linguistic texture of the novels, however, a very different picture begins to emerge: the language of social and political debate actively informs the depiction of the individual psyche.

On publication, *Jane Eyre* was greeted by reviewers as a wonderfully 'natural' and 'real' depiction of emotional life. Its appeal, I would suggest, was less that it managed to capture as never before the inner workings of the mind, than that it incorporated into the novel contemporary psychological discourse, thus offering the dual appeal of familiarity and originality, and establishing a reassuring sensation of realism. With the depiction of a heroine's psyche that follows the rise and fall of physiological energies, and of a romantic engagement which is less of a harmonious union between souls than a power struggle that centres on the ability of each partner to read, unseen, the hidden secrets of the other, we are clearly in new novelistic territory. Such terrain was to be found, however, in the context of medical and economic debates, and in the fields of psychiatry and the popular sciences of physiognomy and phrenology. As Foucault has argued, the nineteenth century witnessed the emergence of a new economy of individual and social life, centered on the regulation of the forces of the body and controlled through surveillance.[4] A new interiorized notion of selfhood arose and, concomitantly, new techniques of power designed to penetrate the inner secrets of this hidden domain.[5] Psychiatry and phrenology emerged as sciences, dedicated to decoding the external signs of the body in order to reveal the concealed inner play of forces which constitute individual subjectivity. Brontë's novels operate within this paradigm. When Rochester asks Jane to read his character from his brow, or Crimsworth scathingly notes the horrendous propensities indicated by the cranial configuration of one of his pupils, we are not being introduced to mere esoteric details, tangential to the novel as a whole. Such references are not epiphenomenal, but are rather constitutive elements of the social, psychological and economic framework which structures the novels.

Brontë's interest in phrenology has drawn the attention of several critics in recent years, but in conflating the science with physiognomy, and thus reducing its doctrines to a mere interest in external appearance, they have failed to take account of its social functions, and thus emptied the terms of social and political relevance.[6] In tracing the impact of phrenology on Brontë's fiction, this study will explore its social role, as the basis of a popular self-help movement, and its position within the wider framework of Victorian psychological debate. The discourse of psychology in mid-nineteenth-century Britain did not function as a monumental, invariant structure. Heated arguments arose concerning the conflicting claims of competing models, but perhaps the most significant conflicts, which were internal to the theories themselves, were never explicitly articulated, obscured from view by their very centrality. Contradictions within the ideologies governing the expansion of industrial capitalism were focused and played out in the domain of psychology, pre-eminently in the sphere of gender.

While always crucial to the ideological formation of society, theories of gender division took on in the nineteenth century a near unprecedented power and importance, metonymically projecting and condensing the contradictions of wider social debate. The ideological separation of public and private, work and home, which underpinned the rise of the Victorian middle classes, was predicated upon a fundamental division between male and female spheres. Furthermore, economic ideologies of the free, independent agent, the self-controlled actor in charge of his own destiny, were supported and sustained by theories of gender division which contrasted male self-control with female subjection to the forces of the body. Medical science presided over this increasingly rigid demarcation of gender roles, lending and indeed deriving prestige and authority from its involvement. The growing body of literature on the powers of self-control was complemented by the rise of gynaecological science which emphasized the uncontrollable processes of the uterine economy. Psychiatry, or as it was then known, mental science, was another emergent area of knowledge which similarly focused on female hysteria and insanity and the unstable processes of the female body. This study will explore the diverse ways in which these two conflicting models of selfhood, of mental control and physiological instability, are played out in Brontë's fiction, heightening and intensifying the erotic struggles for control which centre on the issue of legibility, on decoding and penetrating the secrets of the other.

While placing a very unFoucauldian emphasis on gender and economic power, this work is nonetheless indebted to the ideas and methodology of Foucault, particularly in the sphere of discourse theory. In considering the relationship between Brontë's fiction and Victorian psychological discourse, I have tried, however, to move beyond the notion of a general textual economy, operating largely within disciplinary boundaries, in order to construct a more precise, localized picture of how contemporary theories percolated through to the people of Haworth. As far as records permit, I have attempted to build up an in-depth picture of reading patterns in the parsonage and surrounding community, examining library holdings, periodicals and lectures delivered on the local circuit. I have also looked at the crucial role of the local press in transmitting contemporary notions of psychology, whether in the graphic sexual details often included in trial reports, or in the assumptions encoded in advertisements for medical remedies. My aim has been to break down the hierarchical model which envisages 'official' scientific pronouncements being gradually diluted as they are passed down the cultural chain and to substitute in its place a more dynamic, interactive model which takes into account the social and economic conditions underlying the diverse formulations and specific appropriations of psychological concepts.

The limitations of ahistoricist approaches to Brontë's works are not to be countered by generalized appeals to an overarching, undifferentiated cultural domain. Combining close textual analysis with historical specificity of reference, this study also extends investigation of the textual economy beyond narrow disciplinary boundaries, pursuing it in all the dimensions of its relevance, from newspaper copy and fiction to medical tracts. Brontë's own writing formed an integral part of this wider textual economy. In tracing the relationship between her work and contemporary psychological discourse I will not be charting a process of passive absorption, but rather investigating the ways in which Brontë, as a female writer, both assimilated and challenged Victorian constructs, interrogating received notions, exploring their contradictions, and breaking the bounds of contemporary discourse in the complex structures of her fiction.

The work of Charlotte Brontë clearly has much in common with that of her sisters. All three explore the experience of social marginality, and the constraining effects of gender ideology. Phrenology, and the culture of self-control are foregrounded in Anne's work, while *Wuthering Heights*, like *Jane Eyre*, charts the histories of its protagonists through an economics of energy flow. Heathcliff, that figure who so appalled Charlotte, is nonetheless an alternate embodiment of Bertha: an imaginative projection of what may happen if the energy of the oppressed is harnessed and controlled in the service of aggressive individualism and upward mobility. As Charlotte's negative responses to both *Wuthering Heights* and *The Tenant of Wildfell Hall* suggest, however, there were also very strong differences between her work and that of both sisters. More timid than Emily in some ways, more radical in others, she was also more openly confrontational, as her devotion to the social satire of Thackeray suggests. Rather than treat the writings of the Brontës as different manifestations of one local voice, I have chosen to focus on Charlotte's fiction and to trace through, from the early writings to *Villette*, the different forms of her involvement with contemporary psychological thought.

The first section of this book is a study of aspects of Victorian psychology, chosen initially and framed with reference to their significance for Brontë's work, but possessing relevance for all mid-Victorian writing. While no one writer brings together these psychological strands in quite the same way, or with quite the same intensity, they all play a significant role in the evolution of Victorian fiction. In Dickens, for example, one finds a similar economics of energy, and concern with the fragmentation of the mind, while George Eliot develops Brontë's preoccupation with surveillance and the interiorized space of selfhood. Medical theories of nervous disorder and the workings of the female body feed through, in various forms, into virtually all the fiction of the period.

What renders Brontë's work so significant, with regard to Victorian psychology, is the way in which she so powerfully condenses and explores in her work the dominant paradigms of her era. Writing as a woman, with few social prospects, and outside any socially supportive intellectual milieu, she is placed very differently to either Dickens or Eliot: her very marginality serves to heighten and expose the contradictory formulations of contemporary culture. Eagerly subscribing to ideals of self-help, and inborn talent, she is then paralysed by her sense of social impossibility, and by cultural and medical constructions of female instability and powerlessness. Her fierce desire for social justice is also at odds with her familial allegiance to a Conservative social stance. The resulting fiction draws its imaginative energy from the ways in which it wrestles with cultural contradiction, operating always within the terms of Victorian thought, but giving rise, ultimately, to new ways of expressing and conceptualizing the embodied self.

PART ONE

Psychological discourse in the Victorian era

CHAPTER I

The art of surveillance

In a crucial scene in *Villette*, Dr John directs onto Lucy Snowe the interpretative gaze of medical science: 'I look on you now from a professional point of view, and I read, perhaps, all you would conceal – in your eye, which is curiously vivid and restless; in your cheek, which the blood has forsaken; in your hand, which you cannot steady'.[1] He speaks with unshakeable authority, calmly confident of his professional ability to reveal the hidden meaning of Lucy's inner state. As text, Lucy opens herself up to his readerly skills. Every outer sign becomes an active invitation to his interpretative penetration. The exchange presents a literal enactment of the metaphorical structure of western science: male science here unveils female nature, piercing through her outer layers to reveal her hidden secrets.[2] Within this wider historical framework, however, the scene possesses a more immediate specificity, drawing attention to the new theories of subjectivity which arose in the nineteenth century. Selfhood no longer resided in the open texture of social act and exchange, but within a new interior space, hidden from view, inaccessible even to the subject's own consciousness. Nor was inner self necessarily legible from or immanent within outer sign. The book of the self was not laid open for all to read; specific knowledge and skills were required to decode its language.

This interiorized model of selfhood laid the foundations for later Freudian theory which still dominates our understanding of subjectivity. Its historical emergence was marked by the concomitant rise of medical psychiatry as a science, but as today its ramifications were not restricted to the specific interactions of doctor and patient, but profoundly altered cultural understanding of the self, and the rules of social interaction. In Brontë's fiction the power dynamics implicit in the exchange between Dr John and Lucy form part of a wider pattern of interpretative struggle. William Crimsworth in *The Professor*

9

fearlessly presents his face before his tyrannical brother, feeling 'as secure against his scrutiny as if I had had on a casque with the visor down'.[3] On a less overtly conflictual plane, Jane Eyre's erotic struggles with Rochester are initiated by her phrenological reading of his brow, a scene which is then countered when Rochester, disguised as a female gypsy, reads Jane's forehead. St John later takes up the struggle, attempting 'to read my face, as if its features and lines were characters on a page' and examining Jane 'like a physician watching with the eye of science an expected and fully-understood crisis in a patient's malady'.[4] In each case power resides with the figure who can unveil the hidden secrets of the other whilst preserving the self unread. Supreme interpretative authority, however, as the latter image of St John suggests, is vested symbolically in the figure of the doctor who enshrines his judgments within the hallowed domain of science.

As a literary character, the doctor takes on new prominence in the Victorian era, playing a crucial role in later sensation fiction, usually hovering in the wings, waiting to diagnose the incipient signs of latent insanity or mental disorder.[5] Although Brontë waited until her final novel to offer her first fully fledged portrait of a doctor, her preoccupation with medical knowledge and power is evinced in her earliest writing. In one of the first known pieces of early writing, Charlotte chose as one of her heroes, alongside the Duke of Wellington, the celebrated physiologist, Abernethy. Anne and Branwell further endorsed the prestige of medical science by including a famous physician in their three choices.[6] In addition, the infamous Dr Hume Badry, noted for his devotion to the savage art of dissection, makes frequent appearances within the corpus of early writing, figuring as an inhumane repository of scientific authority who displays 'as much feeling as a stone'.[7] While less of a macabre figure than Dr Hume Badry, the golden-haired Dr John is nonetheless a disturbing presence, threatening mental, rather than physical integrity. Lucy fears the dissecting power of his gaze: 'my identity would have been grasped between his never tyrannous, but always powerful hands' (p. 416). For all its expressions of humane concern, Victorian psychiatry still operated a system of control which was all the more powerful for its covert form.

The authority with which Dr John is endowed held a peculiar significance for Brontë. His name, John Graham, is drawn from the text which held the place of secular Bible in the Brontë household:

Thomas John Graham's *Domestic Medicine*.[8] Virtually every page of this work has been annotated by the Reverend Brontë, offering a moving testimonial to the rigid regimen which governed the life of the household. Patrick records not only his family's physical ailments and the remedies employed, but also his preoccupation with the threat of nervous disease and insanity. Mind and body were subject to minute scrutiny and medical intervention. Patrick threw his whole weight of patriarchal endorsement behind the authority of the medical word. As Foucault has argued, the Victorian preoccupation with control did not emanate initially from a desire to discipline the working classes; the Victorian middle classes were obsessed with the health and regulation of their own minds and bodies.[9] Brontë's novels work within and against this framework of obsession, exploring the implications of this rhetoric of control in all its physical, psychological and social aspects, looking in particular at its effects in the domain of gender.

On the surface, Brontë does not seem an obvious candidate for an interdiscplinary study of Victorian psychological discourse. Unlike her contemporaries, George Eliot or Wilkie Collins, for example, she did not explicitly record her indebtedness to contemporary scientific theory.[10] Nor, as far as we know, did she commence writing her fiction armed by extensive reading in scientific and medical texts. Yet, her novels are permeated by the psychological language and theory of the time, the texture of her fiction belying the myths of her social and cultural isolation. For anyone interested in the inter-penetration of literature and science, Brontë's work offers an interesting challenge: to trace the interconnections with wider psychological discourse one must move outside the mainstream of intellectual culture to plot the subtle pathways of exchange and appropriation which operate within the wider textual economy.

Brontë's fiction shared with Victorian psychiatry a preoccupation with the realms of excess: with the workings of insanity and nervous disease, and the unstable constitution of female identity. Threats to incarcerate characters in lunatic asylums abound in the early writings, matched by frequent displays of insane behaviour, which often arise, significantly, when the boundaries of gender have been destabilized. Charles Wellesley, narrator of the 1834 story, 'The Spell, An Extravaganza' asks us to imagine the early writings' dashing hero, Zamorna, 'a crowned maniac, dying dethroned, forsaken, desolate, in the shrieking gloom of a mad-house'.[11] Brontë's interest in the borderlands of sanity is not confined to her early work but is manifest throughout her fiction: Crimsworth suffers from hypochondria, Caroline Helstone from brain fever, and Lucy Snowe from 'constitutional nervousness'. *Jane Eyre* focuses on two of the classic images of excess in Victorian psychiatry: the passionate child and the hysterical, insane woman. The novel itself contributed powerfully to this discourse; following the publication of *Jane Eyre*, Bertha, the 'mad wife', quickly achieved the mythic status of a cultural symbol, influencing not only subsequent fiction but also the language of medical psychiatry.[12]

It is not only in the realm of excess, however, that Brontë's fiction engages with contemporary psychological discourse; the same rhetoric of regulation and control, and of deciphering the outer signs of concealed inner states, ran throughout medical discussions of physiological and psychological health. Indeed nineteenth-century physiology and psychiatry broke down earlier absolute divides between the normal and pathological, insisting that disease arose merely from an excess or deficiency of elements integral to normal functioning.[13] Excessive activity in one sphere might engender physical or mental breakdown; valuable qualities might turn into agents of pollution if developed to too high a degree. Wealth might turn to waste, if not properly regulated within the economy of the whole. Victorian social economists and medical men shared the same concerns, and employed the same models of analysis; whether in the social or the individual body they sought to bring health through organized management of resources. In Brontë's fiction one can see the same language and categories at work. Health and disease, sanity and disorder, shade imperceptibly into one another; the rhetoric of regulation and control, and the power of decipherment, govern the representation of both social and psychological action.

To trace the operations of psychological discourse in mid-Victorian England one must look beyond the narrow sphere of medical psychiatry to the wider textual economy of which it forms a part. Increasing medical interest in sleep, dreams and hallucinations, for example, was paralleled in the stories carried, in the 1830s and 40s, on the pages of *Blackwood's*, the young Brontës' favourite reading material. Literary and medical texts played a crucial role in mid-nineteenth-century society, offering an arena where cultural meanings could be negotiated, and anxieties expressed and explored. In the constant cycle of textual exchange, social images were endorsed and modified, strengthened by repetition, and subtly transformed to suggest new meanings. Psychiatry was just beginning to emerge as a science, but had not yet covered over its links with literature, or obscured its ideological assumptions under a cloak of specialized language.

Many of these early psychological works drew repeatedly on literary texts for their 'evidence' (Shakespeare was a firm favourite here) or offered long narrative accounts of supposedly true stories. In a cultural equivalent of the monetary economy, psychological stories were endlessly recirculated between writers, their scientific validity, or credit-worthiness, deriving entirely from their previous appearance in a scientific context, and from the narrative coherence of their presentation. Like fictions, they had to convince their readers who formed the sole court of appeal. Entry into this circle of exchange was determined by their conformity to recognized social archetypes, or to the more finely tuned register of social plausibility. No psychological account with any pretensions to scientific status was complete, it seems, without a repetition of the saga of Nicholai of Berlin who, whilst being assailed by horrific hallucinations, managed to retain his sense of their delusory quality, and thus preserved his sanity. The story operates as a perfect moral and scientific exemplum of the social doctrines of self-control.[14]

Where women were concerned, textual borrowings were more likely to be used to demonstrate their animal, or uncontrolled nature. Thus Bucknill and Tuke, in their standard textbook, *A Manual of Psychological Medicine*, supported their explanation of the phenomenon of moral insanity by reference to an account of a 'snake woman' originally published in the *American Journal of Insanity* (October, 1846). The girl, they suggest, possessed intelligence but was destitute of moral feelings. She is granted 'nothing human...but her form', but even this tangential claim to membership of the human race is then severely qualified: 'She is stated to have resembled a serpent in her movements. Her skin was cold – circulation very slow; her skin was also "spotted like a common snake".'[15] With this vision of Eve and Satan rolled into one, the oldest cultural and literary archetype of the western world is sanctified by the imprimatur of science, revealing all too clearly some of the social anxieties which underpinned the rise of psychiatry in the Victorian era. Although the example might appear ludicrous in our eyes, it nonetheless formed part of the ideological process whereby the gender divisions of the bourgeois economy were justified and sustained by the newly emerging sciences of psychiatry and anthropology which offered 'scientific' proof that women were closer to the animal chain than men.[16]

Although sceptical of many of psychiatry's claims, Brontë was not immune to the charms of its unanswerable authority. Responding to criticism of her representation of Bertha Mason, Brontë defends her creation on the grounds of medical 'truth': 'I agree . . . that the character is shocking, but I know that it is but too natural. There is a phase of insanity which may be called moral madness, in which all that is good or even human seems to disappear from the mind and a fiend-nature replaces it.'[17] The idea of insanity which Brontë invokes with such authority is that of the category of 'moral insanity' with which Bucknill and Tuke were concerned in their description of the snake-woman, and which was introduced by James Cowle Prichard in 1835.[18] Both her conception and defence of 'the Maniac' (as she terms Bertha in the letter), are framed by contemporary patriarchal culture: male medical theory acts as guarantee of the verisimilitude of her writing.

Medical science was not an autonomous domain, however. Medical writers themselves turned to literary texts for case studies, offering, in a tautological move, these prior cultural constructions as self-evident demonstration of the validity of their own, dependent, cultural categories.[19] Literary texts were also raided for theoretical pronouncements: Johnson's *Rasselas*, which makes a significant appearance in *Jane Eyre*, was repeatedly cited, for example, as an authoritative text in discussions of the ever-present threat of latent insanity. In a converse shift, characters from psychological works found embodiment in literary texts. Thus John Conolly's observations on the insane figures, 'in strange costume, and full of fancied consequence', who haunt the courts 'in the expectation of acquiring vast possessions' are later given expression in his friend Dickens' creation of Miss Flite in *Bleak House*.[20]

The novelist and physician shared similar ground in mid-Victorian culture. The era had witnessed the simultaneous rise to cultural prominence of both medical and fictional discourse: the novelist, newly released into the sphere of social respectability, took on the role of social sage, empowered to diagnose the moral and social ills of the society, while the physician emerged as the supreme arbiter of mental and physiological health. Such territorial demarcations are clearly nominal, however, since both sides ranged freely across the terrain.

They shared, moreover, the same central metaphors for their proceedings, drawn, pre-eminently, from the sphere of science: surgical dissection, and penetration of the inner recesses of mind and body. Brontë's thematic and methodological concerns here converge, as her comments on other writers suggest. She commends, for example, at the very time when she was being troubled by the over-zealous attentions of her doctor, the 'relentless dissection of diseased subjects' in Thackeray, though she is rather perturbed by the evident relish with which this 'savage surgeon' proceeds to his work: he 'likes to dissect an ulcer or an aneurism; he has pleasure in putting his cruel knife or probe into quivering living flesh'.[21] With less physiological specificity, she also praises Balzac for his 'subtle perception of the most obscure and secret workings of the mind'.[22] The goal of the novelist, like that of the physician, is to penetrate hidden recesses, to unveil the concealed inner processes of the social body or the individual mind.

As a methodological principle, this goal bears witness to fundamental changes which had taken place across the disciplinary field. For Fielding, there had been no divergence between outer form and inner self, no hidden sphere of the psyche which he undertook to disclose.[23] Identity in his novels is constituted in the overt field of social action; and physical appearance, where invoked, is directly expressive of character. Skilful decoding is not required. A similar shift in orientation occurred within the natural sciences: natural history which measured the visible surface of nature was supplanted by physiology which focused on the hidden domain of the 'milieu interieur'.[24] The beginning of modern medicine at the end of the eighteenth century can be traced, Foucault has argued, to the changing structure of relation between the visible and the invisible. The clinic's task was no longer 'simply to read the visible: it has to discover its secrets'.[25] This preoccupation with a secret inner domain, signalled but not fully revealed by the details of outer form, similarly underpinned new conceptions of psychology, which ranged across the spectrum of normality. Insanity was no longer a self-evident disease which demarcated the sufferer from the rest of humanity; it could lurk, Victorian psychiatrists suggested, within the most respectable breasts, to be spotted only by the trained eye. Identity, for the sane and the insane alike, was vested within the privacy of an internal space.

Novelists and physicians took on the mantle of social authority, dedicated to revealing the hidden pathways of social and psychological

life.[26] Dickens, for example, defines his work as a moral extension of
medical science. Following the practice of 'those who study the
physical sciences and bring them to bear upon the health of Man', he
calls for a good spirit to take off the house-tops, to disclose to public
view the haunts where 'Vice and Fever propagate together', thus
rendering visible the black cloud of 'moral pestilence' which ferments
in the hidden recesses of the city.[27] While novelists in France actively
aligned themselves with the sphere of medical practice, English
novelists were generally more circumspect. The shared premises of
the two fields are strikingly revealed, however, in *Middlemarch*, where
Eliot's description of Lydgate's scientific ideals simultaneously outlines
the aims of literary realism:

> he wanted to pierce the obscurity of those minute processes which prepare
> human misery and joy, those invisible thoroughfares which are the first
> lurking-places of anguish, mania, and crime, that delicate poise and
> transition which determine the growth of happy or unhappy consciousness.[28]

A world invisible to the untrained eye bears the secrets of psychological
and social life which the scientist and novelist are committed to
unveiling. In an illuminating elision of categories, the body is here
pathologized as a dangerous city, where mania and crime lurk in
hidden alley-ways, ever ready to leap out and disturb the tenuous
surface calm of life. Eliot's description draws attention to the shared
rhetorical field of Victorian social and psychological analysis: the
same metaphors and vocabulary were employed in each sphere,
whether the threats perceived were of working-class power, disease,
or female sexuality.

The shared vocabulary and metaphoric base of social and
psychological rhetoric permitted a constant slippage and displacement
of categories as the Victorians sought to come to terms with perceived
social ills. Yet the shifting back and forth from bodily to social
diagnosis was not based solely on linguistic sleight of hand: the newly
established theories of physiological psychology gave scientific validity
to the belief that the same laws of circulation animated the individual
organism and psyche as operated in the wider social economy.[29] As
the passage from *Middlemarch* suggests, these physiological premises
gave currency to the belief that social and psychological ills could be
traced back to the workings of the individual body, thus reinforcing
the individualist premises of Victorian social philosophy. Science and
the novel meet in their representation of the individual as a
microcosm of the social realm.

Brontë's fiction is preoccupied, both thematically and method-ologically, with the relationship between the visible and the invisible. Surveillance and interpretative penetration are not represented however, as in the Eliot passage, as innocent activities. The medical viewpoint, Rothfield suggests, offers the paradigm for literary realism: the omniscient, detached observer reveals an 'immanent power to penetrate and know the embodied self it treats'.[30] Not only do Brontë's characters spend their time attempting to baffle such penetration, the texts themselves function at a formal level to challenge such will to knowledge. Suspicion of interpretative authority is embedded methodologically in the narrative form of Brontë's works. In all her works except *Shirley* Brontë eschews the omniscient third person, with its authoritative claims to lay bare the hidden workings of the inner self, and even in this text she plays with generic conventions, interweaving the language of ghosts and visions with that of economic discourse, for example, so that no one voice can claim ultimate priority.

Brontë's challenge to realism is manifest from her early writings onwards: a whole host of unreliable narrators are employed in her first stories to cloud and obfuscate interpretation, whilst in the later autobiographical fictions her narrators are devoted as much to concealing as to revealing the self. Jane Eyre's story is set in counterpoint to that of Bertha, and in *Villette* Lucy is shown deliberately to mislead and withhold information from her readers as she weaves her elusive story. Brontë's interrogation of realism's penetrative authority is given direct embodiment in *Villette* in the scenes between Dr John and Lucy. Unlike Eliot, Brontë here brings her physician into direct confrontation with his subject of study, revealing the power dynamics which lie behind the medical rhetoric of disclosure. The spirit of scientific inquiry is far from disinterested, the text suggests, but carries with it specific relations of power. Literary realism, by extension, is not an innocent practice but is tied in to the structures of surveillance which, Brontë reveals, dominated the internal workings of both personal and institutional life in Victorian England. Her interrogation of realist form and medical authority is thus a political act.

Throughout her writing Brontë explores the gender and class politics which underpin the activities of surveillance, for its functions are not uniform but multivariant. Women and men stand in a very different relationship to the mastery of the gaze, and to the powers of social ascendancy it seems to convey. To understand these differences one must look beyond the surface texture of the novels to the conflicting ideologies of self-control and female sexuality which permeated Victorian economic and psychological discourse, and inevitably affected not only Brontë's representations of her heroines, but also her attitudes to her own authorial role. Brontë, as a female writer, occupying a highly marginalized social position, and brought up in a household where medical authority was constantly brought to bear, had a vested interest in both exploring and defying the forces of literary and social surveillance.

Before moving to an analysis of the novels, I will consider in some detail the contextual framework of Brontë's writing, looking first at the specific culture of Haworth and the parsonage, and then in broader perspective, tracing the rise of medical psychiatry and various models of psychology in the mid-Victorian era, with particular reference to phrenology as a social and psychological movement. The final chapter in this first section will examine the ways in which economic and social ideologies converged in figurations of the female body.

CHAPTER 2

The Haworth context

According to one particularly infatuated Brontë critic of the 1940s, 'These sisters owed less than any other great writers to contemporary currents of religious and political opinion, and more perhaps than any to gifts descending direct to them from heaven with no human intermediary.'[1] The political and sexual underpinnings of such hagiography are fascinating. It presumably rests on a reading of the novels which marginalizes the Luddite framework of *Shirley* and the virulent anti-Catholicism of *Villette*, and entirely disregards the mid-Victorian ideology of self-help which imbues *The Professor*. Such readings persist, even in contemporary criticism, because they continue to fulfil crucial ideological functions, though their origins lie far back in the original mid-nineteenth-century accounts which similarly emphasized the Brontës' cultural isolation.[2] Elizabeth Gaskell's biography, for example, carefully chronicles the fact that the entire road from Keighley to Haworth was built up, and then speaks of the dreamy, supernatural cast of mind the children acquired from dwelling in such seclusion.[3] Harriet Martineau for her part attributes the 'coarseness' of Charlotte Brontë's fiction to the fact of her living 'among the wild Yorkshire hills, with a father who was too much absorbed in his studies to notice her occupations, in a place where newspapers were never seen (or where she never saw any)'.[4]

Although readers in the south of England might still subscribe to myths of Yorkshire wildness, Martineau's assertions held no basis in fact even in the nineteenth century. Charlotte Brontë, as we know from her letters, avidly read two newspapers from early childhood, and responded ardently to the political issues of the day. In the pages of the Tory *Leeds Intelligencer*, and the Whig *Leeds Mercury*, she followed with keen interest the debates on Catholic emancipation and the Reform Bill in her early years, and the progress of the Chartists and the 1848 Revolution in France, in her later years.[5] Her father was no retiring clergyman but an active political campaigner, writing numerous letters to the local newspapers: on Catholic emancipation in 1829, for example (a step to which he gave cautious approval), and a plea for the revision of England's 'bloody' criminal code in 1830.[6] Nor did he conduct his campaigns solely from within the privacy of his study; his public speech indicting the new Poor Law Act was featured in *The Times* in 1837, and in 1832, during agitation for the Reform Bill, he crossed swords with Lord Morpeth in a stormy public debate.[7]

The two Leeds newspapers were no local rags but offered detailed coverage of both national political debates and local economic news. The *Leeds Mercury*, run by the prominent liberal campaigner, Edward Baines, was a paper of national importance. In 1830, for example, it published Richard Oastler's letter on 'Yorkshire Slavery' – an examination of the condition of the children employed in the Bradford textile industry which inaugurated the Ten Hours Movement and the social controversies over factory labour in the 1830s and 40s. Edward Baines played no glorious role in the debates, functioning primarily as an apologetic mouth-piece for the mill-owners, but in the pages of both newspapers the issues received full coverage. Each paper also meticulously traced the movements of labour unrest which inevitably followed the introduction of machinery and the factory system into the textile industry of West Yorkshire. The famous Bradford combers and weavers strike, for example, which involved 20,000 people and lasted for twenty-three weeks between 1825 and 1826, ending with a complete defeat for the strikers, was reported in great detail. At the same time, the economic crash, brought on by joint stock ventures and reckless financial speculation, led to widespread riots in industrial cities in the spring of 1826. On 4 May 1826, the *Leeds Intelligencer* included a chart of all the riots and disturbances which had recently taken place in the region, and Edward Baines published his 'Letter to the Unemployed Workmen of Lancashire and Yorkshire' which warned of the dangers of machine breaking in encouraging foreign competitors (a warning which he then repeated in lectures to the Leeds Mechanics' Institute in the autumn of 1830).[8] Machine wrecking and political discontent in the West Riding was not confined to the Luddite era which Brontë was to feature in *Shirley*, but continued sporadically throughout the first half of the nineteenth century, forming part of the texture of local Haworth life.

As daughter of the rector of Haworth, a village whose economy depended on the worsted industry, Brontë was inevitably caught up in the cycles of poverty and economic distress which shook the region in the 1820s, 30s and 40s. The 1834 Commons Select Committee heard evidence of unprecedented suffering amongst the outworkers in the villages around Bradford and Keighley which had 'for years continued to an extent and intensity scarcely to be credited or conceived'.[9] It has been estimated that there were around 1200 hand-loom weavers in Haworth in 1838 (in a community that numbered 6303 in the 1841 census, with 2431 resident in the village itself).[10] All would have been working for a small fraction of the wages they could previously have commanded before the advent of power looms. By 1850 there were three factories in Haworth itself, two fairly small ones, employing 134, and 39 hands respectively, and one recently established one which anticipated employing up to 1000 hands.[11] A large proportion of the Haworth population, however, would have been involved in wool combing in their own homes, a job which, since the Bradford strike, had lost its economic privileges and social status, and which entailed hot, close work over charcoal stoves in unventilated houses for entire families.

In his younger days the Reverend Brontë had been a fierce anti-Luddite (although he is meant to have turned a blind eye on the Luddites burying their dead companions in the graveyard outside his house).[12] During his time at Haworth, however, he is said to have defended striking workers, much to the annoyance of the local mill-owners, and to have given them financial assistance.[13] Strikes and riots were not confined to the larger industrial centres but found their way also in to Haworth life. Notes of a vestry meeting in 1822 record the determination of the participants to take measures against the numbers of the community who had destroyed property and endangered the lives of the peaceable inhabitants of the township. The Reverend Brontë lived in fear of an eruption of widescale social disorder; he supported the Reform Bill on those grounds, and in responding to the new Poor Law he called on Yorkshire men to rouse themselves to resistance, 'for their laws, and bodies, and souls, were equally concerned in that matter – and country too, for if dear times and general distress should come on, starvation, deprived of relief, would break into open rebellion'.[14] Linking the health of the individual to that of the social body, he concluded that the 'time for healthy action was now or never'.

The stricken workers of Haworth did not live in picturesque

poverty, but rather in physical conditions which intensified their plight. The Reverend Brontë concerned himself not only with the moral and social health of his parishioners, but also with their physical well-being. In response to his petition for pure water, a Board of Health inquiry was held into the sanitary conditions of Haworth which found that, at 25.8 years, the average age of death in the community was on a par with some of the unhealthiest districts of London. A percentage of 41.6 of the population died before they were six years old. Babbage's report paints a graphic picture of the sanitary conditions in Haworth which should dispel any lingering notions of quaint moorland villages. There were no sewers in the village, no water closets, and far too few privies. The latter flowed over into the street, and midden heaps were piled against houses. Although the Brontë sisters might have had their minds on thoughts coming from 'above', their eyes and noses must inevitably have been assailed in the Haworth streets by unavoidable evidence of the realm 'below'. Babbage records with horror the lack of privacy accorded to bodily functions:

Two of the privies used, by a dozen families each, are in the public street, not only within view of the houses, but exposed to the gaze of the passers by, whilst a third, as though even such a situation were too private, is perched upon an eminence, commanding the whole length of the main street.[15]

Such a public enthronement of the body offered a defiant challenge to middle-class Victorian attempts to segregate the life of the mind from that of the lowly body.

In the public debates on the physical conditions of the workers, conducted both in the pages of the local newspapers, and in the periodicals to which the Brontës subscribed, two different models of psychological identity underpinned the conflicting arguments. Should the worker be viewed as physical capital, an extension of the machinery on which he worked, or as an autonomous being and independent agent? The Tory *Blackwood's Magazine* expressed its indignation, in an 1830 article, that 'the working classes are set down as animated machines, from the use of which it is sound policy to draw the greatest amount of profit at the least cost'.[16] Edward Baines, for his part, used the pages of the *Leeds Mercury* for a Whig defence of free trade and the industrial system. In two open letters to Robert Peel, in response to the proposed Factory Education Bill of 1843, he acknowledges the south's fears that under the 'repulsive exterior' of the manufacturing districts there lies 'a fearful mass of disease' but suggests that the workers have never before held such advantageous positions; industrial advance is not at the worker's expense since the factory system 'links with him, in an indissoluble bond of interest, capitalists of the largest means and greatest skill and experience'.[17] In this formulation, the workers form the material cog in the wonderful machine of commerce, organized and directed by middle-class capital and intelligence. Although they might form part of industry's 'repulsive exterior', they are nonetheless ennobled by their participation within this imperial enterprise.

These arguments on the role of the labourer, which are given explicit formulation in *Shirley*, form part of a wider tissue of concern in mid-nineteenth-century economic and psychological thought. The question of whether the individual is a self-determined agent, or merely a part of a larger machine, hinges on the crucial issue of self-control – that sacrosanct principle of Victorian culture. All psychological texts of the era, and many economic discussions, take their starting point from this principle, whether the issue involved is the lurking threat of insanity or the arrangement of industrial practices. Tory concerns for individual autonomy, and Whig preoccupations with industrial interests meet, indeed, on the ground of self-control. Both sides enthusiastically championed the self-help movements of the mid-Victorian era which incarnated both sets of concerns: rigorous control and regulation of the machinery of mind and body would offer a passport to autonomous selfhood and economic liberty. Simple (and familiar) as this formula might appear, it infiltrated Victorian culture at all levels, reconciled Whig and Tory concerns, and offered a developmental model not only for working-class but also for middle-class culture.

Charlotte Brontë's letters, from her youthful days onwards, bear witness to her determined adoption of these ruthless principles of self-regulation, in despite of, or even because of, the psychological pain inflicted. She writes, for example, in defence of the sufferings inflicted on the governess: 'A governess's experience is frequently indeed bitter, but its results are precious: the mind, feeling, temper are there subjected to a discipline equally painful and priceless.'[18] Discipline and regulation formed the keynotes of the general culture in which Brontë moved. Its rhetoric, however, tended to emphasize achievement and endless potentiality, rather than the more negative aspects of control. But, as Brontë's comments suggest, the middle-class woman held a very different relation to these doctrines than her male counterparts: without an external field to exercise her harnessed energies, repressive self-control became a goal in its own right, and internal pain a source of pride.

Despite Brontë's vaunted isolation, and our fairly sparse records of her life, it is relatively easy to trace many tantalizing examples of her connections with local self-help culture, and its more grandiose equivalents in the scientific domain. Thus we find her, at the height of her fame, being conducted around that supreme tribute to scientific imperialism, the Great Exhibition, by Sir David Brewster, self-proclaimed publicist for the wonders of science.[19] The phenomenal popularity of the Great Exhibition derived in no small part from its ideological role as supreme symbolic expression of the principles of self-help: individual ingenuity, when backed by scientific knowledge, would prove invincible. These principles lay behind the founding of both the Society for the Diffusion of Useful Knowledge and the Mechanics' Institutes, and here on a more humble, yet more direct local level, we also find Brontë involved. The annual report in 1852 of the Haworth Mechanics' Institute records that 'Our Annual Soirée was held on Easter Monday, when about 150 partook of an excellent tea; and we were honoured, as usual, by the kind services of the talented authoress of "Jane Eyre", "Shirley", &c.'[20]

The Reverend Brontë and his family were involved in the local network of the intelligentsia who were devoted to the idea of self-improvement and control through the acquisition of knowledge and the principles of science. Their close friends included the Reverend Theodore Dury, one of the prime movers behind the founding of the Keighley Mechanics' Institute (which the Reverend Brontë joined in 1833)[21] and inaugurator of the magazine, *The Monthly Teacher*, designed expressly to bring learning in 'natural history and the arts and sciences' to the local populace.[22] Other acquaintances involved in the local lecturing circuit of scientific proselytizers included numerous medical figures, most notably the surgeon, Mr Milligan of Keighley, who lectured, for example, to the Keighley Mechanics' Institute in 1847 on the sanitary conditions in larger towns.[23]

The West Riding proved a particularly energetic centre of self-help ideology and activity. Edward Baines, one of the prime exponents of these doctrines, and founder of the Yorkshire Union of Mechanics' Institutes, used the pages of the *Leeds Mercury* tirelessly to proclaim the virtues of self-help through the development and control of the mental faculties. Thus in an editorial in 1851 he waxed particularly rhapsodic on the decency and order created in working-class lives through the spread of education, maintaining that despite the material glories of industrial progress 'the advance of mind has outstripped that of wealth and industry'.[24] The local lectures of the indefatigable Samuel Smiles were also widely featured in both papers, as were his letters. In the *Leeds Intelligencer* of 9 November 1850 he writes to support the idea of a local library and museum on the grounds that 'it is absolutely necessary that the intelligence of our population, including our operatives and skilled workmen, should be liberally fed, if we would maintain our manufacturing supremacy among nations'. In the pronouncements of Baines and Smiles, the ideological connections drawn between mental and material wealth are always to the fore: regulation of the mental energy of the workforce is the essential prerequisite for national economic success.

The annual reports of the Keighley Mechanics' Institute reveal how decisively the doctrines of self-help were internalized by aspiring workers and the middle classes. The first annual report in 1825 alludes to the unprecedented commercial distress in the area, but pins its hopes on the benefits to be accrued from knowledge: 'Latent genius may be excited and prompted to action. The dormant abilities of individuals, yet unknown, may be roused, brought to light, improved, and exerted for the general good.'[25] Ever optimistic, the report in 1830 affirms that latent genius and dormant abilities do seem to have been aroused. Membership of the society was drawn from the upper ranks of the working classes and the middle classes, with some aristocratic patrons (Miss Currer, of Eshton Hall, for example, was a member). Its doctrines blended together a defiant challenge to upper-class privilege, with a meek acceptance of individual responsibility for one's social position. The report for 1831 proclaims in rousing tones, that 'Knowledge can...no longer be considered as the exclusive characteristic of any particular caste or profession. No rank is too high to be placed above the sphere of its jurisdiction; and no rank is too humble to be admitted within the precinct of its privileges.'[26] Such inspirational addresses were matched, however, by stern moral lectures; the rule book, for example, carried the forbidding epigraph: 'It is better to be unborn than untaught, for ignorance is the root of misfortune.' Those failing to take advantage of the Institute's services were firmly berated: 'Ignorance is by no means respectable, on the contrary it degrades its possessors; however, in these days ignorance is wilful, and therefore inexcusable, since the door to knowledge is open to all.'[27]

The Institute's panacea for all ills was self-improvement through the development and exertion of the mental faculties (a rhetoric, which, as I will suggest later, was popularized by the phrenology movement). The report for 1832 warns that 'the faculties of the mind, like those of the body, can only be preserved in a sound and healthful state by constant exercise'.[28] In Brontë's letters we find similar concerns expressed. Writing to Ellen Nussey in 1846 she laments the fact that by the time she will be free to leave home, 'I shall be quite past the prime of life – my faculties will be rusted – and my few acquirements in a great measure forgotten.'[29]

The library of the Keighley Mechanics' Institute, which formed a major source of books for the Brontë family during Charlotte's adolescence, was primarily devoted to the natural sciences and philosophy, although literary works, such as Scott's novels, were also purchased.[30] Although we cannot recreate the family pattern of borrowing and reading, the work of Barbara Goff on Emily Brontë's engagement with the scientific aspects of natural theology helps to build up a picture of a wide-ranging, and fairly detailed acquaintance with the resources of the Keighley Mechanics' Institute Library on the part of the sisters.[31]

On the shelves of the library, works on electricity and the development of manufactures mingled with more practical guides to self-improvement such as *Strive and Thrive* or phrenology manuals, while the obverse side of the culture of self-improvement was represented by the treatise of the influential French physician, Esquirol, on insanity.[32] Lectures at the Institute seem to have followed the common pattern: exhortations to self-development alternated with more practical lectures on magnetism and geology, or, in less scientific vein, on the life of Napoleon. Instructional classes were also held, including, in 1849, the foundation of a Female Improvement Society for 'the benefit of young women connected with our factories'.[33] The Haworth Mechanics' Institute, founded in the late 1840s, followed suit, offering nine public lectures in 1851 and classes in the four fundamentals: Reading, Mutual Improvement, Writing and Arithmetic.[34] Charlotte Brontë's own degree of involvement in these improving activities is difficult to gauge, though a letter to Ellen Nussey in 1831 regretting that she cannot attend some lectures on galvanism, suggests that such lectures formed part of her education and social life.[35] Her father certainly lectured to the Keighley Mechanics' Institute, though it is unclear how many times; he and his curate, William Weightman, both gave talks in 1840, and in early 1841 he spoke on 'The Influence of Circumstances'. The only record we have of Charlotte's own attendance, however, is at William Weightman's lecture on 'The Advantage of Classical Studies' in 1840.

The culture of self-regulation entered directly into the Brontë home through both the theory and practice of medicine. Scientific authority, the secular theology of the Mechanics' Institutes, was here brought to bear on the regulation of the inner economy in a decisive physical form. The constant presence of illness in the Brontë family ensured that the medical man held a dominating, authoritative position in their household, but his pre-eminence was reinforced by Patrick Brontë's respect for medical science. Writing to the local surgeon, John Milligan, to explain why he had needed a prescription in written form, he observes, 'The truth is – I wished to have *Medical Authority*, for what I might do.' The letter continues modestly to play down his own medical competence: 'I profess to have no great skill in medicine, though I have studied it both at the university and since I left.'[36] As clergyman, the Reverend Brontë would have been expected to play a role in parish medical care (his *Domestic Medicine* was intended for the use of 'clergymen, families, and students in medicine'). His fascination with medical science, and with the inter-relations between the body and mind, went far beyond the bounds of professional duty, however, leading him to impose a rigorous regime on his entire family. Every symptom, whether of mental or physical ill-health, was closely scrutinized, and checked against the near-infallible word of his secular Bible, Graham's *Domestic Medicine*, which was in turn then checked against the wisdom of other medical texts. Virtually every page of the Graham is covered with annotations, noting the success of remedies, disputing interpretations, and recording alternative theories from other medical experts.[37] All the ailments of the family are noted and explored: Anne's consumption, Patrick's eye problems and rupture, Branwell's drinking, Emily's dog-bite, and Charlotte's tic douloureux. (In the case of the latter, which is described as 'a dreadfully painful affection of the nerves of the face', Patrick turns to other medical accounts which attributed the complaint less to physical than to mental causes, aligning it with hysteria and insanity.[38] The words, he notes, signify a 'convulsive fit'.)

Every aspect of the family's daily life was regulated by the dictates of medical science; not only their diet but even their sleeping habits were subject to control. Patrick twice records that though 'nervous people, from polar attraction, sleep best, with their heads towards the north – this might not suit apoplectic persons, owing to the properties of iron, in the blood'.[39] The bodily system is projected here as helpless materiality, at the mercy of external physical forces. The two conflicting models of psychology found in Victorian economic discourse also figure in the medical rhetoric of the time: the individual is figured both as an autonomous unit, gifted with powers of self-control, and also as a powerless material organism, caught within the operations of a wider field of force.

The Reverend Brontë's fascination with the interplay of body and mind led him to explore the nether-world of control – the arenas where action or response can no longer be controlled by the conscious mind. Drawing on his own experience and Robert Macnish's *Philosophy of Sleep* he makes extensive notes on the terrible visitations of nightmare (including the recommended sleeping position), while in a slightly different vein, he also explores the new medical discoveries in anaesthesia, and the potentiality of mesmerism.[40] His notes reveal that he delegated Charlotte to consult John Forbes, one of the country's most distinguished physicians, on the effects of the newly discovered anaesthetizing powers of chloroform.[41] A clipping from the *Leeds Mercury* on the use of chloroform (a subject followed with great interest by both the Leeds newspapers) was also inserted in the text and the advice of the eminent obstetrician, Dr James Young Simpson, on the use of ether and chloroform was also noted.

Reasons for Patrick's preoccupation with this issue can be gleaned from his extensive jottings on the use of sulphuric ether in operations which when inhaled 'destroys, for some minutes, all consciousness – so that all surgical operations, may now be effected without any sense of pain. Limbs have been amputated, teeth extracted, and persons have been operated on for hernia and the stone, without their having any knowledge whatever of what had been done.' Patrick's interest focuses on the separation of mind and body, on the possibility of acting upon, controlling, and even performing amputations on the body of another without their knowledge. In the case of chloroform, a specific sexual dimension underpinned the controversy concerning its use. It was believed that women, lying insensible under doctors' hands, were liable to reveal unbecoming sexual excitement.[42]

Similar stories of female impropriety had previously circulated with reference to ether. In response to a letter from Ellen Nussey, for example, Charlotte wrote, 'What you say about the effects of ether on Catherine Swaine rather startled me – I had always consoled myself with the idea of having my front teeth extracted and rearranged some day under its soothing influence – but now I should think twice before I consented to inhale; one would not like to make a fool of oneself.'[43] The discovery of the effects of ether and chloroform heightened existing Victorian interest in dreams and hallucinations, and the unconscious movements of the mind, reinforcing belief in a concealed realm of interiority where true selfhood lay. For women, fears of self-revelation were doubly motivated: unveiled and penetrated, the inner domain might prove to contain the very sexual secrets male medical ideology now so insistently proclaimed. Deprived literally of self-control, women might also reveal their innate incapacity ever to attain this goal.

Mesmerism, which also drew the Reverend Brontë's interest, attracted similar forms of controversy. An article on 'Electro-Biology' in the *Westminster Review*, 1851, spoke scathingly of a 'Mesmeric epidemic': 'In a fashionable assembly, experiments on the mental functions take the place of quadrilles. Ladies of sensitive and "susceptible" organization, gratify a drawing-room with the exhibition of "involuntary emotions", instead of a fantasia on the piano.'[44] Whereas women used to reveal their sensibilities through the medium of a piano, their own bodies now become instruments for others to play upon, revealing to the public gaze the spectacle of female lack of control. Objections to mesmerism focused on its 'tendency to take from man his responsibility'.[45] The moral philosopher J. F. Ferrier commented in distaste on the physical and moral infirmity of the people who were willing to 'abandon themselves to a disgusting condition which is characteristic only of the most abject specimens of our species'.[46]

Despite the alarm engendered by these flagrant displays of the fragility of self-control, mesmerism was none the less accepted as further evidence of the fact that 'the imaginative faculties, the nervous sensations and muscular motions, are not always under the control of the judgment or of the will'.[47] Even its fiercest opponents accepted that it brought new evidence to light on the operations of the mind.[48] Thomas Laycock, one of the mid-Victorian authorities on the female mind and body, began his *Treatise on the Nervous Diseases of*

Women with the observation that mesmerism suggests that forms of understanding of 'the whole of the relation of mind to body require a thorough revision'.[49]

Seemingly undaunted by the criticisms of the power mesmerism conferred on its practitioners, Patrick Brontë pursued his researches into the hidden processes of the mind into this domain. His notes record that he read a treatise on mesmerism in 1850 and summarize in graphic detail the various steps involved in inducing mesmeric sleep in a patient, concluding with the words, 'there is no danger'.[50] Whether he experimented on Charlotte is unclear; she did, however, undergo a 'personal experiment' whilst staying with Harriet Martineau, a mesmeric devotee, in December 1850. She records that although 'the result was not absolutely clear, it was inferred that in time I should prove an excellent subject'.[51] Charlotte is quick to insist that she is not a 'convert', yet, as with that other popular psychological movement of the mid-Victorian era, phrenology, one finds the vocabulary and assumptions of mesmerism permeating her fiction.

Scepticism as to the larger claims of mesmerism (such as clairvoyance) was generally accompanied in mid-Victorian responses with a willing acceptance of the fact that, as one reviewer remarked, 'the fabled effects of the basilisk, the serpent, and the evil eye, have probably all some facts for their foundation'.[52] Even fiercely antagonistic writers were yet willing to concede that there might exist an invisible force, analogous to a magnetic field or electric current, which could grant powers to unlock the secrets of the mind.[53] Although many doctors did explore the possibilities of mesmerism, the most decisive opponents of the mesmeric idea and its popular practitioners were the medical men whose licensed authority to explore the concealed territory of the mind was being usurped by the mesmeric entertainers.[54] With its public demonstrations of the control exercised by one mind over another, mesmerism fed into and reinforced contemporary preoccupations with the power of the gaze, and the threat of psychic unveiling.[55]

Although medical authority received the full weight of patriarchal endorsement within the Brontë household, it met with fierce resistance from the younger generation. Emily's famous refusal to see a doctor when she was dying must be placed in the context of Charlotte's observation that 'My sister Emily was not a person of demonstrative character, nor one, on the recesses of whose mind and feelings, even those nearest and dearest to her could, with impunity, intrude unlicensed.'[56] The evocative language links the power of knowledge and sexuality: the inner recesses of the self are to be guarded against intrusion, whether from members of her own family, or, by extension, from medical men professionally empowered to diagnose the inner secrets of the mind and body.

Charlotte's own responses to medical practice were highly ambivalent. On the one hand she fought the controlling hand of Mr Ruddock, whom she aptly describes as 'stick[ing] like a leech'.[57] But, on the other hand, the fears aroused by Emily's illness drew her into collusion with the medical establishment. Knowing that Emily would not consult the eminent London physicians, Forbes and Elliotson, recommended by George Smith, she nonetheless sent a detailed account of Emily's symptoms to another London doctor, Dr Epps, hoping for a helpful response.[58] Almost despite herself, Charlotte turns to medical science for aid. She is markedly impressed by the fact that the distinguished Dr Teale of Leeds, brought in to examine Anne, employed the new implement of medical technology, the stethoscope, and in later letters is eager to cite medical authority both for the treatment of her sisters, and in her own medical, and moral, advice to friends.[59]

Following the death of her sisters, Charlotte becomes preoccupied with the state of her own health, describing her nervousness as a 'horrid phantom'.[60] Her letters recording her illness of the winter 1851–2 possess an obsessive quality, as she works and reworks her own diagnosis of its causes. Interestingly, as the different versions evolve, she shifts from a largely physiological account to one that foregrounds a mental cause: 'That depression of spirits...came back with a heavy recoil; internal congestion ensued, and then inflammation.'[61] Cutting across her own doctor's purely physiological diagnosis of a liver complaint, Brontë adopts the premises of alternative contemporary accounts of the body (and in particular the female body) which maintained a direct relation between the physiological and emotional: the lowering of animal spirits would affect the whole bodily economy.

While resisting Dr Ruddock's *physical* control of her body, Brontë nonetheless subscribes to a theory of physiology which highlights the impossibility of *mental* self-control. In an earlier letter to Elizabeth Gaskell, Brontë had explicitly outlined her belief in this psycho-physical interconnection. Drawing on contemporary theories of the impact of the winds and seasons on the nervous forces of the body (theories which are to figure both in *Jane Eyre* and *Villette*) she writes:

For a month or six weeks about the equinox (autumnal or vernal) is a period of the year which, I have noticed, strangely tries me. Sometimes the strain falls on the mental, sometimes on the physical part of me; I am ill with neuralgic headache, or I am ground to the dust with deep dejection of spirits.[62]

The letter evinces a tremendous sense of powerlessness. Although the medical theories to which Brontë here subscribes take away any sense of guilt for her condition, they also lead to an image of self as a mere plaything in the hands of larger, uncontrollable forces. With her system subject to the operations of the equinox, Brontë can neither predict nor control what form her prostration will take.

Brontë's siblings, Emily and Branwell, offered two entirely different models with reference to self-control and psycho-physical interconnection. Emily's determined defence of her psychological and physical integrity was matched by what Charlotte deemed to be Branwell's entire lack of the 'faculty of self-government'.[63] Whereas Emily was calm and controlled until the last, Branwell's decline was punctuated by the wild torments and hallucinations produced by his drug and drink addiction. As with the health of his other children, the Reverend Brontë anxiously monitored Branwell's condition in the pages of his *Domestic Medicine*. Under the heading of insanity he inserts his own category, 'delirium tremens' with specific details of the symptoms: 'The patient thinks himself haunted; by demons, sees luminous substans, [sic] in his imagination, has frequent tremors of the limbs.'[64] Although paternal anxiety for Branwell clearly motivated Patrick's researches in this area, his fears are not focused on his wayward son alone. Numerous annotations point to his concern with his own state of mental health. Under the heading of 'Hypochondriasis, or Low Spirits' he records his own experience of 'distressing gloom' but concludes, in the peculiar mixture of Latin and English he reserves for commentary on his own ailments, that hypochondriasis is not his own complaint, but rather the more general 'Nervous disorders', defined by Graham as 'a general weakness and derangement of the nerves'.[65] A similar notation occurs under the heading of 'Melancholy', which, for Graham, constitutes a sub-division of insanity. Under 'Causes of Insanity' the Reverend Brontë carefully underlines *hereditary disposition*, thus unveiling the double layer of anxiety which lay behind his concerns with his own nervous complaints.

The section on Nervous Disorders in Graham's *Domestic Medicine* opens with the observation that 'Weakness and irregular action of the greater part or whole of the nervous system' is now common, and its symptoms, which largely duplicate those he ascribes to Melancholy Insanity, will be 'well known to most delicate people in a greater or less degree'.[66] Such calm assertions of widespread mental disorder might appear surprising to us, but are yet fairly representative of received assumptions in the early Victorian era. Fear of mental instability was not a peculiar quirk of the Brontë household, occasioned by Branwell's illness and too much isolation in a moorland landscape, but was rather a widespread cultural phenomenon. To understand the preoccupation with nervous disorder in Brontë's fiction, it is essential to place her work in this wider social context.

The ways in which a society chooses to formalize its categories of the abnormal, crystallize in clearest form the social and psychological assumptions underlying its theories of selfhood. The emphasis on self-control so prevalent in the economic and psychological rhetoric of the time had its reflex in the ever-present fears of loss of control. Such fears, as the subsequent analysis will suggest, were complicated by issues of gender, for men and women were placed in very different relation to the doctrines of control. The following sections will consider in some detail the Victorian psychological context which frames Brontë's work.

CHAPTER 3

Insanity and selfhood

In the year of the publication of *Villette*, a writer in *The Times* offered the following observations on insanity: 'Nothing can be more slightly defined than the line of demarcation between sanity and insanity . . . Make the definition too narrow, it becomes meaningless; make it too wide, the whole human race are involved in the drag-net.'[1] The sentiments expressed are indicative of mid-Victorian fears concerning the delimitation of insanity: no longer were the insane regarded as an outcast group, a sub-human species to be locked away with paupers and criminals. During the first half of the nineteenth century a radical transformation had occurred in attitudes towards insanity which culminated in the passing of the two Lunatic Acts in 1845, and the setting up of public asylums. For the first time the insane were to be radically distinguished from the criminal or indigent. These developments were accompanied by the rise of theories for the treatment of the insane which stressed the possibility of recuperation. Under the regime of 'moral management' the mentally disturbed could be healed and returned to society. Whilst earlier theorists had tended to emphasize the animal nature of the insane, the moral managers now stressed their membership of a common humanity.[2] Thus at the same time that insanity was being constructed as a distinct social category, the borders separating it from sanity were also being eroded.

Medical writings of the period constantly drew attention to the lurking threat of insanity which menaced all individuals. As John Conolly observed in his introduction to *An Inquiry Concerning the Indications of Insanity* (1830), 'Every man is interested in this subject; for no man can confidently reckon on the continuance of his perfect reason.'[3] With the development of the century, this sense of the omnipresent threat of insanity seems to increase, rather than decline, as theories of mental degeneration and inherited brain disease come to the fore. In the post-Darwinian period, Henry Maudsley and

34

others emphasized the *inherited* qualities of brain disease: the individual was powerless in the grip of an inherited constitution. In the earlier period, although the idea of inherited disease was certainly present, more emphasis was placed on notions of self-control. According to Conolly, 'It is only when the passion so impairs one or more faculties of the mind as to prevent the exercise of comparison, that the reason is overturned; and then the man is mad. He is mad only whilst this state continues.'[4] Madness is envisaged less as an inescapable physiological destiny, than as a partial state, to which anyone under stress is liable, and which endures only so long as passion overturns reason. An individual can thus move in and out of a state of insanity. Underlying Conolly's theories is the preoccupation with recuperation and cure which he shared with the other early Victorian alienists (as this professional group was then known). If insanity is not a fixed physiological state, but rather a temporary overwhelming of normal control, it can clearly be subject to medical healing. The corollary of this position, however, was that all individuals (but particularly women) lived under the constant threat of mental derangement. Only the ever-vigilant maintenance of self-control demarcated the boundaries of insanity.

While the category of insanity functioned in earlier historical periods as a social division, establishing the criteria of normality and creating an outcast group, in the nineteenth century it became increasingly an internal, psychological divide. The border to be policed was not so much between self and other, as between the conscious and unconscious self. If all individuals were liable to eruptions of insanity, the only visible sign one could cling to that one was not insane would be one's capacity to exert self-control. Social conformity thus became an index of sanity; the only measure available to the individual fearful of his or her own normality would be a willing obedience to designated social roles. The fears of incipient insanity suggested in the Reverend Brontë's annotations in his *Domestic Medicine*, and given forceful expression in Charlotte's early writings and later fiction, must be placed within this context of socially engendered insecurity of selfhood.

Although a preoccupation with insanity might appear, on the surface, an entirely private matter, the product of purely personal details of biography, its origins are nonetheless irreducibly social. Public and private meet in the domain of selfhood. In the eighteenth century, George Cheyne's *The English Malady* (1733) had linked the growth of nervous disorders to the development of the mercantile economy. In the nineteenth century, the growing concern with insanity was firmly linked to the transformations of England under industrialism. Dramatic shifts in the country's economic and social organization gave rise, in the economic sphere, to a new concern with regulating and channelling the country's material resources and, in the psychological sphere, to ideologies of selfhood which focused on inner regulation and the acquisition of self-control.[5]

Throughout Brontë's fiction, repeated emphasis is placed on the necessity for self-control: mastery of the inner promptings of the psyche is represented as leading directly to opportunities of social control, as each outcast or orphan acquires an impervious external demeanour and moves gradually into a position of social respectability and power. The rhetoric involved in each case is simultaneously that of contemporary economic and psychological discourse: self-control, as I have suggested, operated as a key term in each field. In that quintessential text of moral management, *On Man's Power Over Himself to Prevent or Control Insanity* (1843), John Barlow broke down any notion of an absolute divide between normal and abnormal psychological states, arguing that the difference between sanity and insanity consisted entirely 'in the degree of self-control exercised'. He advises the reader who remains unconvinced to 'note for a short time the thoughts that pass through his mind, and the feelings that agitate him: and he will find that, were they all expressed and indulged, they would be as wild, and perhaps as frightful in their consequences as those of any madman'.[6] The distinction between sanity and insanity rests entirely on the individual's ability to maintain surface control and to direct psychic energy into defined social channels.

The principles of laissez-faire economics were similarly founded on notions of the productive channelling of energy, and the discovery of enlightened 'self-interest'. As Andrew Scull has suggested, the shift in the treatment of the insane at the end of the eighteenth century, when the external mechanisms of restraint such as whips and chains were replaced by an emphasis on internal control and the inner discipline of the mind, can be related to changes in the country's economic base.[7] Lunatics, like the industrial workforce, were to be taught the principles of rational self-interest which governed the marketplace. The individualist principles later encapsulated in Samuel Smiles' doctrines of self-help dominated the treatment of the insane in the first half of the nineteenth century. Although the individual now bore the burden of responsibility and personal guilt for insanity, with medical help he or she could be restored to a productive role in the community and workplace. The shifting curve of attitudes towards mental illness in nineteenth-century England can be plotted directly against the changing patterns of industrial prosperity. The brash confidence of early Victorian optimism which gave rise to theories of moral management and the infinite malleability of the human psyche, gradually shades into the increasingly pessimistic visions of inherited brain disease and social degeneration propounded by Maudsley and other post-Darwinian theorists writing in the era of economic decline in the latter part of the century. Against Brontë's mid-Victorian belief in her protagonists' ability to determine their own destiny we must set the imprisoning biological cycles of Hardy's later fiction, where all attempts to assert control are thwarted by the cumulative forces of history expressed through familial and racial genealogy.

SELF-CONTROL AND THE SOCIAL MASK

In the opening paragraphs of his influential *Treatise on Insanity*, Esquirol asks the philosopher to consider a House for the Insane:

He finds there the same ideas, the same errors, the same passions, the same misfortunes, that elsewhere prevail. It is the same world; but its distinctive characters are more noticeable, its features more marked, its colors more vivid, its effects more striking, because man there displays himself in all his nakedness; dissimulating not his thoughts, nor concealing his defects; lending not to his passions seductive charms, nor to his vices deceitful appearances.[8]

Far from revealing a different world to the gaze of the philosopher, the asylum actually displays a condition of heightened normality. The true distinction which operates between this house and the familial home is not social but moral. The distinguishing condition of asylum life is egoism: 'With no community of thoughts, each lives alone, and for himself. Egotism isolates all.'[9] Esquirol's terms position his work historically. Writing in the wake of the French Revolution, and in response to the seeming failure of the utopia of individual rights proclaimed by the pre-revolutionary ideologues, Esquirol has adopted the nineteenth-century rhetoric of duty and community. The new moral vice is egoism. With the rise of organicist philosophy, writers of all fields and moral persuasions drew stern moral contrasts between egoism and duty: the divisive qualities of individualist impulses were to be subordinated to behaviour directed towards the greater good of the social whole.[10] Social philosophy and psychological theory here converge. Interestingly, Esquirol defines mental cure, the controlling of passion and redirecting of the perverted powers of reason, as the act of 'restor[ing] man to himself'.[11] Selfhood lies not, as one might expect, in the self-enclosed world of egoism, but rather in the directing of energies outward, and participation in the circulating system of the wider social economy.

If we return once more to Esquirol's opening statement, we find the rather disturbing suggestion that the notion of psychological normalcy underlying his work is predicated on a condition of concealment. True selfhood is not the naked display of the insane, but rather the artful concealment and dissimulation of the social creature. Although the insane reveal in more vivid outline the real characteristics of man, to become a social being the individual must learn to overlay and disguise these impulses. Indeed, the condition of selfhood is dependent on having something to conceal: it is the very *disjunction* between inner and outer form which creates the self. The egoist who acts without self-consciousness is self-less. Awareness of an audience, and of one's ability to baffle their penetration, constitutes the essential basis of selfhood.[12]

Esquirol's formulation of selfhood is indicative of the radical shift in conceptions of the psyche which took place at the end of the eighteenth century as theorists tried to balance the respective ideological claims of inner impulse and social demand. The origins of this development are multifold, relating to the new political alignments of the era, and the changing patterns of social organization within an emerging industrial economy which called for a new malleability in its workforce, and more complex networks of interconnection and circulation. Eighteenth-century atomistic and individualistic conceptions of the self, with their emphasis on unified agency, gave way to ideas of social interconnection and determination, and to a new interiorization of the psyche grounded on physiological theories of psychological functioning. In depicting the individual as a multi-levelled site of energy circulation, these theories laid the foundations for later theories of the unconscious. What emerged from these developments was not simply a more complex version of the psychomachia, where reason battles with passion, nor a new grounding of authenticity in the concealed inner realms of body and behaviour. Selfhood, if we follow Esquirol, was situated neither in inner impulse, nor in outer social behaviour, but in the self-conscious awareness of the disjunction between the two. Only with the attempt to conceal the inner psychic workings from the prying eyes of surrounding humanity does true selfhood come into being. The Victorian conception of selfhood is then, paradoxically, of a private state of being which is constituted only within the social act of exchange.

Brontë's fiction circles obsessively around the relationship between concealment and selfhood, from the earliest writings onwards. One early fragment opens with the statement: 'But it is not in society that the real character is revealed.' As readers we are then aligned with the heroine's enemies, invited to gaze voyeuristically on her in the privacy of her bedroom and to decipher the signs of her unguarded visage. Our heroine, Miss West, is aware that, to the judging, 'penetrating eye', there must appear 'something sinister in [the] constant mask which hid and smoothed her natural features'.[13] She is clearly caught up in the double-bind of Victorian femininity, forced to conceal, but convinced that such concealment is sinister. At a deeper level, however, the passage suggests that she comes to self-conscious awareness only through her sense of her self as an object to an external eye, whose gaze she must nonetheless baffle if she is to retain integrity of selfhood. The external gaze simultaneously constitutes and threatens to dissolve the self. The erotic interplay which occurs throughout Brontë's fiction is similarly not just a defensive game designed to protect the boundaries of a pre-existent self, but is rather actually constitutive of selfhood.

THE PENETRATING GAZE

The preoccupation with the power of the penetrating gaze in Brontë's fiction is not peculiar to her writing but can be located historically within a wider field of literary and social concern. The rhetoric of the penetrating gaze seems to come into prominence in the decades of the 1780s and 90s across a whole network of disciplinary fields. Bichat, defining the premises of the newly emerging science of physiology, stated that the goals of anatomists would be attained 'when the opaque envelopes that cover our parts are no more for their practised eyes than a transparent veil revealing the whole and the relations between the parts'.[14] The language of the body was no longer deemed to be self-evident: knowledge was required to decipher its signs.

Indeed, its opaque surface spoke only when properly interrogated by experts. The gaze of the clinician, Foucault suggests, was not that of passive observation but rather an active agency, like fire in chemical combustion, which operated to free 'an implicit structure'.[15] A similar epistemological framework is discernible in nineteenth-century psychology and Brontë's fiction: the observer does not simply read the inner secrets of the self, but functions as an active agency to release an 'implicit structure' previously outside the subject's grasp.

Within the domain of the novel, a similar shift in attitudes towards the external signs of the body is discernible; the notion of the gaze takes on new significance and importance in the late eighteenth century. As Graeme Tytler has pointed out, the mid-eighteenth-century novel offered few detailed physical descriptions of characters, presenting instead rather generalized statements about beauty or ugliness.[16] By the last decades of the century detailed physiognomical analysis is beginning to emerge, but the English Gothic fiction of that period tends, I would suggest, to be preoccupied more with the power of the gaze, than with specific delineation of features. The owner of the fierce, interrogatory gaze in Gothic fiction is frequently a monk or Roman Catholic priest (an association perpetuated in *Villette*). In Ann Radcliffe's *The Italian* (1796), the hero is subjected to the 'piercing eye' (201) of both the monk Schedoni and the Inquisitor who both claim (rightly in Schedoni's case) to possess greater knowledge of his inner self than Vivaldi himself.[17] The structure of power which Radcliffe highlights through the archaic threat of the inquisition, found its late eighteenth and early nineteenth-century equivalent in the new science of psychiatry, and the related practices of physiognomy and phrenology.

Opposition to Roman Catholicism, so prevalent in Gothic fiction, flared up in social debate periodically throughout the nineteenth century, but often in peculiarly subjective terms which were mirrored in the anti-Catholicism of Brontë's texts.[18] The proposal for Catholic Emancipation in the late 1820s, for example, was greeted as a threat to national independence, but newspaper reporting tended to focus on the threats to psychological independence suggested by the practice of confession. The *Leeds Intelligencer*, 26 January 1826, speaks in disgust of the '*slavish dependence, destructive of all mental vigor*' which resulted from confession to these 'Scavengers of the Conscience'. The vigour and virility of the self-contained man of economic ideology is clearly seen to be under threat. Resistance to unlicensed priestly intrusion takes on decisive sexual overtones. The *Intelligencer* suggests that priests exercise over penitents 'the power of wringing from them in detail every secret action of their daily existence. This, from the close relation which it establishes between the priest and his female penitents, has been for ages considered a fertile source of immorality.' In Catholic countries, the report continues, 'it is notorious that the Catholic Priesthood are esteemed the grand authors of female corruption'.[19] Confession, which for men was merely a threat to virile self-containment, becomes for women the inevitable prelude to sexual fall. To enter into the hidden secrets of another is to rob them of control: knowledge becomes absolute power. The Reverend Brontë, entering into the fray with a letter to the *Intelligencer* in 1829, concluded that 'the Church of Rome, by taking away all the right of private judgment, has pressed and must ever press as an incubus on the human mind'.[20] The term 'incubus' with its associations of nightmare, and predatory sexual activity (associations later mobilized by Charlotte in *Villette*) highlights once more the perceived relation between knowledge, violation, and control.

The preoccupation in Gothic fiction with the power of the gaze, and the insidious forces of the Catholic church, bears witness to the new notions of an interiorized selfhood which were to dominate Victorian psychological thought. Opening the second section of his *History of English Literature*, the literary critic Taine demanded, 'When you observe the visible man with your eyes, what do you look for? The hidden man.'[21] Selfhood is separated from appearance. The form and movements of the body have become a system of signs to be decoded in order to reveal the hidden self lying below. Literary criticism, Taine suggests, must follow social practice in its decipherment of visible signs. The power relations embedded in this approach to social interaction are made manifest in a work by the engraver, Thomas Woolnoth, who instructs the close observer to distrust speech and to watch instead the 'shifting process of the face' which cannot help 'betraying its own secrets, for even one unguarded look from the chambers of the eye, may be sufficient to bring into suspicion the most studied harangue'.[22] Portraiture is conceived as a system of espionage, capturing the 'true' self by reading against the social mask. His art possesses, Woolnoth warns, a 'power over the secret consciousness of the soul, that may be called the rendering of 'darkness visible'.[23] The quotation from *Paradise Lost* suggests god-like powers being extended to expose the murky depths of the human psyche.

The power of unveiling which Woolnoth attributes to portraiture, and which Gothic fiction invested in the Roman Catholic priest, was the explicit goal of nineteenth-century psychiatry which sought to explore, in the words of John Reid, 'the invisible world in which we may properly be said to live and have our being'.[24] The preoccupation with rendering visible the invisible which runs throughout nineteenth-century psychological discourse received, in medical psychiatry, its most authoritative expression. To many eyes, the physician had taken over the role of the priest. The relationship between medical and priestly surveillance, which Brontë explores in *Villette*, was the subject of explicit contemporary debate. An 1848 article on 'Moral Physiology; or, the Priest and the Physician' concludes that medical science has rendered the role of the priest all but redundant. The secrets of the self are displaced from the spiritual to the physical domain, and healing is construed as a physiological process to which only the physician holds the key.[25]

With the rise of medical alienism in the early nineteenth century, and the growing professionalization of medical practice, physicians claimed for themselves the exclusive right to treat diseases of the mind and body. Their bid for authority was supported by developments in physiological research which designated the brain and nervous system as the site of mental life.[26] No longer was the mind viewed as an immaterial or spiritual essence, but was placed firmly within the workings of the body. Increasingly, social problems and individual deviance were medicalized, traced back to a physiological base. The physician, in consequence, was raised to a new eminence: the arbiter of normalcy, and licensed interpreter of the hidden secrets of individual and social life.

Psychological texts of the era are riddled with physicians' overt statements of their interpretative authority. John Reid implicitly likens the gaze of the physician to that of the physiologists' instrument, the microscope: 'There are floating atoms or minute embryos of insanity, which cannot be discerned by the naked or uneducated eye. One of the most important requisites in the character of the Physician, is the capacity of detecting the earliest rudiments and the scarcely formed filaments of disease.'[27] Insanity hangs in the air, waiting incubus-like to take over the body of its unsuspecting victims and enact the ghastly process of reproduction menaced by its 'minute embryos.' Men and women alike are to be turned into demonic mother figures, nursing within themselves, quite unsuspectingly, the seeds of a hideous new self. As in the current scare with the AIDS epidemic, the most terrifying aspect of this lurking insanity was its invisibility: it might lie incubating for years within the bodies of the most respectable citizens, showing no signs of the ravages it is about to commit. According to nineteenth-century alienists, only the physician, with his educated eye, could detect the signs of this germination before it was too late and body and mind were beyond redemption. The public, Reid insists, must remain ever-vigilant, ready to call in the medical expert at the slightest sign: 'the smallest speck on the edge of the horizon ought to be regarded with awe, as portending, if not speedily dispersed, an universal and impenetrable gloom'.[28] The alarmist rhetoric of the self-justifying professional suggests the possibility of sweeping contagion.

The language and symbols employed in the cultural representation of epidemics always crystallize the fears and concerns of the defining culture, but all the more so in the case of insanity where no physical symptoms might arise to give the lie to professional judgment, and fear of the disease might itself be the source of infection. Showing a perfect instinct for the market, popular remedies were advertised in the newspapers which claimed to cure not only insanity, but also 'fears of insanity'.[29] Unlike that other epidemic which galvanized Victorian fears, cholera, insanity need not manifest any material signs. Its spread could only be monitored by the professionals who could gaze into the recesses of the soul. Mind was thus set against mind in a confrontation whose fundamental issue was the demarcation of the social boundaries of normality. The ever-present threat of insanity constituted the sub-text of the culture of self-control. Nor was the physicians' power of defining insanity entirely metaphysical: they also possessed the power of forcible committal to an insane asylum. The mid-century press gave a blaze of publicity to cases, such as that of Miss Nottridge in 1849, where patients sued for wrongful committal.[30] The plot line of many sensation novels in the 1860s, where protagonists are repeatedly wrongfully incarcerated in asylums, picked up on this element of social fear which evidently spread far beyond that warranted by actual events.

Physicians' claims for their authoritative role in treating insanity were founded on the grounds both of training and morality. Haslam, outlining the principles of moral management, suggested that female insanity could only be treated with true propriety by the medical profession.[31] While priests might have been entrusted with the secrets of the soul, the physician is given access to the secrets of that even more unspeakable realm, the body: 'the most virtuous women unreservedly communicate to their [doctor] their feelings and complaints, when they would shudder at imparting their disorders to a male of any other profession; or even to their own husbands'. By reinforcing women's sense of shame, and thus perpetuating their isolation, the medical profession established their empire. Haslam envisages a state of female dependency or 'confidence' engendered by medical science and the 'decorous manners' of its practitioners, such that the doctor becomes 'the friend of the afflicted, and the depository of their secrets'.[32]

In acting as the 'depository' of secrets the medical man is clearly taking over the role of the Catholic priest, but unlike his earlier counterpart, his knowledge goes beyond the aural testament of the confessees' self-knowledge.[33] The physiological training and educated eye and ear of the physician gives him access to an understanding denied the patient. Self-knowledge, once the most intimate sphere and kernel of selfhood, is passed out of the control of the individual and into the hands of the experts.

The new role of the physician coincides with the development of theories of moral management which assumed not only that the patient could be cured, but that the personal influence of the doctor was a crucial factor in effecting a recovery. From the 1790s onwards alienists practised the technique of quelling the insane with their gaze.[34] As a method of control, the gaze was but a literal extension of the new attitudes towards insanity adopted by the moral managers: the insane were to be regarded not as criminals but rather as embodiments of mental disorders presented to the calm, observing eye of science.[35] As Foucault has suggested, this transformation in the mechanisms and target of control was not confined to the treatment of insanity but formed part of a wider pattern of social change, epitomized in Bentham's plans for the Panopticon, or inspection-house, which offered, Bentham claimed, 'A new mode of obtaining power of mind over mind, in a quantity hitherto without example.'[36] Bentham's words are echoed in the mid-nineteenth century by Bucknill and Tuke in their description of the personal qualities and social role of the alienist which they liken to that of the clergyman or teacher:

A faculty of seeing that which is passing in the minds of men is the first requisite of moral power and discipline, whether in asylums, schools, parishes, or elsewhere. Add to this a firm will, the faculty of self-control, a sympathizing distress at moral pain, a strong desire to remove it, and that fascinating, biologizing power is elicited, which enables men to domineer for good purposes over the minds of others.[37]

The stark outline of the aims and processes of domination is quickly qualified by the phrase 'good purposes', suggesting an underlying uneasiness with such overt claims to power. Social control is now seen as a function of the interaction of individual minds. The personal qualities of the professional, the ability to preserve self-control, and thus retain the interstices of his own mind unread, are crucial to the operation of 'moral' power and discipline. (The term 'moral' here clearly elides the descriptive meaning of 'psychological' with a highly charged evaluative sense.) In this process of domination, the gaze of the physician is sharply distinguished from that of priest or teacher, for to the medical practitioner alone belongs that 'fascinating, biologizing power'. A wealth of meaning is suggested by this enigmatic phrase: the gaze of the physician fascinates and entraps its victims, both by its intrinsic power and by the patient's deference to its scientific authority.[38] The medical practitioner not only sees into the depths of the patient's mind, but reads there the biological processes, unknown to the patient, which actually compose the self. The mind is dissolved into biology, and only the doctor holds the key to its secrets. To arrive at self-understanding, and thus mental cure, the patient must place his or herself entirely in the hands of the physician. Power to confer integrity of selfhood, an understanding of the relationship between inner mind and outward show, now rests, it is claimed, within the hands of the medical profession.

For the 'soi-disant sane' (in Barlow's phrase) and the insane alike, the physician looms large as a threatening figure, ever ready to destroy the defences constructed to ensure the privacy of the interiorized self, and to ward off intrusive eyes. In the sensation novels of the 1860s, the figure of the doctor, and the associated threat of mental unveiling, haunts many of the female protagonists.[39] This structure of power relations was not, however, confined to medical figures, nor to the sensation novel. The preoccupation with spying and surveillance which we find in Brontë's novels was common to much Victorian fiction. From the 'piercing gaze' of Gothic fiction we move to more developed forms of social surveillance in the mid-Victorian novel, where figures such as the rusty Tulkinghorn in *Bleak House* accrue and hoard details of others' lives, knowing that knowledge is power. The whole rise of detective fiction as a genre is premised, indeed, on a form of symptomatic reading: the skilled eye of the detective, like that of the doctor, unlocks the details of external form invisible to the untrained eye, which reveal the secret history hidden below.

As Alexander Welsh has pointed out in his work on George Eliot, blackmail, bribery based on knowledge of the hidden self, now begins to feature prominently in Victorian fiction.[40] The model of social interaction employed is conflictual: power resides with the figure who can read the other whilst preserving the illegibility of the self. Crimsworth can thus endure his brother's tyranny with equanimity, knowing that the signs of his countenance are as Greek to an unlearned man.[41] According to Bentham, the power of the panopticon lay in the fact that it offered contrivances for 'seeing without being seen'.[42] This principle defines not simply a new structure for social control, but also a new structure of the psyche which is evident in Brontë's fiction: the self does not exist prior to social interaction, but is actually *constituted* in the social struggle to baffle penetration. The desire of the other to read the self, brings to the subject of surveillance a reassuring sense of self-'possession': a sense of selfhood is actively produced through the experience of the power to withhold.

THE RHETORIC OF MENTAL DISORDER

According to the Victorian alienist, the entire psychological health of the nation rested on the population's willingness to submit their minds to medical control. Conolly observes that without the aid of medical men, the influences to which men were subjected would necessarily give rise to mental disorder and would 'soon render the greater part of mankind helpless and miserable'.[43] His vision of an exponential increase in insanity was echoed throughout the medical and popular press of the period. Thus Barlow wrote in panic that 'The cases of insanity, we are told, have nearly tripled within the last twenty years! – a fearful increase, even after allowing the utmost for a larger population.'[44] Although later analysis has suggested that the apparent rise was more to do with practices of confinement than with any actual increase, the literal accounting is less significant than the societal self-image suggested by this prevalent fear.[45] The eighteenth century had regarded the apparent rise of nervous disorders amongst the upper classes with semi-complacency, considering them primarily as a tax on luxury, an index of civilization to be regarded almost with pride.[46] By the nineteenth century nervous disorders had become nervous disease, a threatening state of organic pathology which seemed to menace bodily, mental and social health.

In one of the first studies of the effects on health of various jobs and professions, Charles Turner Thackrah, a leading medical practitioner in Brontë's local city, Leeds, argued that 'Civilization has changed our character of mind as well as of body. We live in a state of unnatural excitement; – unnatural, because it is partial, irregular, and excessive. Our muscles waste for *want* of action: our nervous system is worn out by *excess* of action.'[47] Thackrah is offering a moral, or psychological, reading of Cuvier's dictum that 'Life is a state of Force.'[48] Following the premises of physiological psychology, the mind and body are regarded as an indivisible circulating system which, like the social economy, demands careful regulation: over-development in one area could lead to dearth in another, wealth could rapidly turn to waste. The association between the mental and social economy in Victorian rhetoric was not merely one of analogy. The life of the mind was believed to be linked to that of the social body in one unified system of force: irregularities in the body's circulating system would produce insanity which would in turn undermine the health of the social economy.

Earlier in the century Thomas Trotter had made a plea that the British population endeavour to preserve Great Britain's 'commercial greatness' and that 'ascendancy, which is so essential to our welfare in the convulsed condition of Europe' by recurring to simplicity of living 'so as to check the increasing prevalence of nervous disorders; which, if not restrained soon, must inevitably sap our physical strength of constitution; make us an easy conquest to our invaders; and ultimately convert us into a nation of slaves and idiots'.[49] The strength of the political and economic constitution is seen as directly dependent upon the health of the individual constitution. Commercial ascendancy, the domination of markets, can only be retained by carefully regulating the flow of psychological and bodily energy. If the physiological 'convulsions' of Europe are not to be repeated in England, the mental life of the entire body politic must be policed. Slavery and idiocy are not linked metaphorically, as expressions of a state without self-determination and control, but in a causal chain. The era accordingly saw the development of an institution known as 'medical police' concerned with the regulation of all matters of public health and hygiene.[50]

The rhetoric of the nineteenth century insistently linked the political health of a nation and its psychological state. With the increase of political and social agitation in England in the 1840s, theorists such as Barlow reiterated the accepted dogma that insanity increased 'to a frightful extent' with the French Revolution and declined with the restoration of order.[51] Charlotte Brontë's response to the European revolutionary activity of 1848 reveals how decisively she has imbibed the notion that physiological, psychological and social pathology are all interconnected. In a letter to Margaret Wooler in March 1848 regarding these 'convulsive revolutions' she observes:

it appears to me that insurrections and battles are the acute diseases of nations, and that their tendency is to exhaust by their violence the vital energies of the countries where they occur. That England may be spared the spasms, cramps, and frenzy-fits now contorting the Continent and threatening Ireland, I earnestly pray![52]

Having fallen into a state of disease, the vital organism of the French nation displays all the contorted behaviour of a lunatic left without the beneficial care of moral management, flailing around in 'spasms, cramps, and frenzy-fits'. Without proper political regulation, the 'vital energy' of the nation is dissipated in the wild, unproductive excesses of insanity.

In the symbiotic relationship between political and psychological life established in nineteenth-century discourse, political deviancy was figured in psychological terms, and categories of insanity were grounded in diagnoses of social pathology. Introducing his new theories of monomania (the belief that lunacy could be a partial state, restricted to one particular subject area), Esquirol suggested that it was a form of disease which followed the contours of social development: 'The more the understanding is developed, and the more active the brain becomes, the more is monomania to be feared. There has been no advancement in the sciences, no invention in the arts, nor any important innovation, which has not served as a cause of monomania, or lent to it, its peculiar character.'[53] Each shift in social organization produces its own specific effect on the patterns of mental stability. Lunacy offers an ever-changing relief map of the social body. Far from being the excluded, outside term, lunacy has become the interiorized space of society; to understand the workings of its hidden recesses is to hold the key to social knowledge.

INVISIBLE INSANITY: MORAL INSANITY AND MONOMANIA

The designation of new categories of insanity in the nineteenth century reflected these changing attitudes to mental disorder. Following the work of Pinel and Esquirol, English theorists developed the notion of what Prichard termed 'moral insanity' which he defines as: 'a morbid perversion of the natural feelings, affections, inclinations, temper, habits, moral dispositions, and natural impulses, without any remarkable disorder or defect of the intellect or knowing and reasoning faculties, and particularly without any insane illusion or hallucination.'[54] The description suggests a revolution in conceptions of insanity. No longer need there be any of the usual outward signs of lunacy; madness is compatible with a total absence of illusion, and an ability to reason without any discernible flaws in logic or understanding. The individual could thus function perfectly well within society; lunacy would be attested solely by a failure to conform to the increasingly rigid social and moral prescriptions of Victorian culture. While the eighteenth century imprisoned the madness of unreason, focusing on its outward effects, the nineteenth century adopted a more privatized sense of lunacy. The diagnosis of moral insanity was not a straightforward affair of decoding outer signs, but rested crucially on the observer's *interpretation* and assessment of the relationship between outward behaviour and inner motivation. Outward conformity was no longer sufficient. Insanity could still be adduced if the underlying emotional attitude was judged to be unsatisfactory. The emergence of theories of moral insanity is symptomatic of the tightening networks of social control in the Victorian era as the inner self becomes the target of ideological surveillance. The instability thus engendered in the heart of the self is suggested in *Jane Eyre* where the seeming outward conformity of Jane is counterpointed by the eruptions of 'moral madness' from Bertha.

Prichard's category of moral insanity was founded on an intransigent model of psychological continuity: decisive changes in behaviour patterns could offer evidence of lunacy, even though the behaviour itself was judged socially acceptable. A miser who turned philanthropist could run the risk of committal.[55] At a more fundamental level, theories of moral insanity enshrined normative judgments of 'natural' feelings and responses. Behind all the case histories offered in the various medical texts one can trace the uncompromising outlines of Victorian models of manhood and femininity. Women in particular were sufferers under this regime; one of the early examples Prichard quotes is that of 'a female, modest and circumspect, [who] becomes violent and abrupt in her manners, loquacious, impetuous, talks loudly and abusively against her relations and guardians, before perfect strangers. Sometimes she uses indecent expressions, and betrays without reserve unbecoming feelings and trains of thought.'[56] All the imprisoning Victorian assumptions concerning true femininity are encapsulated in this notion of the 'unbecoming' which shades directly into insanity.

Equivalent constraints were imposed upon young men: failure to show sufficient enterprise in the realm of commerce was judged sufficient evidence of insanity. Conolly cites the example of men who have talents but fail to show ambition :'They have no violent desires nor perturbations, and they never ripen. Neither ambition nor pride can rouse them to sustained efforts.'[57] The passivity, so desirable in young women, becomes pathological in men. Prichard similarly records the case of a young man whose attempts to avoid entering his father's business land him in an asylum where he is judged 'in every way a man calculated for business, excepting in the estimate he entertained of himself'. Despite his stay in the asylum, he still reveals symptoms of moral insanity in his patently unnatural display of resentment: 'he avoids his father, speaks harshly to him and angrily of him, and is suspicious of the rest of his family'.[58] With such an unwarranted display of familial distrust towards those who have incarcerated him, the young man fails the tests of social normality on two counts: business competency, and filial obedience.

The test of sanity for women rests almost entirely in the realm of emotional restraint. Bucknill and Tuke quote the words of a woman's self-diagnosis: '"I have my reason, but I have not the command of my feelings. Circumstances in life create feelings and prejudices which prevent my passing through life smoothly. My *intellect* is not insane; it is my *feelings* I cannot control." It would have been impossible to have described her case more correctly.'[59] The patient has internalized the social values and assumptions underlying notions of moral insanity. Rather than forcing a diagnosis on a reluctant client, the alienists merely have to stand back and admire the degree to which medical rhetoric has entered into the domain of self-understanding. Medical practitioners joined with other writers of the period in promulgating the new restricted standards of true womanhood, helping to promote the internal self-policing of emotional energy.

As Brontë's authoritative explanation of 'moral madness' in her letter concerning the depiction of Bertha suggests, notions of moral insanity passed rapidly into general social currency, offering scientific form and validity to the more vaguely defined social beliefs which had, in their turn, originally fuelled the psychiatrists' formulation of this category. Another psychological concept which caught the popular imagination was that of monomania, a term first formulated by Esquirol in France. From the late 1830s onwards, references to monomania recur throughout the literature and periodical writing of the period. In Brontë's work the term figures both in the early writings and in *Villette*, while in *Wuthering Heights*, Ellen, that voice of local lore, speaks of Heathcliff as having had 'a monomania on the subject of his departed idol', Cathy.[60] Together with the notion of moral insanity, the idea of monomania constituted one of the most decisive innovations in nineteenth-century psychiatry. Although monomania and moral insanity were rather different concepts, they were frequently associated, both in the popular and scientific literature of the time, since they both suggested ideas of partial insanity.[61]

Prichard defines monomania as a form of Intellectual Insanity 'in which the understanding is partially disordered or under the influence of some particular illusion, referring to one subject, and involving one train of ideas, while the intellectual powers appear, when exercised on other subjects, to be in a great measure unimpaired'.[62] On the surface, monomania can thus appear even more circumscribed a form of mental derangement than moral insanity. Lunacy could be signalled by one particular preoccupation or obsession, while perfect sanity is revealed in all other spheres. This notion of highly localized insanity caught the popular imagination, and monomania quickly became a commonly used term to designate fanaticism or obsession: a practising medium, for example, is described in *Blackwood's*, 1833, as 'a case of monomania well worthy the attention of Phrenologists'.[63]

The rise of notions of monomania and partial insanity had several important social and psychological implications. While the idea of moral insanity had suggested the possibility of a complete division between the moral and emotional aspects of the mind and the purely intellectual, monomania implied an even greater degree of mental division. No longer was the mind to be regarded as a unified entity. Cartesian man ceased to exist. In his place theorists suggested a model of the individual grounded entirely in physiology. The mind was placed firmly in the brain, which itself was then regarded as segregated, an aggregate of different parts without any necessary channels of communication between each section. In England, phrenological theory, which divided the brain into a congerie of different organs or faculties, helped facilitate the ready acceptance of theories of monomania. As Roger Cooter has shown, a large percentage of the British alienists and asylum keepers in the early Victorian period subscribed to some form of phrenological theory.[64] Although Esquirol himself was not a believer in phrenology, Andrew Combe returned to England having studied Esquirol's work with the firm conviction that the existence of monomania or partial insanity demonstrated the validity of the phrenological division of faculties. According to George Combe, the existence of monomania appeared 'to exclude the possibility of one organ executing the functions of all the mental faculties'.[65]

The introduction of ideas of monomania and phrenology held important implications for the representation of psychology in the novel. No longer was the individual to be viewed as a unified agent: action and feeling could be dictated by different parts of the mind which held no necessary interconnection or even awareness of the other parts' existence. In *Jane Eyre*, for example, battles are fought out between different faculties in the mind without any input from a controlling agency. With the development of notions of a fragmented, non-integrated mind, concepts of individual sovereignty were undermined. In place of the absolute ruler, dominating and controlling the processes of the body, a more malleable and also more tenuous model of the self was established. This shift in psychological theory parallels a similar development in social philosophy. Just as the eighteenth-century individualist doctrine of rights was supplanted in the nineteenth by an emphasis on social duty and membership of the wider social whole, so, in the psychological sphere, ideas of autonomy and control gave way to an image of self based on the interrelationship between the different organs of the mind. The problems of reconciling the conflicting demands of social integration and personal control, foregrounded in economic debate, also surface in the domain of psychological thought.

The social emergence of conceptions of a divided mind was directly correlated with a new form of public intrusion into the inner realm of the psyche. If the part was no longer identical with the whole, and outer form no longer gave expression to a unified inner self, since different selves might lurk behind the social mask, then public policing was required to root out the undesirable elements. The spectre of invisible insanity gave even further power to the rising profession of medical alienism. According to Esquirol,

There are some insane persons so reasonable that it is necessary to live with them, and to follow them in every action of their life, before pronouncing them mad. Some of them know so well how to disguise their situation, and to justify their actions, that it becomes extremely difficult even for judges to pronounce whether they are insane or not.[66]

Medical policing must now intrude even into the sanctity of the home. So complete is the insane person's capacity for disguise, that only a professional alienist, keeping the individual under careful surveillance in an asylum, can authoritatively pronounce on their state of mental health. Esquirol frequently extended this system to watching patients all night, convinced that they would reveal the secrets of their insanity in their sleep.[67] People were now likely to learn, from the voice of the expert, that family members with whom they had lived closely for years had in fact been maniacs all that time. Prichard cites the case of the man who had believed his wife had been insane for six months, but was at length convinced by Pinel that she had actually been insane for fifteen years.[68] Self-distrust and watchfulness must be accompanied by careful surveillance of all one's closest friends and relatives. Esquirol's translator, Liddel, inserts a footnote into the text to warn readers that 'Insanity is sometimes so insidious in its attack as to escape the notice of even the nearest relatives for a considerable period. As a general rule, any change from the usual habits of the individual should excite suspicion.'[69] With such incitements to vigilance, it is little wonder that the Reverend Brontë subjected himself and his family to such rigorous medical scrutiny, filling the margins of his *Domestic Medicine* with worried jottings on nervous disease. Far from indicating a state of pathology, his anxieties, and Charlotte's own preoccupation with nervous disorder in her fiction, suggest rather their immersion in the currents of contemporary concern.

The interest manifest in Brontë's fiction in the possibilities of reading the mind from the details of external form must also be placed within this nexus of psychological thought. Once the possibility of invisible insanity emerges, the interpretation and decoding of external signs takes on an unprecedented importance. The first medical illustrations of insanity emerged in the nineteenth century (and the first atlas of insanity was appended to Esquirol's *Des Maladies Mentales* in 1838).[70] Virtually all the manuals of psychological medicine of the era offered guidelines as to how the physician should interpret the physiognomical and pathognomic signs of their patients' outward appearance. Conolly suggests that even the 'most masterly dissembling' of patients cannot hide their true condition from the physician skilled in the interpretation of psychological signs. Such are the legible indicators of the inner state that 'the very mode of wearing the hat will differ in the same man, in his sane and in his insane state'.[71]

Further implications of notions of monomania and partial insanity, and of a related nineteenth-century conception, instinctive insanity, can be traced in the sphere of legal discourse. As Roger Smith has shown, the early part of the century witnessed a dramatic increase in the use of the insanity plea in court.[72] Within the court room, and in the accompanying publicity given to the celebrated cases, ethical and social issues surrounding the concepts of individual responsibility and self-control were debated and given form. Notions of instinctive insanity suggested that an individual might be insane only at the moment of committing a criminal act, and monomania was compatible with a life of apparent total normality, apart from within the circumscribed area where behaviour had moved into the criminal sphere. Pursuing this logic, Prichard cited absence of motive for a crime as a criterion of insanity.[73] The debates brought into direct confrontation the two associated sets of premises underlying contemporary economic and psychological theory. Maudsley defined the problem as a conflict between medical determinism and legal voluntarism: 'medicine deals with matter, force, and necessity; law deals with mind, duty, and responsibility'.[74] The legal debate merely crystallized, however, the contradictions already present in Victorian economic theory. The individualist rhetoric of laissez-faire economics made each individual firmly responsible for his or her own actions. Yet the same economic theory also suggested that, far from being autonomous, the mind and body of the individual worker merely formed part of the general circulation of energy in the social economy. The individual was deemed to be both 'responsible', and also a simple cog within the operation of the social machine, a mere conflux of forces without any determining control. In Brontë's fiction one finds a similar alternation: fierce assertions of self-determination are followed by statements of powerlessness, where the self is projected as a mere product of uncontrollable energies.

With the increasing use of medical evidence in trials, public debate focused on the social implications of recent developments in the categorization of insanity. Medical journals, and popular periodicals alike carried articles exploring contemporary issues in medical jurisprudence.[75] An article on 'The Plea of Monomania in Criminal Cases' in the *Journal of Psychological Medicine and Mental Pathology* pointed out the worrying aspects of a position where 'Men of Science declare that monomania is consistent with sanity in all other points, and a jury acquits.'[76] A writer in a later edition of the same journal defines the central issue as hinging on the 'solidarity' of the mind: whether it is *one* or, as the supporters of the theory of monomania maintain, a '*compound*, consisting of many distinct faculties or attributes, any one of which may be disordered or subverted independently of the others'.[77] Judgment of mental derangement must rest, he suggests, on a measure of responsibility: genuine disorder must be carefully distinguished from 'mere unbridled passion and *unresisted*, but not *irresistible* impulse'.[78] Yet the distinction between a resistible and irresistible impulse does not solve but merely highlights the problems surrounding the notion of responsibility, since the idea of a resistible impulse necessarily implies a unified subject as the source of resistance.

To illustrate the category of *genuine* disorder, the writer cites the case of a murderer who, once 'the orgasm has passed away', remains by the victim, 'aimless and motiveless'.[79] The use of the term 'orgasm' suggests the onrush of desire which overtakes the mind, and then leaves the individual helpless and drained of energy. In depicting the rise and fall of her protagonists' emotions, Brontë uses similar terms: Jane Eyre, when confronting Mrs Reed, feels a surge of power, quickly followed by feelings of utter helplessness. Medical texts of the era associated such attacks primarily with familial relations; the writer quotes Esquirol on monomania: 'The Impulse is sudden, instantaneous, unconsidered, *stronger than the will*; the murder is committed without interest, without motive, most frequently upon those most dear to them.'[80] The description enshrines the ideological assumptions underlying conceptions of the disease: attacks on family are 'motiveless' since the sane hold these relations 'most dear'. Jane Eyre is similarly held by her aunt to possess an 'unnatural disposition'. Jane's narrative constitutes a defiant refutation of this charge, although it rests, significantly, on the same framework of psychological thought: Jane challenges the reading but retains the psychological premises on which it was based. She casts herself as the bewildered product of forces she cannot control.

The social debates surrounding the emergence of monomania and moral insanity as diagnostic categories offer an excellent guide to the significant issues and transformations within Victorian psychological discourse. By raising the spectre of invisible insanity, both categories pushed further the notion of interiorized selfhood; and by emphasizing the fragmentation of the mind they offered a decisive challenge to earlier models of unified agency. Understanding of these debates is crucial for an interpretation of Brontë's fiction, where the problems associated with the decipherment of external form are linked to a wider exploration of the issues of individual responsibility and control. Her first-person narrators in particular employ the rhetoric of contemporary psychological discourse in their explanations of act and impulse, shifting the ground of analysis as it suits their purposes. The self is projected variously as a unified, self-determining agent, and as a fragmented site of conflicting forces. Such oscillations between feelings of autonomy and of helplessness encapsulate the contradictory positions articulated not only within Victorian psychological discourse, but also in its economic ideology. Even at the times when Brontë's fiction appears most removed from the spheres of politics and economics, the language of psychological representation nonetheless draws on the terms of economic and social debate.

Popular acceptance of ideas of monomania and partial insanity was facilitated, I suggested, by the rise of phrenological theory which offered an explanatory framework for the segregated structure of the mind. It is within the domain of phrenology, which functioned both as a theory of mind, and as an explicit social movement, with its own journals and platform of social reform, that social and psychological theory in Victorian culture became most tightly enmeshed. Brontë's letters and fictional writings bear witness to her interest in phrenology from an early age, an interest, I will argue, which encompassed both the social and psychological aspects of its doctrines. In the following section, I will look in detail at the relationship between the physiological and social dimensions of phrenological theory, and its role within Brontë's local culture.

CHAPTER 4

Reading the mind: physiognomy and phrenology

Brontë's fiction is permeated by the language and assumptions of phrenology. Her novels, as one critic has remarked, 'contain passages of pure phrenological jargonese'.[1] It is not, however, just in the explicit descriptions of cranial form and organs that one can trace the influence of phrenology, but also in the more widespread references to the development and exertion of mental faculties, a form of talking about the self as a collection of heterogeneous elements which was popularized by phrenology. On one of her trips to London Brontë paid a visit with her publisher, George Smith, to a phrenologist, who gave a surprisingly accurate diagnosis of his anonymous caller's character.[2] Long before this time, however, we can trace her interest in phrenological ideas: Jane Moore is credited with possessing too large an organ of secretiveness in a story of 1838 (the Keighley Mechanics' Institute had acquired a *Manual of Phrenology* in the preceding year).[3] Throughout her letters Brontë adopts a segmented view of the self, alluding to the contest of faculties, their individual recalcitrance, and the impact of well-developed organs on social behaviour: she describes Harriet Martineau's amused response to Joe Taylor's 'organ of combativeness and contradiction' and attributes Dr Arnold's success to his 'giant faculty of labour'.[4] Thackeray's writing suffers, in her judgment, when his 'master-faculty' of observation is 'thrust into a subordinate position'.[5] With reference to herself, Brontë, writing to Wordsworth, speaks of possessing in childhood, a 'very strong faculty of admiration, but a very weak one of criticism'.[6] Active exercise of the 'faculty of imagination' she tells W. S. Williams in 1849, lifts her up when she is sinking. Her language in this letter highlights the ways in which phrenology assimilated the Protestant culture of self-advancement. She informs Williams that 'I am thankful to God who gave me the faculty; and it is for me a part of my religion to defend this gift and to profit by its possession.'[7] In 1850 she writes to

G. H. Lewes of her longing for some invention to enable distressed authors 'to compel to obedience their refractory faculties'.[8] Extending her tendency to speak of Currer Bell as a separate existence to her own, outside of her control, she suggests that even this shadowy figure cannot control his faculties: the production of a new book 'is between him and his position, his faculties and his fate'.[9] The comments vary from the serious to the humorous, but whether Brontë is offering heartfelt moral advice to her friends, or comically deploring her own deficiencies, she adheres to the same model of the psyche, stressing the fragmented nature of the mind, and the value of mental exercise.

Critics have already examined Brontë's interest in phrenology but have tended to elide its doctrines with those of physiognomy, considering it merely as a form of generalized concern with external appearance without any particular social or political import.[10] The impact of phrenology on Victorian culture was far more decisive than these analyses suggest. Phrenology, as Brontë would have encountered it, was not a neutral system of character classification and description: one thrust of the phrenological movement was to inscribe psychological questions directly in the domain of politics. In the hands of the social adherents of phrenology, the reading of inner character from outer form became an overtly political act, with the explicit goal of redrawing the map of social hierarchy.

In its dual role of scientific theory of the mind, and popular social movement, phrenology played a significant part in Victorian scientific, social and economic life. As a scientific doctrine of the materialist functioning of the mind, it established the foundations for later developments in physiological psychology; and in its more popular guise, as the foundations of a widespread social movement, it helped inculcate the tenets of that crucial economic ideology of Victorian England: self-help.[11] Phrenology also served, however, as a platform for the articulation of social dissent: its doctrines were susceptible to diverse social and political interpretations. Brontë's fiction exploits this diversity, particularly in the field of gender politics, using the phrenological framework both to sustain bourgeois ideologies of self-help and control, and to offer a radical challenge.

One of the attractions of phrenology for Brontë was that it supplied a coherent framework for conceptualizing and speaking of the intersection between social and psychological life. The play of internal physiological energy could be linked to a wider pattern of social advancement, and the dynamics of personal interaction, where power hinged on the issue of legibility, could similarly be transposed into a larger political field. Phrenology was not entirely unique in this respect, however, and in offering a detailed analysis of its social functions, I do not wish to appear to be overestimating its role, either by isolating it or endowing it with exclusive influence. Many of the tenets of phrenology were not original, and indeed drew their strength from the fact that they reinforced dominant ideological strands in Victorian culture (and were thus available to Brontë in other forms). The significance of phrenology for Brontë, and for Victorian culture as a whole, lies not so much within its originality as in its function as a paradigmatic discourse of the era, condensing within one framework psychological, social, economic, and textual concerns.

The rise of physiognomy and phrenology at the end of the eighteenth century, and the re-emergence of interest in the decoding of physical form, can be linked, together with the concomitant development of medical psychiatry, to the fundamental transformations in social and cultural organization and systems of control taking place at that era, and to the correlated emergence of new interiorized models of selfhood. Although the two systems of physiognomy and phrenology clearly overlapped in popular usage, they sprang from very different roots, and were associated with quite distinct world views. While physiognomy, as defined by Lavater and other eighteenth-century theorists, was an extension of theology; phrenology, in its English incarnation, was based on a materialist system of the mind and was linked to a specific political and and social platform.[12]

English nineteenth-century interest in physiognomy was stimulated primarily by the writings of Lavater, translations of whose work flooded into England in the 1780s and 90s, under the title *Essays on Physiognomy*.[13] According to Lavater, physiognomy was 'the science or knowledge of the correspondence between the external and internal man, the visible superficies and the invisible contents'.[14] The premises of his doctrine were religious: God had inscribed a language on the face of nature for all to read. It necessarily followed, therefore, that an absolute correspondence existed between outer human form and inner moral quality, since otherwise, 'eternal order is degraded to a juggler, whose purpose it is to deceive'.[15] Lavater's vision of a science of physiognomy arises from his conception of a new interiority and invisibility in nature, exemplified pre-eminently in the constitution of man. True knowledge must now rest on an understanding of the relationship between outer sign and inner content, body and spirit.[16] Thus Lavater castigates the 'mere literal readers' of the general populace: 'The herd satiate themselves with words without meaning, externals without power, body without mind, and figure without essence.'[17] The signs of nature are meaningless unless read in the light of the animating spirit of the divine Word which is 'the very soul of knowledge, and the secret of secrets'.[18] The book of nature has been transformed into a repository of secrets which require expert decoding: mere 'literal' classification is to be replaced by skilled reading and interpretation. Man is simultaneously accorded both a new invisibility and increased legibility: no matter how spiritual his essence might be, he is 'only visible and conceivable from the harmony of his constituent parts' hence 'this material man must become the subject of observation. All knowledge we can obtain of man must be gained through the medium of our senses.'[19] With the suggestion that the individual is only 'conceivable' if read through the details of external form, we are offered a fundamentally new theory of the self which will also underpin the development of medical psychiatry. Not only is the individual transformed into a material object to be defined and controlled through observation; selfhood is predicated on the social interaction of the gaze.

The science of phrenology which evolved from the writings of Franz Joseph Gall in the 1790s held much in common with physiognomy, but its fundamental premises were neither essentialist nor idealist but rather defiantly materialist. Although phrenology shared with physiognomy an interest in the decipherment of external signs, Gall's primary concern was with the physiological functioning of the brain. He poured scorn on the work of Lavater and other physiognomists who were not 'guided by the knowledge of anatomy and of physiology' and knew nothing of 'the laws of the organisation of the nervous system, and of the brain'.[20] Gall was interested in the external formation of the skull only as a means of demonstrating his theories of cerebral localization: his belief that the mind was divided into distinct faculties, each of which had a specific location in the brain. The size of each bump on the skull indicated, he believed, the strength of the individual organ lying below.

The phrenological interpretation of external form thus differs substantially from that of physiognomy. Lavater believed that outer form directly expressed, or embodied, inner quality. Like the German *Naturphilosophen*, he emphasized the harmony and unity of the whole:

'Each part of an organized body is an image of the whole, has the character of the whole.'[21] There was thus no space for division between sign and signified, nor for any psychological multiplicity or internal contradiction. The moral character of an individual was imprinted unambiguously on the face for all, who were able, to see. Phrenology, however, treated the external only as a system of signs to be decoded to determine what lay below: the sign itself was not directly expressive of inner quality, but was only an indicator of quantity.[22] Contrary to physiognomical principles, a large bump of amativeness, for example, would not in itself possess a particularly amative character. While physiognomy claimed to be based on an extension of intuitive understanding, on evidence open for all to see, phrenology necessitated the acquisition of a special body of knowledge in order to interpret skull formation. Taken singly, the individual contours of each cranial organ, like elements in a language, held no meaning, their significance lay entirely in the observer's interpretation of their pattern of relationship. Against the physiognomical insistence on unity between part and whole, sign and signified, phrenology proclaimed the arbitrariness of the sign and the inner multiplicity of the mind.

Physiognomy and phrenology thus offered two contrasting forms of semiosis. Physiognomy was essentialist, idealist, and open of access; phrenology was relational, materialist, and closed of access to the uninitiated. As semiotic systems, operating upon different social and intellectual axes, they presented quite distinct models of character interpretation. Gall's theories held no place for the physiognomists' belief in an animating soul. He ridiculed their belief that the soul actually builds its own external envelope; they 'suppose that the cause of the difference of the qualities and faculties of the soul depends on the soul itself, and not on the material organs'.[23] Such unrelenting physiological determinism roused the ire of the German Romantic Philosophers, who had enthusiastically embraced the essentialist premises of physiognomy, and also gave rise to strong political opposition. In 1801–2 Gall was forbidden by the government to deliver his public lectures in Vienna on the grounds that he was endangering morality and religion.[24]

The greatest impact of Gall's work stemmed from his materialist insistence that the brain was the 'organ of the mind'.[25] Although many nineteenth-century physiologists had severe reservations about other aspects of phrenological doctrine, Gall's theories stimulated research into the nervous system and the physiological basis of psychology so that by 1857 G. H. Lewes could observe that 'now there is no physiologist who openly denies that mental phenomena are directly connected with nervous structure'.[26] Far from endorsing earlier theories of the mind as an immaterial, indivisible entity, Gall insisted on its physicality and multiplicity: 'the brain', he argued, 'is composed of as many particular and independent organs, as there are powers of the mind'.[27]

The phrenological conception of the mind was based, like contemporary models of the economy, on the idea of fiercely competing energies; it thus grounded man's sense of identity in the experience of internal division. In explaining how the mind could simultaneously contain faculties of Benevolence and Destructiveness, George Combe, the Scottish populariser of phrenology, observed, 'Man is confessedly an assemblage of contradictions.'[28] Such a conception marks a significant departure from earlier associationist models of a cumulative unity in the mind. The phrenologists' model of mind held no space for a unifying, directing ego. The individual was, for the phrenologist, the site of warring forces, the conflux of different flows of energy. Internal contradiction was not simply an occasional occurrence, but a necessary state of being.

By undermining ideas of intrinsic psychological unity, and establishing the notion of internal multiplicity, phrenology laid the foundations for later nineteenth-century explorations into the complexities of the unconscious. In the suggestive words of Gall, phrenology 'will explain the double man within you, and the reason why your propensities and your intellect, or your propensities and your reason are so often opposed to each other'.[29] As I suggested earlier, phrenology played a significant role in many of the central debates within nineteenth-century psychological discourse: its premises helped facilitate acceptance of notions of partial insanity, and underpinned social and judicial discussions of the complex issues of individual responsibility and physiological determinism. Phrenology offered an explanatory structure for the experience of internal division which was crucial to Brontë's work. Her fiction draws on the vocabulary and assumptions of phrenology in exploring the relationship between physiological force and mental control: her protagonists shift constantly between a sense of power and autonomy and its converse, a feeling of helplessness in the face of irresistible internal forces.

Phrenology was not, however, merely a psychological theory: on

importation into Britain by Spurzheim and George Combe in the
1820s, it was transformed into an explicit social programme.[30] While
Gall had adhered to a relatively static conception of the faculties,
Combe emphasized their potentiality for development through
exercise.[31] In Combe's hands, phrenology was turned into a scientific
authorization of the doctrine of self-improvement. Reversing the
apparently determinist component of phrenology, Combe argued
that there was no end to possible human advancement, once man had
fully grasped the laws of nature revealed by phrenology and had
altered his behaviour accordingly. Although faculty endowment was
given by nature, each individual could, by studying the laws of
phrenology, learn to maximize their full potential, developing areas
of strength and controlling weaknesses. Combe and his followers
extended their activities into the social arena, campaigning for social
reforms to facilitate individual development. Phrenological adherents
were at the forefront of mid-century agitation for social and legislative
change, using its doctrines as a platform from which to fight for
reform in penal institutions and lunatic asylums, and for radical
changes in the educational system (including education for women)
and in factory legislation.

From the perspective of the twentieth century, when the term
phrenology primarily conjures up associations with a peculiar craze
for examining bumps on heads, it is perhaps difficult to grasp the
immense social influence and popularity of phrenology in the
mid-nineteenth century. By 1851 Combe's *Constitution of Man*
(published in 1828) had sold 90,000 copies and was, according to
Harriet Martineau, outstripped in all time readership only by the
Bible, *Pilgrim's Progress* and *Robinson Crusoe*.[32] Few people in mid-
nineteenth-century England could have remained unaware of the
doctrines of phrenology, and the debates surrounding its emergence.
From the 1820s onwards, phrenology received constant attention in
newspapers and the periodical press, both of a supportive and
fiercely condemnatory nature. Brontë herself would have read
innumerable articles in *Blackwood's* and *Fraser's*, and in her local
papers where trial reports now frequently included phrenological
analyses of the accused.[33]

The lecture tour was another important means by which the
doctrines of phrenology permeated through to the general public. In
mechanics' institutes phrenology was one of the most popular
subjects, and Keighley Mechanics' Institute proved no exception. In

1836 they had their obligatory lecture; a phrenological bust was then duly acquired and a *Manual of Phrenology* placed in the library.[34] Local interest in the Leeds area was not only confined to mechanics' institutes however; the more socially elevated Leeds Philosophical and Literary Society had repeated lectures on the topic between 1821 and 1852,[35] and provided the forum for the nationally famous debate between Wildsmith and Hamilton on the materialist tendencies in phrenology which further intensified local interest.[36] Yorkshire seems to have been a centre of popular publishing in phrenology; innumerable layman's guides were published and distributed in the area, while the local newspapers carried frequent detailed reports of Samuel Smiles' 'impassioned speeches on the virtues of self-help, doctrines he had modelled on Combean philosophy.[37]

To answer the question of why phrenology should have proved so popular we must look at the social groups to which it appealed. Recent research suggests that it primarily appealed to socially marginal and upwardly mobile groups, though clear distinctions must be made here between the responses of medical and lay audiences.[38] As a social philosophy, phrenology offered a new system of classification. Against social divisions based on rank and privilege, it offered a new mode of measurement based on innate endowment. According to one hostile commentator of the time, the object of phrenology was 'to render the great mass of the community discontented with their condition, and with the existing relations of society . . . Phrenology . . . now appears as the disturber of the peace and well-being of society.'[39] In similar vein, a reviewer in *Fraser's* lumped together the doctrines of the 'Materialists, the Owenites and the Craniologists'.[40]

The actual social functions of phrenology were far less radical than these images and associations might suggest; they were, as both Temkin and Cooter have argued, reformist rather than revolutionary.[41] Phrenology offered a perfect philosophy for the new industrial economy: whilst challenging privileged interests, it suggested in their place not a levelling, but a new social hierarchy, which claimed for itself the legitimating authority of science. With its emphasis on individual improvement, phrenology diverted attention away from the possibility of class-based social action. The motto adopted by the *Phrenological Journal*: 'Know thyself' encoded their assumption that the road to social advancement lay primarily within self-analysis and introspection.

In the hands of Combe, the division of faculties was transformed into a natural hierarchy which in turn supported his progressivist theories of social advancement: the march of civilization could be measured by the degree to which men managed to subjugate their lower animal propensities to the control of their higher sentiments and intellectual faculties. By defining the clergy who criticised *Shirley* as 'men in whom the animal obviously predominates over the intellectual' Brontë was consigning them to the bottom of the social heap, identifying them as the enemies of social progress who would inevitably be thrust aside once talent, rather than innate privilege, became the determinant of social success.[42] In Combe's writings social control is seen to devolve naturally from the acquisition of self-control, a pattern, I will suggest, which is repeated in the structure of Brontë's fiction.

Combe's hierarchical, and hence politically reformist vision of the faculties did not go unchallenged, however. The popular lecturer, Mrs Hamilton, toured England and Scotland, taking her message that phrenology, in confirming the mental equality of the sexes, bestowed on woman the 'power to break the chains of the [male] tyrant and the oppressor and set [woman] completely free'.[43] While for men, the doctrines of phrenology might merely reinforce the emergent structure of social relations in industrial England, for women, they offered exciting new visions of social power and control, extending the horizons of social possibility.[44] The input of gender radically destabilizes the symbiotic relationship between phrenological doctrine and bourgeois ideology. Analysis of the complex functions of phrenology in Brontë's fiction suggests a similar dichotomy: although at one level the texts endorse Combean ideology, they also exploit, with reference to gender, the subversive potential of notions of equality and free faculty development.

The reasons for Charlotte Brontë's initial attraction to the doctrines of phrenology can be fairly easily discerned. Her social status, like that of the phrenological adherents analysed by Cooter and Shapin, was decidedly marginal: middle-class and educated, but with few surrounding social peers, and constantly under the threat of genteel poverty, she had, as a woman, no legitimate social outlet for her talents. Her first attempt to enter into the professional literary world was met by Southey's crippling rebuff, which she was initially willing to endorse: 'Literature cannot be the business of a woman's life, and it ought not to be.'[45] Her second-class status was reinforced by the favouritism shown towards her pampered brother, Branwell, whose extravagance forced her to become, for a time, a governess – a social role which, in placing her in a limbo between employer and servant, further reinforced her sense of social liminality. In phrenology she would have found a philosophy which offered a legitimating faith in hidden talent, and suggested the possibility of an individual resolution to the social impasse. Both her letters and fiction use the vocabulary of phrenology to dramatize the possibilities of psychological transcendence of social limitations. Mary Taylor's description of life in Brussels awakens in her a wish for wings, 'such an urgent thirst to see – to know – to learn – something internal seemed to expand boldly for a minute – I was tantalized with the consciousness of faculties unexercised – then all collapsed and I despaired.'[46] Although the feeling is only transitory, Brontë's articulation of the experience draws on the Combean model of self-improvement and social advancement through the exercise of unused faculties.

In letters to her friends, Brontë repeatedly cites the wisdom of faculty exertion, however distasteful the object of labour might be.[47] She worries about Mary Taylor's 'flightiness' but feels that once she is occupied in 'serious business' then 'her powerful faculties will be put to their right use'.[48] Faculties possess their own energies which can clearly be disruptive if not rigidly controlled. The same model of mind can also be used, however, to legitimate unorthodox action, under the banner of personal powerlessness. Brontë defends her artistic practice to G. H. Lewes on the grounds not of personal choice, but rather of impotence: 'imagination is a strong, restless faculty, which claims to be heard and exercised'.[49] On a more charged, emotional plain, Brontë writes to M. Heger of the impossibility of keeping silent and thrusting suffering down: 'quand on ne se plaint pas et qu'on veut se dominer en tyran – les facultés se revoltent – et on paie le calme exterieur par une lutte intérieure presque insupportable'.[50] The language of the faculties allows her to draw a distinction between conscious desire and unruly internal energies, in terms here which draw attention to the ways in which the patriarchal controls on female behaviour re-enact the political structures of social tyranny.

Brontë's most explicit response to phrenological theory occurs in her letter of advice to George Smith in which she endorses the moral to be drawn from the phrenological reading of his character produced by Dr Browne, the phrenologist they had both visited (she judged the reading to be 'a sort of miracle – *like* – *like* – *like* as the very life itself'.[51]

If I had a right to whisper a word of counsel, it should be merely this: whatever your present self may be, resolve with all your strength of resolution never to degenerate thence. Be jealous of a shadow of falling off. Determine rather to look above that standard, and to strive beyond it. Everybody appreciates certain social properties, and likes his neighbour for possessing them; but perhaps few dwell upon a friend's capacity for the intellectual, or care how this might expand, if there were but facilities allowed for cultivation, and space given for growth. It seems to me that, even should such space and facilities be denied by stringent circumstances and a rigid fate, still it should do you good fully to know and tenaciously to remember, that you have such a capacity.[52]

Such self-revelatory 'advice' suggests the powerful attractions of the phrenological creed which Brontë has clearly internalized as her own: in despite of all outward circumstances one can rest assured of one's own self-worth. The language of self-cultivation, and the defiant insistence on personal superiority, which characterizes the prose of Brontë's first-person narrators is here given particularized expression. On an even more revealing note, Brontë warns Smith that he must not allow himself to be overwhelmed by people with acquired knowledge: like herself, he should rest confident in the powers with which he has been endowed by Nature which distinguish them both from the common run. Phrenology offered a double-edged sword: one need not despair of one's present situation, since the potentiality for self-improvement was unbounded; but, in addition, one could also comfort oneself with the sense of the superiority of one's innate endowment.

One of the clearest statements of the phrenological doctrine of self-improvement is to be found in Anne Brontë's novel, *The Tenant of Wildfell Hall*, which foregrounds the lamentable figure of Arthur Huntingdon who, like Branwell, loses his 'faculty of self-government' and becomes locked in 'absolute bondage' to his 'detestable propensity' for drink (phrenologists were also leading lights in the temperance movement).[53] In an erotically charged scene, which parallels that between Jane and Rochester, Arthur offers his head to his wife's inspection: 'The head looked right enough, but when he placed my hand on the top of it, it sunk in a bed of curls, rather alarmingly low, especially in the middle.'[54] The sensuous mop of curls hides the significant absence of Arthur's 'organ of veneration' (an absence, notably, which would not be disclosed in a purely visual, physiognomical inspection). Helen's answer draws on the Victorians' favourite Biblical parable, revealing the ideological process by which Biblical teachings are always recast within the dominant social paradigms of an era:

> You are not without the capacity of veneration, and faith and hope, and conscience and reason, and every other requisite to a Christian's character, if you choose to employ them; but all our talents increase in the using, and every faculty, both good and bad, strengthens by exercise; therefore, if you choose to use the bad – or those which tend to evil till they become your masters – and neglect the good till they dwindle away, you have only yourself to blame. But you *have* talents, Arthur – natural endowments, both of heart and mind, and temper such as many a better Christian would be glad to possess – if you would only employ them in God's service.[55]

As in the scene in *Jane Eyre*, phrenological analysis empowers the reader, conferring the right both to interpret and judge the unfortunate subject (a similar dynamic is in play in Brontë's rather bold response to Smith's phrenological reading). The seriousness of Helen's response, however, defuses the erotic tension which is actively heightened in *Jane Eyre* by this penetration into the concealed depths of another's psyche.

Phrenology did not simply offer a philosophy of self-advancement, it also constituted a system of power relations. Although this aspect of the science has received little attention from historians, it was nonetheless central to Brontë's fictional explorations. As systems of bodily decipherment which aimed to render visible the concealed inner domain of the psyche, physiognomy and phrenology shared, in this regard, some common ground. An article on Lavater in the *Encyclopaedia Britannica* recounted how, 'in many places, where the study of human character from the face became an epidemic, the people went masked through the streets'.[56] Phrenology, with its overt social aim of redrawing the lines of the social hierarchy, represented an even greater threat to the security of selfhood. In a sympathetic review of the doctrines of phrenology, Chevenix summarizes their position in the following terms: 'We will tell the men of every country their faults and their vices, their virtues and their talents, and hold them up, as clearly as size and form can be held up, to the notice of mankind. None shall escape us.'[57] Although the phrenologists themselves were more cautious about proclaiming their power, their detractors focused on this threatening aspect of their system. Thus an only partially facetious reviewer in *Blackwood's*, 1851, argues that one might see in the doctrines of phreno-mesmerism 'the consummation of "knowledge is power."'[58] A more moderate version of this claim is offered by the physician John Elliotson who suggests that the individual who acquires skill and knowledge in this field will 'feel himself to be possessed of a power in his intercourse with men and books relating to the human character, to which those unacquainted with phrenology are perfect strangers'.[59]

The different semiotic theories of physiognomy and phrenology gave rise to distinct power dynamics. Unlike physiognomy, which claimed to be based on an extension of intuitive understanding, and thus on evidence open for all to see, phrenology operated according to a set of rules which were closed to the uninitiated. Phrenological adherents could thus stand in judgment over their less knowledgeable counterparts, claiming, moreover, the validating authority of science for their verdicts. While physiognomy merely recast in verbal terms the unambiguous statement imprinted in the features, phrenology delved below the surface, examining the secrets of a psyche which was no longer figured as one uniform essence, but rather a contradictory, fragmented system. A phrenological reading would explore not only present attainment, but also potentiality (hence M. Paul's rather enigmatic decipherment of Lucy's character in *Villette*), and would offer an emphatic judgment on the position each individual should hold within the social hierarchy. Reading the inner self had become an overtly political act.

Phrenology, I have suggested, functioned as a condensation of many of the dominant strands in Victorian psychological discourse. It gave new political meaning to the power struggles focused on unveiling the inner self, on the acquisition of control through knowledge; and in emphasizing the material and segmented basis of mind, it offered theoretical grounding for ideas of partial insanity, leading the way in the development of theories of physiological psychology which were similarly to undermine ideas of psychic unity and integration. In place of the unified ego, it installed complex systems of circulating energy (in terms which directly paralleled the concerns of contemporary economic rhetoric). Phrenology seemed to offer a scientific basis for the ideologies of self-control which dominated Victorian culture. Yet while calling for ever greater self-command and faculty development, it created a model of perpetual internal faculty conflict which, while reproducing the Victorian ethos of competition, nonetheless clearly conflicted with the theoretical need for some model of hierarchical control. Phrenology canonized the principles of self-control, while simultaneously undercutting all notions of a unified, directed self. Its doctrines thus offered a perfect encapsulation of the ideological conflict which dominated Victorian economic and psychological discourse: ideas of responsibility and control are set in uneasy juxtaposition with material, determinist models of the mind.

In many ways, phrenology could function as an empowering doctrine for women: it could be read as a statement of the mental equality between the sexes, and it seemed to offer new vistas of social power and opportunity to be obtained through the careful nurturing of the inner faculties and the cultivation of self-control. Yet the whole rhetoric of self-control, so crucial to the socialization of Victorian men and women, was nonetheless in direct conflict with an alternative strand of psychological discourse which stressed woman's innate lack of self-control, and her subjection to the forces of the body. This conflict, with its dichotomous models of the female body and mind, underpins much of Brontë's fiction, where female self-assertion is invariably twinned with a sense of powerlessness and self-aversion. The following chapter will explore in detail the internal contradictions within Victorian formulations of femininity.

CHAPTER 5

The female bodily economy

Throughout Charlotte Brontë's fiction, her heroines relentlessly pursue their quest for self-definition and identity. Although they invoke a rhetoric of freedom, their language and categories of thought are nonetheless inevitably caught up within the contradictions of Victorian discourses on femininity. Brontë's heroines tread, either warily or defiantly, onto the field of self-assertion, only to be assailed immediately by profound remorse. They speak openly of their sexual feelings and are then consumed with shame for their unfeminine behaviour. Caroline Helstone believes that such open speech would be 'self-treachery', a defiance of 'Nature's' instincts, and Jane Eyre habitually uses the language of abortion and monstrous motherhood to define the 'deformed thing' produced by her rebellious thoughts and desires.[1] The internal dynamic of these oscillations forms one aspect of a wider field of ideological contradictions condensed within Victorian projections of gender identity.

The social and economic rhetoric of self-help and improvement upon which Brontë's protagonists draw was countered for women by an equally prominent strand of discourse which emphasized female powerlessness and subjection to the forces of the body. Even that seemingly most private act, self-definition, is yet inextricably interwoven within the wider material and linguistic field of economic and cultural practice. To understand why, for example, Victorian medicine focused on the pathology of the female body and its resistance to mental control, we must look beyond the narrow sphere of medical discourse to consider the ways in which ideas of gender division functioned to underpin the emergent social division of labour in industrial England. Similarly, at a more specific level, to account for the medical preoccupation with circulation (and particularly the menstrual cycle) within the female economy one must set physiological accounts of female reproduction against laissez-faire analyses of material production and economic circulation. None of these fields existed in isolation; all mutually informed the others. Language and assumptions passed from one sphere to another, eliding distinctions of category and creating associative clusters of thought. Ideologies of gender operated across the entire spectrum of Victorian thought, from botany to social hygiene, offering an interpretative grid which could function, through displacement, to offer apparent resolutions of intractable social problems. This chapter will explore in some depth the ideological deployment of theories and images of the female body, looking in particular at the intersections between economic and psychological discourse which define the framework of Brontë's novels.

The issue of legibility, of reading the inner psyche from the traces of outer form, which figures so prominently in Brontë's fiction, was also of central importance, I have suggested, in the social and psychiatric discourse of the era. Women and men were situated differently, however, with reference to the interpretative gaze: the condition of femininity was dependent on the woman retaining her impenetrability. In one of the many double-binds which characterize Victorian ideas on womanhood, a woman was deemed to be feminine (and thus truly woman) only if sexually responsive to a man; but should she disclose that responsiveness before the requisite time she would also forfeit her feminine status. Femininity was thus predicated on a condition of concealment, on a disjunction between surface control and inner sexuality.

This duality of womanhood is graphically presented in one of Brontë's early stories, 'A Peep into a Picture Book'. The narrator is arrested by a portrait of the charismatic Zenobia Percy, the 'most learned woman of her age' but also a figure given to hysteria and passionate outbursts:

Who would think that grand form of feminine majesty could launch out into the unbridled excesses of passion in which her ladyship not unfrequently indulges?...As I turn from this pictured representation of the Countess I must say she is a noble creature both in mind and body, though* full of the blackest defects: a flawed diamond; a magnificent landscape trenched with dark drains; virgin gold* basely adulterated with brass; a beautiful intellectual woman, but an infidel.[2]

Surface promise is belied by eruptions from the 'dark drains' of her inner recesses. Victorian attitudes to female sexuality cannot be summarized according to any simple division between virgin and whore; both attitudes were simultaneously deployed. The rhetoric of drains and sewers was not reserved for that outcast group of women, the prostitutes, but applied to all female bodies.[3] As one physician expressed it, the uterus is 'the sewer of all the excrements existing in the body'.[4] Zenobia's explosive energies merely offer for public display the internal corruption which characterizes all womanhood.

The language of the passage, with its depiction of 'a magnificent landscape trenched with dark drains' suggests the ways in which the female body came to function as a metonymic representation of the industrial organism in the mid-Victorian era. Both the city and the woman were figured as bodies containing within them dark hidden recesses harbouring disease or crime, liable to burst out at any moment in excesses of passion or social discontent. Like the industrial social body itself, the body of woman promised virgin gold, but then contaminated prospectors with the muckiness of brass. The noble progress of industrial development carried with it a threatening inner pollution, spawned in the dark alleys of the slums, which had to be controlled, purged and cleansed or even removed by surgery. According to an article in the *Lancet*, 'Towns, indeed, may be looked upon, and ought to be treated, as individuals; but in their present state they are diseased individuals, carrying about on their persons festering, malignant sores, sores which not only threaten to poison, but actually do poison, the rest of the economy'.[5] The notion of the industrial city as a polluted body was carried even further by that prime ideologue of Victorian laissez-faire economics, Herbert Spencer. He observed, with reference to the social disease engendered by the socially useless poor who were clogging and obstructing the system, that a surgeon would be foolish 'to let his patient's disease progress to a fatal issue, rather than inflict pain by an operation'. Indeed in a natural social order, unencumbered by state interference in the form of poor laws, society would 'excrete' its useless and unhealthy members.[6] Women, with their concealed inner recesses, and harbouring of polluted blood, contained naturally within them the sewers which so preoccupied the sanitary reformers of the mid nineteenth century and which figured in contemporary rhetoric as the breeding ground of social disease.

The preoccupation with hygiene, with cleansing and controlling, operated at all levels of social discourse. Calls for social sanitary reform were matched by those for 'mental sanitary reform' of which the disruptive working classes and women, with their unstable physical systems and predisposition to insanity, were to be the prime targets.[7] In the medical domain, the Victorian era witnessed the growth of a new specialism: the diseases of women and children (a category grouping suggestive of women's uncontrolled state) which heralded unprecedented medical interference in the regulation of the female uterine economy, a regulation which stretched at its most extreme into the sphere of surgical excision.[8] Surveillance and interpretative penetration were now to move beyond the surface of the female body to uncover the hidden secrets of sexuality. As John Power observed in his *Essays on the Female Economy* with reference to the mysteries of menstruation, 'it is to be hoped that the light of truth will eventually be enabled to penetrate into the more secret, and hitherto unexplored, recesses of Nature'.[9] Just as Henry Mayhew sought to expose the hidden corners of London slums to the light of social investigation, so medical practitioners attempted to illuminate the unexplored territory of the female body. The sanitary reformers and medical men shared the same language and assumptions, investing particular terms with an associative freight of meaning.

In responding to Mayhew's papers on the London poor, Brontë echoes the rhetoric of *Blackwood's* and *Fraser's* and other contemporary accounts. She finds the articles, 'singularly interesting; to me they open up a new and strange world, very dark, very dreary, very noisome in some of its recesses, a world that is fostering such a future as I scarcely dare to imagine'.[10] Her vision of the city as a pathological organism, a form of demonic mother breeding unspeakable offspring reproduces popular representations of the 'noisome alleys' of the slums, giving birth to the 'heaving of the mindless behemoth'.[11] Brontë is less willing to endorse, however, medical theories of female pathology. In a letter to Ellen Nussey, she praises her friend for possessing as honest a soul 'as ever animated human carcase – and a clean one for it is not ashamed of showing its inmost recesses.'[12] The swift transition from carcase to cleanliness suggests a troubled resistance to contemporary medical theories of hidden female pollution. Similarly, in her fiction she returns again and again to the neatness and inner cleanliness of her heroines: they might be slightly untidy on the outside, but when their desks are opened up to male inspection they reveal an exquisite neatness and unsullied purity.[13] Running counter to this insistent representation of female neatness and control, however, we find repeated explorations of female passion which employ the language of pollution, and figures such as Zenobia and Bertha who display only too clearly the condition of palpitating excess which medical discourse attributed to all women.

The discourse of disease in the Victorian era drew directly on notions of polluted internal space. Cholera, which seemed to pass mysteriously and invisibly across all known barriers, was associated with syphilis which could lurk invisibly within the female body, turning even the innocent wife into a diseased receptacle who would unwittingly poison her children. Suggested cures for cholera ranged from industry and education (thus converting the 'pestilential marsh' and 'stagnant waters' of 'ignorance and sloth' into 'flowing and irrigating streams') and mental self-control (developing a disposition that would keep it at bay).[14] In the late 1840s public attention turned specifically to syphilis and the role of prostitutes in transmitting the disease. According to W. R. Greg, with an estimated 50,000 prostitutes in England, 'spreading infection on every side of them, quarantines against the plague, and costly precautions against the cholera, seem very like straining at gnats and swallowing camels'.[15] Greg's alarmist calculations suggested that ten per cent of the male population of England acquired syphilis by this means. Prostitution seemed to reveal, through a form of ghastly parody, the interconnected, distributive networks of the social organism. Sexuality, and specifically female sexuality, appeared to lie at the heart of the corruption of the industrial social body. These associative connections are given fictional embodiment in Dickens' novel, *Bleak House*, where the mouldering diseases of capitalism and female sexual passion are drawn into one circle. Esther Summerson learns of her origins in sexual sin and is immediately struck down by a disease bred in the horrifying recesses of Tom-all-Alone's, 'a villainous street, undrained, unventilated, deep in black mud and corrupt water'.[16] Lack of due regulation has created both this stagnant human cesspit, which threatens to pollute the entire social organism, and the self-destructive consequences of Lady Dedlock's sexuality. The two finally come together with her death amidst the miasma of the graveyard.

To understand Victorian attitudes to female sexuality we must move beyond simple dichotomous divisions, to explore the diverse, often mutually conflicting models of womanhood which were brought into play. Just as Dickens' novel, with its complex sets of character doubling, breaks down any rigid divide between angelic innocence and sexual guilt, so in the wider field of social discourse we find contradictory formulations of womanhood. We are all familiar with the Victorian trope of the angel in the house: the male returns from his contaminating material labours in the outer world to be spiritually refreshed by his angel within the inner sanctum of the home. This outer/inner polarity existed, however, in direct conjunction with another formulation of the inner/outer divide suggested by Brontë's representation of Zenobia: women were outwardly fair, but internally they contained threatening sources of pollution. The Victorian ability to maintain seemingly contradictory models of femininity is starkly revealed in Dr J. G. Millingen's 1848 work, *The Passions; or Mind and Matter*:

If corporeal agency is thus powerful in man, its tyrannic influence will more frequently cause the misery of the gentler sex. Woman, with her exalted spiritualism, is more forcibly under the control of matter; her sensations are more vivid and acute, her sympathies more irresistible. She is less under the influence of the brain than the uterine system, the plexi of abdominal nerves, and irritation of the spinal cord; in her, a hysteric predisposition is incessantly predominating from the dawn of puberty.[17]

Two traditional tropes are here combined: Victorian medical textbooks demonstrated not only woman's biological fitness and adaptation to the sacred role of homemaker, but also her terrifying subjection to the forces of the body. While man is deemed to occupy the central defining position of rationality and control, woman is assigned to the two contrary poles of spirituality and bodily subjection. At once angel and demon, woman came to represent both the civilizing power which would cleanse the male from contamination in the brutal world of the economic market, and also the rampant, uncontrolled excesses of the material economy. The medical specificity of Millingen's terms, of uterine system and spinal irritation, gives scientific authority to notions of female pathology. Woman, with her constant predisposition to hysteria, is a figure of radical instability. As in the social economy, surface order rests on a precarious balancing of forces, ready to be disrupted and thrown into convulsions at the slightest disturbance of equilibrium.

The internal mysteries of the female body drew unprecedented medical attention in the early nineteenth century: the physiological processes of pregnancy, childbirth and lactation all became the focus of intense medical research and analysis. It was the functioning of menstruation, however, whose dark flow still remained threateningly inexplicable well into the latter part of the century, that seemed to haunt the male imagination.[18] According to the physician George Man Burrows in his 1828 work, *Commentaries on Insanity*, 'Every body of the least experience must be sensible of the influence of menstruation on the operations of the mind. In truth, it is the moral and physical barometer of the female constitution.'[19] Menstruation acted as an external sign system, or instrument, by which doctors could read the internal health, both *mental* and physical, of their patients.[20] It was believed, moreover, to play a uniquely causative role in the unified circulating system of body and mind. The physiological, mental and emotional economies of womanhood were all regarded as interdependent. Any aberration in the menstrual flow, Burrows continues, must inevitably create an equivalent form of mental disorder. Similarly, strong emotions could cause menstrual obstructions which could in turn lead to insanity and death. Burrows cites two noted cases of women who literally died of shame. He distinguishes the mere blush of modesty from the 'suffusion of shame': 'the blood is here retained, in a peculiar manner, in the capillary vessels, as if the veins were constringed. This sensation will suppress the menses, or other secretions, has occasioned insanity, and in some instances has even produced death.' Thus one woman 'became insane on the wedding-night, from shame on sleeping with a man'.[21] The medical and psychological literature of the era focused on the inter-relations of the nervous and vascular systems in the enclosed system of the female economy. If the menstrual flow were obstructed, and hence denied its usual exit it would, doctors warned, be forced to flood the brain and thus lead to irreparable psychological breakdown. Although the emerging state of the field meant that there were divergent theories of the female reproductive system at this time, there was remarkable unanimity with regard to the importance placed on menstrual flow.

Medical theories of the role of menstruation in the female economy were used in fairly overt ways to police the boundaries of gender identity. Burrows warns, for example, that intellectual study for a woman could lead to suppressed menstruation, and thence, to the eruption of nymphomania (a connection which suggests the associations drawn between sexual energy and menstruation).[22] Similar arguments were employed later in the century, to bar female entry into higher education: withdrawing physiological energy from the reproductive organs, and directing it instead into intellectual pursuits would lead, physicians argued, to a complete breakdown of female health.[23] The weight of social disapproval directed towards female intellectual ambition is given full medical endorsement. Southey's warnings to Brontë concerning her 'unfeminine' desires to embark on a literary career, were underpinned, in contemporary medical ideology, by a more sinister, alarming message.

The problems associated with menstrual flow were not confined to a small percentage of unlucky women. As Thomas Laycock, one of the most pre-eminent Victorian experts on the female body, observed, with reference to that 'peculiar secretion' of the uterus, the menses: 'The first appearance of this secretion is almost always accompanied with symptoms of hysteria, more or less severe; recurring also occasionally at each monthly period'.[24] Inner excess and uncontrollable flow gives rise to outward symptoms of disorder (a similar association can be traced in the imagery which surrounds Jane Eyre's first explosion of passion, and subsequent imprisonment in the symbolic red room at Gateshead).[25] Like insanity, menstruation was seen as a physiological marker of social disruption. Just as insanity was believed to rise with the onset of the French Revolution, so 'The siege of Paris by the allies, in 1814, occasioned in the female inhabitants much irregularity in the menstrual flux'.[26] Such was the fragility of the female economy, any disorder in the outer social sphere was inevitably re-enacted in the internal processes of the body, thus metonymically reproducing the ailments of the social body.

The physician's Word on the instability of the female economy was also matched by deed, as women became increasingly the subject of medical regulation and control. Public medical writings, and private diaries and letters of the era suggest that we must discard completely our customary image of Victorian middle-class women as isolated from physical contact and understanding of their own bodies, and in its place substitute a perhaps even more disturbing picture of women anxiously monitoring every slight aspect of their bodily functions, constantly under threat of medical intervention in the most overtly physical forms. Brontë's own encounter with contemporary popular and medical theories of the female body was inevitable, whether through the numerous medical men who trailed through the house (including the distinguished Dr Teale, from Leeds, author of a treatise on hysteria), her father's collection of domestic medical texts, or the pages of the local newspapers.[27]

The entries under menstruation in the Reverend Brontë's beloved *Domestic Medicine* form alarming reading. With the first appearance of this discharge, Graham observes, the 'greatest care is then necessary, as the future health and happiness of the female depends in a great measure upon her conduct at that period'. The greatest danger, Graham warns, is that of causing an obstruction of the discharge, and extreme care should therefore be taken to avoid this eventuality. His examples help to explain why the Victorian heroine is always so solicitously guarded from the cold. Exposure to cold during menstruation will 'often be sufficient entirely to ruin their health and constitution . . . I have lately heard of a young lady, in my neighbourhood, who was suddenly seized with mental derangement after the improper use of cold water at this particular time; and all the means hitherto employed to restore her health and reason have altogether failed.'[28] Such dire warnings are by no means uncommon but are to be found throughout the medical and popular health literature, echoing the strictures set out in the eighteenth century by William Buchan in his *Domestic Medicine*, the other primary medical text to which the Reverend Brontë habitually turned, and which was still very influential in the Victorian era. A woman's delicacy at the beginning of her menses is so pronounced, Buchan suggests, that 'taking improper food, violent affections of the mind, or catching cold . . . is often sufficient to ruin the health, or render the female ever after incapable of procreation'.[29] Women ignored their menses at their peril; not only might their physical health break down, but they could be excluded forever from the social category of womanhood, whether through the loss of their sanity, or from the onset of barrenness, and the cessation of their reproductive powers.

Popular iteration of such doom-laden messages was not lacking. In the pages of the two local newspapers which formed one of the main staples of Brontë's reading from early childhood onwards, one can find similar views promulgated, pre-eminently, through the constant bombardment of advertisements for medical remedies. Within the explicit reporting of these two papers, the *Leeds Mercury*, and the *Leeds Intelligencer*, women rarely figure as active agents, they enter the pages rather as passive bodies, victims, for example, of sexual crimes, or subjects of medical experiments with chloroform. Where they are ascribed active roles, these are invariably associated with sexuality and mental derangement: accounts on the flourishing state of prostitution are set alongside reports on women being incarcerated in lunatic asylums, breaking out into hysteria or puerperal mania, and committing infanticide or suicide 'while the balance of the mind was disturbed' (the causes were often deemed to be shame after they had been sexually assaulted).[30] The female sexual body is graphically portrayed in these papers; no concern for the 'cheek of the young person' holds in check the often gruesome descriptions of sexual crimes and murders. Court reports frequently offer verbatim transcriptions of testimony, with a level of detail which our contemporary press entirely fails to match. For a female reader, the papers create an image of a world of sexual violence and female powerlessness, where even the workings of her own body and mind lie outside her control. The latter impression is further reinforced by the only sections of the paper specifically addressed to a female readership: the advertisements for remedies for female ailments. (Some measure of the impact of this advertising on the Brontë household can be gleaned from the fact that the Reverend Brontë recorded in his copy of Graham's *Domestic Medicine* his family's use of and response to, various of these remedies, while Charlotte and Branwell in their early writings frequently imitate and burlesque the format of the papers and their specific advertising copy).[31]

The advertisements targeted at female complaints were distinguished by their lengthy preambles and 'medical' justifications which reiterated and confirmed contemporary beliefs in the peculiar delicacy of the female system, and the pernicious impact of menstruation. Thus an 1837 advertisement for 'Lady Huntingdon's female pills' proclaims that they have 'rescued many thousand young persons from an early grave'. Their particular efficacy was to be found in 'cases of general Debility of the Constitution, in creating appetite, by strengthening the system, removing obstructions, giving relief to those troubled with fainting fits, nervous giddiness, pains in the head'.[32] Such recitations of symptoms functioned almost as a prescriptive list for femininity. In each case, the various forms of female ailments were all associated with 'obstructions', with the suppression or the irregularity of the menses. Pursuing a common practice, this advertisement reinforced its message with dire warnings purportedly drawn from contemporary medical opinion:

A learned Physician very justly observes that the health of females depending on circumstances more complicated and uncertain than that of the other sex, it is the duty of persons entrusted with their care to instruct them in the course they ought to pursue at those periods of life which require the utmost attention to prevent consequences which may render them sickly, infirm, and miserable for the rest of their existence.[33]

In the copy of these advertisements, the alarmist rhetoric of 'respectable' medical texts is heightened and given mass circulation.[34]

The same citation from a 'learned physician' occurred eight years later in an advertisement for the aptly named 'Croskell's female corrective pills', (phrasing which suggests that it is the very condition of being female that the pills are trying to correct, or punish) which were 'adapted to those morbid periodic affections peculiar to females'.[35] The reiterated refrain throughout the advertisements of this period is that of female vulnerability, and the determining impact of menstrual obstruction.[36] Thus an 1850 advertisement for 'Dr Locock's Female Pills' which prevent consumption, remove chlorosis and 'all nervous and hysterical affections', cites the opinion of six doctors that 'most of the diseases of women are caused by irregularities.'[37] All advertisements for female pills assume a direct continuity between the operation of the menstrual cycle, and mental health. To compound the image of female subjection to the tyrannous operations of the body, these threats and warnings were supplemented by advertisements for remedies for nervous affections which, if left untreated, the readers are informed, are liable to result in insanity.[38]

Medical advertising did not offer its message in isolation, however; to appreciate fully its impact it must be read in conjunction with the social and political reporting which defined its context. The medical remedies and texts touted in the *Leeds Intelligencer* of 4 January 1851, for example, include *The Medical Adviser*, which offers help with extirpating the evils of masturbation and venereal disease, Kearsley's Original Widow Welch's Female Pills, 'a safe and reliable Medicine in effectually removing obstructions, and relieving all other inconveniences to which the female frame is liable', and Holloway's Pills. These were billed as 'an infallible cure for female complaints'. They were 'searching, cleansing, and yet invigorating' for 'the maiden, the mother and the middle aged'; swiftly undertaking their task to 'remove every species of irregularity'. Under the mellifluous three 'm's lie the three biological stages of womanhood: puberty, pregnancy, and what was termed the 'climacteric', or menopause. In each case the dark obstructions within the body which cause irregular flow are to be sought out and 'cleansed': invigorating purity will result from this ritual purgation which rids the body of 'morbid blood', restoring the modest maiden to a state where surface appearance is not belied by the state of her bodily secretions.

Set against these advertisements was an account of the recent lectures at the Leeds Mechanics' Institute, including that by Dr Samuel Smiles on 'Self-Help in Man' and the Reverend W. M. Guest on 'Mental Improvement and Discipline'. In both instances, the activities of control and regulation are at issue; there is, however, a crucial gender distinction. Whereas the woman, rendered helpless by the tyranny of her body, must resort to external medication and supervision to regulate the flow of her secretions, and hence her physical and mental health, the man in Smilesian ideology needs nothing more than his own internal resources to bring about the requisite self-control which will enable him to climb the social ladder. With enough 'self-help' the labourer will become the 'self-made' man of mid-Victorian ideology – an expression which perpetuates the ideological erasure of female agency.

These juxtaposed images of female helplessness and male self-help are indicative of the increasingly rigid demarcation of gender roles which was taking place in the nineteenth century; a transformation over which the medical establishment presided, lending and indeed also in part deriving their growing prestige and authority from this process. Extending their purview beyond the simple processes of the female body, medical textbooks in the Victorian era gave scientific authority to contemporary ideological constructions of class and gender divisions. Thus John Elliotson, in *Human Physiology*, offers a description of sexual roles worthy of Sarah Stickney Ellis: 'The male is formed for corporeal and intellectual power; the female for gentleness, affection, and delicacy of feeling'.[39] Elliotson gives grave warning that woman is 'not intended for the rough business of the *world*'. Buttressing his argument with quotations from *Paradise Lost*, Elliotson calls to task those women who seek a wider sphere of activity: 'Women ill appreciate the true loveliness of their sex who wish to resemble man in their mind and occupations'.[40] Woman's role, according to Victorian medical opinion, was entirely bounded by her reproductive functions.

Brontë's heroines who enter the labour market have already broken the social prescriptions for femininity; but in making them small, slight and nervous, Brontë places them even further outside the charmed circle of acceptable womanhood. The social and medical emphasis on woman as reproductive vehicle heavily influenced social perceptions of female beauty and marriageability. Medical texts warned men to select their wives carefully, avoiding those who were pale or slight; William Acton warmly recommended the choice of a bouncing country girl.[41] The Victorian ideal of female beauty focused strongly on the procreative organs: a well developed bust and hips, set off by a narrow waist. Medical texts of the period sought to offer physiological grounds for this ideal. Thus one writer extolls the beauty of the wide female pelvis, 'the encasing of the procreative organs', and the 'voluptuous contours' of the bosom 'on which the organs for nutrition of the tender offspring are developed'.[42] Male erotic arousal is given acceptable social form by linking it entirely with the social duty of procreation. No longer need the male worry about his sexual response to female beauty, or the problems of selecting a fit mate: the external physical indicators of breeding capacity are all that should count since 'the Creator has provided that all the most attractive traits in woman's person shall indicate either *moral* or *physical fitness* for her duties as woman'.[43] Long before Darwin, and the late nineteenth-century eugenicist debates, the question of the healthy perpetuation of the species had become a focus of public attention. It was primarily the female, however, who was cast in this biological light, as if she alone were the agent of reproduction. The external signs of the female body were to be read not simply as indices of hidden secrets of character, but also as markers of reproductive potential, signals that a female was not merely masquerading, but did indeed have a right to be regarded truly as a woman. Brontë's heroines, by their very physique, are thus put on the margins of womanhood.[44] Their relationship to femininity is figured in their acquisition, or loss of flesh: Jane Eyre, as she falls in love with Rochester, 'gather[s] flesh and strength',[45] while Caroline Helstone's recovery from her illness is signalled by a restoration of those curves which had previously marked her reproductive fitness.[46]

The Victorian belief that woman should be subordinated to her reproductive role was nowhere more clearly demonstrated than in the medical profession itself, where midwives and female asylum keepers were ruthlessly attacked, hounded out and demoted.[47] A blatant ideological defence of this practice was offered by the obstetrician, W. Tyler Smith, who argued in *The Lancet* that the social value accorded to women, as demonstrated in their treatment in childbirth, was an index of a country's state of civilization. To preserve this 'value', however, women had to be excluded from the obstetrical labour market, which they 'degraded' by their presence, and restricted to the 'natural' sphere of reproductive labour. True 'respect' towards women, and thus the triumph of civilization, was signalled by the transference of 'the allegiance of the lying-in woman from Lucina to Apollo', from the incompetent female midwife, to omnicompetent male science.[48] Such a seemingly contradictory formulation, with its simultaneous elevation and abasement of the woman, reducing her from an active participant in the labour market to a passive bodily existence to be controlled by male expertise, is indicative of the ways in which the ideological deployment of gender roles operated to facilitate and sustain the changing structure of familial and market relations in Victorian England.

The social effectiveness of Victorian gender ideology derived to a large degree from the lack of apparent novelty in the formulations. Women were not for the first time being associated with the forces of the body; and nor were they thereby being cast forth from their other ideological role of spiritualizing and civilizing force. Throughout western culture the male/female divide has operated as a crucial site of ideological deployment. Although it has been articulated through a fairly constant set of interrelated oppositions, most notably those of mind/body and culture/nature, its formulations are never stable. Woman, for example, though rarely identified with mind, can emerge on either side of the nature/culture divide, depending on the specific historical and social context of the argument. With changing economic and social formations, different aspects of these polarities are mobilized, often in seemingly contradictory conjunctions, their articulation both containing and contributing to wider social tensions and conflicts. What we find from the late eighteenth century onwards is that the traditional, rather undefined associations between woman and the body are strengthened, particularized and codified in medical science. The introduction by Linnaeus of a sexual system of plant classification in the eighteenth century was indicative of the shape of things to come. Victorian scientists and social theorists increasingly sought out and extolled biological evidence of the sexual division of functions in all forms of life, transforming the interpretative map of both natural and social existence into one continuous chart of gender polarity.[49]

To try to explain why the study of biological differentiation should have been invested with such urgency at this period is to become involved in a complex network of determinants whose interconnections and formations have not yet been fully explored.[50] One obvious impetus for this interest, however, was the changing structure of social relations under the emerging industrial economy: the increasing social division of labour which took place both on the factory floor and in the growing bureaucracy which sustained the industrial system, and the concomitant further domestication of the middle-class woman. The intersection of class and gender ideology at this era is peculiarly instructive. Although middle- and working-class women were clearly situated in different relations to the labour market, both were equally subject to the reigning ideology which operated across class lines, emphasizing domesticity, and woman's role as biological reproducer of labour, rather than productive participant in the labour market. While middle-class women were thus held firmly within the confines of the home, supplying (in accordance with Malthusian notions of underconsumption) a leisured class of consumers, women of the working class were transformed into a more docile workforce who could be slotted into or retired out of the labour market, in accordance with the specific demands of each industry and the cycles of trade. Within this ideological formation, woman was figured simultaneously as angel, divorced from the material realm of the marketplace, and as body, devoted to the fundamental processes of material reproduction. The potential contradictions between these two models emerge strongly within Victorian formulations of gender roles.

Until recently, feminist criticism has tended to argue that the Victorian ideology of female domesticity was designed to suppress and control the threat of female sexuality. The problem should, however, be posed the other way round: why, at this specific historical period, should women have been perceived as being in possession of a disruptive sexuality which needed to be disciplined and controlled? Given that there was not an upsurge of female sexual rampancy at this period, and no more than the first rustlings of female social discontent, the answer would seem to lie outside the domain of female sexuality *per se*. Although many factors are once again in play (including the displacement of class antagonisms into gender terms), I would suggest that one strong impetus behind Victorian ideologies of womanhood springs not from the need to control women, but rather from the problems involved in assimilating *men* to the new conditions of the labour market.

With the increasing social division of labour, the question of sexual difference became the focus of ideological attention as concern with the partitioning of economic roles was displaced metonymically onto the individual body. By the early Victorian period gender demarcations in social and medical texts were mobilized within forms that responded directly to the contradictory formulations of laissez-faire economics. As I suggested earlier, man figured in the social and economic discourse of the era both as a self-interested actor, in full control of his own destiny, and also as a mere cog within the larger machinery of industrial labour, without free agency or self-determination. By the 1820s and 30s the speed of industrial transformation had accelerated, and revivified notions of the division of labour were brought to bear on the disciplining of the labour force. Political economists such as Ure and Babbage extolled the virtues of the machine as a corrective to the indiscipline of labour, and portrayed in loving terms the industrial ideal as that of 'a vast automaton, composed of various mechanical and intellectual organs, acting in uninterrupted concert for the production of a common object, all of them being subordinated to a self-regulated moving force'.[51] Both Tory and radical opponents of contemporary developments in industrialism focused their criticisms on this construction of man as a mere machine. Peter Gaskell expressed the fear that human labour under the industrial system would lose all social value: man 'will have lost all free agency, and will be as much a part of the machines around him as the wheels on cranks which communicate motion'.[52] Critics and apologists of industrialism alike proposed a similar model of man as automaton, a model seemingly confirmed on the factory floor with its endless subdivision of manual tasks and the subordination of human labour to the requirements of machinery.

The early Victorians were forced to address, in terms very different to those employed by Descartes, the interface between man and machinery. Yet at the same time that man was being spoken of as mindless machine, or automaton, he was also being celebrated, in accordance with the ideology of laissez-faire economics, as a rational, independent actor, exercising full control over his own activities in the marketplace, and capable of rising upwards through the social ranks solely through the exertion of his own powers. In the light of these social contradictions, Victorian ideologies of gender functioned as displaced forms of resolution. Notions of gender differentiation fulfilled the ideological role of allowing the male sex to confirm their faith in personal autonomy and control. Unlike women, they were not prey to the forces of the body, the unsteady oscillations of which mirrored the uncertain flux of social circulation, but rather their own masters; not an automaton or mindless part of the social machinery, but a self-willed individual, the living incarnation of the rational individualist and self-made man of economic theory. The disruptive social forces which had to be so decisively channelled and regulated to ensure mastery and controlled circulation in the economic sphere were metonymically represented, however, in the domestic realm, in the internal bodily processes of the woman in the home.

In medical discussions of the female mind and body, woman was figured frequently as an automaton, a category which linked her also to a whole series of unruly social 'others': infants, savages, and the working classes. Writing on hypochondriasis in 1821, John Reid observed that 'the savage, the rustic, the mechanical drudge, and the infant whose faculties have not had time to unfold themselves, or which (to make use of physiological language) have not as yet been *secreted*, may, for the most part, be regarded as machines, regulated principally by physical agents'.[53] As the century progressed, women were increasingly added to this list of machines, of peoples dominated by the workings of the body. Existing on the border between sanity and insanity, woman was ruled, Laycock argued, not by conscious control, but rather by the processes of reflex, or instinctive action which governed her physiological economy.[54] When Jane Eyre demands of Rochester, 'Do you think I am an automaton? – a machine without feelings?' her question carries a whole cultural freight of associative class and gender meanings.[55]

The ideological distinction between male self-control and female powerlessness which operated at a social level to sustain their differential positions within the wider social economy, also figured in more precise physiological terms in medical analyses of the female circulating system. Intuitively, one might assume that, as in other cultures, the sense of pollution associated with menstruation in Victorian England would be focused on the flow itself, on the mysterious out-pouring of blood. Contrary to such expectations, however, it seems that it was not the menstrual flow *per se* which caused alarm, but rather its suppression and retention. In this regard the marketing of female remedies mirrored the concerns of the medical establishment: the primary ill the pills were designed to alleviate was not the menstrual flow itself, and any accompanying physical pain, but rather its obstruction and suppression. Whereas the primary categories of male sexual disfunction in the Victorian era, masturbation and spermatorrhea, focused on the male need to retain vital force, to expend capital only in productive fashion, the primary form of female pathology was that of the *retention* of internal secretions.

Spermatorrhoea was itself an invention of the Victorian economic and sexual imaginary; a dreaded 'disease' whose definitive symptom was the uncontrolled emission of semen.[56] The medical elaboration of this disease drew on earlier strictures against the undisciplined 'spending' of vital force in masturbation, a vice which functioned in turn as a primary ideological figure of the horrors awaiting men who violated the sacred economic and social rules of self-control.[57] As in the case of representations of female 'obstructions', doctors and quacks alike participated in the social popularization of ideas of spermatorrhoea. Although some doctors dissented, and others tried to distance themselves from the unscrupulous ways in which quacks were manipulating worried males, both sides of medical practice basically collaborated in fanning the social fears focused on this particularly worrying disruption of self-control.

The fashionable diseases of mid-nineteenth-century England were thus marked by a crucial gender distinction. While male health was believed to be based on self-control, woman's health depended on her very *inability* to control her body. Any exertion of the mind, whether of intellectual effort, or fierce emotion, might prove fatal, it was suggested, in creating a stoppage of menstrual flow. Women should therefore concentrate on dulling the mind, allowing the processes of their body to proceed unimpeded by mental obstruction. Indeed the very possibility of female health depended on the woman's ultimate inability consciously to interrupt her menstrual flow. As in Brontë's vision of Zenobia, female identity was defined by the condition of *excess*, an excess which had to be sluiced away through her 'dark drains' if it was not to flow back and pollute the entire system. Samuel Hibbert, writing on woman's predisposition to hysteria in the early part of the nineteenth century, observed that 'when the growth of the form is nearly completed, the circulating fluid necessary for the future support of the body is in superabundance, and unless corrected in the delicate system of the female, must . . . necessarily acquire a power of rendering unduly intense the feelings of the mind'.[58] The intensity of emotion associated with womanhood is directly aligned with the flow of bodily fluids; only if such 'superabundance' is drained from the body can emotional tranquillity be preserved.

By the mid century this model of female 'excess' was incorporated into the new theories of the relationship between the sympathetic and spinal nervous systems, and physiological theories of the conservation of energy which, in regarding the body as a closed system, suggested the ready translatability of emotional and physiological force. In his 1853 study of hysteria, Robert Carter argues that there existed a 'natural tendency of an emotion to discharge itself either through the muscular, the secreting, or the sanguiferous system'.[59] Following through this notion of the interchangeability of emotional and physiological energy, he suggests that if women lack social outlets for sexual expression, they will be thrown into a state of hysteria.[60] Although arguments have been made for the modernity of Carter's thought, his arguments are solidly based on a development of mid-Victorian theories on the 'perversion of the secretions'.[61] In common with his contemporaries, he believed that the mental and physical health of woman depended on ridding the body of any obstructions to the free circulation of internal energy.

The fears of obstruction, accumulated waste, and stockpiling which dominated Victorian theories of the female economy were not confined to this one arena of concern. Like the rhetoric of male self-control which spread across medical and economic discourse, these preoccupations also featured prominently in contemporary writings on laissez-faire economics, suggesting a direct homology between certain physiological and economic models of circulation. Herbert Spencer argued fiercely for a literal, rather than a simple metaphorical relationship, between the internal dynamics of a physiological and a social organism. The two organizing categories for the social, as for the bodily organism, were, he maintained, those of waste and repair: 'what in commercial affairs we call *profit*, answers to the excess of nutrition over waste in a living body'.[62] Spencer proposes a direct analogy between the circulation of blood and that of money, concluding that there is a homologous relation between 'the blood in a living body and the consumable and circulating commodities in the body-politic'.[63] Viewed within these terms, the retention of the menstrual discharge would thus be the overwhelming of profit and nutrition by the poisonous attributes of waste. Free, unimpeded flow is Spencer's primary category of social health, any blockage or interference would overthrow the system as a whole. Thus government action to block the issue of notes by local banks would lead to extensive disruption elsewhere: wild unregulated forms of speculation would threaten the stability of the entire system.[64] Just as blockage in the female economy would lead to hysteria and insanity, so in the wider social system it led to its equivalent economic form: uncontrolled speculation. Spencer's physiological theories of the social economy place on a material base the traditional associations between the fickle, uncontrollable operations of credit, and the female sex.

Although Spencer himself did not explicitly address the relationship between the female and the social body, one finds throughout the medical and social rhetoric of this era an increasing intensity of focus on this issue. The cycles of production and reproduction are repeatedly aligned and compared. According to the obstetrician, Tyler Smith, in an article in *The Lancet*, the uterus was the 'organ of circulation of the species'.[65] The cycle of reproduction had to be policed and controlled to ensure the quality and continuity of social production. A woman's womb was figured both as a sacred font originating life, and as a crucial stage in the machinery of material social manufacture. Contemporary medical accounts emphasized the criteria of efficiency and the productive channelling of physiological force. Class anxieties fuelled these discussions. The idle middle-class woman, a direct product of the increasing social division of labour, was yet made the subject of attack by the self-same classes which had produced her. The alarming fertility of the working classes was contrasted with the supposed barrenness of the middle-class woman, whose idle and luxurious life style created the internal obstructions of secretions which led both to insanity and sterility.

William Buchan's *Domestic Medicine* outlined the complaint against the middle-class woman which was to gain a groundswell of popular support in the Victorian era. Barrenness, which was 'chiefly owing to an obstruction or irregularity of the menstrual flux' was to be regarded as a disease, which afflicted only the indolent and affluent female; the poor remained free from its effects.[66] Early nineteenth-century accounts added the 'savage' to this list, contrasting the seeming fertility and lack of labour pains of 'primitive' females to that of their diseased, 'civilized' counterparts. Buchan's observations on menstruation offer a perfect exemplum of the contradictory injunctions which were to govern Victorian prescriptions for womanhood. Women are simultaneously castigated for idleness and yet also warned that they must treat themselves with great delicacy during menstruation, making sure not only that they protect the body from cold and exertion, but that they also similarly protect the mind. The female should force herself to keep calm and cheerful during her menses since 'Every part of the animal economy is influenced by the passions, but none more so than this. Anger, fear, grief, and other affections of the mind, often occasion obstructions of the menstrual flux, which prove absolutely incurable'.[67] The foundations of the cherished Victorian image of female placidity are here being laid. Woman's 'mission' is to try and suppress all mental life so that the self-regulating processes of her animal economy can proceed in peace. Female thought and passion, like government intervention in the Spencerian model of the economy, created blockages and interference, throwing the whole organism into a state of disease.

With the development of medical specialization in the diseases of women during the Victorian era, the preoccupation with the functions and role of menstruation became more intense. Despite extensive research, however, the menstrual flow still remained, by the 1850s, disturbingly inexplicable.[68] Perhaps more than the self-evident functions of childbirth, menstruation became an obsessive focus for the male imagination, symbolizing, with its bloody, uncontrollable flow, the dark otherness of womanhood, the suppressed term behind the ideological projections of female purity and spirituality. The state of medical ignorance surrounding menstruation in the 1840s is illustrated by Elliotson's observation that the physical origins and *causes* of this 'hemorrhage', were still unknown.[69] He concedes, however, that 'To regard women as unclean during menstruation is certainly very useful'.[70] Less circumspect contemporary accounts elaborated on these notions of uncleanliness, developing traditional associations between menstruation and the state of sexual heat in animals. Locock in his article on menstruation in John Forbes' 1833 *Cyclopaedia of Practical Medicine*, bases his theory of menstruation on the resemblance between the state of the uterus in a woman menstruating, and the appearance in 'rabbits killed during the state of genital excitement, usually called the time of heat'.[71]

Menstruation was regarded as an outward sign of the threatening sexual and reproductive excess of the female body, an excess which caused her to vibrate indiscriminately to all external stimuli.[72] In the popular mind, then, menstruation was linked not just with reproductive functions, but with a more disturbing image of palpitating sexuality, existing independently of any specific object of desire – the male is not the cause or origin, but rather the belated, arbitrary target of female sexual passion. Medical textbooks of the era reinforced this sexualized view of menstruation, as in the account of the 'enchantment' exercised by the sight of a soldier's red uniform, or the charms of the 'manly sensualist', on the body of 'a young female just bursting into womanhood':

This *enchantment* – which it literally is – this infatuation, is often due to the unrecognised reaction of the physical appearance of the tempter upon the mind of his victim, untrained to self-control, predisposed to the allurement by an excess of reproductive energy, and irresistibly impelled forward to the gratification of the obscure, deep-felt longings he excites by an over-stimulated nervous system.[73]

The traditional scenario of the fairy tale is reversed: the princess is not lulled to sleep or imprisoned by enchantment, but rather stimulated into frenetic activity. Behind the careful regulation of Victorian girls' lives lay the ever-present fear of their promiscuous libidinal energy. While scarcely flattering to the male recipients of female desire, this construction of femininity nonetheless confirmed the fundamental opposition between male self-control and female powerlessness, and reinforced the perceived need for patriarchal policing of the female body. Overwhelmed by the uncontrollable processes of her own physiological economy, the young female must place herself under male medical guidance (or imbibe popular remedies) if she is to avoid precipitating herself into a state of permanent nervous disease or insanity. The obstruction of menstruation, viewed as the outward sign of sexual heat, represented the damming up of sexuality, causing pollution, and implosion throughout the entire mental, emotional and physiological economy.

For women themselves, the double binds involved in these prescriptions for femininity were legion. They were expected to be more controlled than men, but were also presumed to be physiologically incapable of imposing control. As vessels of receptivity, doomed to vibrate indiscriminately to external stimuli, and to the functions of their uterine system, they were helpless prisoners of their own bodies. All paths of active self-help also seemed foreclosed. Self-control was depicted as directly harmful in its effects: if the internal 'excess' of reproductive energy were suppressed or obstructed in its outward flow, then insanity would ensue. If, however, it were acted on, the resulting 'immodest' behaviour would immediately call for the certification of insanity.

For the Victorian woman, the threat of insanity loomed large, figuring in the rhetoric of some medical practitioners as almost the determining condition of womanhood. Women increasingly internalized the self-distrust inculcated by such discourse. In a graphic depiction of the overweening influence culturally ascribed to the medical profession in the mid-Victorian era, an article in *Fraser's*, 1848, observed, 'No one possesses such absolute power as the medical man over his patients; that which the veriest despot in the world exercises over his slave does not equal it.' The prime example of the patient's powerlessness in the face of irresistible medical opinion is that of a woman:

A person – say a young female, say a mother – is haunted with the fear of hereditary insanity. If she feels low-spirited, she dreads it; if she feels more than ordinarily happy, in the midst of her joy the thought strikes her that perhaps her merriment is morbid; if her children gambol, and laugh, and shout, more than usual, she trembles lest each ebullition of joy be not the first symptom of the the object of her dread, or they may retire from their rougher sports, and she again apprehends the worst.[74]

While drawing attention to the potential abuses of medical power, should the doctor choose to play upon the young mother's fears, the vignette nonetheless endorses cultural images of female helplessness in the face of the lurking threat of insanity. That impossible golden mean, normalcy, becomes the only convincing evidence of sanity: slight deviations, excess of any form, become worrying symptoms whose tyrannous grip on the psyche only the doctor can dispel. For all its expressed concern, the article yet reproduces the cultural assumption that the state of Victorian womanhood would inevitably be one of tortured self-doubt.

Victorian psychiatrists, or alienists as they were known, frequently debated amongst themselves whether women were actually more prone to insanity, and whether they did constitute a larger proportion of inmates in asylums, but such measured discussion was over-balanced by their own examples and illustrations, and indeed the very categories of insanity that were formulated. A list of forms of insanity, drawn up in the 1860s by Dr Skae, includes as separate categories, hysterical mania, amenorrhoeal mania, puerperal mania, mania of pregnancy, mania of lactation, climacteric mania, ovario-mania and the intriguing category of 'post-connubial mania'.[75] The male reproductive system drew no equivalent listing; there was no form of insanity specifically theorized as a male disease. Throughout mid-Victorian discussions this gender discrepancy was maintained. Although spermatorrhoea became an obsessive concern in the mid-nineteenth century it never entered medical lists as an independent cause of insanity. Masturbation was specified as a prevalent cause, but the literature here referred (contrary to our commonly accepted notions) both to male and female figures.[76]

In a table of the causes of insanity published in *The Lancet*, 1845, the only sex-specific causes are associated with the physical processes of the female body, including, notably, the suppression of the habitual evacuation of menstruation.[77] According to Bucknill and Tuke, uterine disorders, and suppressed or irregular menstruation, accounted for ten per cent of all female admissions to asylums.[78] Even higher figures were offered in other works. Accounts by alienists of their female patients all gave extraordinary narrative prominence to the state of the menstrual flow. Esquirol's diagnoses include a girl who was in a state of dementia for ten years with the suppression of her menses and was cured on the day that they flowed.[79]

A preoccupation with menstrual flow was not confined, however, to the arena of mental pathology. It was equally prevalent in the various *Domestic Medicines* produced for home consumption, and more general medical discussions of female health. In that representative guide to mid-nineteenth-century perceptions of the female body, John Forbes' 1833 *Cyclopaedia of Practical Medicine*, the list of specific female diseases, and particularly those connected with menstruation, is of impressive length. To read through the entries is to gain an impression of a near hysterical male anxiety focused on the flow of female secretions, and in particular those of menstruation, a hysteria whose impact on the female psyche must inevitably have been to create a sense of existing in an almost permanent state of pathology. The catamenia (or discharge) could be too thick or too thin, too profuse or too scanty, too frequent or too scarce; though when they ceased to flow, womanhood itself was at an end, since medical texts insistently told their readers that women were attractive to men (and thus truly female) only during the period of activity of their reproductive organs.[80] Womanhood itself is thus figured as a form of pathology: only when polluted and out of control (and thus not 'feminine') could females be socially accredited with the title of true woman. An extension of this form of thought is given in Laycock's assertion that the most desirable female qualities of grace, soft skin, and embonpoint are to be found pre-eminently in prostitutes and hysterical females (women, in other words, who are not suppressing their sexuality).[81] Medical literature warned of the dangers surrounding the period of the climacteric or menopause which, it was believed, would often put an end not only to womanhood, but to life itself.[82]

Worry about menstruation for the Victorian woman could not be confined solely to its commencement or its surcease. Locock, the famous accoucheur to Queen Victoria, who contributed virtually all the articles on the female secretions in the *Cyclopaedia*, informs his readers that 'during the menstrual period, when quite regularly and properly performed, no medical treatment is required'.[83] The question of proper 'performance' he continues, however, should always be the focus of careful attention of both the woman and her medical adviser who should always enquire as to their state. Despite Locock's disclaimer, the very suggestion that medical treatment might be required under normal circumstances, offers some inkling of the degree of medical intervention to which middle-class Victorian women were subject. Given the innumerable criteria of quality control applied to the menstrual flow, and the difficulties of assessing normality, female anxiety could only be allayed by medical opinion, or by ingesting 'female corrective pills'. The 'gynaecological tyranny' of which Clifford Allbutt was later to complain, which fastened its 'morbid chains' around the woman, forcing her into a state of fearful physical introspection, and sowing the seeds of hypochondria, is here set in motion.[84]

The measures suggested by Locock for inducing normal flow in the female body might appear to us quite draconian, but his descriptions, for example, of treating amenorrhoea by applications of electricity to the pelvis, and of applying leeches once a month to the groins, labia, uterus, or (interestingly) the feet, are reiterated in the practical medical advice disseminated in the *Lancet* and Braithwaite's *Retrospect of Practical Medicine and Surgery* (a national journal which came out of the Leeds School of Medicine).[85] An 1847 article on uterine diseases in the *Retrospect* suggests that either leeches or the lancet should be used if the 'menses are interrupted . . . the period ought not to pass over without detracting some blood, either from the uterus or its immediate neighbourhood'.[86] The article suggests the terror aroused by the idea of menstrual obstruction. Blood should be drawn from even neighbouring areas, rather than let a month pass by without flow.

The controversy surrounding the use of the speculum in the 1840s gives further indication of the degree of medical intervention to which middle-class Victorian women were subject. The more research was pursued, the more it seemed to be established that a majority of

English women were in fact suffering from some form of uterine disease. Robert Lee's objections, in 1850, to the current practice of using the speculum to cauterize the cervix as often as thrice weekly for nine months gives an indication of its widespread nature.[87] Similar confirmation is offered by Carter's ill-humoured observation that, 'It is scarcely possible at present for an hysterical girl to have no acquaintances among the many women who are subjected to the speculum and caustic, and who love to discuss their symptoms and to narrate the sensations which attend upon the treatment.'[88] Carter's vision is that of lascivious women, luring men on to examine their sexual organs, and to delight their feelings by applying caustic to their cervix. Such practices can lead respectable, middle-class and unmarried females, he observes, into the 'mental and moral condition of prostitutes'.[89] Subjected to such forcible medical penetration, women are doubly victimized – made to bear the burden of guilt evoked by male anxiety over their own erotic arousal. While no doubt exaggerated, Carter's claims do draw attention to the ways in which the rising medical industry devoted to investigating female diseases created and confirmed its object, establishing on medical authority that a majority of the female population of England was in a state of pathological disorder.

Although subject to virulent attack, the speculum did have its enthusiastic supporters, however, as evidenced in Protheroe Smith's lyrical depiction of the virtues of his new design of speculum which 'accomplishes the object, never heretofore attained, of employing *simultaneously* both visual inspection and tactile examination'.[90] Technology here offers the fulfilment of the male erotic dream: the male gaze could follow the fingers into the most hidden recesses of the female anatomy, unveiling the fundamental secrets of femininity. While physiognomy and phrenology were still restricted to decoding inner secrets from external signs, the speculum, in its vulgar materiality, created the ultimate penetration of the male gaze. The 'discoveries' which ensued, however, merely reproduced dominant cultural assumptions, revealing in full physiological splendour, that women were the harbourers of hidden pollution.

Brontë's fiction, with its emphasis on the unveiling of inner secrets, and its assertion of the sexuality of its heroines, participates within and contributes to Victorian discourses on the body. For Brontë, forced to watch the successive deaths of all her sisters, the issue of the female body and illness loomed large (many medical accounts attributed consumption, significantly, to the obstruction of menstruation, and hence a damming up of sexuality).[91] Her heroines, with their oscillations between self-assertion and self-doubt, fall prey to the double binds of Victorian femininity: whether overtly expressed, or inwardly contained and restricted, sexual energy was inevitably harmful.

In keeping with economic and social ideologies of male self-help and self-control, the fashionable male diseases of the era, masturbation and spermatorrhoea, were concerned, I have suggested, with the problems of loss, and the need to *conserve* vital force. Medical discussions of spermatorrhoea argued, in a physiological version of Freud's later theories of sublimation and displacement, that unused sperm could actually be absorbed back into the bodily economy.[92] Notions of female pathology, however, focused on woman's need to maintain free flow, to ensure that she did not withhold or retain within her the polluting and disruptive forces of sexual energy. Behind the obsessive return to the issue of menstrual flow in Victorian discourse lies a model of the female bodily economy which maps the disturbing forces of sexuality and reproduction onto a chart of economic circulation. Though the menses are distasteful in themselves, reeking as they do of animality and sexuality, their obstruction threatens to cause violent internal disruptions: a stockpiling which would similarly cause putrefaction and disease in the social organism. Only by constant sluicing through her 'dark drains' could woman retain even a semblance of physical or mental purity.

These polarized views of the male and female mind and bodily economy can only be fully comprehended, I have suggested, if viewed in the light of the increasing social division of labour under industrial capitalism, and the inherent contradictions within the ideological projections of laissez-faire economics. Ideologies of gender differentiation offered a displaced resolution to the contradictory economic figuration of man as both autonomous, rational actor, in control of his own destiny, and also as a mere unit controlled and determined by the wider operations of the social organism of which he formed a part. Manhood was articulated against and defined by its opposite: whilst the attributes of self-control and self-help were aligned with masculinity, woman was increasingly viewed as an automaton at the mercy of her body. Like the material economy, however, she also represented a threatening instability of physical forces which needed to be externally regulated and controlled. In Brontë's fiction the internal dilemmas of her heroines cannot be resolved into a simple conflict between reason and passion: medical, social and economic theories of the relationship between womanhood and control all inform the representation of their struggles. Brontë, in charting the histories of her unusual female protagonists, both works within and against the highly charged notions of gender differentiation to be found throughout Victorian discourse.

PART TWO

Charlotte Brontë's Fiction

CHAPTER 6

The early writings: penetrating power

Charlotte Brontë's early writings, which preoccupied her from early adolescence to her late twenties, lay the groundwork for the psychological concerns of her later fiction. We find here the same sense of embattled selfhood, shying away from interpretative penetration, the same concerns with the instabilities of psychological and gender identity, which fuel the later work. In these playful, unconstrained works we find expressed, in more direct and less mediated form than subsequently, the concerns of contemporary psychological debate. Like the Victorian alienists, Brontë is concerned with the realms of social and psychological excess; where they sought to delimit and define the boundaries of the normal, however, Brontë opens them up to interrogation.

The world Brontë creates in these early stories is one dominated by the power of the 'penetrating' and 'scrutinous' gaze[1], where the secrets of identity often lie in the hands of another, and the glittering eye of insanity is frequently displayed. Doubles, and alter-egos abound; and the boundaries of masculine and feminine identity are subject to constant questioning and dissolution. Charlotte's well known 'Farewell to Angria', in which she evinces her desire to 'quit that burning clime where we have sojourned too long' for a 'cooler region where the dawn breaks grey and sober', has led to the common misapprehension that all her early writing takes place amidst exotic climes in a heady atmosphere of emotional intensity.[2] Romanticism, however, is kept firmly under the control of a humorous and cynical narration, and the imaginative landscape of Angria itself is interwoven with the harsh realities of life in industrial Yorkshire. Romantic drama is played out amidst the social and political disruptions of the era. Smoke-vomiting factories, strikes, and political insurrections trouble the social stability of this African land. Far from representing an escapist realm, the world of Angria gives Brontë the imaginative licence to move outside the constraints of realism to explore, in heightened form, the social and psychological figurations of Victorian England. Not until *Shirley* does Brontë attempt again to link so overtly the upheavals within an industrial state with the emotional life of her protagonists, to trace the interconnections between the individual psychological economy and that of the wider social body. As in science fiction, the geographical and temporal displacement of the narrative, with its extreme formulations, serves not to lessen but rather to intensify its focus on specific aspects of the Victorian economic and symbolic order.

Brontë's long devotion to the form of the early writings can be explained in part by the freedom it allowed her. Writing pre-eminently for herself and Branwell, rather than for a public audience, she was able to range freely outside the conventional structures of writing, exploring and testing the boundaries of Victorian literary realism. The manuscripts playfully test and transgress the conventions governing the representation of character and psychology. Brontë showed no compunction about resuscitating her characters from the dead, changing their past histories, or altering their future formation. Not content, however, with such disruption of the sacred principles of narrative continuity, she also subjects her characters to synchronic dispersion: overt doublings, baffling contradictions, and eruptions of insanity all disturb the psychological principles of linear, unified identity upon which literary realism is grounded.[3] Her challenge to the constraining categories of psychological normality is encoded in the form of her fiction.

At first glance it might seem as if these early stories merely recycle certain gender stereotypes of the era: dashing, Byronic males treat with contempt the women whose lives are entirely bound up in theirs. Close analysis, however, reveals a more complex picture, where an interrogation (rather than simple confirmation) of gender boundaries is set firmly within the context of political and social events. 'Something about Arthur' (1833), for example, interweaves the casting off of effeminacy by Douro (later the Duke of Zamorna, principal hero of the tales) with his leading role in an industrial uprising. Angria is a land constantly under threat of social rebellion: from a discontented industrial workforce, from racial rebellion of the oppressed Ashantee, led by Quashia, and from a political challenge, modelled on the French Revolution, fermented by Alexander Rogue. Virtually all the romantic tales are set within this context of actual or impending social disruption, with varying forms and degrees of explicit interconnection. The dramas of selfhood are invested with political significance, drawing out in overt terms the unacknowledged linguistic associations which framed contemporary depictions of the unruly energies of the individual body and of wider social disorder.

One tale which overtly integrates the sexual and the political is 'The Bridal' (1832), where female madness is aligned directly with working-class rebellion. The noble Zenobia, possessed by wild sexual jealousy due to Douro's impending marriage, figures in the classic pose of a mad woman, with tattered clothes, dishevelled hair, and emaciated features; a 'ghastly apparition' who speaks in 'wild, maniacal accents'.[4] Unlike Bertha, however, she is able to move in and out of this frenzy, maintaining her elevated social position all the while. Hers is a latent insanity, which only breaks out on provocation. With the news of Douro's wedding, her actions are paralleled in the political sphere, where the Great Rebellion is fermenting:

Unequivocal symptoms of dissatisfaction began to appear at the same time among the lower orders in Verdopolis. The workmen at the principal mills and furnaces struck for an advance of wages, and, the masters refusing to comply with their exorbitant demands, they all turned out simultaneously. Shortly after, Colonel Grenville, one of the great mill-owners, was shot.[5]

The material is clearly that deployed, from a more sympathetic stance, in *Shirley*. In this early tale it is possible to trace the overt operation of an ideological alignment between the uncontrolled responses of femininity and the working classes. Thus Douro proclaims in his 'sublime' speech that,

There is a latent flame of rebellion smouldering in our city, which blood alone can quench! The hot blood of ourselves and our enemies freely poured forth! We daily see in our streets men whose brows were once open as the day, but which are now wrinkled with dark dissatisfaction, and the light of whose eyes, formerly free as sunshine, is now dimmed by restless suspicion.[6]

This extraordinary speech highlights the parallels, and mutual reinforcement, of Victorian political and psychiatric discourse. From images of concealed, smouldering fires and latent disruption, we move to those of blood-letting (where associative resonances link the female economy with the political sphere) and to the question which so preoccupied the Victorian alienists – that of bodily legibility. Like women, who have dammed up their menstrual flow, and allowed the processes of their bodies to overtake their reason, the workers move from an open transparency of expression, where innocence is inscribed, to the distorted visage found in insanity. Political rebellion, like insanity, is figured by changes in the bodily text. In this tale, as throughout the early writings, Brontë aligns the operations of political and sexual power. Responsibility for the political rebellion is placed firmly at the door of Alexander Rogue (also called Percy, Ellrington and later Northangerland), Douro's political and sexual rival and Zenobia's husband. Douro makes a stirring speech which reinstates his political and sexual dominance over Rogue, and ensures the defeat of the rebellion. It also leads, however, to the overthrow of Zenobia's reason once more. She accosts him 'with the same wild, unnatural expression of countenance [which] had before convulsed her features', asserting that his eloquence had made her 'no longer mistress of myself'.[7] Using magic, she attempts to prevent his wedding. The virile suppression of working-class discontent only leads, it seems, to renewed convulsions in the female sphere, where the marks of excessive adoration are indistinguishable from political revolt. Passionate excess, both political and sexual, is set in opposition to dominant, patriarchal order.

The interconnection of insanity and political revolt is made even more explicit in the later 'History of Angria' where the social disruption of the African kingdom is aligned with the mental disease of Percy. Insanity, significantly, is not solely the province of the female in the early writings, but operates as a constant undertow of both masculine and feminine identity. The narrator informs us that, 'All the body politic of Africa seems delirious with raging fever: the members war against each other. Parties are confounded.'[8] Much of this disease in the body politic is attributed to the impact of Percy's 'wild impulses' on the 'undefined masses of followers' who figure only as a form of 'fluctuating movement' in the social organism. According to the narrator, 'His late disreputable and eccentric proceedings are not a disease in themselves, but merely the symptoms of some grand latent malady.'[9] The wild, seemingly purposeless, gyrations of the social body are figured as the external symptoms of Percy's psychic disorder which, in accordance with Victorian views of insanity, can be present without sign: an invisible insanity, lurking, in latency, spreading disease throughout the mind and body before any external manifestation can raise the alarm. Brontë's tale gives literal expression to the rhetorical projection of social disorder as a form of mental disease. 'Percy' exists as a condensed term and metonymical embodiment of the mysterious forces of social disruption. Here, as throughout the early writings, Brontë transgresses the ordering conventions of realist fiction, dissolving the boundaries of discrete and unified identity, and collapsing hierarchical distinctions between the personal and the social order.

Another text which explicitly links the trajectory of a personal life with that of social disruption is 'Something about Arthur'. In this tale the emphasis falls primarily on gender construction. The narrator is Lord Charles Wellesley, the witty, cynical and jealous younger brother of Arthur Wellesley. He treats us to his memories of the young Arthur who had a complexion of 'effeminate delicacy and transparency' and who, in feminine fashion, used to throw fits, completely losing self-control.[10] Arthur's rites of passage into true masculinity proceed in three stages. The first is a bloodthirsty fight with his enemy, Lord Caversham, which takes place, with rather obvious symbolism, at the top of a gigantic pillar.[11] In the second stage, Arthur takes on the role of incendiary, leading an attack against and then setting fire to Lord Caversham's mill, and releasing the workers from their slavery: 'the roll and rattle of machinery proclaimed the presence of the miserable captives whose unceasing labour was ever prolonged "from morn, till dewy eve; from eve, till morn"'.[12] As in 'The Bridal', the material is again clearly that employed later in *Shirley*, but sympathy in this case lies unequivocally with the down-trodden workers. Femininity and social rebellion are, in the figure of Arthur, directly aligned: the potentially radical import of the tale is destabilized, however, by its gender focus. The firing of the mill functions primarily as an index of Arthur's lingering femininity which he has to transcend. This time it is he, not the mill owner, who is shot. After undergoing the ritual purgation of delirious fever, he emerges in the end as a fully fledged masculine hero: convalescing in the mountains he loses 'the delicate transparency of complexion which had before given him a very effeminate appearance' and acquires a 'lofty heroic stature and free, bold, chivalric bearing' which enables him to consummate his manhood by making his first seduction (of Mina Laury, the first in his long line of mistresses).[13]

The parallels between 'The Bridal', 'Something about Arthur' and *Shirley* point to the difficulties inherent in any attempt to impose a stable political meaning on Brontë's texts. Throughout her work the economic and class issues involved in industrial unrest are refracted through gender concerns. Although the associations between incendiarism and political uprisings and the feminine remain constant, their valency shifts in accordance with the narrative frame: feminization of the hero, as in this case, leads to a more positive valuation of revolt, but a simultaneous downplaying of its political significance. In their playfulness, Brontë's early texts highlight the shifting, metaphorical associations which underpinned Victorian ideologies of gender and class. The associations persist, but they can be mobilized in different ways to produce seemingly very divergent political implications.

Brontë's fascination with the construction and operations of masculine dominance, as revealed in the above tales, is expressed both in the thematic content and narrative presentation of her tales. Her narrators in the early writings are almost invariably male, and the tales themselves are frequently cast within the comic framework of the coarse exchanges of a male pot-house fraternity. Puzzled by this persistent choice of a male voice, critics have tended to treat it as an aberration, an attempt to enter a male realm of power and privilege which precedes Brontë's discovery of her 'own' voice.[14] Such a formulation closes off analysis of the ways in which the male persona and narrative frame actively contribute to the tales' interrogation of masculinity and the male *abuse* of power and privilege. The cynicism both of Charles Wellesley and of the later persona, Charles Townsend, displays, in a lower and hence more obviously distasteful register, the exploitative operations of male dominance depicted in the main tales. 'Henry Hastings', for example, begins with Charles Townsend's advertisement for a wife – physical deformities ignored as long as she is possessed of CASH.[15] His misogyny provides a fitting frame for his subsequent depiction of the unhappy life of Elizabeth Hastings, harried by her profligate brother, and subjected to the sexual importunity of William Percy. Over the years, as the heroic Douro transformed into the dissolute Zamorna, Brontë's framing narratives take on an increasingly cynical tone which, in their coarse replication of the main action, function as a double-layered de-mystification of the 'romantic' plot.

The interrogation of masculinity in Brontë's tales is complemented by an analysis of the construction of femininity. The character who draws the most commentary from the assembled male characters is that living embodiment of dualism and internal schism, the passionate Zenobia.[16] Emotional excess is combined with formidable learning. Alone of the female characters in the early writings she trespasses on the male sphere of power and privilege, daring, like her creator, to write. Male judgments on Zenobia hence become part of Brontë's self-reflexive preoccupation with her own role as female author, as she wrestles with contemporary beliefs that such self-exposure constitutes a violation of femininity.

In 'Visits in Verreopolis' (1830) Arthur, Marquis of Douro (the later Zamorna) heatedly defends Zenobia against his companions' slights, accusing them of jealousy 'because a human being of the feminine gender has displayed such wonderful abilities'.[17] Captain Tree (an author himself and occasional narrative persona in the tales), deflects this challenge by focusing on Zenobia's physical appearance, likening her swarthy complexion to that of a Martinique scullion (a parallel which links Zenobia to that later transgressive figure, Bertha). The Duke of Wellington also intercedes, comparing women to swans, graceful and dignified in their natural element, the water, or home, but once they 'presume' to leave it their 'unseemly waddle' entitles every creature 'to laugh till their sides split at the ludicrous spectacle'.[18] Brontë's witty dissection of the operations of patriarchal ideology, written seven years before Southey dashed her own literary hopes, registers some of the unease she felt in entering the male literary realm.[19] Her female characters' fears of self-exposure, which indeed increase as Brontë's fame grows and her career progresses, express her concerns that writing, as a form of outward self-articulation, becomes hence a de-sexing, public activity, a thrusting aside of the veils which should conceal the inner secrets of femininity. This same fear might also have been one of the factors governing Brontë's extraordinary perseverance with the miniscule handwriting of the early writings.

Douro, although acting as Zenobia's defender, nonetheless makes brutally clear that her intellectual attainments, in robbing her of her femininity, also render her undesirable. Sending Zenobia one of his manuscripts to correct and polish, he adds insult to injury by implicitly comparing her to his beloved wife who has the sense to remain within the domestic sphere:

> The peal within the shell concealed
> Oft sheds a fairer light
> Than that whose beauties are revealed
> To our restricted sight.[20]

The anatomically suggestive image of the concealed peal draws attention to the mutual reinforcement of ideological projections of the female body and of woman's designated social sphere. Women who too freely expose their wares, cease to have any exchange value in the social marketplace and become instead the butt of male ridicule.

Zenobia further forfeits male respect by her unfeminine physical attack on Lord Charles (she boots him down the stairs). Douro defends her again, but not, significantly, on the grounds of justified anger, but rather that of insanity, 'She was not to blame, sir. Repeated insults of the most aggravated nature had stung her to desperation, and she committed the act in a moment of insanity' (p. 314). Douro follows the lines of Victorian psychiatric thought: over-straining of the female mind leads to the disruption of self-containment and control; intellectual excess will produce a parallel result in the emotional sphere.

The women in the early writings can be divided into two camps, in accordance with the cultural theories of the female body traced in the preceding chapter. Either they release their energies, and are branded immodest and insane, or they contain them internally and are subject to a form of self-consuming insanity – morbid fantasies destroy their peace and health. The double bind in Victorian prescriptions for femininity is starkly depicted; whichever course of action the women pursue it seems to end in insanity. Within the first camp we find Zenobia, subject to intellectual and passionate excess, and Louisa Vernon, the ex-actress who gives voice to 'hysterical and fiendish' screams, and whose utterances even her daughter dismisses as 'wild, mad trash'.[21] Kept prisoner by Zamorna, Louisa, as hysterical woman, from the lowly ranks of actresses, brings together aspects of female excess which are separated out in *Jane Eyre* to produce the two seemingly very different models of femininity represented by the insane Bertha and Adele's despised, actress mother, Céline Varens. Their combination in Louisa casts light on Rochester's role as figure of patriarchal restraint. Louisa's lower-class status, which aligns her ideologically with sexual rapacity, coupled with her capacity to earn money through public self-display, clearly signals her as a figure requiring patriarchal control. In significant contrast, in *Jane Eyre* it is Céline Varens' very sexual freedom and capacity to earn money through marketing her body which places her outside Rochester's control which is exerted instead on Bertha who is constrained by marital bonds (and who is given racial rather than class origins for her licentiousness and rebellious behaviour).

The second camp of women in the early writings contains virtually all of the mistresses and wives of Zamorna, whether they retain virtue and exist within the sanctions of marriage, or have thrown virtue to the winds in their passionate devotion to their lord. Rosamund Wellesley, seduced by her guardian and tutor, Zamorna, is a classic case of self-consuming energy. She dies we learn, from the violence of her own contained feelings: 'Shame and Horror, I suppose, had worked her feelings into Delirium and she died very suddenly'.[22] Zamorna's first wife, Marian, suffers silently from fears of his infidelity (fears exacerbated by the feeling that the eye of her 'evil genius', Percy, is always upon her): 'Her mental sufferings were made particularly fearful by the spectral – "the ghostly gloom by which they were invested by a far too vivid imagination and a morbid nervous system".'[23] Marian's true femininity, revealed by her 'morbid nervous system', directly causes her downfall: she falls prey to the physiological consequences of this morbidly retained energy, consumption, and dies. Zamorna's next wife, Mary, survives a little longer, but suffers much the same fate (although she is later resuscitated). She seems to live permanently in a state of shattered nerves, questioning her own sanity, bewildered by Zamorna's behaviour, but never willing to violate her feminine role and articulate her fears. In 'The Return of Zamorna' we find her, during Zamorna's exile, doubting her own sanity, subject to 'superstitious horror', 'shattered nerves' and a 'morbid imagination' – symptoms which all lead her into a state of consumption, from which she miraculously recovers when Zamorna returns, thus highlighting the sexual freight of meaning carried by consumption in Victorian culture.[24]

The landscape of Angria is populated by a whole series of imprisoned women, Zamorna's mistresses, all shut up in lonely houses, pining away, consumed by their own emotions to which they cannot give vent. Interestingly, their sexual fall is seen as natural and inevitable, and not a subject for moral comment. Whereas outwardly expressive figures like Zenobia forfeit, through their insane rages, membership of their sex, the self-denying, self-restraining heroines who block all outflow of unrequired emotion prove their essential femininity by developing morbid nervous systems and dying of emotional exhaustion and consumption.

Brontë's representations of femininity in her early writings dramatize, in uncompromising form, the negative and constraining implications of cultural constructions of the feminine in Victorian culture. Both the discourse and practices of Victorian psychiatry are placed overtly in the domain of sexual politics. Surveillance and visual penetration, for example, are presented neither as objective nor gender neutral, but rather as instruments of power in the struggles between the sexes. All dominant men, whether heroic or villainous, are given penetrating, piercing eyes. The women, on the contrary, are assessed entirely in terms of their capacities for self-enclosure and concealment. Not even Zenobia is granted a penetrating eye. The men dominate the women through their fierce gazes which lay bare the hidden secrets of their victims, thus rendering them their slaves.

The complex sexual politics of surveillance are demonstrated in 'The Green Dwarf' (1833) where the heroine, Emily, attempting to elope with the virtuous St Clair, is actually carried off by the villainous Percy, and placed under the surveillance of the wretched Bertha, a 'withered hag' whose 'small red eyes gleamed with fiend-like malignity'.[25] Once more we are offered anticipatory elements of *Jane Eyre*, only in this case Bertha, the fiend, is not the prisoner, but rather the keeper, confining one of her own sex under patriarchal instruction. Brontë's placement of the fiend-like Bertha in *Jane Eyre* in the position occupied in the early tale by the chaste and innocent Emily is highly suggestive, reinforcing feminist readings of the novel which highlight the textual parallels between Jane and her apparent opposite. Furthermore, the implied relationship between racial and gender oppression in *Jane Eyre*, signalled by Bertha's Jamaican origins, is given explicit form in the earlier manuscript.

'The Green Dwarf' intercuts the romantic drama of Emily with the racial uprising of the Ashantee. Emily is left abandoned, 'a touching picture of beauty in distress' whilst the narrative cuts to a history of the 'subjugation' and 'annihilation' of the Ashantee people, and an account of the current wars.[26] Hero and villain alike have gone off to fight the Ashantee who are represented, significantly, in a sympathetic light as victims of Angrian brutality and lust for dominance. St Clair had returned to Angria both to capture Emily and to conquer the Ashantee, a dual purpose which inevitably highlights the relationship between racial and gender oppression. He is rewarded for his imperial prowess on the battlefield by the gift of Emily to grace his home. In similar fashion, Quashia, the indomitable leader of the Ashantee, had been part of the 'booty' of an earlier battle, and been placed within the bosom of the Duke of Wellington's family. Quashia's position, as a surrogate member of the ruling member of the ruling family who rebels against its constraints, highlights even further the parallels between race and gender in the tale. Characters' responses to such 'ungrateful' and unreasonable behaviour mirror Victorian psychiatric discussions of what was deemed to be wilful hysteria and unwarranted aggression to their families by adolescent girls. The figure of Bertha in *Jane Eyre* can be seen as a rewriting of Quashia: as a member of a subordinate and subjected group and race, she is taken into the heart of the familial structures of white patriarchy, but rebels in defiant form against its constraints.[27]

The preoccupation with the practices and effects of domination in the early writings, both by visual penetration of the body's textual surface and by physical violation of its materiality, is crystallized in the early obsession with dissection, both of live and dead bodies.[28] The impetus for this concern certainly came from the contemporary scandal concerning the resurrection men, and the famous case, which came to light in 1829, of Burke and Hare who had murdered their victims then sold their bodies for medical dissection. Its prominence in the early writings, however, can be traced to the ways in which the historical event condensed, and gave symbolic expression to, many of the concerns already motivating Brontë's writing both as regards the politics of gender, and her own authorial role. In 'The Adventures of Mon Edouard de Crack', for example, the hero's initiation into manhood is accomplished through five years spent in the underworld of Paris, years represented not, as one might expect, through sexual exploits, but rather, in a symbolic displacement, through his encounters with dissection.[29]

The symbolic multi-valency of dissection is demonstrated in another tale where it is linked to writing and textuality. In 'An Interesting Passage in the Lives of Some Eminent Men of the Present Time', the narrator, Charles Wellesley, boasts of all the secrets he could unveil of the grandees of Glass Town. After building up our hopes and expectations what he actually offers us is a semi-comic tale of the theft of some library books. Captain Tree (a fellow author) stages a mysterious midnight funeral which has all the trappings of a political conspiracy. The coffin turns out to contain, however, not a body, but rather stolen library books. Tree's fraud is discovered by the 'resurrectionists', Dr Hume Badry, Young Man Naughty and Ned Laury, who are raiding the graveyard for bodies. The frightened Tree promises 'to procure you a living subject every week' as the price for their silence (although he nonetheless still gets stuck in Dr Badry's macerating tub).[30] Power, knowledge, word and body are brought together in this strange tale, where the greatest secret concerns not the violation and dissection of the body, but rather the concealment and burial of the written word. Like later surrealist texts, Brontë's tales offer bizarre conjunctions whose symbolic potency is strengthened by a complete absence of any explanatory structure. The symbolic interchange of book and body gives literal expression to the dominant psychological trope in Brontë's fiction in which mind and body are figured as texts to be read. In addition, the alignment of the author, Tree, with the resurrecting doctor underscores the parallels drawn in contemporary rhetoric between the practices of fiction, in its penetration and unveiling of the human mind, and medical dissection. Body, text and surveillance are indeed all brought together in one of Tree's romances which bears the wonderfully Foucauldian title of 'The Incorporeal Watcher'.[31]

Although the above tale functions more by symbolic association than by explicit elaboration, it does point to the ways in which Brontë's concerns with power, knowledge and the unveiling of the self circle back self-reflexively to include her own creative role. Far from merely endorsing realist assumptions of an external, controlling authorial presence, Brontë suggests in one text that writing can be a form of disempowerment that actively entrammels its producer. 'Four Years Ago' offers us a model of the creative process in the figures of Douro and Ellrington who create their Elysium or Pandemonium: 'these were the Magicians who sent across the surface of society scenes so gorgeous and so polluted' that one had to be armed with supernatural strength to resist.[32] Such power brings its own curse, however; they never dare absent themselves from their created world:

That was one of the curses which this monument of their own guilt entailed upon them – it exacted a constant attendance, and incessant surveillance – neglect would have been followed by ruin – the bands of Hell were not so easily kept in subordination – there would have been fierce disputes then a blow up then an exposure – all laid open to the glaring light of day.[33]

This emblematic projection of writing as an external monument of authorial guilt reverses the customary image of writing as the surveillance and exposure of others. Brontë's dedication to her early writings can be read in similar terms: she was enchained to her own creation, never able to cease surveillance in case the release of unruly meanings should lead to her exposure.

Brontë's explorations in her early tales of the interface between writing and selfhood, and the symbiotic relationship between character and creation, lead to a direct interrogation of the conventions of realism.[34] One of her most intriguing tales, 'The Spell, an Extravaganza', (1834) calls into question the realist commitment to a model of an autonomous, unitary self and the assumed distinction between reference and referent, text and character, upon which realism is predicated. The reader is given due warning of his or her constructive and participatory role by the prefatory epigraph on the frontispiece: 'I give you the raw material, Words; to your own ingenuity I leave the eliciting of the manufactured article, Sense'.[35] The narrator, Lord Charles Wellesley, sets out in this tale to convince his audience that his brother, the Duke of Zamorna, is mad. Following a preamble which raises doubts as to his own sanity, he announces that his tale is a form of revenge on his brother: 'In this book I have tampered with his heart-strings.'[36] This enigmatic statement functions on two levels: first, and most simply, it suggests that the tale will upset the pre-existent Zamorna by revealing his true character; but at a deeper level it also suggests that Zamorna is solely a textual construct and Charles, as author, has the power actively to tamper with his puppet. As readers we too are to be implicated in creating a mad Zamorna; we are not allowed to retain our innocence, our illusions of detachment and passive readerly consumption are directly assailed. Charles instructs us that the evidence is to be found not in overt declaration but only in 'hints interwoven with the whole surface'. Authorial injunction transforms us into symptomatic readers. On finishing the book the reader is enjoined to shut it 'and, dismissing from his mind every fictitious circumstance, let him choose such only as have self-evident marks of reality about them. Then, after due consideration, let him deliver his opinion. Is the Duke of Zamorna sane or insane?'[37] The reader is placed in the same position as that of the Victorian alienist presented with a case history; the reader's judgment must determine fiction from fact, insanity from sanity.

By aligning the boundaries between fiction and fact with those of sanity, the text clearly suggests that the deciding factor in both cases is solely that of normative judgment. Out of a given texture of narrative, the reader weaves his or her own reality according to preconceived notions of psychological normalcy. Lord Charles' overt textual strategy casts light on the ways in which psychological identity in the social realm is similarly the product of textual construction: insanity is a label imposed by the interpretative judgment of others. 'The Spell' draws our attention to the inseparability and mutual reinforcement of Victorian literary realism and medical ideology: both discursive practices construct and maintain, and indeed are predicated upon, a model of discrete, unified selfhood. In this text, as in her later fiction, Brontë violates realistic convention in order to suggest a more disruptive, challenging model both of psychology and of writing and reading practice. The autonomy of the text, and the distinction between text and reader is broken down. The narrative strategy anticipates *Villette* where the obvious unreliability of Lucy Snowe's text tempts the reader into assuming the position of medical authority occupied by Dr John and offering a diagnosis of the pathology of the proferred tale and its author. The possibility of such interpretative authority is rapidly undermined, however, by the multiplicity of the text with its Gothic disruptions of realism. In similar vein, 'The Spell', openly tempts the reader into the exercise of interpretative power, whilst simultaneously signalling the dangers of this trap: the text is, after all, possibly itself the work of a madman.

Lord Charles sets out initially a reading of his brother which draws directly on contemporary diagnoses of lunacy:

Serfs of Angria! Freemen of Verdopolis! I tell you that your tyrant and your idol is mad. Yes, there are black veins of utter perversion of intellect born with him and running through his whole soul. He acts at times under the control of impulses that he cannot resist; displays all the strange variableness and versatility which characterize possessed lunatics; runs head-strong forwards in dark by-paths sharply angular from the straight road of common use and custom; and is, in short, an ungovernable, fiery fool.[38]

Like Barlow and the moral managers, Charles highlights the lack of self-control of his subject. His evidence, like that of the alienists, is drawn from an external assessment of apparent inconsistency in behaviour, and of a departure from 'common use and custom'. Since his diagnosis forms part of a political address designed to discredit his opponent, however, attention is inevitably drawn to the relative nature of such normative judgments.

The content of Lord Charles' tale is that of a high drama of death, disease and passion. Taunted by a 'stranger' with killing his wife through his infidelity, Zamorna defends his libidinous excess as a demonstration of love: 'For if I had permitted her to remain an impediment to my inclinations, I should soon have hated her – lovely, devoted and innocent as she was.'[39] Zamorna and his mocking 'familiar' dramatize the two conflicting sides of Victorian ideologies of manhood: ruthless conquest and self-assertion and necessary sexual excess are set against the values of conjugal harmony and self-control. The interest of the tale lies in its disempowering of Zamorna: he is punished for his sexual aggression by feminization. The ravages he commits, in a highly voyeuristic scene, on Zenobia's desk, are in turn visited upon himself. His wife's curiosity about his concealed life precipitates him towards death: '"Who has been tampering with my private affairs? Who has been prying into that which I chose to keep a sealed and solemn secret? Whose hand picked the lock? Whose eye gazed on the treasure?"'[40] The language of the passage, with its physical images of lock-picking and concealed treasure, highlights the sexual associations underpinning notions of unveiling the inner self in Victorian culture. Once exposed to another's gaze, Zamorna takes on the powerlessness associated with the cultural position of femininity.

Although the veteran of so many sexual skirmishes, the heroic Zamorna now regresses to the effeminacy of his adolescence: 'Yes, hear it, ye ladies of Africa, the Duke of Zamorna was once like a girl!'[41] The two stages of Zamorna's life are connected, Lord Charles informs us, by his fits of passion or tantrums, when his veins would swell and throb and 'his slight pliant form would strain and writhe while he struggled with his opponent (commonly Quashia) as though the spirit strove in mortal agony to accomplish that by force of desire which it[s] clay casket was unequal to from fragility'.[42] Zamorna's struggles to assert masculine self-control are figured in terms of the suppression of the feminine within and the racial other without.[43] The racial dynamics of Brontë's exploration of gender identity are further reinforced by the representation of the Duke's servant, Finic, a misshapen, deaf and dumb dwarf, given to fits of jealous rage, who, we learn elsewhere, is the miscegenic product of Zamorna's liaison with a Moorish woman.[44] The tale's concern with the impossibility of stable definitions of identity is highlighted linguistically through Finic's role as speechless messenger between the Duke and his wife, and by his capacity to actually embody their respective emotions. Although the symbolic intricacies of his role are too convoluted to bear complete unpacking here, he clearly operates as yet another alter ego for our hero, a darker self signalled by both racial and gender otherness.

When confronted by the evidence of the 'insolent curiosity' of womanhood which has pryed into his secrets, Zamorna observes that 'Thus have they always overthrown the greatest fabrics of man's construction.' To delve below is to bring the whole facade of masculinity crashing down. Such action, according to Zamorna, is sufficent to 'breathe insane life into the lungs of a corpse'.[45] His words are prophetic; his feminization is completed as he becomes by stages 'raging mad', held to his bed by force, and finally a near-lifeless corpse. The secret that Mary, Zamorna's wife, has unwittingly stumbled upon (but which she is not allowed, in masculine fashion, to unveil) is not, as she suspects, a covert sexual liaison with another woman, but rather, in a further destabilizing twist of gender identity, Zamorna's intense love-hate relationship with his male twin, whose existence has hitherto been concealed. Whereas the 'treasure' Victorian women always concealed from view was that of their suppressed sexuality, Zamorna's secret seems to be that of homoerotic bonding.[46] He and his mysterious twin are linked not as body and spirit, or opposing personalities, but rather by a threatening oneness. According to their father, 'they agree much better than for the convenience of society it could be wished they did'.[47] Such extended selfhood represents an explosive challenge to the romantic ideal of union through the extreme heightening, rather than nullification, of gender difference which underpinned the Victorian social order.

The revelations of Zamorna's duality evoke a mixed response. While Mary, the mistreated wife, clings to the evidence of duality in order to sustain her illusion of Zamorna's fidelity, Valdacella neatly deflates the romantic illusions of the rest of the assembled company by informing them that their cherished private relations with Zamorna have also been conducted with him: 'I know you all, body, mind and estate.'[48] The duplication of Zamorna not only breaks down the image of discrete selfhood of realistic fiction and romantic ideology, it also intensifies the social threat of surveillance. Intimate self-revelation takes on a frightening new aspect if the eyes that are watching are not those of a self-confirming 'other', but rather an extended social network of omniscience. 'Zamorna' becomes less a character than a system of power. This aspect of 'The Spell' again anticipates *Villette*, where the challenge to notions of atomized, unified selfhood projected through the Gothic machinery of the nun is directly interwoven with the projection of a society dominated by surveillance, whether through the machinery of education (in Madame Beck's school), religion (Père Silas and Catholicism) or medicine (Dr John). Both texts highlight the ways in which the social operations of surveillance at first intensify, but finally shatter, illusions of discrete selfhood.

As in *Villette*, Brontë uses the question of possible insanity in 'The Spell' to focus her challenge to the psychological tenets of literary realism, a challenge which is reinforced in the structure and narrative methodology of both texts. Unlike Lucy Snowe, the narrator of this early tale openly proclaims his own unreliability, drawing our attention to the ways in which he has deliberately flouted the realist code of truthful depiction. In his concluding remarks, Charles Wellesley maintains that he has kept his pledge to show that the Duke of Zamorna is partially insane. His 'proof', however, turns out to be the fictionality of his own discourse: 'Reader, if there is no Valdacella there ought to be one. If the young King of Angria has no alter ego he ought to have such a convenient representative' since no single being should 'speak and act in that capricious, double-dealing, unfathomable, incomprehensible, torturing, sphinx-like manner'.[49] The critical industry devoted to unearthing the presence of psychological 'doubles' in Brontë's novels is here unceremoniously pre-empted. While the narrative device used to represent psychology in the tale is openly identified, the text also makes clear that the notion of an *alter ego* operates not as an underlying theoretical guide, but rather as another useful fiction. 'The Spell', indeed, points to the limitations of psychological notions of doubling since they perpetuate, albeit in binary form, ideas of discrete selfhood. With the representation of Zamorna as the personification of a social system of surveillance, we have moved well beyond ideas of either unitary or dual selfhood.

Charles' final descriptions of his brother continue the text's challenge to notions of discrete identity by dissolving distinctions between the self and social order, and collapsing the operations of mind and the social state into one. Zamorna, he suggests, has 'too many reins in his hands':

He has gathered the symbols of dominion in a mighty grasp; he strains all the energy, all the power, all the talent of his soul to retain them; he struggles...to hold the empire he has established in so many lands, so many hearts, so many interests. He strives to keep them under one rule and government and to prevent them, if possible, from coming into collision. His brain throbs, his blood boils, when they wince and grow restive under his control, which they often do, for should they once break loose, should the talisman of his influence once fail – !50

The problem of retaining empire is represented as simultaneously one of social and psychological organization. The figure 'Zamorna' ceases to represent a discrete individual, and expresses instead a system of

social power and control. Should Zamorna succumb for one moment
to his throbbing brain, relax for one instant his control of conflicting
inner psychological forces then the consequences, Charles warns,
would be social cataclysm. As in the representation of Percy examined
earlier, Brontë has appropriated the political rhetoric associated with
the French Revolution, which figured political instability in psychological terms, and given it literal instantiation in the character of her
ruler. There is no protective allegorical distance separating one level
from another: analysis functions simultaneously in social and
psychological terms. The name 'Zamorna' thus expresses a radically
unstable, hierarchical system of social control, threatened at every
moment with internal disruption.

Charles perpetuates the challenge offered to the tenets of realism by
painting not one but two possible conclusions to his tale: the first is
that of total social disorder; the second is the psychological parallel to
this scenario:

Reader, what say you to the image of a crowned maniac, dying dethroned,
forsaken, desolate, in the shrieking gloom of a mad-house. No light around
him but the discoloured beam which falls through grated windows on
scattered straw; his kingdom gone, his crown a mockery, those who
worshipped him dead or estranged.[51]

The reader, as active participant and creator of this drama, is asked to
select the appropriate ending, which here is a graphic pictorial image
of the classic madhouse before non-restraint and moral management.
Confined as a madman, Zamorna has lost the last vestiges of control;
even his thoughts no longer submit to command. Such an ending still
has too much glamour to Charles' mind, however; he rewrites the
conclusion once again to create a more prosaic impression:

Zamorna, a young man of promise. He attempted, however, more than he
could perform; his affairs grew embarrassed and perplexed; he became
insane and died in a private mad-house at the early age of twenty-two.[52]

From a heroic monarch, Zamorna is transformed into a typical
example of a failure figure in Victorian bourgeois life. Like the many
narratives offered by Esquirol and Conolly of young men who failed
to live up to their social position and the business expectations of their
fathers, he becomes routinely insane from trying to accomplish too
much. His story is not the stuff of tragedy, but rather the all too
familiar saga, for Victorian readers, of the regrettable results of
inadequate self-control.

By challenging readers to select their own desired ending, Lord Charles highlights both the fictionality of his own discourse and the role played by readers' ideological assumptions in the interpretation and construction of a text. Like *Villette* which similarly offers multiple possibilities of closure, 'The Spell' points to the illusory nature of assumed distinctions between the realms of the imagination and the Real, text and world, and of the fictions of discrete, unified identity which are predicated upon that divide. Both texts invoke insanity as a form of explanation of their own waywardness, both materially and methodologically, but insanity too is quickly exposed as only a useful fiction which allows readers to impose definitional coherence on disruptive material. Just as *Villette* undermines realist conventions by the use of Gothic and external dramatizations of the inner workings of the psyche, so 'The Spell' also openly flaunts its own unconventionality with dramatic shifts in tone and genre. Thus the high point of drama, when the hidden story is being revealed, is interspersed with comic narrative: the arch-villain, like any self-respecting Victorian business man, leaves a visiting card whose inscription underscores the disruptive and playful tone of the whole composition: 'Henri Nicolai, Flesher and Spirit Merchant, Styx-Wharf, Close by the Gates of Hades – 18 of July – Cycle of Eternity.'[53]

'The Spell' anticipates later developments in Brontë's fiction in both methodological and thematic terms. Her depiction of the intense bond and yet all-consuming rivalry which links Zamorna and Valdacella, prepares the way for later analyses of the social construction of masculinity. Throughout the early writings, male intensity of feeling is associated not with women, but with other men. Thus Percy is driven by an insane hatred of his male children, William and Edward, who are themselves locked in mutual antagonism and whose relationship provides the groundwork both for *The Professor* and for the two later novel fragments, 'John Henry' and 'The Story of Willie Ellin'.[54] 'The Spell' presents male rivalry in perhaps its purest form: Zamorna and Valdacella are not, like the Crimsworth brothers, divided by differences of character or class, but are rather two identical figures struggling for possession of the same social space. In this regard their relationship mirrors that between Zamorna and Percy whose perpetual battles for political and sexual predominance impose an overriding structure on the early tales.

The central organizing trope for the early writings is not, as critics have tended to assume, the ideology of romantic love to which the female characters so desperately cling, but rather the dynamics of male struggles for power. Romantic ideas are exposed as useful fictions that help maintain female subordination, but are largely irrelevant with regard to the main operations of male social interest and power. Women function primarily as pawns between men, or mediums through which battles for emotional and social ascendancy can be played out. Struggles for gender identity are frequently enacted, however, solely between men. Zamorna's social and psychological empire is always under threat, whether from social rebellion or incipient madness, and both of these are customarily identified as the work of Percy. In 'My Angria and the Angrians', a letter from Percy, begging to be released from exile,[55] kindles in Zamorna 'that tinge of insanity which certainly mingles with his blood'.[56] From an ecstatic vision of his union with Percy, he progresses to terrified imaginings of his own death and the end of his greatness. True union would imply annihilation.

The intense, mutually-defining engagement of Zamorna and Percy is dissected in the extraordinary poem, 'And When You Left Me' (1836), which reads initially as a standard female plaint to the man who has abandoned her; only as it progresses does it become clear that it is written by the exiled Zamorna to the militarily triumphant Percy. Zamorna 'confesses' to all the secrets he would not tell Percy to his face:

> How oft we rung each other's callous hearts,
> Conscious none else could so effectively
> Waken the pain, or venom the keen darts
> We shot so thickly, so unsparingly
> Into those sensitive and tender parts
> That, veiled from all besides, ourselves could see
> Like eating cankers, pains that Heaven had dealt
> On devotees to crime, sworn slaves of guilt.[57]

Zamorna confesses that he married Mary because she was Percy's daughter, and in waking her 'nature's wildest play' his aim was to evoke 'intense passion' in Percy's breast. Now, in revenge for his exile, he vows 'To break her father's heart by Mary's death!'[58] In a repetitive pattern throughout the early tales, Zamorna steals Percy's women, and attempts to make him suffer through his mistreatment of them. Sexual desire itself seems to play little role in these exchanges; women are the insignificant conduit of the males' mutual absorption.

Although clearly fascinated by these male power struggles, Brontë does not idealize them; her heroes are increasingly depicted as ridiculous at times. In 'Four Years Ago' they are shown repeatedly beating each other up in the street, and being 'carried to their respective homes insensible bleeding and bruised from head to foot' for no greater cause than rivalry over a shopgirl.[59] The 1839 tale, 'Caroline Vernon' offers an equally cynical representation: Zamorna is introduced as an aging roué, crassly pursuing, for the benefit of his cronies, the girls at work in his hayfield. He is figured, in comic fashion, as a 'large Tom-cat'.[60] Unable to resist temptation, he mercilessly seduces and abducts his ward, and Percy's daughter, Caroline. The final scene is a confrontation between Percy and Zamorna. To Percy's dire threats of vengeance Zamorna coolly replies, 'In nature there is no such thing as annihilation – blow me up and I shall live again.'[61] Stripped of his heroic qualities, Zamorna is the non-individuated instantiation of the unsavoury lust for power which governs the gender and social politics of this 'mythical' realm.

Brontë establishes necessary distance from her subject matter both by the cynical, digressive form of narration, and by her incisive exploration of the costs exacted of her vibrant women trapped within this world. The women are shown as caught in a double bind; power accrues to them only to the degree that they subordinate themselves to the male. Such subordination, however, and the dependency it implies, ensures the future tyrannizing contempt of their 'master'. In *The Spell*, the power balance momentarily seems to shift as Zamorna's mistress, Mina Laury, through renewed self-sacrifice, ransoms his life: 'It seemed as if she thought she had acquired a right to look at him undaunted.' Such audacity quickly vanishes, however, 'and then again she was the doomed slave of infatuation, devoted, stricken, absorbed in one idea, finding a kind of strange pleasure in bearing the burden and carrying the yoke of him whose fascinations fettered her so strongly'.[62] Critical embarrassment in relation to the early writings possibly stems from the fact that it reveals all too plainly the social causes and production of female masochism. Taught to value themselves only as objects of male desire, women actively contribute to their own enslavement, channelling all their energies into a devotion towards the masculine source of their own perceived value, and thus locking themselves into a vicious cycle where the more they attempt to affirm their worth, the more they actively devalue themselves in the eyes of their chosen master.

Female identity in the early writings is shown to reside, in a very literal sense, in the hands of men. The plot, for example, of *The Secret*

(1834) which forms an interesting companion piece to *The Spell*, revolves around the struggle between male and female figures for ownership of the identity of Marian Hume (Zamorna's first wife). Significantly, the primary opponent to Zamorna here is a subversive female figure, the governess Miss Foxley, whom, he believes, holds Marian under her 'inexplicable spell'. All the negative cultural associations surrounding the governess in Victorian culture are mobilized around this figure whose threat to familial and marital order is reinforced by the sexual connotations attached to her wage-earning power.[63] Like Zenobia, who is also associated with independent incursions into the male field of wisdom, Miss Foxley is seen to be ruled by the dangerous, destabilizing forces of sexual passion, and, in a further parallel, she is given the power to impose illusions on others, thus aligning her with her 'Geni' creator, the future governess, Charlotte.

The hold which Miss Foxley exerts over Marian is that she claims to be able to tell her 'who and what you are, a circumstance of which you have hitherto been ignorant'.[64] Miss Foxley's bid for power is grounded on nothing less than an overt challenge to male control over language, naming and self-definition. In an even more convoluted development of the usual power struggles and gender politics of the early tales, Marian has to enter the 'sanctum sanctorum' of Percy at night, in order to gain material possession of the secret of her supposed identity. Once there she is forced to view Percy's collections of swords, those that have already done their slaughter, and the sharp, unsheathed one without a spot of blood: 'This is a virgin sword; it has pierced no heart, freed no spirit. But it lies bare and ready; it bides its time. A voice and a power is in that weapon: the voice shall speak the doom of nations; the power shall execute it.'[65] The implications of this passage, with its explicit interweaving of militaristic and sexual self-aggrandizement, scarcely need glossing. The sexual politics of the scene are rendered even more disturbing when we later discover that Marian was under the impression (later revealed to be false) that Percy was actually her father. 'The Secret', with its continuous series of broken taboos, highlights the ways in which incestuous patterns of desire were culturally produced by the patriarchal formation of the Victorian family structure: the discourses of sexuality and social control were intimately interwoven.

The scene with Percy does not, however, merely dramatize female helplessness in the face of masculine dominance, but rather highlights the conflict between two different forms of power. The supposed secret of Marian's identity is kept in the casket of Percy's late wife which only Marian knows how to open. According to Miss Foxley, Lady Percy had, unknown to Percy, agreed to exchange her child with Lady Hume, and had left a written agreement of the affair in a casket 'fastened by a secret spring'.[66] The precise physical details of the description inevitably evoke associations with the female body, reinforcing men's worst fears: the secrets of female sexuality and procreativity will always evade the questing male, hungry for knowledge and control. In the happy denouement of the tale, which corrects all Miss Foxley's disinformation and restores Marian to her previous identity as wife and daughter, only the governess is punished for daring to usurp Zamorna's control over Marian. The implied violation of his wife by Percy counts as nothing in the face of threatened female ascendancy.

Throughout the early writing Brontë addresses themes and issues which are to re-emerge in altered form in her later works. Her questioning of psychological and gender identity goes hand in hand with her interrogation of literary conventions of representation. These early texts repeatedly and defiantly break taboos, with reference both to content and to form. There is no felt obligation to provide an acceptably neat ending, to disguise the throbbings of sexual desire, or to construct characters as carefully packaged, unified identities. As in the novels, the central concern lies with the workings of power: the operations of sexual, class, and racial power and their intricate intertwinings, all come under scrutiny. Amidst all the drama of industrial unrest, racial uprisings and sexual excess one image of the workings of power remains paramount: the unveiling of the hidden secrets of selfhood. This sexually charged, condensation of Victorian social politics lies at the heart of the major fiction, but pursued now into an analysis of the inner workings of subjectivity. In her first novel, *The Professor*, Brontë retains her male focus, but thereafter the disruptive potential of female rebellion, kept on the margins in the early writings, is brought centre stage.

CHAPTER 7

The Professor: *'the art of self-control'*

Charlotte Brontë's first major fictional work, *The Professor*, is centrally concerned, as its working title 'The Master' suggests, with questions of mastery and control.[1] Social, economic, and psychological discourses of regulation and control furnish the discursive framework for this quintessential Victorian tale of social success. Our hero, William Crimsworth, offers a self-justificatory narrative of his rise from the position of penniless outcast to that of country gentleman with independent means. The trajectory of the plot, and the autobiographical form, anticipate Brontë's subsequent novel, *Jane Eyre*. The difference in gender of the protagonists is crucial, however: whereas Jane Eyre's social marginality duplicates and intensifies her gender position, there is, for Crimsworth, an acute disjunction between the two. His social powerlessness, by robbing him of the essential attributes of the Victorian male's gender identity – mastery and control – effectively feminizes him.

Crimsworth's tale of class mobility is informed throughout by gender anxiety and ambivalences. Problems of interpretation are intensified for the reader by awareness of the division between the male speaking voice who claims interpretative authority, and the shadowy female author who controls and exposes him. In a further interpretative twist, Crimsworth's autobiography is framed by another level of autobiography: material from Brontë's own life is assimilated across the gender and power divide, informing the representation of both master and pupil, William Crimsworth and his subsequent bride, Frances Henri. The result is a highly self-reflexive text which tests and explores the interrelations between Victorian ideologies of gender and the operations of social power.

Crimsworth's tale of social betterment draws directly on the Victorian ideologies of economic and psychological regulation which found popular expression in the social doctrines of the phrenological movement. His social success, he suggests, stems directly from his ability to regulate his inner psychological and physiological economy. To this materialist model of energy regulation is added another level, that of information control. Knowledge, for Crimsworth, is power. He sites his struggles for pre-eminence on the battleground of psychological legibility. Social control resides with the figure who possesses the power to read the inner state of the other, whilst maintaining the illegibility of the self. As a discourse which focused the material and informational, interpretative aspects of Victorian ideologies of regulative control, bringing together theories of social betterment with those of self-regulation and psychological decipherment, phrenology provided the framework and language for Brontë's exploration of the unstable groundings of class and gender identity. Her fictional development works to expose, however, some of the latent ideological contradictions within these theories. The novel works both within and beyond the phrenological framework, straining its boundaries, developing its language in potentially subversive terms, and shifting into a rhetorical space of psychic geography which owns no theoretical parallel.

Crimsworth frames his account of his social ascent through a series of professional and erotic struggles focused on the act of reading the inner psychological state from outer form. Placed in such a charged context, the rhetoric of penetration and control employed within medical and phrenological texts takes on specific, gender-differentiated, forms of erotic meaning. Economic, social and sexual discourses of control, secrecy and power, intersect in Crimsworth's dramatized representations of his battles to gain social acknowledgement of his interpretative supremacy. As consumers of the text, engaged in a second-order level of reading and interpretation, we are necessarily implicated in these dynamics.

Crimsworth's interpretative powers underwrite his ascent from his initial highly ambivalent gender and class position to that of confirmed masculinity and social power. The text works through the imposition of a whole series of boundaries and hierarchical divisions whose very multiplicity highlights their instability. Ideologies of class and gender intersect in a constantly shifting network of relations involving the oppositional formulations of masculine/feminine, bourgeois/aristocrat, plebian/patrician, power/powerlessness, self-made man/son, female pollution/purity, working-class female sexuality/upper-class angel, animal/spiritual. Crimsworth's attempts to resolve the contradictions and ambivalence which inform his gender and class identity are enacted through a constant series of displacements of these binary terms.

On approaching his brother's mill, Crimsworth reads the landscape in both class and sexual terms. Where he had hoped to find 'romance and seclusion' he finds instead an active, fertile body, cradling cylindrical chimneys, and hiding in its sooty hollow Edward's 'Concern' (p. 15). Nature, as veiled, aristocratic bride, has been transformed into a productive, bourgeois wife who threatens to engulf him: '"Look at the sooty smoke in that hollow and know that there is your post! There you cannot dream, you cannot speculate and theorise – there you shall out and work!"' (p. 15). William aligns himself with the feminized, aristocratic values of romance, seclusion, and imagination, against the masculine, bourgeois, values of trade, manufacture, and work. These binary oppositions are then in turn predicated on two opposing views of the female body: spiritual and asexual, the shrine of imagination, or dark, dirty and sexually rapacious.

William's scrutiny of the landscape sets the terms for the interpretative analysis of his relations with his brother which immediately follows. Crimsworth turns himself and his brother into 'pictures'. Although possessing a 'broader brow' he is greatly inferior 'in form' to his brother: 'As an animal, Edward excelled me far – should he prove as paramount in mind as in person I must be his slave' (p. 16). Edward's robust masculinity emphasizes William's feminine form, but the deft assimilation of Edward's virility to the sphere of animality leaves the way open for William to claim the higher ground of mental superiority (as signalled, phrenologically, by his 'broader brow').

In yet a third scene of reading, this time involving the portrait of William and Edward's mother, the class and gender dynamics underlying their relationship are spelt out. William retires from a dance at Crimsworth Hall feeling 'weary, solitary, kept-down – like some desolate tutor or governess' (p. 23), an image which clearly reflects his dependent, feminized position. Failing to find a female partner, he communes instead with the portrait of his mother, tracing his own image in her lineaments. The semiotic analysis is this time furnished by the manufacturer, Yorke Hunsden, who traces the effects of the ill-assorted marriage of the elder Crimsworths in the material inheritance of their children: Edward inherits the handsome, animal vigour of his 'plebian', manufacturing father, and William the traits of his 'sen-si-tive' mother who has 'Aristocrat written on the brow and defined in the figure' (p. 26). The divisions between the two are drawn across a whole series of binary oppositions. Edward's inheritance is unproblematic, confirming his alignment with the values of masculinity, power, and bourgeois manufacturing. His social status of self-made man intensifies his dissociation from the sphere of femininity: masculine control of production, rather than the legacy of female reproduction, operates as the governing principle of his life. William, by contrast, is aligned with femininity, powerlessness, and the aristocracy. His inherited traits actively render him unfit for the world of trade and manufacture. As Hunsden demands: 'What good can your bumps of ideality, comparison, self-esteem, conscientiousness, do you here?' (p. 27). William is not, however, merely an aristocrat but a hybrid: although he disdains the world of trade, he has enthusiastically embraced the bourgeois ideology of self-improvement. His problems of self-definition are indexed very precisely to a specific social formation: a fallen aristocracy seeking to reinvigorate itself without becoming subsumed within the bourgeois sphere of trade and manufacturing. For William there is a disjunction between the femininity inscribed on his form and features and reinforced by his social position, and his internal sense of innate power and authority. The narrative plots the reordering of these elements until his external social position can stand testimony to an achieved sense of masculinity and social power.

Crimsworth's simultaneous struggles for coherent masculine identity and social power and control are enacted through the dual exercise of self-control and interpretative power. He not only participates in the outward forms of social surveillance, but has also internalized its structures to his own psyche. He defeats his brother, he suggests, by his ability to police internally his own mental traits: 'I was guarded by three faculties; Caution, Tact, Observation; and prowling and prying as was Edward's malignity, it could never baffle the lynx-eyes of these – my natural sentinels' (p. 31). In this dual layering of surveillance, the phrenological theory of discrete faculties is co-opted to suggest an internal regime of surveillance which guards an inner sanctum of selfhood. Crimsworth's language underscores the interdependence of theories of interiorized selfhood and external structures of surveillance. His sense of the primacy of a pre-existent realm of selfhood is illusory. As Foucault has argued, the modern interiorized subject is itself actively produced by the internalization of the social structures of surveillance.[2]

William shifts the grounds of his struggles with Edward for masculine predominance from economic power and animal prowess to a more interiorized terrain. His brother, he suggests,

> was trying to read my character but I felt as secure against his scrutiny as if I had had on a casque with the visor down – or rather I showed him my countenance with the confidence that one would show an unlearned man a letter written in Greek – he might see lines, and trace characters, but he could make nothing of them – my nature was not his nature, and its signs were to him like the words of an unknown tongue.(p. 21)

William's vigilant self-control gives him a triumphant illegibility which defies his brother's penetration, translating his state of social powerlessness into one of empowerment. The description mobilizes class assumptions, of aristocratic culture which remains impenetrable to the bourgeois philistines. But its ideological functions are more complex than a simple defence of upper-class privilege, for it draws specifically on the discursive framework of phrenology which operated to legitimate the rising middle classes' claims to social power. The semiotic system in play is not that of physiognomy where signs were open for all to read, but the more competitive system of phrenology: bodily form still articulates inner qualities, but the signs hold meaning only for the initiated, schooled in the rules of translation. Crimsworth's rhetoric highlights the ways in which phrenological claims to interpretative authority were directly indexed to aspirations for upward social mobility, giving dramatic form to the claims that phrenology represented 'the consummation of "knowledge is power"'.

The primary threat to William's sense of his own identity and integrity comes not, however, from his brother, but from the enigmatic Hunsden who offers an unpleasant mirror image of the curious hybrid he may himself become. At once patrician and manufacturer, Hunsden's straddling of class and economic roles is directly associated with his problematic physiological and sexual identity. Alone of all the characters he encounters, Hunsden seems to defy William's descriptive and classificatory powers. The initial impression he gives of something 'powerful and massive' is belied by his small, and feminine lineaments, a contrast which suggests to Crimsworth a sense of 'incompatibilities of the "physique" with the "morale"' which could explain the 'secret of that fitful gloom' which could eclipse his countenance. Crimsworth is obsessed by Hunsden's sexual amorphism. After returning repeatedly to the subject, he finally concludes that 'There is no use in attempting to describe what is indescribable' (p. 200). There followed in the manuscript a passage which Brontë subsequently deleted: 'I can only say that the face [or 'form'?] and countenance of Hunsden Yorke Hunsden Esq resembled more the result of a cross between Oliver Cromwell and a French grisette, than anything else in Heaven above or in the Earth beneath' (p. 200). The sexual indecipherability of Hunsden is transposed into a whole series of further oppositions: angel/devil, English/French, sexual repression/licentiousness. Hunsden seems to unite the extremes of masculine dominance and control with those of loose female sexuality.

The timing of Crimsworth's acknowledgement of this defeat of his classificatory powers is significant. It is immediately followed by Hunsden's definitive triumph: the delivery of the portrait of Crimsworth's mother which has presided symbolically over their personal conflict. Economic, class, and gender determinants all figure in this complex exchange over the body of the mother. Hunsden's act and humiliating note underscore Crimsworth's problematic relations to his mother. In communing with his own reflection in the portrait, Crimsworth is locked into a feminine and infantilizing position which is associated on the one hand with the idolization of female purity, and on the other with the economic and social powerlessness of a bankrupt aristocracy.

The sexual dynamics which underpin the association between William and Hunsden, and in particular the role played by the mother, are prefigured in the opening page of William's narrative, in his letter to Charles which never reaches its destination. Although critics habitually complain about the technical awkwardness of this narrative device, its insistent redundancy draws attention to the psychic dramas in which William is still enlocked, and which he is committed to re-enacting. William's sexual uncertainties are exposed in his anxious, unsolicited denial that he possessed 'romantic regard' or 'anything of the Pylades and Orestes sentiment' for Charles whose qualities, 'sarcastic, observant, shrewd, cold-blooded' seem to align him both with Hunsden and the social image Crimsworth himself would like to project (p. 5). By summoning to mind these mythic figures who cement their friendship by the brutal stabbing of Orestes' mother, Clytemnestra, the letter establishes a symbolic association between male bonding and matricide. In Aeschylus' play, *The Choephori*, Pylades urges his friend on to the murder, and stands with him over the mutilated body of Clytemnestra as Orestes, in language redolent with sexual disgust, gives vent to his horror at her deeds.[3] Such disgust finds its parallel in *The Professor* not in the actual depiction of the mother, but rather transposed onto Crimsworth's responses to the Belgium schoolgirls over whom he is set in the role of master. Brontë gives to her hero an extreme version of the dichotomized attitudes to female sexuality expressed in contemporary medical and social writing: idolization of the purity of the mother is set against the animal nature of the sexualized schoolgirls. Yet as the opening reference to Orestes and Pylades suggests, the magnificent landscape of the mother is also feared to enclose dark drains.

The text works once more through a series of binary oppositions and transpositions as it negotiates the complex interweavings of class and gender ideologies. Crimsworth's change in attitude to female sexuality presages his own transformation into an economically successful and fully masculinized figure. Once set in the role of master over the Belgium schoolgirls he ceases to regard the female body as a mirror-like reflection of his own purity, but looks instead beneath the representational surface to unveil the animal sexuality which lurks below. This gaze of sexual mastery initiates his ascent up the economic and social ladder. Hunsden's taunting note, which shatters his identification with his mother, completes the process: he immediately goes out and procures the job which leads to financial independence, and to the affirmation of an unproblematic heterosexual identity through his marriage to Frances Henri.

Crimsworth's transformation from powerless aristocrat to bourgeois self-improver is directly indexed to his changing relations to female sexuality. As in the tale of Orestes and Pylades, however, the ritual slaying and purging of the mother is achieved through the agency of another male, in this case Hunsden. The homoerotic dimension of their relations is explicitly underscored by Hunsden who, on encountering William rushing out of town after a violent, sexually charged scene, in which his brother attacked him with a whip, suggests that 'Just so must Lot have left Sodom' (p. 32). The threat of sodomy to William's sexual subjectivity lies less with his brother and the world of manufactures, however, than with Hunsden himself. Hunsden announces that he had been waiting for the gift of a woman, 'Rebecca on a camel's hump, with bracelets on her arms and a ring in her nose', but will have to make do with William instead (p. 32).[4] Hunsden's house, which, in keeping with his ambivalent social and sexual status, is situated in liminal territory, on the border between country and city, nature and manufacture, provides the site of seduction. As in Brontë's later work, where rooms and desks function as external projections of inner body spaces, the interior space of Hunsden's parlour carries a symbolic freight of sexual meaning. Its neat orderliness and red glowing coals appeal to Crimsworth: here is neither the pale ashes which 'that slut of a servant' had left in his own grate (p. 31) nor the roaring conflagration with which Bertha Mason is later associated. The attractions of Hunsden's clean, carefully controlled sexuality are rendered menacing, however, by his gender. William's extreme rudeness to Hunsden in all their encounters is testimony of the degree to which he feels, socially and sexually, under threat.

In exploring the problems of masculine identity, Brontë is entering relatively uncharted territory. Although ideals of masculinity underpinned much of the social, psychological and economic discourse of the era, they received little theoretical attention, their very centrality, indeed, ensuring freedom from discursive interrogation. Medical literature frequently drew attention to the conflict between social prescriptions for femininity and the workings of the female body,[5] but did not engage with the problems created for men by the dictates of manliness.[6] The discursive attention paid to masculinity focuses pre-eminently on fears of its loss, as in the extensive popular literature on spermatorrhea and masturbation. In accordance with the economic theories of control which regulated social and psychological discourses of the era, masculinity becomes a function of the practices of containment and control. Fears were also voiced that masculinity could be lost by men being feminized, either through too strong an association with the mother, or through undertaking 'women's work.'[7] In *The Tenant of Wildfell Hall*, all the advice Mrs Graham receives as to the rearing of her son rehearses the contemporary view that keeping a boy too much with his mother would inhibit the unfolding of his innate manhood, and thus undermine his will to power.[8] Crimsworth is governed by similar arguments when he decides, at the conclusion of *The Professor*, to send his son, optimistically named Victor, to Eton, away from the influence of his wife and Hunsden. Once more, Hunsden is seen to exert a destabilizing influence on the social and sexual bases of masculine identity, whilst Crimsworth's wife, Frances, is given the emasculatory role previously associated with his own mother.

In her exploration of the complex determinants of Crimsworth's subjectivity, Brontë highlights the ways in which questions of social and economic positioning were refracted through the domain of the sexual. The picture she draws is not of an innate, assured masculinity, but rather of a social and gender identity created and sustained only through violence: the violence of self-repression and of repudiation of all who might threaten the carefully nurtured illusion of self-control.

With the shifting of the action to Belgium, the ambivalences which have framed Crimsworth's gender and class identity in England are transposed into the simpler terms of sex and race. In England William was an aristocrat without land or power, but in Belgium, he appears to accede, symbolically, to his natural birth-right. Taking upon himself the mantle of England's imperial greatness, he enters into his self-imposed task, of classifying the Belgian people as a whole, with all the zest of an anthropologist assured of his own evolutionary supremacy. From a phrenological contemplation of a few details of outer form of his 'selected specimens' he is quickly able to define the characteristics of the entire 'youth of Brabant': 'Their intellectual faculties were generally weak, their animal propensities strong; thus there was at once an impotence and a kind of inert force in their natures' (p. 67). Judging by the evolutionary scale laid down by Combe, where ascendancy was conferred according to the degree to which 'animal propensities' were held in check by the intellectual faculties, these schoolboys are clearly near the very bottom of the ladder. Crimsworth's earlier sense of his own impotence is clearly held in check by his crass exercise in cultural chauvinism which anticipates some of the worst excesses of the ways in which phrenology, and the later science of craniology, were later deployed in evolutionary anthropology.[9] History, and the issues of material inheritance, which radically destabilized Crimsworth's sense of identity in England are no longer seen as operative. The features of his pupils, according to Crimsworth, offer a retroactive explanation of 'the political history of their ancestors. Pelet's school was merely an epitome of the Belgian Nation' (p. 68). Belgian culture is reduced to a reiterative pattern formed by a single psyche which illuminates Crimsworth's own intrinsic superiority.

Crimsworth's problems with respect to sexuality are not so easily resolved, however. His early responses to his female pupils enact the schizophrenic qualities of Victorian cultural definitions of femininity, oscillating wildly between visions of purity, and disgusted repudiations of female sexuality. The initial fantasies which Brontë gives to her hero are founded on an idolization of female purity; his imaginings at this stage are tentative and restrained. Faced with the stern reality of a boarded-up window, Crimsworth hopes to find 'some chink or crevice which I might enlarge and so get a peep at the consecrated ground' (p. 65). Crimsworth's role is portrayed in intriguingly feminine terms. He had hoped, 'to have studied female character in a variety of phases, myself the while, sheltered from view by a modest muslin curtain' (p. 66). Like a woman, Crimsworth must drape himself with 'modest' muslin in order to remain hidden and inviolate. His accession to his true role as 'master' in the girls' school marks an end to all such emasculatory fantasies. Openly confronting the girls with his gaze, he establishes control over the class by ridding himself of all notions of female purity and mystery. The secrets of womanhood are now opened to him, and their essence revealed to be 'precocious impurity' (p. 99). In exorcizing his awe for the female body, Crimsworth has taken one more step towards emancipating himself from the hold of his aristocratic mother, and launching himself on the bourgeois path of masculine self-creation and advancement.

Although Crimsworth's primary responses to his female pupils are clearly those of sexual disgust, it is a disgust which is displaced onto a cerebral location. Phrenology, once more, supplies the validating authority for his judgments. Of Juanna Trista he observes,

I wonder that any one, looking at that girl's head and countenance, would have received her under their roof. She had precisely the same shape of skull as Pope Alexander the sixth: her organs of benevolence, veneration, conscientiousness, adhesiveness were singularly small, those of self-esteem, firmness, destructiveness, combativeness preposterously large; her head sloped up in the penthouse shape, was contracted about the forehead and prominent behind.(pp. 101–2)

In *The Constitution of Man*, Combe prints a picture of Pope Alexander the Sixth accompanied by Spurzheim's original analysis:

'This cerebral organisation', says Dr Spurzheim, 'is despicable in the eyes of a phrenologist . . . The cervical and whole basilar region of the head are particularly developed; the organs of the perceptive faculties are pretty large; but the sincipital (or coronal) region is exceedingly low, particularly at the organs of benevolence, veneration, and conscientiousness. Such a head is unfit for any employment of a superior kind, and never gives birth to sentiments of humanity. The sphere of its activity does not extend beyond those enjoyments which minister to the animal portion of human nature.'[10]

Brontë's account delineates the contours revealed in the illustration, not merely reproducing Spurzheim's analysis of the faculties, but developing and extending its range, in line with Combe's chart of the thirty-five phrenological organs and the principles of phrenological analysis. The additional area of deficiency ascribed to Juanna for instance is that of 'adhesiveness', defined by Combe as the capacity for attachment which underlies friendship and society. It is also the only faculty which he specifically associates with the condition of femininity.[11] (Frances is later to prove her intrinsic femininity and moral quality in her debate with Hunsden when she insists that association, and the emotional processes of attachment, are the only sources of social value.)

From goddesses, the schoolgirls are quickly turned into animals. Unlike the boys they are carefully differentiated, but all to the same end: to demonstrate diverse varieties of animal behaviour and propensities. From the almost loving detail Crimsworth lavishes on their bodily figures, there is an abrupt shift each time as he moves to decipher the secrets of their heads and faces. The shift from lascivious gaze to disgusted analysis enacts his own confusion, highlighting the ways in which male 'knowledge' of the female is used to police the male's own sexuality. Adele Dronsart, whose initial description suggests a 'dumpy but good-looking damsel' is transformed into a mythological beast as Crimsworth's gaze meets hers: 'She was an unnatural-looking being, so young, fresh, blooming, yet so Gorgon-like. Suspicion, sullen ill-temper were on her forehead, vicious propensities in her eye, envy and panther-like deceit about her mouth' (p. 100). To avoid being turned to stone, Crimsworth employs the same defence as in his confrontation with his brother, buckling on 'a breast-plate of steelly indifference' (p. 86). His armour against the challenging, unabashed gaze of femininity is his claim to knowledge of their inner secrets. The gendered ideology of early modern science underpins his stance: male scientific mastery is displayed by the unveiling of female nature.[12] Phrenology proves a vital ally in this quest for control. Once character can be discerned from outer form, the power of secrecy (the only mode of power ever allotted to women) is transferred to the active decoder. Crimsworth's own fears of being read take on new meaning in this light: in the sexually charged dynamics associated with the legible body, to be read is to be feminized. Male power lies not in the physiological secrets of the body, and its powers of creation, but in the domain of knowledge and its social control.[13]

The narrative function of Crimsworth's detailed phrenological analyses of his male and female pupils is to shift the boundaries of self-definition from the problematic arenas of class and gender to the more simplistic registers of race and sex. His racial superiority over the Flemish male dissolves the problems of class identity which had assailed him in England, whilst the overweening, coarse sexuality of his female pupils acts to stabilize his own gender identity. In the complex, intersecting realms of Victorian ideology, the problem of female sexuality was partially resolved on a class base, shunted off onto the lower orders, yet the fears of ubiquitous contamination remained. Crimsworth's depictions of his Belgium pupils confirm those fears: girls from all social spheres, from farm girls through to countesses, are all aligned with rampant sexuality. By transposing this sexuality into the realm of the 'foreign', Crimsworth is able to free himself from emasculating fantasies of female purity, whilst simultaneously retaining, uncompromised, his sense of his maternal, aristocratic inheritance.

Crimsworth's struggles for social and psychological dominance are replayed in Belgium, but this time within a more explicitly sexual frame. The dominating figure of his brother Edward is replaced by that of his new 'master', Pelet, who fails to pose an equivalent threat to William's virility, either in terms of bourgeois manufacturing power or animal vigour (his name means 'bald' or 'plucked'). The taunting, sexually hybrid role of Hunsden is now played by Zoraide Reuter, the female directrice with the political powers of Talleyrand (p. 90), while the presiding figure of female purity is transposed from his mother to Frances Henri. The sexual politics are now less threatening. Unlike Hunsden, Zoraide, as a woman, can be openly desired, and rejected, by William, whilst Frances can be appropriated and controlled without threat to his heterosexual identity.

As an antagonist Pelet is soon disposed of. The same window through which Crimsworth had hoped to gaze on the schoolgirl 'angels and their Eden' (p. 76) allows him to unveil Pelet's 'secret': like the female pupils, he is found to be 'indelibly stained' (p. 112). On encountering Pelet's 'false glance and insinuating smile' Crimsworth thanks heaven that he had read 'the true meaning of that guileful countenance; I felt half his master, because the reality of his nature was now known to me' (p. 114). Possession of knowledge, in our narrator's eyes, reverses their material social relation.

Crimsworth's relations with Zoraide herself are more complex. As a combination of masculine force within an alluring female frame she is potentially more threatening than the hybrid figure of Hunsden. On meeting her, Crimsworth is guilty of his only significant misreading in the text. Mistakenly perceiving openness and elevation in her forehead, he jumps to the conclusion that some 'upward-tending career were even then opening to me' (p. 81). Her features are made to bear a literal inscription of his future prospects. Whereas Jane Eyre's situation as governess only reinforces her lowly status in the sexual hierarchy, Crimsworth, as employee of a woman, hopes to rectify his anomalous position by reinstating the traditional pattern of masculine dominance through sexual control of his 'mistress'.

His subsequent interactions with Zoraide highlight the erotic dimensions of the power play which directs all his social actions. The excitement of pursuit is heightened by Mdlle Reuter's employment of male weapons: calm inscrutability and an 'astute, penetrating' eye which speaks to Crimsworth the language of dominance: 'Be as close as you like – I am not dependent on your candour – but what you would conceal – I already know' (p. 89). Like Jane with Rochester, Crimsworth derives pleasure from their mutual attempts to penetrate the other. Far from withdrawing in disgust, he actively enters into the fray, 'I enjoyed the game much and did not hasten its conclusion' (p. 90). His pleasure stems froms the ways in which their interpretative struggles actively produce and confirm his sense of possession of an interiorized selfhood.

Crimsworth is saved from the consequences of his misreading of Zoraide, by the 'open lattice' which functions as literal window into the secrets of sexuality, rendering Mdlle Reuter 'transparent' (p. 153). Disgust at her sexuality, and his own initial entrapment, fuels Crimsworth's analysis as he turns her phrenological configuration into an anatomy of social perversion: 'to Violence, Injustice, Tyranny she succumbed – they were her natural masters; she had no propensity to hate, no impulse to resist them' (p. 132). Crimsworth's revenge on this self-controlled, masculine woman is to turn her into a slave of her own body. Crimsworth's triumphant unveiling does not release him from her thralls, however, but, paradoxically, intensifies her power. Brontë's text traces through, in all their subtle contortions, the psychic structures of dominance produced by Victorian models of social and self-control. Zoraide's 'servility', gives Crimsworth 'an irritating sense of degradation in the very experience of the pleasure' (p. 184). Crimsworth's social interactions are based on a public playing out of the internal dynamics of self-control: only in the experience of the tension of resistance is his own sense of agency and power affirmed. Mdlle Reuter's excessive subservience thus produces a double defeat for Crimsworth: far from exerting mastery he is reduced to a slavish response, at the mercy of the 'degrading,' animal promptings of his body. By offering herself 'self-given' to this Victorian male, Mdlle Reuter deprives him of his manhood.

Crimsworth's sense of loss of control extends self-reflexively into the arena of narrative. He decides to leave Pelet's residence, once the latter is married to Zoraide, rather than become involved in a 'practical Modern French novel' (p. 192). Like Jane who decides to flee from Rochester, rather than become one more in his line of mistresses, Crimsworth withdraws from the scene once it becomes clear that he will no longer be able to control his own narrative, but will be forced to live within the constraints of an undesirable genre. Crimsworth turns instead to an alternative female figure to represent his social prospects, and an alternate text: *Pilgrim's Progress*. In his secular reworking of this text, economic progress is directly indexed to female sexuality. While Mdlle Reuter represents the 'mossy and declining . . . green way along which Temptation strewed flowers' Frances offers the 'rough and steep . . . path' of upward mobility, inspiring Crimsworth's 'hopes to win and possess, my resolutions to work and rise' (p. 193). Sexual and economic possession are intertwined. Against the sloth and ease of sensual temptation, and economic reward without labour offered by Zenobia, the non-threatening, self-contained figure of Frances suggests a form of untainted sexuality, and the social rewards of labour and self-control.

The features and characteristics given to Frances are those of Crimsworth's mother, so in becoming her 'master' he effectively demonstrates his ability to command his feminizing aristocratic traits in the service of his bourgeois progress. His own hybrid class status is duplicated in Frances' mixed racial origin which, in contradistinction to that of all his other pupils, offers a positive blend. Frances' sensitivity, and innate superiority are inscribed outwardly in her phrenological profile: 'the shape of her head . . . was different, the superior part more developed, the base considerably less' (p. 124). Indeed, she represents for Crimsworth such a desirable configuration of faculties that he portrays his quest of her through Brussels as a search, not for a woman, but for a combination of signs: 'an ample space of brow and a large, dark and serious eye with a fine but decided line of eye-brow traced above' (p. 164). As one of nature's aristocrats, occupying but a lowly position on the social ladder, Frances represents both a female mirror image of Crimsworth, and an external site upon which he can project his own internal struggles.

As readers we are not allowed to be complicit with Crimsworth: his courtship of Frances displays all the aggressive will to power that ruled his earlier associations.[14] William's early exercise of mastery over Frances is played out in the domain of language. In *Villette*, Lucy Snowe's developing bilingualism functions as a mode of empowerment, allowing her to triumph over the mono-lingual M. Paul.[15] Bilingualism is constraining to Frances, however, subduing her to the role of perfect mate for Crimsworth. Once married, Frances chooses French as the language of her rebellion, and is forced by Crimsworth 'to read English to me for an hour by way of penance' (p. 253).[16] Frances is granted the same ambitions as Crimsworth, the same desires for faculty development, but all agency is taken from her. In Crimsworth's eyes, Frances exists as a physiological economy whose fixed sum of resources require his careful regulation in order to inhibit 'a wasteful expense of energy and labour' (p. 131). He advises her to 'cultivate' her faculties (p. 137), but then depicts her development as a consequence entirely of his own gardening skills (p. 148). In a deft twist, the phrenological theory of faculty cultivation with its correlated notion of the organic laws governing mental life, is assimilated to traditional images of women as flowers and plants, female nature waiting to be governed by masculine control.[17]

Frances' true potential is signalled by her literary ambition which, as in Brontë's early writings, becomes an explicit focus of debate. Mdlle Reuter insists on the absolute impropriety of a woman entering the public domain of writing: 'even in celibacy it would be better for her to retain the character and habits of a respectable, decorous female' (p. 151). Brontë's own response to these views is actively encoded by their placement in the mouth of the treacherous Zoraide Reuter. Yet the ambivalence of her initial response to Southey, where she set writing in opposition to 'all the duties a woman ought to fulfil' is nonetheless present in the text.[18] Frances' writing is placed specifically within the constraints of the private sphere: its form violates none of the interdictions placed on female ambition or self-absorption. Indeed, where ambition is acknowledged in her poem it is then instantly paired with the opening of a bleeding 'secret, inward wound', an image, which suggests that female flow and outpouring is to be confined to the private space of the body.[19] Her poem is designed not for a public audience but for her ears alone, and in recasting her experience it ensures that 'while egotism was avoided, the fancy was exercised, and the heart satisfied' (p. 217). Far from violating Frances' essential femininity, her writing actively confirms it. The enunciation of her poem, overheard by Crimsworth, leads directly to his decision to change her role from that of pupil to that of wife.

In contrast to the repressive Mdlle Reuter, Crimsworth, as nurturer of his precious plant, seems to offer a more positive model of female education. The message he claims to 'read' on Frances' brow whilst she is reciting the 'language of her own heart', however, downgrades female creativity to an inadequate substitute for a male lover. Crimsworth proceeds to define female fulfilment in terms of a destined biological role. He directs his readers to 'Look at the rigid and formal race of old maids – the race whom all despise'. Far from challenging such a viewpoint he clearly endorses it, reinforcing the social ideology which places women and men in very different relations to the doctrines of self-control. Women who 'have fed themselves, from youth upwards, on maxims of resignation and endurance' become,

ossified with the dry diet; Self-Control is so continually their thought, so perpetually their object that at last it absorbs the softer and more agreeable qualities of their nature, and they die mere models of austerity, fashioned out of a little parchment and much bone. Anatomists will tell you that there is a heart in the withered old maid's carcass – the same as in that of any cherished wife or proud mother in the land – can this be so? I really don't know – but feel inclined to doubt it.(p. 216)

Whereas man's task is to control and to contain, to subjugate the lower animal propensities to the higher intellectual faculties, woman's goal is to ensure that thought and mental control do not block and impede the fundamental reproductive processes of the body. Self-control (here equated with a pattern of life outside male control) leads to self-negation, a destruction of female identity and a literal withering of the body. Crimsworth denies old maids all active agency; they do not control their own destiny by writing but are rather passively 'fashioned' into parchment, reduced to a material base for male inscription. Sexual disgust reverberates throughout the passage; Crimsworth's penetrating eye not only unveils but also dissects the old maid's anatomy for his readers, exposing her inner organs to view in an image which draws on that ultimate symbol of male mastery, the pictorial representation of the anatomy lesson.[20]

Crimsworth's analysis reduces the 'soft' attributes associated with the feminine psyche to literal qualities of the flesh. Frances' development functions primarily as a demonstration of Crimsworth's sexual power; under his tutelage she acquires the external signs of reproductive fitness (the plumpness and embonpoint so frequently extolled by physiologists) which indicate her readiness to fulfil her designated female role (pp. 147–8). Her literary creativity drops from view, having served its purpose, in Crimsworth's eyes, as a mode of self-revelation which renders her more sexually pliable. Following interaction with her 'master', her 'old maid's' state of withered self-control and obstructed flow is transformed into one of vital animal health. Their exchanges over the sharpening of pencils (a symbolic sexual terrain which recurs throughout Brontë's opus) cause her spirits to 'maintain their flow, often, for some hours, and . . . her health therefrom took a sustenance and vigour which . . . had almost recreated her whole frame' (p. 177). 'Recreated' by Crimsworth, Frances evolves into his perfect mate, gently affirming his masculine identity without subjecting him to the sexual challenge offered by Zoraide Reuter and the collective gaze of her shameless pupils. Frances, by contrast, possesses a gaze 'where affection tempered penetration' (p. 174).

Brontë's representation of the workings of Crimsworth's sexual imagination explores and delineates the forms of erotic ideal to which the Victorian philosophy of masculine self-help and control gave rise. Frances is for Crimsworth alternately a plant to cherish, a patch of ground to cultivate, or, more straightforwardly, a storage vessel in which to preserve his own life force: 'my ideal of the shrine in which to seal my stores of love' (p. 169). The image reinforces theories of reproduction which assigned to male sperm the active, creative force, women merely supplying the conditions of nurturance.[21] Although Crimsworth attributes to Frances the traits of 'self-denial and self-control' their primary purpose is to ensure the predominance of his own control; they are to act as 'those guardians, those trusty keepers of the gift I longed to confer on her'. The decorous prose, with its enigmatic framing of this 'gift', nonetheless draws on the symbiotic relation between semen and selfhood in Victorian ideology. Frances herself is also endowed with sexuality, but of a non-menacing 'silent' form that neither clamours nor challenges, nor threatens to engulf: 'silent possessor of a well of tenderness, of a flame as genial as still, as pure as quenchless'. In Frances, sexuality is subordinated to the home-making instincts; her 'dangerous flame' is self-subdued, suggesting the perfect workings of an internalized structure of political oppression: 'I had seen Reason reduce the rebel and humble its blaze to embers' (p. 169). Sexual humiliation is not to be feared from Frances, she inflicts its force rather on her own psyche.

Crimsworth seeks to portray his history as one steady ascent towards his desired goals of social and sexual control. There is one extraordinary section, however, where this control breaks down. Once Frances has been secured, Crimsworth is at pains to point out he derives 'a pleasure purely material' from contemplating her body (p. 227). This admission is immediately followed, however, by his description of his subjection to a 'dreaded and ghastly concubine', the spirit of Hypochondria.[22] For once, Crimsworth's explanatory powers fail him. It is worthwhile dwelling at length on the ideological context which framed Crimsworth's self-projections in order to understand this dual breakdown.

As a term in Victorian medicine, hypochondria had more extensive connotations than in contemporary usage, encompassing both the sense of imaginary perceptions of illness, and the 'incurable despair' and 'melancholy forebodings' earlier defined by Sydenham.[23] Dismissing any form of supernatural account, Crimsworth initially adopts the explanatory terms of Victorian medicine: his earlier ecstasy had 'jarred' his nerves, and his 'soul' had 'overstrained the body's comparative weakness'. While the notion of nervous strain draws on contemporary medical accounts, the reference to an incompatibility between 'soul' and body directly recalls the descriptions of Hunsden, and his ambiguous sexual identity. Crimsworth is unable to account for the fact that hypochondria, the companion of his unhappy youth, should now recur at the moment of his greatest fulfilment. The imagery suggests, however, that the very relaxation of control consequent on his sense of achievement brings to the fore all his unacknowledged fears surrounding his social and sexual identity.

By allowing himself to indulge in fantasies of sensual pleasure, Crimsworth shatters the fragile equilibrium of his psychic structure which was grounded entirely on restraint. His ensuing fears of annihilation and engulfment are focused on threatening images of female sexuality. The dreaded concubine who now shares his life and bed, whispering to him of death, leads him, as in boyhood, into the symbolic terrain of the female body, 'shewing me nooks in woods, hollows in hills, where we could sit together, and where she could drop her drear veil over me, and so hide sky and sun, grass and green tree; taking me entirely to her death-cold bosom' (p. 228). Crimsworth's terrors of being trapped, veiled from life within secret nooks, and grasped in the smothering female embrace of death, dramatize two of the central thematic strands in mid-Victorian popular texts on 'manhood' where the expenditure of sexual energy, both as aroused by and demanded by the female, was figured as a form of psychological and physiological death.

Within mainstream medical writing, male hypochondriasis was frequently related to forms of sexual fear. Bucknill and Tuke quote a case of a 'gentleman' who 'was firmly convinced that the testicles had wasted away, and brooded over the supposed loss of reproductive power. This is a very common notion with hypochondriacal men.'[24] Gloomy forebodings of death, and loss of a sense of purposive existence, were commonly linked to sexual fears within the ideological nexus which grounded the social identity of the male in his role of producer. Within this framework, in which manhood, and hence a confirmed sense of self-identity, depended on the production and controlled retention of the life force, both women and masturbation could constitute a threat to masculine integrity. The dreaded vice of masturbation, which figured so largely in Victorian projections of the male sexual economy, was frequently cited as itself a cause of hypochondriasis. According to the widely-read, popular text of Deslandes, on *Manhood; the Causes of its Premature Decline, with directions for its Perfect Restoration*, the practise of onanism would frequently lead to hysteria and hypochondriasis, and a state of extreme nervous irritability and sensitivity throughout the system.[25]

Deslandes' work also offers significant observations on the dangers of heterosexual activity. The text opens with dire warnings concerning the expense to the male system of the 'convulsions' which accompany the act of emitting semen. Women, however, are less affected, as is clearly demonstrated by their ability to serve as 'public women'. Any man would quickly be brought to his death-bed by such repeated sexual activity.[26] In drawing together, in this image of the asexual prostitute, the two opposing Victorian constructions of womanhood, as asexual being or voracious consuming sexual beast, Deslandes draws attention to their ideological synonymity. The polar opposition of angel and whore upon which the Victorian sexual hierarchy has been deemed to be based thus founders. Both projections of womanhood function in response to the perceived fragility of the male sexual economy. Crimsworth's attack of hypochondria, once sexual union with Frances becomes certain, thus operates as a structural challenge to the narrative trajectory he has constructed in which the lures of the sensual Zoraide are replaced by the safe attractions of his chaste pupil, Frances.

In order to understand the operation of Crimsworth's sexual anxieties it is necessary to recast our understanding of Victorian projections of female asexuality. Critical analyses of Victorian sexual attitudes over the last twenty years have drawn a great deal of mileage from William Acton's famous pronouncements that 'the majority of women (happily for them) are not very much troubled with sexual feeling of any kind'.[27] If these comments are considered in context, however, they suggest that Acton's primary concern actually lay with the operation of the male sexual system and its role in the social economy. Like W. R. Greg in his essay on 'redundant' women, Acton attempts to persuade the reluctant male into the socially requisite expenditure (both of semen and money) of marriage.[28] His primary tactic is to reassure would-be spouses that the 'modest English girl' will not make the sexual demands they have been accustomed to from their mistresses, and they therefore need not fear that 'the marital duties they will have to undertake are beyond their exhausted strength'.[29] Acton offers this polarized view of female sexual appetite in response to the perceived male fear that the self, conceived as a fixed sum of retained energy, would literally be consumed in marriage. In order to stabilize the social flow of material energy, and hence ensure the requisite channelling of property, the ideological emphasis on the dangers of sexual spending had to be negated in relation to the domestic sphere. Men had to be convinced that marriage to an asexual angel would not lead to a cannibalistic orgy of consumption.

As the foregoing suggests, Victorian ideologies of manhood were more complex than is usually recognized. Like those of femininity, they were not unified, but multiple, offering contradictory positions of subjectivity in relation to the social and economic structure.[30] Theories of 'respectable' female asexuality were directly related to models of the male sexual economy which stressed the excessive drain of orgasm on the system where passion and mental exertion were both involved. In the crude, highly explicit terms of the quack medical texts one finds spelt out in all their crass simplicity many of the assumptions which underpin subtler, more refined constructions of

Victorian sexual ideologies. Deslandes, for example, establishes a hierarchy of desirable forms of sexual release: onanism was the most pernicious since it required the greatest effort on the part of the mind; intercourse involving passion, and thus the active participation of the emotional economy was the second most deadly; and at the bottom of the scale the least threatening forms of release were those with 'public' women, or asexual wives who did not stir up the emotions.[31] Contrary to our intuitive understanding of the Victorian period, wives and prostitutes here occupy the same position in relation to the male sexual economy. This sense of synonymity lies, unarticulated, behind the argument, to be found across the entire range of medical writings, from professional journals to popular tracts, that it is far better to frequent prostitutes than to commit the sin of onanism.[32] Although Acton does not go so far as openly to advise the use of prostitutes, he does warn against the dangers of long betrothals which lead to sexually exciting ideas, without the calming possibility of controlled emission. At whatever level they are framed, all early Victorian texts on manhood share the ideological work of constructing a model of the male sexual and psychic economy which tries to balance the demands of retention and emission within an overall structure of control.

Crimsworth's puzzlement as to why hypochondria should accost him at the precise moment when his desires had 'alighted on the very lap of fruition' must be set in the context of these Victorian ideologies of masculinity which figured sexual release both as the necessary completion of manhood, and as the basis of its destruction. The 'ghastly concubine' which comes 'to embitter a husband's heart toward his young bride' gives vivid psychological enactment to the two associated, but contradictory, ideological figurations of womanhood which the Victorian male had to negotiate. Crimsworth's account follows the medical emphasis on the waste and dissipation, through internal friction and conflict, of physiological force. In youth hypochondria had attacked him when he had 'strong desires and slender hopes' and her onslaught now is described in terms of dissipated energy. He begins to return to normalcy not when he starts to understand the psychological grounds for his terror, but when 'my spirits began slowly to recover their tone' (p. 229). From this moment on, Crimsworth depicts his life as a steady climb to social ascendancy, founded on the principles of regulation and control. The extended attention paid to his hypochondria, which remains unexplained, signals, however, a disturbance which is not resolved in the text, cutting across Crimsworth's much vaunted beliefs in the powers of self-control.

Crimsworth's depiction of his married life could well act as an exemplum in a phrenological text. The tone is smugly self-righteous. By hard labour, and rigorously subordinating the lower animal propensities to the higher faculties, he and Frances regain social caste, and acquire an 'independency' which allows them to purchase property adjacent to that of Yorke Hunsden. Their self-command is reflected in their position of social command; no longer are their energies dissipated in unproductive causes. The terms of their personal relationship suggest a balancing of forces which mirrors both the internal hierarchy of faculties and the social division of labour. William's economic success is also used to vindicate his masculinity. He and Edward have reversed their positions: William has proved his virility by hard labour (albeit outside the tainted field of trade) and judicious 'investment', whilst Edward has entered into a feminized periodic cycle of economic rise and fall, placing himself at the mercy of the fluctuations of the market, and trusting not to hard work but to the alluring wiles of speculation. We learn in the final paragraph that he is getting 'richer than Croesus by railway speculations' (p. 268). Edward is finally aligned not with masculine labour, containment and control but with threatening, uncontrolled excess and the hysteria of the imaginary realm of stocks and shares.

The solidity of William Crimsworth's attainment of an unproblematic social and sexual identity is put into question, however, by the presence of the restless Hunsden who looms large in the closing pages of the narrative, breaking the confines of the bourgeois domestic idyll Crimsworth is attempting to construct. Unlike Crimsworth he has not succumbed to the lures of compulsory heterosexuality, but remains stubbornly unmarried. His uncertain sexuality is directly highlighted in a scene which recalls once more William's problematic relationship to the figure of his mother. Hunsden unveils a portrait of Lucia which, in structural parallel to William's mental obsession with his mother's picture, he carries always about him. Both men are locked in a circuit of desire for unattainable women, a desire which signals their own unease in their social and sexual identity. William has sought both to exorcize and control his aristocratic mother, and the contamination of his own undesired femininity, through his re-creation of Frances into his desired model of chaste wife and bourgeois mother. Frances' eager interpretation of the portrait, however, suggests an alternate reading of the Crimsworths' marriage. Lucia is, for Frances, a sexual and social rebel, one who, on entering into a career on the stage, had been forced to forfeit her place in society. Her face, 'is that of one who has made an effort, and a successful and triumphant effort, to wrest some vigorous and valued faculty from insupportable constraint' (p. 262). Frances draws on the phrenological language of faculty development, but to very different ends than Crimsworth's paternalist vision of plant cultivation. The Italian Lucia of Frances' imagination is an earlier model of Vashti, but unlike Lucy Snowe, Frances regards her achievements and charismatic power as wholly admirable, rather than demonic (an interpretation which casts light on Frances' previous endorsement of a reversed *Othello*, where Desdemona takes the active role and smothers her spouse).[33] Frances' celebration of Lucia's rebellious programme of self-development casts an unflattering light on her own marriage, undermining Crimsworth's complacent projection of the harmonious hierarchy of their relations.

Hunsden similarly acts as a destabilizing figure in relation to William's role as father. The concluding pages of the novel are overshadowed by a disturbing act of violence: Crimsworth's shooting of his son's beloved dog, Yorke, which was a present from Yorke Hunsden. Symbolically, the scene can be read as Crimsworth's ruthless attempt to exorcize the feared contaminating influence of Hunsden on his son (he fears the dog is rabid). The narrative emphasis of these final pages falls on the violent restraint which underpins the attainment and construction of self-controlled masculinity. The bitter irony underlying Crimsworth's naming of this son Victor, is soon manifest. Crimsworth is plagued by restless fears that both Frances and Hunsden will hinder the development of his son's masculinity. Hunsden will foster his rebelliousness, his 'electrical ardour and power' (traits which ally him then with the enigmatic Lucia) while Frances will run the danger of making a 'milksop' of him (p. 266). Crimsworth resolves to send Victor to Eton, knowing full well that his son will be unhappy. He is determined to render him a respectable English gentleman at all cost, whipping the 'offending Adam' out of him: 'he will be cheap of any amount of either bodily or mental suffering which will ground him radically in the art of self-control' (p. 266).[34]

Although Crimsworth constructs his narrative as a textbook account of the social and psychological value of self-control, it functions rather to highlight the structural violence implicit in these ideological formations. His own ambiguities of class and gender identity were displaced narratively into the more containable terms of race and sex, yet his anxieties were not resolved but merely displaced onto the next generation. His vision of Victor's future education draws out the irony of ideologies of 'self' control. Only by subjection to the most extreme form of institutional discipline will Victor be crushed into the required state of class and gender subjectivity, whose defining attribute is deemed to be 'the art of self-control'.

CHAPTER 8

Jane Eyre: *lurid hieroglyphics*

In *Jane Eyre* Brontë extends her analysis of the ways in which ideological pressures of class, gender and economics are played out in the domain of subjectivity. Traditional readings of the novel which regard it primarily as a drama of the psyche, where society is consigned to the role of backdrop, fail to register the ways in which the language of psychology in the novel is itself politically defined and charged. Similarly, feminist celebrations of Brontë's depictions of sexual rebellion fail to take into account the ways in which the novel is framed by the discourses of Victorian psychology.[1] Medical texts of the era foregrounded the same three concerns which dominate Brontë's novel: the mechanics of self-control, the female body and sexuality, and the insurgence of insanity.

Psychology however, has never been an innocent discipline: in the Victorian period, as today, the writing of the self is a political act. In this conflict-ridden tale of upward female mobility, and flagrant female rebellion, Brontë's own political ambivalences are recorded in the ways in which she mobilizes contemporary psychological discourse. Cutting across the overarching narrative of self-improvement through self-control, one finds depictions of internal struggle cast in terms of both racial and class conflict. Although Brontë does not, as in *Shirley*, foreground the political dimensions of class and gender polarities in this novel, the realm of psychic struggle is clearly associated in her mind with the dynamics of social struggle and insurrection. The drama of social interaction is played out, however, on the terrain of the female body, which is treated, by Jane's antagonists and lovers alike, as an object to be regulated, controlled and decoded.

Jane Eyre follows a similar social trajectory to *The Professor*. Each text records the transition of an outcast figure from a position of social marginality to confirmed membership of the gentry. Both Jane and Crimsworth make their way by hard work, thus avoiding the taint of upper-class idleness, and the overt money-grubbing of trade. The relationship between this plot and the analysis of surges of energy within Jane's inner emotional life, and the depiction of Bertha's madness is not tangential, I will argue, but fundamental. The issue of 'madness' or female sexuality cannot be isolated out from this wider social and economic context which actively defines them.[2]

The drama of social ascent and erotic exchange is once more focused on the activities of reading and surveillance. Jane's courtships with both Rochester and St. John, for example, are competitive exercises in interpretative penetration. A preoccupation with unveiling is not restricted to the thematics of the text, however. In the preface to the second edition of *Jane Eyre*, Brontë, responding to those who had criticized the religious tendency of the book, significantly aligns her own authorial stance with the act of unmasking: 'To pluck the mask from the face of the Pharisee, is not to lift an impious hand to the Crown of Thorns'.[3] Invoking the authority of the Bible for her own stance, Brontë warns that her work will constitute a radical, political act of unveiling. The world, 'may hate him who dares to scrutinize and expose – to rase the gilding, and show base metal under it – to penetrate the sepulchre, and reveal charnel relics: but, hate as it will, it is indebted to him' (p. xxxi).[4] The connections of this sexualized rhetoric of unveiling to the overt political sphere are made explicit in Brontë's own comments on the preface, which she had concluded with a eulogy of Thackeray as the 'first social regenerator of the day'. In a letter to W. S. Williams, Brontë makes clear that she had associated Thackeray's role as regenerator, mastering and rectifying a warped social body, with the contemporary revolution in France. The letter passes from praise of Thackeray as the high priest of the goddess of truth to the observation that 'I read my preface over with some pain – I did not like it. I wrote it when I was a little enthusiastic, like you, about the French Revolution.'[5]

For Brontë, the connection between the rhetoric of unveiling the truth and an overt political movement of insurrection is painfully evident. Writing again two weeks later, Brontë returns once more to the topic of the French Revolution, contrasting her scepticism about the end results with her faith in the Germans' 'rational and justifiable efforts for liberty'. Using the language of earthquakes and tremors, which occurs throughout *Jane Eyre* to describe upheavals in the psychological domain, she makes clear that she perceives England to lie under similar threat of social insurrection:

It seems, as you say, as if change drew near England too. She is divided by the sea from the lands where it is making thrones rock, but earthquakes roll lower than the ocean, and we know neither the day nor the hour when the tremor and heat, passing beneath our island, may unsettle and dissolve its foundations.

Like the forces of female violence and insanity in *Jane Eyre*, that 'crime . . . that lived incarnate in this sequestered mansion, and could neither be expelled nor subdued by the owner . . . [but] broke out, now in fire and now in blood, at the deadest hours of night' (p. 264) the forces of political rebellion are figured as latent, secretive, and beyond control. England might be 'sequestered' by the sea, but is nonetheless liable to find her foundations shaken and her mansion rased by fire to the ground. The implicit associative connections in this letter between the psychological and political domains are confirmed in the ensuing praise of Thackeray whose power stems from his calm 'self-control': '*he* borrows nothing from fever, his is never the energy of delirium – his energy is sane energy, deliberate energy, thoughtful energy . . . Thackeray is never borne away by his own ardour – he has it under control.'[6] Thackeray's activities as social unveiler are thus aligned not with the delirium of revolution but with the Germans' 'rational and justifiable efforts for liberty', not with female excess but masculine control. The text of *Jane Eyre* itself, however, is by no means so clear-cut with reference either to social and gender politics, or authorial stance, as these subsequent reflections might imply. The firm distinctions Brontë is proposing here are themselves the subject of interrogation in the novel.

Brontë's observations on the different forms of energy reveal the ideological hegemony established in nineteenth-century discourse by ideas of the controlled circulation of energy: the same model could be applied to the economy, the social body and the psyche, or the production of writing; to working-class riots in England, political revolutions in France, or slave rebellions in the colonies; to the processes of the female body and the eruptions of insanity, or the novels of Thackeray. The dividing line between the forceful, useful channelling of energy, the full utilization of all resources, and the overspill into revolution or insanity was a thin one. The problem was particularly acute because the nineteenth century had witnessed the dissolution of binary divisions between health and sickness, both social and physiological. The new paradigm emerging in physiological and social discourse was one in which the old 'Manichean' divide between health and sickness, good and ill, had been supplanted by a sliding scale of the normal and pathological.[7] The differentiation between activities which would lead to health or disease was now only one of degree; depending on the state of the organism, the same activity could lead to perfect health or dangerous excess. Central to this new discursive regime was the elusive concept of the 'normal': the power to determine and define the normative state hence became crucial.

In the discourses of both political economy and psychiatry one can see the same preoccupation with the normal, the same attempt to define when control modulates into hysteria. Political economy concerned itself with that indefinable line which marked the transition from a healthy, expanding economy producing useful goods, to a sick system characterized by gluts, overstocked markets and financial panic. Psychiatry employed a similar economic model of the psyche, exploring the ways in which healthy attempts to develop all the faculties to the full could quickly shade over into monomania, delirium, insanity; the only demarcating factors would be those of balance, and control. Insanity and ill-health were not absolutes, but rather states of health pushed to extremes. The discourses of political economy, medicine and psychology all converged in their preoccupation with the balanced channelling of energy within the individual body.

Brontë's depiction of Thackeray's 'sane', 'deliberate energy' contrasts the useless waste of energy in the delirious movements of insanity, with the social power and productivity deriving from self-control. In *Jane Eyre* she brings a similar model of interpretation to bear. The incipient parallel which runs throughout the novel between Jane and the 'mad' Bertha turns on the issue of the flow of energy: at what point does productive forcefulness turn into self-destructive anarchy? For a Victorian woman the question was peculiarly fraught since women were biologically defined as creatures of excess, throbbing with reproductive energy which had to be sluiced away each month, and yet could not be dammed up or controlled without real threat to the balance of the psyche. In constructing the parallel histories of Jane and Bertha, Brontë constantly negotiates between these different models of womanhood, trying to find an image of female empowerment and control which would not also be a negation of femininity.

Although the question of energy control is played out primarily on the terrain of the female body, its ramifications in the text concern all social groups who seek to overturn the established lines of demarcation between 'normal' and 'pathological' behaviour; between praiseworthy exertion and self-help, and destabilizing 'revolutionary' activity. The famous passage in *Jane Eyre* where Jane compares the plight of women, condemned to lives of inactivity, to that of workers who are forced by the social paralysis imposed on their faculties into revolutionary action, is not merely an isolated allusion, but rather raises to the level of explicit statement the implied parallels which run through the text.

At a linguistic level, the narrative of *Jane Eyre* enacts the novel's central thematic: order and structure are imposed on disruptive, inchoate material. Jane's claims to have achieved social success, to have moved out of her initial state of social and psychological marginality, are vindicated by her ability to tell a 'credible' tale and thus win from readers a conviction of her probity and sanity. The measure of her success is the degree to which we as readers believe we are listening to the workings of 'sane energy', rather than the ravings of delirium. Syntactically, Jane's prose gives the impression of surges of energy which are yet restrained within legitimate social bounds. As Margot Peters has pointed out, Brontë's style is characterized by a practice of syntactic inversion, which creates a sense of pervasive tension.[8] The novel replicates linguistically Jane's attempts to transgress social boundaries whilst remaining within an accepted social framework; to maintain energy at the highest level of excitation without bursting through into pathology.

Like its predecessor, the history of 'Jane Eyre' describes an arc through a whole series of problematic social boundaries. As a child Jane occupies the difficult terrain between servant and kin: kept at a distance from the family she is also 'less than a servant, for you do nothing for your keep' (p. 9). Her life as an adult repeats this pattern: as a governess, she is again neither servant nor kin. Fulfilling the role of wife or mother for monetary gain, she is aligned with the members of that other 'anathematized race', prostitutes, who similarly substitute an economic relation for a familial one, and who together with that other marginal female figure, the madwoman, haunted the Victorian imagination.[9] With her flight from Thornfield, Jane transgresses the social demarcations of class, occupying simultaneously the positions of lady and beggar; the Rivers' servant, Hannah, immediately places her once more in recognized categories of social liminality, prostitution and criminality: 'You are not what you ought to be' (p. 428).

In traversing the domains of social and psychological marginality,

Jane Eyre explores the intersection of models of the psyche and of social order. Jane's problematic status in the social and economic sphere is replicated in the psychological domain where she is aligned with the two figures from the discourse of Victorian psychiatry who demarcated the sphere of excess: the passionate child and madwoman. Following her eruption of childhood temper she comes to reside, in the household's eyes, within the borderland of insanity, and on the cusp between humanity and animality, thus preparing for her later association with Bertha. In both the social and psychological domains, wasteful, polluting excess is set against productive, healthy regulation. Jane depicts her history as a battle on two fronts: the internal struggle to regulate her own flow of energy, and the external, social fight to wrest control of the power of social definition. Her battle with the Reeds concerns the issue of denomination: where the boundary demarcating the normal and 'natural' should be drawn. As in *The Professor*, the site of struggle rests in the dual sphere of control and penetration: regulating the self and unveiling the other.

From the opening paragraphs of the novel, where a defiant note of self-assertion is quickly introduced, it becomes clear that the narrator of *Jane Eyre* is a figure involved in the processes of self-legitimation. Jane's reference to her sense of being 'humbled by the consciousness of my physical inferiority' to her cousins actually suggests an opposing sense of *mental* superiority. Her account of her alienation from the family circle reveals a curious blend of envy and disdain. Jane is writing as an outsider who longs to be included, but yet whose self-definition and sense of self-worth stems precisely from her position of exclusion and sense of difference. Like the upwardly-mobile middle classes, Jane is fighting a battle for definitional control. Her relatives, the Reeds, have usurped the categories of both society and nature: Jane is to be excluded, Mrs Reed declares, until she learns, paradoxically, to acquire a 'more natural' disposition. At issue is the clash between two models of mind and the 'natural'. Against Mrs Reed's identification of the 'natural' with her own social expectations, Jane, by contrast, identifies herself with an independent realm of physiological energy and innate capacity: a 'natural' endowment which cannot, without violence, be constrained within the gentry's normative rules for social behaviour. Her physiological model of the self thus aligns her with the phrenologists, and the social economists who sought to analyse social dynamics entirely in terms of energy circulation.

Brontë's representation of Jane's adolescence draws on two fundamental strands in nineteenth-century psychology: the phrenological depiction of the mind as the site of warring faculties, conceived not as abstract intellectual powers but as distinct sources of physiological energy; and a separate tradition which focused on the female reproductive system as the source of destabilizing energies. Whereas the phrenologists emphasized the goals of self-control, and the hierarchical ordering and directing of mental energies, medical theories of the uterine economy suggested that female mental energy would always be overwhelmed by the forces of the reproductive system. Although in practice the two strands often overlapped, it is important, for analytic purposes, to maintain a distinction in order to explain why, in *Jane Eyre*, the rhetoric of liberating energy is also allied to the language of self-defeat and disgust. In dramatizing the ebbs and flows of Jane's internal conflicts, Brontë explores in depth the complex forms of female subjectivity engendered by contradictory formulations within Victorian discourse.

Jane's strategy of response to oppression is concealment, a retreat to a physiologically suggestive interiority, 'enshrined' behind the red curtain. In dragging her out of her shrine and exposing her to public view, John Reed enacts a gross physical parody of the more subtle forms of female unveiling in psychiatric discourse. His literal unveiling is matched, however, by Jane's own figurative unveiling in her sudden eruption into passion, thus confirming Victorian fears of the latent fires within the female body. In the class and gender war in which she is engaged Jane is bound to lose. Her attempts to pit her ideational wealth against his material power prove futile. To John Reed she becomes a 'rat', a term which demotes her from humanity to the animality reserved in contemporary rhetoric for the violence of the lower classes. As a dweller in the sewers, she is, furthermore, associated with both class and sexual contamination.[10]

The red room in which Jane is subsequently imprisoned functions, like the third story of Thornfield, as a spatialized configuration of Victorian notions of female interiority.[11] The flow of blood which had marked Jane's entrance, associates her confinement both with the onset of puberty, and the polluting effects of suppression within the female frame. Jane's responses capture the bewildering, contradictory formulations of femininity in Victorian discourse. Catching sight of herself in the mirror, she is not reassured by a comforting specular identification with the physical coherence of her image, but rather precipitated into spirals of increasing terror.[12] That 'visionary hollow' confirms only her own insubstantiality, an endlessly retreating centre of self (p. 12). The fears of spirits and phantoms it engenders set in motion the extended network of imagery which draws Jane and Bertha together within an associative nexus of the 'non-human'.

Jane's own language for herself in childhood repeatedly stresses her lack of a sense of coherence. She is a 'heterogeneous thing', an 'uncongenial alien' distinguished from her cousins by her innate endowment of 'propensities' (pp. 13–14). Her oscillation between defiant self-assertion and a sense of internal fragmentation can be traced not simply to contradictory constructions of femininity but also to contradictions within the dominant Victorian theories of self-control. According to Combe, 'Man is confessedly an assemblage of contradictions', a conflict-ridden association of 'heterogeneous elements'.[13] His fierce advocacy of the doctrines of self-improvement and advancement is based, paradoxically, on a physiological model of the psyche which undercuts earlier theories of a unified psychological principal. Combe's domain of selfhood is not the originating source of emotion, thought or action, but rather the shifting balance or product of internal conflicts: a battleground of warring, autonomous energies, where conflict is inscribed not as an occasional lapse, but as a necessary principle of existence. As a model of mind it takes to an extreme the principles of laissez-faire economics.

Whereas in *The Professor* Brontë had been content to chart the difficulties attending Crimsworth's ascent to an achieved state of repressive self-control, in *Jane Eyre* she explores the contradictions at the heart of theories of unified selfhood. Jane dwells repeatedly on her internal divisions, her lack of a unifying, controlling centre of self. In her conversations with Mrs Reed, 'something spoke out of me over which I had no control' (p. 28). Although constrained grammatically to the use of 'I', Brontë draws attention to the illusory fiction of unified control connoted by that term. The language of Jane's self-representation at this time emphasizes the implied political parallel between the upsurge of psychic energies, and the swell of revolutionary fervour both in England and Europe, and in the slave revolts in the West Indies. Jane's mood is that of a 'revolted slave', her brain is in 'tumult' and 'my heart in insurrection' (pp. 12–13). Taking the contemporary Tory rhetoric of social revolt as the eruption of animal energies, the convulsive thrashings of insanity, Brontë reverses its import to suggest a necessary, though equally unstoppable, outflow of constrained psychological force, whose release is essential for the health of the organism.

Brontë's analysis of the shifts and turns in Jane's emotions traces the material, physiological flow of her energies. The figure 'Jane' exists not as controlling agent but rather as the site of violent, contradictory charges of material energy. Following the 'gathering' and 'launching' of her energies in a verbal assault on Mrs Reed, Jane depicts her sensation of expansion and exultation: 'It seemed as if an invisible bond had burst, and that I had struggled out into unhoped-for liberty' (p. 39). This notion of an emergence into selfhood occurring with an unleashing of physiological powers is reiterated later by St John Rivers in describing the impact of his decision to become a missionary: 'my cramped existence all at once spread out to a plain without bounds . . . the fetters dissolved and dropped from every faculty' (p. 462). In each case, responsibility for social rebellion is displaced onto a material sphere; it is not the individual, but rather the physiological faculties which act to overthrow the fetters of social constraint.

The phrenological theory of innate, unrealized capacity lies behind this dual image of justified revolt and of the psychological exhilaration to be obtained from faculty exertion. Each faculty, Combe argued, 'has a legitimate sphere of action, and, when properly gratified, is a fountain of pleasure'.[14] Moving beyond the instrumentalist basis of Bentham's 'felicific calculus' with its integrated, associationist model of selfhood, Combe offers the alluring notion of buried treasure within the self, multiple sources of gratification, only waiting to be released. Brontë's novel reveals the seductive attractions of this philosophy which simultaneously privileged ideas of a private, interiorized domain of authenticity, and authorized movements of social revolt – the challenging of entrenched systems of social interest and power. Yet Combe's theories were no more divorced from the sphere of economic interest than those of Bentham. Behind the rhetoric of pleasure and social liberation lies the dominant economic principle of Victorian industrial expansionism: full maximization, utilization and free circulation of all resources.

At the end of *The Professor* Brontë had offered a tantalizing portrait of female self-development in the image of Lucia. *Jane Eyre* looks more chillingly at the difficulties faced by a Victorian woman in fulfilling this goal. In Jane's case the rhetoric of liberation conflicts with her internalized fears of the disruptive forces of female energy. Searching for a fit 'emblem' to depict the processes of her mind she turns to the image of fire, which recurs so frequently in mid-Victorian medical representations of the dangerous, destabilizing energies of the uterine economy: 'A ridge of lighted heath, alive, glancing, devouring, would have been a meet emblem of my mind when I accused and menaced Mrs Reed: the same ridge, black and blasted after the flames are dead, would have represented as meetly my subsequent condition' (pp. 40–1). In Brontë's hands, the common rhetorical image of female sexuality is transformed into an analytic tool to suggest the ways in which the internalization of conflicting models of the psyche creates a sensation of self-defeat, of self-consuming energy. Jane is left once more in fear of herself, and of the seemingly unrestrainable force of her own faculties. She dreads offering an apology to Mrs Reed lest she re-excite, 'every turbulent impulse of my nature. I would fain exercise some better faculty than that of fierce speaking; fain find nourishment for some less fiendish feeling than that of sombre indignation' (p. 41). The language of the passage encapsulates Victorian social hopes and fears: doctrines of self-improvement through the 'nourishment' and 'exercise' of the faculties, are set against more deep-rooted fears of social turbulence, and 'fiendish' female behaviour.

Images of turbulence and fire permeate Victorian discussions of working-class life and political organisation.[15] Sir James Kay Shuttleworth's work, *The Moral and Physical Condition of the Working Classes*, warns of the dangers of 'the turbulent riots of the people – of machine breaking – of the secret and sullen organization which has suddenly lit the torch of incendiarism'.[16] Similar rhetoric occurred in psychiatric texts. The physician Georget gave a more sympathetic warning of the consequences of women's social situation; prohibited from outward expression of their sexual feelings, they are forced 'to feign a calmness and indifference when an inward fire devours them and their whole organization is in tumult'.[17] The association between fire and femininity is not solely metaphorical, however. There were also abundant medical accounts of the 'insane cunning' of women which could be seen in 'the perpetration of *secret* murders by wholesale poisoning, or in secret incendiarism'.[18] The working classes and women alike are accused of secrecy, of suddenly erupting after years of quiescence into turbulence and both literal and figural incendiarism.

Jane's primary crime, in her aunt's eyes, is her sudden flaring into violence which suggests a history of secrecy and concealment. On her deathbed, Mrs Reed recurs once more to her bewilderment as to 'how for nine years you could be patient and quiescent under any treatment, and in the tenth break out all fire and violence' (p. 300). At the time of Jane's outbreak the servants had scrutinized her face 'as credulous of my sanity', wondering how a girl of her age could have 'so much cover' (p. 10). Mrs Reed similarly gazed at her 'as if she really did not know whether I were child or fiend' (p. 28). Jane defies her oppressors' theories of physiognomical correspondence, secretly nursing within her, in a hideous parody of motherhood, the hidden germs or 'minute embryos' of insanity and social disruption.[19] As passionate child, Jane Eyre is one of the first literary embodiments of that new object of fear in Victorian social and medical discourse. Together with the hysterical woman, the passionate child was perceived as a being dominated by the processes of the body, outside rational control; both were therefore viewed as disruptive, marginal groups, on the borders of 'real' humanity.[20] This simultaneously lowly, yet threatening, status was further reinforced by writings within political economy and anthropology which linked women and children together with savages and operatives as figures on the bottom rungs of civilization.[21]

In its focus on passion, *Jane Eyre* has been seen as a very unVictorian text; its organising psychological assumptions, as I have suggested however, are drawn directly from the energy dynamics of nineteenth-century economic and psychological discourse. The problems of an industrial culture, of simultaneously maximizing and restraining energy resources, are replicated in the psychological sphere. According to Combe's Malthusian economy of the psyche, 'All the faculties, when in excess, are insatiable, and, from the constitution of the world, never can be satisfied.'[22] In the mind, as in society, the economics of scarcity and competition are in operation. Development must work hand in hand with control: Jane desires to starve her 'fiendish' feelings and to find 'nourishment' for her more socially acceptable faculties. Her mingled exultation in, and fear of, her new-found powers is mirrored in the social realm where pride in the seemingly endless potentiality of the industrial economy, with its liberation of previously unutilized and imprisoned energies, was indissolubly linked with fear of the monster they had created, whose powers might turn out to be unstoppable.

The psychological correlative of this position is complex. Passion could not, in itself, be dismissed as fiendish. Indeed in Combe's work this preoccupation with energy flow gives rise, significantly, to a validation of passion. 'PASSION', he observes, 'is the highest degree of activity of any faculty . . . Hence there can be no such thing as *factitious* passion.'[23] His model of the mind is of a constant, competitive struggle between different forms of passion. Against the rationalist philosophers who had insisted on the illusory nature of strong emotions, Combe proclaims the psychological and material validity of all passionate sensations. His stance also has significant ramifications with regard to childhood. Whereas Locke had argued that passion could only be the outcome of extensive experience, and thus was an attribute solely of adult life, Combe suggests that it could be experienced with equal force by children.[24] The Victorians' fears of the passionate child, and the enthusiasm with which they policed the borders of childhood, establishing it as an explicit social and psychological category, can be linked to this shattering of the developmental continuum.[25] The sacred ideas of hierarchy and linear progression were under threat: children had now been granted the same unruly energies as undisciplined adults.

The narrative structure of *Jane Eyre* mirrors this challenge to developmental hierarchy. Like that other mid-Victorian portrait of a passionate child, *The Mill on the Floss*, it seems to follow the developmental pattern of a *Bildungsroman*, whilst in actuality offering the very reverse of a progressive, linear history.[26] Jane, as child, presents the same psychological formation as Jane in adulthood. The history she offers is that of a series of moments of conflict, a series, moreover, which does not display the characteristics of progression, but rather the endless reiteration of the same. This non-progressive format is demonstrated most clearly in her comments on her response to the loss of Miss Temple. On the day of Miss Temple's marriage, Jane recounts, 'I altered': 'I tired of the routine of eight years in one afternoon' (pp. 99–101). Jane represents her mind as a microcosm of the asylum in which she had been placed; while it had seemed that 'better regulated feelings had become the inmates of my mind' her mind now 'put[s] off all it had borrowed of Miss Temple . . . I was left in my natural element; and beginning to feel the stirring of old emotions' (pp. 99–100). Jane's life is a history of eternal recurrence, offering a challenge to the forces of institutional order; no matter how firmly the 'inmates' might be subject to external direction and regulation, they remain essentially unchanged, ready at any moment to 'break bounds'. The Freudian model of the mind, and the 'scandalous' notion of infant sexuality, find their roots in mid-Victorian economies of the psyche.

The Victorian preoccupation with simultaneously maximizing and restraining energy, which underlies the repetitive cycle of Jane's history, reverberates throughout contemporary discourse: in debates on the 'machinery question', and the problems of labour or in medical and social discussions of the female role.[27] As with the productive working-class body, the reproductive energies of the female body had to be fully utilized, without transgressing the fine line of regulatory social control. The problem was particularly fraught with regard to women since the very energies which fuelled their essential role of reproduction were also deemed to be dangerously at odds with their required domestic role. Brontë explores in *Jane Eyre* two alternate institutional models for the disciplining and controlling of female energy, two forms of 'asylum': Lowood and the third floor of Thornfield.

The system at Thornfield represents the vestiges of a prior era, when the 'animal' insane were kept hidden and mechanically restrained (as Bertha is after each outbreak) and no attempt was made at cure or recuperation. 'Nature' was given free rein, but the inmates were in consequence cast out from the ranks of humanity. Lowood, by contrast, conforms more to the system of moral management (with a leaven of physical violence); individuals are to be 'saved' for society by the careful regulation of their inner impulses. As Brocklehurst declares, 'we are not to conform to nature' (p. 73). Discipline is achieved both by mortification of the flesh, and constant inspection and surveillance. Jane's punishment for being a liar is to stand on a stool and be displayed to the public gaze.

In depicting events at Lowood, Brontë explores the consequences of restraining female energy. Two models are offered, both associated with death. Whereas the other girls die of the contagious disease of typhus, Helen is granted a more dignified death from consumption, which as I noted earlier, was consistently linked in Victorian medical texts with a repression of sexuality. In physiological terms, her internal productive forces, turned inward upon themselves, become self-consuming. Helen achieves her wish to become a 'disembodied soul', burning in purifying fire the forces of sexual desire (p. 298). The other girls, however, are brought to a death which reeks of putrid animality. Whereas Helen is permitted a form of transcendence, the other girls in the asylum are driven inwards into their own materiality which, once restrained, obstructed in its flow, becomes a source of pollution. The two forms of death prefigure that of Bertha who is not allowed to be consumed, like Helen, by purifying fire, but smashes down to her native earth in an apotheosis of her intrinsic animality: 'dead as the stones on which her brains and blood were scattered' (p. 548).

Surviving the fires of self-consumption, and the diseases of obstruction, Jane depicts her escape from Lowood in terms of the upsurge of clamorous, independent energies. Her initial responses to Thornfield are framed outside any personal sense of agency: 'My faculties...seemed all astir. I cannot precisely define what they expected, but it was something pleasant' (p. 118). The 'I' who speaks is differentiated both from the source and experience of emotion. This famous novel of defiant self-assertion persistently undercuts notions of an originating, unified self. Jane's restlessness, which translates into social discontent, is defended on the grounds of physiology: 'Who blames me? Many no doubt; and I shall be called discontented. I could not help it. The restlessness was in my nature; it agitated me to pain sometimes' (p. 132). Seemingly aware of the accusations which might be levelled at her text, Brontë permits her heroine to draw on the discourse of internal, competing energies in order to absolve herself of responsibility for her rebellious thoughts. It was precisely such passages, however, which caused Elizabeth Rigby to attack the novel as a 'proud and perpetual assertion of the rights of man': 'We do not hesitate to say that the tone of the mind and thought which has overthrown authority and violated every code human and divine abroad, and fostered Chartism and rebellion at home, is the same which has also written *Jane Eyre*.'[28]

Rigby's indignant review picks up on the implied parallels between female and working-class revolt which run through the narrative, and are later to be foregrounded in *Shirley*. Jane's famous assertion of female rights makes these parallels quite explicit:

It is in vain to say human beings ought to be satisfied with tranquillity: they must have action; and they will make it if they cannot find it. Millions are condemned to a stiller doom than mine, and millions are in silent revolt against their lot. Nobody knows how many rebellions besides political rebellions ferment in the masses of life which people earth. Women are supposed to be very calm generally: but women feel just as men feel; they need exercise for their faculties, and a field for their efforts as much as their brothers do; they suffer from too rigid a restraint, too absolute a stagnation, precisely as men would suffer; and it is narrow-minded in their more privileged fellow-creatures to say that they ought to confine themselves to making pudding and knitting stockings, to playing on the piano and embroidering bags. (p. 133)

Ostensibly the passage articulates support for the reformist position adopted by Combe, that women, as well as men, should be allowed to exercise their faculties to the full. The demand is not for radical change, but rather that women should be allowed to participate in the given social order in more decisive fashion. But against this reformist reading we must place the explosive energy of the passage, and the explicit linking of the position of women and workers. The vision is that of a silent but seething revolt, merely waiting to erupt.

Writing in the era of Chartism, and at a time when political revolution was about to explode throughout Europe, Brontë was not employing her terms loosely. Her letters of 1847 and 1848 show a recurrent preoccupation with the phenomenon of political rebellion, though her shifting responses reveal a significant ambivalence. In April 1848 she speaks of Chartism as an 'ill-advised movement . . . judiciously repressed': collective political action should be replaced by 'mutual kindliness' and the 'just estimate of individual character'.[29] Two months later, when the focus of her letter is the more personally implicative issue of the plight of governesses, this individualist perspective and emphasis on restraint is ultimately overthrown. After insisting initially that what governesses most require is 'self-control' and 'the art of self-possession' Brontë reverses her position in the postscript:

I conceive that when patience has done its utmost and industry its best, whether in the case of women or operatives, and when both are baffled, and pain and want triumph, the sufferer is free, is entitled, at last to send up to Heaven any piercing cry for relief, if by that cry he can hope to obtain succour.[30]

This same ambivalent shifting between the politics of control, and the inescapability of rebellion, underlies the passage in *Jane Eyre*.

The ideological power of Combe's phrenological social platform and the whole self-help movement lay in its ability to defuse the political challenge of working-class insurgency: in its individualist focus on self-improvement, it directed attention away from class-based action, and facilitated the internalization of social controls. Yet the reformist implications of this position are only operative if emphasis is placed firmly on the processes of regulation and control. Jane's strident utterance, by contrast, seems to focus rather on the impossibility of restraint and the inevitability of rebellion. Combining ruling-class fears of the animal masses, with the reformist platform of self-development, Brontë articulates a political position which extends beyond, and undercuts, the bourgeois ideology of the dominant narrative. Rebellion is figured as an irresistible physiological process which 'ferments' not in the masses (understood as human subjects) but in 'the masses of life which people earth'. Social and political rebellion is conceived as an inevitable upswelling of a homogeneous animal life-force.

Brontë is drawing here jointly on the rhetoric of the medical obsession with the disruptive potentiality of female reproductive energies, and on depictions of working-class animality. Sir James Kay Shuttleworth, for example, traced many of the problems of society to the working-class body. There was, he maintained, 'a licentiousness capable of corrupting the whole body of society, like an insidious disease, which eludes observation, yet is equally fatal in its effects'. Unlike criminal acts, this disease was so insidious and secretive as to escape even the controlling, classificatory powers of statistics: 'Sensuality has no record, and the relaxation of social obligations may coexist with a half dormant, half restless impulse to rebel against all the preservative principles of society; yet these chaotic elements may long smoulder, accompanied only by partial eruptions of turbulence or crime.'[31] Working-class sensuality stands as a figure of political rebellion; like the workings of latent insanity, and the hidden processes of the female body, it smoulders in secret, gathering its forces of disruption beyond the control of social regulation.

In Brontë's text, the associative connections lying behind Jane's vehement defence of female faculty development are made clear in the continuation of the passage where Jane suggests that it is thoughtless of men to laugh at women,

if they seek to do more or learn more than custom has pronounced necessary for their sex.

When thus alone, I not unfrequently heard Grace Poole's laugh: the same peal, the same low, slow ha! ha! which, when first heard, had thrilled me: I heard, too, her eccentric murmurs; stranger than her laugh. (p. 133)

From men's laughter at women, Jane moves to the uncanny laughter of female response, which she initially locates in a member of the servant class. Her own bodily 'thrill' of response directly implicates her within this disruptive domain.[32] Brontë's attitudes to the sexual and social challenge offered by the figure of Bertha/Grace are, however, far more ambivalent than Rigby's review might lead one to believe.

THE 'MAD WIFE'

Recent feminist criticism has tended to adopt a celebratory response towards Brontë's 'mad-wife', suggesting that the representation offers a clear critique of the Victorian repression of the 'innate' forces of female sexuality.[33] To figure woman as a sexualized creature, liable to outbreaks of insanity, is not to move beyond the parameters of Victorian thought, however, but rather to give them explicit inscription. Setting aside the romanticized view which depicts female madness as the natural rebellion of the oppressed, we should consider rather the ways in which Victorian discourse had pre-defined the forms both of rebellion and conformity. Brontë's originality lies less in her focus on the issue of sexuality, than in her resolute juxtaposition of conflicting formulations within Victorian psychological thought, and her tracing through of the implications of these contradictions for the formation of female subjectivity. The measured rhetoric of self-development and control is placed alongside its feared inverse image, the eruption of uncontrollable energies; in the careful structuring of her narrative, Brontë breaks through the binary divide which policed the borders of category ascription, suggesting that the forces of conformity and rebellion are one and the same. Bertha's laughter and 'eccentric murmurs' constitute another narrative within the text, running in counterpoint to Jane's rational discourse. Yet her voice is not that of the semiotic (as defined by Kristeva), the upswell of madness outside the dominant patriarchal sphere of the symbolic.[34] Rather, as incarnation of an alternate male model of the female psyche, a gendered inflection of the doctrine of control, the figure of Bertha functions to call attention to the tenuous, fragile foundations of Jane's imperialist claims to self-dominion.

The issue of imperial control is one which has both psychological and political dimensions. Bertha is not only mad but is also, a Creole; placed on the border between European and non-European blood and culture, she is a literal realization of Jane's self-depiction as an 'heterogeneous thing', 'an uncongenial alien' within that first upper-class household.[35] Bertha functions less as a 'self-consolidating Other' for Jane than as a destabilizing agent, undermining her attempts to construct a fiction of integrated selfhood.[36] The explicit textual parallels drawn between Jane and Bertha have been well documented in feminist criticism: the red room and the attic, the imagery of blood and fire, the references to Jane as 'mad' and a 'fiend' and her famous question to Mrs Fairfax, 'am I a monster?' (p. 334)[37] To Rochester the division is absolute: Jane is 'my good angel' and Bertha is a 'hideous demon' (p. 402). Yet the very scene in which he hopes to offer a visible demonstration of this polarity to an assembled public audience is ambiguous.[38] Rochester asks the 'spectators' of his physical struggle with Bertha to 'Compare these clear eyes with the red balls yonder – this face with that mask – this form with that bulk' (p. 371). His ostensible meaning is clear: defined form is set against the shapelessness of sheer excess; open transparency against the practices of concealment. Yet if we recall the nineteenth-century rhetoric of insanity, and the rise of interest in the physiognomy of the insane, concealment and deception were the very attributes that the insane were assumed to lack. According to Esquirol, the capacity for concealment was a fundamental pre-condition for a state of sanity, and civilized humanity. It is Jane, the child who possessed 'so much cover' and defied her critics' physiognomical powers, who possesses the ability to 'mask' herself. Bertha's insanity is in fact visible proof of her inability to mask her feelings or actions.

Madness, John Reid argued, stemmed from a 'deficiency in the faculty of self-control', an inability to command the thoughts and passions: 'The veil is rent which concealed, the resistance is overcome which controlled them.'[39] Lacking any form of veil herself, Bertha literally rends Jane's bridal veil in a symbolic gesture which focuses narrative attention on the associated network of interconnections between the exposure of female sexuality and insanity. Jane is saved from casting her hymenal veil aside, and only returns to Rochester once she is veiled from his sight. With Bertha, by contrast, we are presented with the 'lurid hieroglyphics' of a sexuality too evidently displayed. Rochester recounts his meeting with his destiny, a hag, as in Macbeth, who writes in 'lurid hieroglyphics all along the house-front' his memento: 'Like it if you can! Like it if you dare!' (p. 175). The challenge is that of the demon who has usurped the domestic space of the household angel; the threatening 'other' who, refusing to recognize the barriers of race or geographical space, has staked her own territorial claim in the heart of English patriarchal and upper-class culture.

In depicting Bertha, Brontë draws on the animal imagery which pervaded contemporary representations of the 'savage', the working classes and the insane. With the rise of theories of moral management, the insane were no longer automatically assimilated to the category of animal; yet this rhetoric was retained, only in a more subtle register, particularly with reference to female forms. Our first sight of Bertha is not, significantly, as the beast grovelling on all fours, but rather as a woman gazing into Jane's mirror. Her 'savage face' with its 'red eyes and the fearful blackened inflation of the lineaments' (p. 358), her black hair, sanguine colouring, and tremendous strength, all conform to contemporary images of the most violent form of maniac.[40] Her laughter, and propensity to destruction, and attacks on her closest relatives also form part of the contemporary repertoire of images.[41]

On our second sighting of Bertha she has crossed the border from human to animal: 'it grovelled, seemingly, on all fours; it snatched and growled like some strange wild animal: but it was covered with clothing; and a quantity of dark, grizzled hair, wild as a mane, hid its head and face' (p. 370). When the 'clothed hyena' stands on its 'hind feet' it becomes, significantly, a masculinized figure which shows 'virile force' in its contest with Rochester. Following this 'spectacle' Bertha seems irrecuperable for femininity or humanity. Yet Rochester's ensuing reveries on what Jane would be like if she were mad, and Jane's mirroring of Bertha's animal posture, 'crawling forwards on my hands and knees' (p. 410) as she pursues her flight from Thornfield, reduced to a social status lower than that of a lost dog, all suggest a more searching, interrogative attitude towards the social demarcations which separate the animal from the human, and the insane from the sane, underscoring once more the parallels between Jane and Bertha.

The reasons given for Bertha's insanity are all drawn, as Showalter has pointed out, from the discourse of Victorian psychiatry.[42] Rochester's accounts combine two forms of explanation which yoke together the idea of inherited taint with the notion of personal responsibility. Bertha inherits her insanity from her mother, 'the Creole', who was 'both a mad woman and a drunkard' but it was her 'excesses' which had 'prematurely developed the germs of insanity' (p. 391). In addition to her specific legacy from her mother, Bertha is also plagued by the generic functions of her female body, the sexual heat associated with menstrual flow. Her attacks occur, significantly, on occasions when there is a blood red moon,[43] in line with medical belief that, in some women, insanity 'bursts forth at each menstrual period'.[44] Court reports in newspapers and medical texts popularized ideas of the 'insane cunning' of women, when under the influence of their reproductive organs. Laycock's graphic accounts of the 'grotesque

forms' this cunning assumed in the 'hysterical female' cover all the
ground detailed by Rochester in his complaints of his wife who 'is
prompted by her familiar to burn people in their beds at night, to stab
them, to bite their flesh from their bones, and so on' (p. 384).[45]
Incendiarism, and the 'ovarian perversions of appetite' which prompted
the desire to eat human flesh (usually of the husband) were a common
theme.[46] The eruption of Bertha Rochester into the text does not
signify the intrusion of an out-moded Gothic form into a realist novel;
she stands, rather, as the crystallization of the negative images of
womanhood available in contemporary social and scientific discourse.[47]

Given Rochester's eagerness to tell Jane all the details of his affairs
with his previous mistresses, he is curiously inexplicit in his account of
Bertha's early crimes. Her first failings, significantly, are those of
household management: she cannot keep servants, and fails to give
the correct angelic responses to his expansive conversation. To this
image of domestic inadequacy, which already inspires Rochester's
'disgust', is added that of the sexually depraved female: Bertha is 'at
once intemperate and unchaste'. The forms of Bertha's unchastity are
unclear; evidently she displayed too avid a sexual appetite towards
Rochester himself, but it is also possible, as no other partners are
specified, that he is here referring also to the 'vice' of masturbation
which was widely treated as a major cause of insanity, in women as
well as men. Laycock, for example, warns that allowing girls to
associate together at school when they are 'influenced by the same
novel feelings towards the opposite sex' will lead them to 'indulge in
practices injurious to both body and soul'. The 'young female' will
return home, 'a hysterical, wayward, capricious girl; imbecile in
mind, habits, and pursuits'.[48] At a more popular level, a best-selling
tract on female complaints describes 'self-pollution' as 'the *fashionable*
vice of young women' which causes the 'moral economy of the mind
[to be] completely overthrown'.[49] Significantly, the writer, like Freud
in his later theories of child seduction, does not situate the originating
cause of masturbation in the upper-class body, but rather traces it to
the seductive practices of 'depraved servant women'.[50] Bertha, as an
upper-class, but exotic, racial 'other' represents a threatening
conjunction between high breeding, and the sexual depravity attributed
to the lower classes and alien races.[51]

It is significant that Jane explicitly demurs from Rochester's
condemnation of Bertha: she remains for her 'an unfortunate lady'
who 'cannot help being mad' (p. 384). Nowhere does she endorse

Rochester's statements of disgust. Her own revulsion is reserved, rather, for the idea of a sexual connection between Rochester and the lower-class Grace:

> I hastened to drive from my mind the hateful notion I had been conceiving respecting Grace Poole: it disgusted me. I compared myself with her, and found we were different. Bessie Leaven had said I was quite a lady; and she spoke truth: I was a lady.(p. 196)

The child who had not been 'heroic enough to purchase liberty at the price of caste' (p. 24) has not changed. Even in her raging madness Bertha remains to her a 'lady': caste overrides the boundaries of race, and of animal/human, insane/sane behaviour. Despite the mobilization of images of the animal grotesque, Jane places herself, Bertha and Blanche on the same side of the class divide, in opposition to the servant Grace.[52]

It is important to the structure of Jane's narrative of self-improvement that her two rivals, Bertha and Blanche, should both belong to the same social strata, and thus represent alternate models of upper-class womanhood. The parallels between Blanche and Bertha are insistent. Blanche is 'dark as a Spaniard' (p. 216), and serves as a model in Rochester's description of the former appearance of his wife (p. 389). More subtly, Rochester, in the proposal scene, draws attention to the surprising intrusion of a West Indian-looking insect, a 'large and gay ... nightrover', and accuses Jane of questing after the moth as he speaks of his marriage to 'my beautiful Blanche' (pp. 313–14). Such parallels function to suggest that what we see in Bertha is merely the full flowering of the flagrant, 'depraved' sexuality which the upper-class male fears exists not only in the females of exotic races but also amongst the ranks of 'respectable' English ladies.

The fate meted out to Bertha, locked away in an attic as soon as she ceased to please her husband sexually, is a precise enactment of Jane's own fears. In defending her sexually elusive conduct during courtship, Jane refers to the 'books written by men' which assign the period of six months as 'the farthest to which a husband's ardour extends' (p. 327).[53] Jane assumes that she will retain Rochester's liking, but not his 'love' – a distinction which, cutting across Victorian literary niceties, clearly aligns the latter term with sexual interest. Brontë's novel offers a devastating dissection of Victorian constructions of male sexual desire, exposing the ideological double bind which underpins cultural dominance (whether of race, sex or class). Marriage for Rochester, the explicit ownership of an ideologically-constituted inferior, necessarily brings with it a sense of self-loathing and pollution: 'a nature the most gross, impure, depraved I ever saw, was associated with mine, and called by law and by society a part of me' (p. 391). Legal dominance is purchased at the cost of self-hatred which carries over into his subsequent sexual activity: 'I tried dissipation – never debauchery: that I hated, and hate. That was my Indian Messalina's attribute: rooted disgust at it and her restrained me much, even in pleasure' (p. 397). The distinction between dissipation and debauchery might seem to twentieth-century eyes a rather subtle one: for Rochester the crucial differentiation rests in the notion of enjoyment. In this brilliant anatomy of Victorian attitudes to male sexuality, Brontë suggests that pleasure could be legitimately experienced only if wedded to a just sense of degradation. The despised debauchery assumes a frank enjoyment of sex, whilst dissipation is always constrained by a feeling of disgust.

Once Rochester has had connection with Bertha, she becomes 'my secret' which he is afraid will be revealed to the world, and Thornfield, with its 'lurid hieroglyphics' becomes 'this accursed place – this tent of Achan – ... this narrow stone hell, with its one real fiend, worse than a legion of such as we imagine' (p. 383). Brontë turns this Biblical tale against the teller to suggest that his 'narrow stone hell' is of his own making: it is Rochester who has, like Achan, stolen the 'accursed thing' and thus he who is the 'real fiend' who will cause his own house and innocent wife to be destroyed by fire.[54] In defining Bertha as 'accursed' he has prepared for his own (partial) immolation.

Brontë's text offers a fierce critique of the perverted, self-destructive forces of Rochester's sexual tyranny, but also implicates Jane in the act of collusion. In another telling Biblical reference, Rochester locates Jane as Esther, in relation to his own role as King Ahasuerus, an association which then aligns Bertha, the scorned wife, with the defiant figure of Vashti (p. 329). The story could operate as a parable of *Jane Eyre*: Vashti's open rebellion is countered by Esther's strategic pliancy, as she undergoes extensive purification rituals in order to gain control of the king. Esther, in her single-minded defence of her people, has long been a heroine in Jewish and Christian religion, just as Jane, in her quest for self-fulfilment has become the heroine of recent feminist criticism. Jane, like Esther, quietly achieves her aims (with slightly less bloody results), but only at the expense of her rival who represents an alternate model of female power. Bertha, that complex symbol of abused innocence, female rebellion and sexual depravity, must be sacrificed in order for Jane to achieve her ambitions. Brontë, however, does not offer an unambiguous endorsement of Jane's progress. Her fears at the costs exacted, subtly registered through this text, are flamboyantly displayed in *Villette* where Bertha is revived as Vashti, a figure whose 'unholy power' acts even more forcibly than that of her predecessor to destabilize the realist narrative of self-improvement.

COURTSHIP RITUALS

The courtship of Jane and Rochester, over which Bertha presides, is framed in very different terms to that of Rochester's account of his relations with Bertha. The dominant discourse here is not that of sexuality and the body, but rather that of phrenology and the economic and psychological principles of Victorian individualism. Sexuality is displaced into erotic power play. While Jane might not openly defy Rochester, she is not meekly submissive. Both figures treat their association as a fierce battle for the preservation of autonomy. As Rochester says to Jane, shortly after his proposal, 'Encroach, presume, and the game is up' (p. 330). The rules of their 'game' are defined, as in all Brontë's novels, by an attempt to read the inner territory of the other while preserving the self unread. On their first evening together Rochester reads Jane's character from her sketches, and on the second she is invited to read his skull. Her unquestioning assertion that Rochester is not handsome confirms that we are in the domain of phrenology, not physiognomy. Neither Rochester nor Jane, who constantly stresses her own lack of physical beauty, conform to the rules of physiognomy which suggest, as Spurzheim observes, that 'an unsightly person ought to be the concomitant of an unenviable soul'.[55] The external signs of the head and countenance do not directly express inner qualities, but rather offer a language that has to be decoded. Rochester offers his skull for Jane's perusal:

'Criticize me: does my forehead not please you?'
    He lifted up the sable waves of hair which lay horizontally over his brow, and showed a solid enough mass of intellectual organs; but an abrupt deficiency where the suave sign of benevolence should have risen.
    'Now, ma'am, am I a fool?'
    'Far from it, sir. You would perhaps think me rude if I inquired in return whether you are a philanthropist?' (p. 161)

In this phrenological exchange the barriers of class and status are overthrown; all that matters is innate endowment and interpretative proficiency. As an equally skilled reader, Jane is momentarily placed on equal terms with Rochester.

Surveillance and interpretative penetration form the groundworks of Jane and Rochester's erotic struggles. He attempts constantly to baffle her powers of deciphering external signs: he withholds information, offers misleading explanations, and even engages in masquerade, as in his courtship of Blanche, and his impersonation of a gypsy. Jane is never allowed to rest secure in her own interpretative powers. Following Rochester's stories concerning Grace Poole, she is 'amazed – confounded' by the discrepancies between her attributed character of would-be murderer and that suggested by her features and 'hard-forehead' (p. 192). Bodies cease to be legible. Rochester's explanations, indeed, trespass on the tremulous borders of Jane's own sanity. He denies, initially, the physical existence of the woman who tore her veil, thrusting on Jane, rather, the label of hysteric with his suggestion that it was 'the creature of an overstimulated brain' (p. 360). Not content with defining one wife as 'maniac', he places his future bride in that other category of female weakness: the nervous, hysterical woman. Their attempted marriage, in which he attempts to impose a false name and role on Jane, represents the culmination of his bid for control of interpretative and definitional power.

Like Jane, Rochester aims to read the other, while keeping the self firmly veiled. Although critics have celebrated the novel's depiction of a romantic union of souls, close reading suggests that even their moments of greatest apparent union are in fact based on power struggles centered on the withholding of self.[56] In the gypsy scene, which directly parallels Jane's earlier phrenological reading of Rochester, he offers to analyse her destiny from her face and forehead. Disguised as a woman, Rochester enjoys free access to Jane's unprotected interiority. There follows an extraordinary passage, in which the gypsy's ventriloquizing of the 'speech' of Jane's forehead is set in dialogue with her inner self. The divisions of self and other seem to break down, and inner and outer to meld into one. In that external voice Jane believes she hears the 'speech of my own tongue' (p. 253), but as soon as Rochester unveils himself the preceding events take on a different complexion. By exposing herself, unguarded, to his gaze, Jane has betrayed herself, temporarily, into his power, allowed him both to penetrate and control the articulation of her psyche.

Yet the struggle is not all one-sided: the retaining and withholding of self also constitutes part of Jane's 'system' for handling Rochester. Her depiction of this 'system' (as she designates it), represents a decisive innovation in the genre of the novel. Whereas Pamela and Clarissa mobilized their resources of defence to protect their 'hidden treasure' of virginity against a very real physical threat, Jane's system of withholding operates within the domain of knowledge. A physical threat to virginity is no longer even the ostensible issue. The erotic charge created in readers of the eighteenth-century novel, hovering always on the brink of violation, is here openly defined and analysed, and explicitly appropriated by the protagonist as a mode of regulating social and sexual interaction. Jane delights in 'vexing and soothing' Rochester 'by turns'; though 'beyond the verge of provocation I never ventured; on the extreme brink I liked well to try my skill' (p. 197). Such tactical play now figures not only as a goal in itself (to be continued, Jane asserts, even into marriage) but also as a source of pleasure.

Jane Eyre offers an anatomy of the 'perpetual spirals of power and pleasure' which were incited by the nineteenth-century regulation of sexuality.[57] Erotic excitement is produced by evading interpretative penetration, while a sense of selfhood is actively created by the demand for disclosure. Under this regime romantic union is impossible. Rochester's demonstrations of tenderness constitute a threat, rather than desired end: 'Soft scene, daring demonstration, I would not have: and I stood in peril of both: a weapon of defence must be prepared' (p. 343). Jane's 'weapon' is that of language: throughout their courtship she aims constantly to gain control by contradicting his expectations, and challenging his interpretative skills. Only by maintaining herself unread can she maintain the balance of power. Her system is therefore to 'thwart' and 'afflict' him since she realizes that this keeps him 'excellently entertained' (p. 345).

What we are offered in these descriptions is not an invariant, ahistoric model of sexual dynamics, but rather an analysis of the specific forms of erotic enjoyment engendered by nineteenth-century models of economic, psychological and sexual regulation.[58] Although erotic surveillance is clearly to be found in Restoration comedy, for example, it is not tied in with the same economic theory of regulated selfhood. With its dual emphasis on external surveillance and the internal channelling and restraining of competing energies, phrenology may be taken, as I suggested earlier, as the paradigmatic model of the psyche during the rise of the industrial economy. The courtship of

Jane and Rochester, which revolves around the activities of surveillance, and the maintenance of the energies of both self and other in a state of productive, dynamic tension, inscribes these economic principles in the domain of romance. As in the economy, energies were to be both fully maximized, and firmly restrained. Jane's most intense experience of erotic excitement arises not from sexual contact but from involvement in a triadic structure of surveillance. Carefully positioning herself so that she can watch Blanche without being observed, she notes that her scrutiny is being duplicated by 'other eyes besides mine . . . the future bridegroom, Mr. Rochester himself, exercised over his intended a ceaseless surveillance' (p. 232). In feeling united to Rochester by their shared readerly skills, and mutual conviction of Blanche's gross textual incompetence, Jane feels herself to be 'at once under ceaseless excitation and ruthless restraint' (p. 233). Stimulated, but controlled, Jane enacts in her love life the ideologically-prescribed role of the industrial worker. Energy is to be maintained at its highest level without 'breaking bounds'.

To romantic souls, *Jane Eyre* must seem to to offer a very perverted model of interaction. Jane revels in the pleasures of dominance even in the agonised moments after her aborted marriage. Looking at Rochester's incipient frenzy, she realizes that 'the passing second of time – was all I had in which to control and restrain him . . . I felt an inward power; a sense of influence, which supported me. The crisis was perilous; but not without its charm' (p. 386). Brontë cuts through the niceties of romance tradition, daring to give her heroine (and not, as in earlier fiction, just her readers) a sense of enjoyment at the conventional moment of supposed greatest suffering. Control and regulation have moved from being mere agents in the service of wider social concerns to being ends in themselves, and ones which are, on the psychological level, decidedly pleasurable.

THE PLEASURES OF CONTROL

In order to understand the centrality of ideas of regulation and control in *Jane Eyre* it is necessary to place the novel within a wider frame of cultural reference. Throughout nineteenth-century psychological theory one can see the emergence of a new emphasis on the centrality of opposition as the defining category of selfhood: in Esquirol's insistence that selfhood only emerges with the ability to conceal, and in the phrenologists' grounding of self in the experience of conflict, both internal, between the faculties themselves, and external, between the self and the world, a theory which, in turn, bears a strong relation to aspects of German Romantic psychology.[59] Nowhere are these principles of opposition given more prominence than in a series of articles by James Ferrier entitled 'An Introduction to the Philosophy of Consciousness', published in Brontë's favourite periodical, *Blackwood's*, 1838–9. While Brontë would probably have read these articles, I am less concerned with questions of influence, than with Ferrier's role in articulating and isolating one of the emerging principles of nineteenth-century psychological thought which frames Brontë's writing. In Ferrier's work, the German Romantic ideal of striving and becoming is assimilated to the antagonistic, individualistic principles of Victorian economic culture. The self, he insists, only comes into being by an act of opposition or negation.[60] Consciousness is not the 'harmonious accompaniment' but rather 'the antagonist and the violator of sensation'.[61] The violent, implicitly sexual, imagery, which parallels that of Brontë, is indicative: his work is suffused with a sense of perpetual embattlement. In a passage of importance for *Jane Eyre*, Ferrier maintains that one cannot 'lay hold of the good' by remaining unconscious of evil,

for the passions are real madmen, and consciousness is their only keeper; but man's born amiabilities are but painted masks, which, (if consciousness has never occupied its post) are liable to be torn away from the face of his natural corruption, in any dark hour in which the passions may choose to break up from the dungeons of the heart.[62]

Like Esquirol, Ferrier situates selfhood and sanity in the act of masking. He emphasizes the absolute primacy of control; surrender to any passion, whether judged morally 'good' or 'bad' leads to the total erasure of selfhood.[63] In the light of this philosophy, Jane's fears of Rochester's tenderness become clear: to surrender to passion is to surrender the very basis of selfhood. The 'real madwoman' of Thornfield breaks out on each occasion when Jane allows herself to be almost submerged within Rochester. On the night when she follows him 'in thought through the new regions he disclosed', and slips free from her usual 'painful restraint' his bed is set on fire (p. 180). Her sense of union with Rochester in his gypsy guise is similarly followed by the attack on Mason, and the final eruption occurs before the wedding when Jane has been absorbed, imaginatively, in Rochester's world, thinking 'of the life that lay before me – *your* life, sir' (p. 354).

Her nightmares culminate in the tearing of the bridal veil. Jane's amiability is a 'cover' or 'mask' which is liable to be torn away each time she surrenders to passion and loses sense of herself as individualized being, a being defined by the active process of opposition.

The significance of Ferrier's text lies in its separation of the doctrine of self-control from any vestiges of a moral framework. The only category of evil he seems to acknowledge is that of passivity of response, an inertness of control; thus to bask in the warmth of another's love is to become little better than an 'automaton'.[64] Opposition has become an end in itself, to be activated whatever the content or the character of the desires or individual being opposed might be. Jane flees Rochester not because of moral scruples, but so that she can retain her own oppositional sense of self. With Rochester she had felt called to an Edenic 'paradise of union' (p. 321). She had wished to deny separation, the founding condition of selfhood, and to return once more to the harmonious, passive, pre-conscious state of paradisiacal existence which for Ferrier (anticipating contemporary psychoanalysis) defined our original state of union before the emergence of the 'rebellious I' which marked our Fall.[65] Jane has been guilty of trying to create a false Eden; in ceasing to oppose the promptings of her passions she is in danger of becoming, 'an automaton'. She is saved from such a lapse by her pursuit of individualism on the economic front: her letter to her uncle functions as the primary agency in averting the impending wedding.

Her response to this situation is clearly in line with Ferrier's theories of self-suppression; she becomes her own violator: 'you shall, yourself, pluck out your right eye; yourself cut off your right hand: your heart shall be the victim; and you, the priest, to transfix it' (p. 379). Such self-mutilation constitutes for Ferrier the ultimate act of liberty, the only possible way of attaining inviolate selfhood. Its foundation in an ever-vigilant state of opposition and warfare, whether towards inner emotion or external forces, suggests, however, the very essence of slavery. In shifting the definition of freedom from a social and political register to that of a qualitative measure of psychological experience, he, like the phrenologists, has inscribed the social battleground within the self.

Brontë explores the impact of these oppositional principles of selfhood on the genre of romance. If the self is only an unstable point, which exists only to the degree that a sense of conscious opposition between both self and other, and emotional prompting and repressive control, can be instituted, then the romantic ideal of harmonious union between two integral units is firmly undercut. Yet Jane Eyre should not therefore be considered as a heroine of feminist self-fulfilment, overthrowing the tyrannous demands of a patriarchal society for female submission. In subscribing to the oppositional principles of selfhood, seeking power through concealment and self-control, she is adhering to the competitive, individualist principles which underpinned Victorian social and economic theory.

Jane Eyre is a heroine of individualism who exposes the contradictions of individualist ideology. She attempts to found a sense of personal agency and power on a concept of selfhood which, lacking all unity, is merely the shifting relation of internal conflicts. At the very time when individualist theories of social and economic interaction held ideological sway, and contemporary rhetoric was filled with references to individual rights, psychological theories of individuality, applying the competitive principles of the market place to the psychological economy, started to stress internal divisions, and the lack of a unified centre of self. This principle holds true across the wide spectrum of psychological theories, whether in the aggressively individualistic premises of phrenology, which nonetheless rested on a theory of internal contradiction, in the fierce assertiveness of Ferrier's theories which reduced selfhood to a state of negativity, an ever-shifting point of opposition, or in the more popular interest in the unconscious processes of the mind which developed, in the hands of physiological psychology, into an energy-dynamics of the psyche which grounded selfhood in the conflicting flows of physiological force. Selfhood thus becomes, not an invincible bastion of sovereignty, the unshakeable bedrock of the imperialist project, but rather the interiorized site of social conflict.

Jane's narrative plots a series of defiant assertions of a self which threatens, imminently, to fragment and rupture. After her flight from Thornfield, and her experience of being reduced to the level of animal existence on the moors, her re-entry into selfhood is marked not by her articulation of the self, but rather by her experience of the power to withhold. After refusing to offer an account of herself to the Rivers family she remarks, 'I began once more to know myself' (p. 431). The self is only conjured into existence by an act of refusal.

With St John Rivers, Jane enters into a new cycle of her battles for self-definition. As before, the struggles are played out on the field of knowledge, both parties withholding the self while trying to read the other. St John's initial diagnosis of her physical condition is followed by a reading of her character: 'I trace lines of force in her face which make me sceptical of her tractability' (p. 433). Their relationship is founded on the power of the gaze; each treats the other as a text to be decoded. St John seemed 'to read my face, as if its features and lines were characters on a page' (p. 452). Jane refers repeatedly to the qualities of his gaze; to his piercing eyes, and 'coruscating radiance of glance' (p. 452); she finds herself falling 'under the influence of the ever-watchful blue eye' (p. 507). Like Lucy before Dr John, Jane feels reduced to the status of an object, examined and controlled by the scientific gaze. St John waits, 'looking like a physician watching with the eye of science an expected and fully-understood crisis in a patient's malady' (p. 511). Jane becomes the figure of a disease whose external symptoms are monitored, anticipated and controlled by medical expertise.

St John acquires dominion through his own indecipherability. Extending the medical analogy, Jane observes that he uses his eyes, 'rather as instruments to search other people's thoughts, than as agents to reveal his own' (p. 441). Nonetheless, St John is not impervious to interpretation. To Jane's eyes the physiognomical harmony of his Greek features is suggestive not of perfection, but rather of elements 'restless, or hard, or eager' (p. 440). Both characters use the vocabulary of phrenology to diagnose in the other 'insatiate' faculties which need to be 'pruned', 'trained' and 'eradicated'. The force of St John's sermon, 'compressed, condensed, controlled', seems to Jane to spring from 'a depth where lay turbid dregs of disappointment – where moved troubling impulses of insatiate yearnings and disquieting aspirations' (p. 449). The language recalls her own emotional outbreak as a child when angry thoughts 'were turned up in my disturbed mind like a dark deposit in a turbid well' (p. 12). In addition, it associates both figures with the upswell of working-class discontent, the social 'turbulence' of contemporary rhetoric, where the 'dregs' of society seek to further their destructive ambitions (the officers in the nearby town, we learn, are there to control the riots). The minds of both Jane and St John are represented as microcosms of the social whole: an assemblage of conflicting elements, where the higher faculties seek to impose control on the turbulent lower orders.

St John, with his resolute, mechanized timing of a permitted period of submission to the 'nectarous flood' of sensual desire, stands as paradigm of a ruthless, repressive organization of energies, whether in the social or psychological system. In the debates between Jane and St John, the potential subjects of his imperialist mission in India are almost entirely omitted: the social is shifted, metonymically, into the psychological. Discussion focuses on the interaction of the faculties, conceived as an independent sphere of competing energies, distanced both from the control of the speaking subject, and the people who are to be subject to this dominion. Jane colludes with St John in this writing out of the native subjects, shifting the politics of imperialism into an issue of internal psychology and geographical space. She agrees that St John's faculties are 'paralysed' (p. 454) and 'stagnate' in England, and that the 'Himalayan ridge, or Caffre bush' would enable him to develop them to advantage (p. 502). But she refuses, however, to accompany him on the grounds that, 'I want to enjoy my own faculties as well as to cultivate those of other people' (p. 498). Such a 'selfish' demand for enjoyment and pleasure is deemed impermissible by St John who fiercely rebuts Jane's claims to be able to impose harmonious control on her energies: the inner scene of the psyche, and the outer terrain of social action, must always be characterized by conflict and a relentless struggle to control.

Whilst Rochester literally imprisoned his Creole wife, St John fixes Jane with his 'freezing spell', exerting on her the imperial authority he hopes to unleash overseas. Like members of other oppressed groups, Jane nurses sentiments which belie her apparent quiescence: 'I did not love my servitude' (p. 508). The cycle of their mutual struggles for dominance is disrupted by St John's proposal of marriage which shifts the question of control onto an explicit material ground, forcing Jane to confront, finally, the question of the relationship between sexuality and selfhood. The problem of marriage to St John would not lie, as critics sometimes assume, in its asexuality, but rather in his physical obedience to the letter but not the spirit of the marriage contract. In terms remarkably explicit for the Victorian age, Jane wonders whether she could endure for St John to 'scrupulously observe . . . all the forms of love' whilst knowing that his 'spirit was quite absent'. Unlike the later Dorothea Brooke, she decides that 'such a martyrdom would be monstrous' (p. 517).[66] She fears that, as St John's wife, she would be 'forced to keep the fire of my nature continually low, to compel it to burn inwardly and never utter a cry, though the imprisoned flame consumed vital after vital – *this* would be unendurable' (pp. 520–1). Jane's image of the agony of self-consuming energy recalls her early responses when she first discovered her love for Rochester: 'it is madness in all women to let a secret love kindle within them, which, if unreturned and unknown, must devour the life that feeds it' (p. 201).[67] Jane believes that, if forced to marry St John, she could 'imagine the possibility of conceiving an inevitable, strange, torturing kind of love for him' while he would find her exhibition of desire, 'a superfluity, unrequired by him, unbecoming in me' (p. 531). A cultural system which defines women as aggressively sexual beings, but maintains that *both* repression and expression of sexuality will lead to madness, establishes the perfect model for self-mutilation. As the image of 'torturing love' suggests, women are rendered doubly abject, their own persecutors and destroyers.

By forcing Jane to overcome her dualistic model of selfhood and actively confront the question of the relationship between sexuality and self-definition, St John offers her a model of empowerment. Much has been made of the 'Gothic' voice which rescues Jane from self-destructive commitment, but of equal importance here is the way in which Brontë self-confidently intercuts different genres: the supernatural and the theological are directly tied to overtly materialist depictions of energy flow. The supernatural is invoked only to be negated: the voice was, Jane firmly decides, no miracle but 'the work of nature' (p. 536). In one of her most daring Biblical rewritings, Brontë recasts St John the Divine's cry, 'Even so, come Lord Jesus', (which is also to conclude her novel) into overtly secular and sexual terms: 'I am coming! . . . Oh, I will come!' (p. 536). The onrush of sexual energy rouses Jane's senses from their 'torpor' and brings about a total reversal of the power dynamics in her relations with St John. Whereas before she had been tempted to 'rush down the torrent of his will into the gulf of his existence, and there lose my own', she feels it was now '*my* turn to assume ascendancy. *My* powers were in play, and in force' (pp. 534, 536). We have moved swiftly from the Gothic to the social drama of aggressive, competing energies.

Jane's final ascendancy is set against the destruction of 'Bertha', that feared embodiment of female bodily excess, and the mutilation of Rochester whose physical injuries embody the acts of self-violation Jane had previously wished to impose on herself when her 'tyrant' conscience had decreed 'you shall, yourself, pluck out your right eye; yourself cut off your right hand' (p. 379). The depiction of Rochester as 'some wronged and fettered wild-beast or bird, dangerous to approach in his sullen woe' (p. 552) clearly recalls, however, descriptions of the imprisoned Bertha, and of Jane's earlier desires to cast off the fetters from her faculties, setting an ominous note for this final stage in their mutual struggles.

On returning to Rochester, Jane enters directly into a replay of the power games which had marked their earlier relations, only this time it is she who is in command, withholding herself and information, and deliberately allowing him to misconstrue her relations with St John. Her assumption of social dominance is figured in her assertion that 'I was then his vision, as I am still his right hand' (pp. 576–7). She becomes, in terms which confirm Brontë's explicit secular rewriting of the conclusion of Revelations, literally, Rochester's 'alpha and omega' (p. 572).[68] Not only is Jane hidden, through Rochester's blindness, from the controlling power of his gaze; she holds interpretative authority over his entire world: 'He saw nature – he saw books through me; and never did I weary of gazing for his behalf, and of putting into words the effect of field, tree, town, river, cloud, sunbeam' (p. 577). The description recalls Rochester's statement of how he would behave to Jane if she were mad. As her sole 'watcher and nurse' he would 'never weary of gazing into your eyes, though they had no longer a ray of recognition for me' (p. 384). Jane inverts this image of male delight in female powerlessness; where Rochester had committed himself to an inward-looking gaze, striving to find himself in the non-reflecting eyes of female madness, Jane takes more active command, seeking not to find herself directly, but rather through the exercise of interpretative control.[69] Jane begins her autobiographical narrative with her struggle against the Reeds for the power of social definition, and concludes with her attainment of this power. Throughout she has been forced to listen to others' narratives of herself: that of Mrs Reed's which 'obliterates hope' from her future existence, Mr Brocklehurst's account of her to Lowood, Rochester's gypsy reading, and St John's story of one, 'Jane Eyre'. In each case the accounts represent an overt bid for control, offering a narrative which takes over the role of self-definition. The conclusion reverses this situation: Jane literally articulates Rochester's world.

Despite the foregrounding of romance, *Jane Eyre* does not end, as one might expect, with a celebration of Jane's romantic or maternal role. Final place is actually given to St John Rivers, raving in perpetual restlessness, transplanting the bourgeois ideology of self-improvement into an imperial exercise in control: 'full of energy, and zeal, and truth, he labours for his race: he clears their painful way to improvement; he hews down like a giant the prejudices of creed and caste that encumber it' (p. 578). Just as the eruptions of Bertha had earlier disrupted the surface meaning of Jane's text, so this final vision of St John, internally torn and violently hewing down external opposition, undercuts Jane's claims to have achieved harmonious union.

Jane's history, like that of Crimsworth, seems to endorse popular ideologies of self-improvement: by acquiring self-control she is able to move into a position of social power. Her will to control has not been allayed, however, but rather projected outwards more forcibly onto her relations with Rochester. While Jane's calm assertions of domestic serenity endorse the overt moral message of Combe's philosophy, the underlying implications of his world view are more accurately conveyed in the final picture of St John's savage discontent. If, following the conflictual theories of selfhood which emerged in the nineteenth century, the self is not a unified entity, but rather a site of internal struggle between competing energies; and self-consciousness arises only through the experience of oppositional control, then a sense of unified harmony can never be attained. Competition and opposition, as in the economy, are the defining elements of selfhood. Total fulfilment could come, indeed, only with total vanquishment. The novel ends fittingly, therefore, with St John, like his name-sake, calling on God for death. If, in the figure of Rochester, chained and fettered, we have an image of sullen energy, poised to re-enact Jane and Bertha's rebellion against constraint, in Brontë's final return to the words of St John the Divine, we have the startling suggestion that the sexual awakening to which Jane 'comes' is a form of living death.

The brooding, dank atmosphere of Ferndean, with air so 'insalubrious' that Rochester had declined to place Bertha there, forms a setting which ill accords with Jane's attempts to claim happiness for all. Just as the violence of Crimsworth's murder of his son's dog in *The Professor* revealed Brontë's clear awareness of the costs exacted by a culture of control, so the final foregrounding of the figure of St John signals a similar unease. Where Crimsworth sends Victor away to Eton, to subdue his 'electrical ardour', Rochester's ward, Adele, in parallel with the young Jane, is sent away from the family home until she too learns to acquire a more 'natural' disposition. Jane's celebration of the fact that Adele learns to become 'docile, good-tempered and well-principled' places her unnervingly close to the position of the detested Mrs Reed, whose social status she has now assumed. Such statements of happy conformity sit awkwardly in a text whose power and motivating force lies in its clamour against injustice, its desire to 'break bounds' whether of social prescriptions for femininity or the generic conventions of the realist text. The spirit of Bertha is not quite so easily subdued.

The difficulties of interpreting *Jane Eyre* lie in its internal contradictions, which in turn mirror those of the social, psychological and economic discourse of the age. The text yearns towards the powerful ideal of romantic union, whilst simultaneously exposing it as a further expression of the competitive dynamics which govern the marketplace. It seems to take us inward into the most private recesses of selfhood, but then shatters illusions of individual autonomy by showing how even these most private realms are constructed socially, in a silent drama of conflict and withdrawal. It espouses ideologies of self-development and improvement, and economic ideas of energy flow, only to reveal their intrinsic opposition; the self is figured both as a striving, integrated unit, and as the divided, unstable product of conflicting energies. The ideals of self-control are set, furthermore, against alternate models of female subordination to the forces of the body, and their social and psychological implications are explored and interrogated. Jane's defiant assertions of selfhood in the text are cut across by fears of imminent dissolution, and the upsurge of energies which cannot be controlled.

In many ways *Jane Eyre* can be read as a quintessential expression of Victorian individualism. Whilst George Eliot's heroines ask where social duty can lie, Charlotte Brontë's ask only how individual desires and ambitions can be achieved. In the mouth of an industrialist, such sentiments would express the spirit of the age. Coming from a socially-marginal female their import is radical, if not revolutionary. The spirit of defiance can find no social locus, however; the red room and the attic cannot be socially contained. Brontë's novels move reluctantly, defiantly, towards a conventional ending in marriage whose harmony and stasis suggest, to an individual defined by conflict, a form of self-annihilation.

CHAPTER 9

Shirley: *bodies and markets*

The gentlemen turn them into ridicule: they don't want them;
they hold them very cheap: they say – I have heard them say
it with sneering laughs many a time – the matrimonial market
is overstocked.[1]

In *Shirley*, Brontë's most overtly political work, the circulating
economies of psychological and social life are directly interwoven.
Shirley is a novel about overstocked markets, surplus commodities and
blocked circulation. Brontë brings to the fore in this work the parallels
between women and workers which had remained largely implicit in
Jane Eyre. Critics have always been puzzled by the structure of this
work and have generally tried to down-play the industrial side.[2]
Catherine Gallagher, for example, chose not to include *Shirley* in her
excellent *Industrial Reformation of English Fiction* on the grounds that
'industrial conflict in *Shirley* is little more than a historical setting and
does not exert any strong pressure on the form'.[3] In contrast to
Gallagher, I will argue that the analogy between the situation of the
'surplus' middle-class woman and that of the unemployed worker is
central to the structural organization of the novel.

In one of her first references to her new work of fiction, Charlotte
Brontë suggests that it will touch, however tentatively, on the
'"condition of women" question . . . It is quite true enough that the
present market for female labour is quite overstocked, but where or
how could another be opened? . . . When a woman has a little family
to rear and educate and a household to conduct, her hands are full,
her vocation is evident; when her destiny isolates her, I suppose she
must do what she can, complain as little, bear as much, work as well as
possible.' From this contemplation of the situation of the 'redundant'
old maid, Brontë moves directly into the impassioned statement
quoted earlier 'that when patience has done its utmost and industry

its best, whether in the case of women or operatives' then 'the sufferer
is free, is entitled, at last to send up to Heaven any piercing cry for
relief, if by that cry he can hope to obtain succour'.[4] The sequence of
thought is clear. The parallel proposed between the situation of the
unmarried middle-class women and that of the 'operative' is not
founded on a vague or generalized sense of shared oppression, but
rather on their homologous structural position in relation to the social
economy. Both the labour and marriage markets are overstocked.
Middle-class women and mill workers are alike made redundant,
transformed from valued producers into worthless commodities by
the operation of economic factors over which they have no control.
For the 'old maid' (a figure who is, by definition, middle class) such
negative placement is doubly determined. She is placed outside the
cycles of both production and reproduction, denied entry into the
former, and made redundant in the latter.

Shirley represents a working through of this structural homology.
The critical bewilderment created by the novel is perhaps due to the
fact that Brontë has not followed the generic pattern of the emerging
industrial novel in creating social interaction between her two classes,
however forced or implausible. The love plot in this work does not
straddle the class divide, nor is the class conflict transmuted into
gender terms so that a concluding marriage and reconciliation of the
sexes can be presented as a healing of class antagonism.[5] The two
classes are kept largely distinct in *Shirley*, meeting primarily through
violence. Brontë has also eschewed the sentimental reductionism
which would suggest that the interests of middle-class women and
workers are identical. The structure of *Shirley* is stark and uncompromising; the impetus of plot is not allowed to obscure the operations of
class division and conflict. Caroline and Shirley can never cross class
lines in either thought or deed. Analogy rather than plot forms the
unifying principle of the text. Without annulling difference, it offers a
determined exploration of the ways in which the lives of middle-class
women, like those of the lower classes, are governed by the harshness
of the market economy. Caroline's observations, cited above, on the
closure of labour markets to women and the overstocked matrimonial
market form the centre around which the rest of the text revolves.
'Old maids', she notes bitterly, 'like the houseless and unemployed
poor, should not ask for a place and an occupation in the world: the
demand disturbs the happy and rich: it disturbs parents' (p. 441).
Brontë's text focuses on the multiple ways in which the demands of old

maids and the unemployed are suppressed, both socially and economically.

Although Brontë was writing in the 'hungry forties' when economic distress amongst weavers in the Haworth area had reached unprecedented proportions, and newspapers and periodicals were full of speculations as to whether the revolutions on the continent were going to sweep through Britain, she chose to set her study of unemployment in 1811–12, at the time of the Luddite riots. The reasons for this choice have been much debated. The historical setting allowed her to draw on material known to her from childhood, both from her father's recollections and local memory in the area of Roe Head, her school, where the attack on Cartwright's mill took place. It also offered all the advantages of historical distance. Moreover, the issues raised by Luddism were far clearer for Brontë's purposes than those present in the agitation of the 1840s. Chartism had raised the spectre of workers' social and political rights and transformed the context of the economic debate. The grounds of conflict in the Luddite era were sharper and more economically focused. No attempts were being made to redraw the political map. Rioters were merely claiming the right to a place, as before, in the labour market. The political context of the Orders in Council acted to intensify the economic factors at work, taking pressure, for Brontë, off the question of class conflict. The problem of economic circulation is central to her text. Goods stock-pile in the warehouses, and workers are laid off in consequence, reduced themselves to the worthless status of unwanted goods. Circulation in the marriage market is in an analogous state. In a cynical move, Brontë highlighted the relationship between the economic and matrimonial markets by tying Caroline's position as unwanted goods directly to that of the warehouse stockpiles. The Orders in Council are lifted, 'Stocks, which had been accumulating for years, now went off in a moment, in the twinkling of an eye' (pp. 728–9) and Caroline instantly receives a marriage proposal. The tone and structure of Brontë's 'winding-up' are deeply ironic, and we are warned that the hopes at this time are 'delusive' (p. 729). The conclusion of the novel does not resolve but merely exacerbates the novel's sense of the shared powerlessness of women and workers within the operations of economic markets.

Economic concepts of speculation and circulation are central to Brontë's treatment. Shirley rebukes Robert for wanting 'to make a speculation of me. You would immolate me to that mill – your

Molloch!' (p. 608). His proposal to Caroline is similarly an extension of his financial speculation, subsequent to the lifting of the Orders in Council. All merchants, Brontë cuttingly observes, 'like wise men, at this first moment of prosperity, prepared to rush into the bowels of speculation, and to delve new difficulties, in whose depths they might lose themselves at some future day' (p. 728). Caroline merely exchanges one perilous economic position for another; as purchased stock her future is tied to the speculative fortunes of her owner. Without training for employment, Brontë observed in a letter of 1848, women were 'piteously degraded', 'reared on speculation with a view to their making mercenary marriages'.[6] Caroline's unhappy position is clearly portrayed as a result of this form of speculation which, by denying women access to the labour market, reduces them to the status of objects in the economic nexus of the matrimonial market, mere vehicles for others' speculation. Trapped in a stagnant economy, where the market is glutted and circulation has ceased, Caroline is powerless to change her situation. Her energies, which should be directed outward, are obstructed, turned inwards against herself, causing a near total breakdown of her physiological and psychological health.

Circulation proves the key to the intersection of the economic and psychological dimensions of the text. Brontë's depiction of Caroline's illness follows the language and diagnoses of Victorian medical accounts of the 'female economy'. Obstructed circulation leads to a breakdown of the system. While social and medical writers drew frequent attention to the correlation between the nation's political and psychological health, Brontë takes the correlation one stage further, pinpointing a precise causal relationship between the political and economic state of the nation and the physiological and psychological health of her heroine. In *Jane Eyre* Brontë had offered two contrasting models of female energy: the imploding, self-consuming energy of Helen Burns, and the disruptive, exploding energies of Bertha Mason. *Shirley* employs the same division but shifts its axis from internal gender coordinates to those of class and gender. The working-class rioters take over the role of Bertha Mason, as socially marginalized figures who are nonetheless violently disruptive of bourgeois order, while Caroline fulfils the self-negating model of Helen Burns. The shift from madwoman to riotous workers highlights the economic force of the structural homology employed in *Shirley*: those denied access to economic power and a legitimate outlet for their energies will erupt in violence against the system which constrains them. Alternatively, as in the case of Helen and Caroline, the violence will be directed against themselves.

Shirley herself is a figure set above the situational powerlessness which defines Caroline and the working class. Given wealth, land and ownership of Moore's mill she possesses all the material, non-gender specific bases upon which social power is grounded. 'Captain Keeldar' is an experiment on Brontë's part to investigate the relationship between gender, class and social power. The novel, however, is pessimistic in its conclusions, reversing the trajectory of *Jane Eyre* and offering a study in disempowerment. Material power is insufficient to defeat the forces of patriarchy. Jane's initial sense of her own insubstantiality and spirit-like existence, as reflected in the 'visionary hollow', is gradually reversed as she acquires psychological coherence, independent material wealth, and ultimate control over the maimed Rochester. The two heroines of *Shirley*, however, move into increasing insubstantiality. Caroline is threatened by the ultimate form of insubstantiality, death, whilst Shirley becomes, in conclusion, virtually a figment of Louis' mind: her capitulation to his control is presented entirely through Louis' eyes, in the form of his notebook entries.

Structurally, *Shirley* is a more radical and innovative work than *Jane Eyre*. Brontë deliberately eschews unity of focus and of voice. We are no longer offered the comfort of an autobiographical account in which the continuity of voice acts to maintain an illusion of the continuity of the subject. This text is split across divided sites and multiple protagonists whose shifting relations are plotted directly against the wider operations of class and economic conflict. The language is also split, mingling complex analyses of the economic consequences of the Order in Council with invocations of visions, wraiths, and spirits which cut across the economic fiction of the rational, unified actor in control of his destiny. Brontë is not here merely resorting to a Gothic mode which rests uneasily in a materialist tale of markets, but is striving to create a narrative form and language which gives expression to the novel's challenge to the certainties of social and psychological identity, its sense of the insubstantiality of our most assured reference points. Division and uncertainty characterize both the society and the four principal protagonists who seem to be defined less by any centre of selfhood than by their positioning in relation to each other. Not only is Moore divided socially into Robert and Gerard, he also acquires a double, Louis, who is introduced as if a figment in Caroline's waking dream.[7] Multiplicity breaks down the certitude of identity, both of self and other.

With Shirley herself, in whom one might expect to find a defined centre for the novel, we are offered rather a psyche whose centre seems endlessly recessive. Not only is she silenced and exiled from the conclusion of her own story, she is also absent for the first third of the novel, existing rather as a social and psychological space to be filled. Even her material presence is marked by a peculiar distancing; we are given her speech but never, as with Caroline, enter directly into her inner thoughts. We are offered instead a series of others' readings of Shirley.[8] Against the emphatic certitude of men such as Helstone, Moore and Yorke, who view women and the economy with the same dogmatic narrowness, Brontë stresses the difficulties and ambivalence of interpretation. Subjective desires occlude vision, whether in judgments on the economic laws of circulation or on the secrets of womanhood. In contrast to these inflexible patriarchal constructions of the 'real', Brontë sets up the alternative space of vision and dream which cuts across divisions of gender and class. The obnoxious curates address themselves in the opening chapter to the visions of Mike Hartley, the Antinomian weaver, visions of soldiers which are later fulfilled when Shirley's visions, in turn, of a Titan-Eve are interrupted by the glitter of 'martial scarlet' and the crude chauvinism of Joe Scott. The circle is completed when Hartley shoots Moore (at the very moment when he has confessed his crime against Shirley). The function of the visionary element in the text is not to displace or deny the force of the material power and violence marshalled against the labourers and their feminine counterparts, but rather to offer an alternative voice, an alternative interpretation of the merchants' seemingly fixed laws of economic and gender interaction, and, finally, an alternative source of violence.

Brontë repeatedly violates realist 'decorum' in *Shirley*, though perhaps nowhere quite so decisively as in the opening chapter which she insisted on retaining against the advice of her publishers.[9] The anger which fuels the text is evident in these scenes which, far from being irrelevant, offer a condensation of many of the central issues of the text. The politics of superfluity are addressed through the position of these curates, who existed in 'abundant shower[s]' at Brontë's time of writing, but were reckoned in 1811–12 to be highly desirable items of scarcity. The unproductive, self-regarding lives of these favoured beings are set against the sufferings of the unwanted, surplus women and workers of the parishes. This contrast is heightened by the fact that, ignoring all spiritual duties, these parasites actively *choose* a life of social visits which rivals in monotony 'the toil of the weaver at his loom' (p. 40) and mirrors in outward form that of women, like Caroline, denied access to the labour market. With a wealth of social possibilities open to them, the curates waste their days, frittering away the opportunities offered solely to them and denied their female counterparts. Although these curates lived too early, Brontë notes, to have been influenced by the Oxford Movement's ideas on preordination and apostolic succession, they seem, nonetheless, to be laying claims to special grace which parallel those of the mill owners in the material sphere. The crude physicality of these curates' lives suggests the spiritual bankruptcy of the church: not only is it unable to resolve a material dilemma, it is itself part of the problem.[10] As part of her bargain with the reader, Brontë promises 'something real, cool, solid'; there is to be no resolution through the mists of feeling, no narrative transubstantiation to invoke a higher spiritual plane. The reader is to be offered a repast of 'unleavened bread with bitter herbs', a textual menu which underscores the novel's radical intent. The remembrance of Passover is a remembrance of a fight against social oppression.

'More bread!': the first spoken words of the text, uttered by Malone, echo throughout the novel. The social conflict between the millowners and the workers is essentially a conflict over the right to bread: 'As to the sufferers, whose sole inheritance was labour, and who had lost that inheritance – who could not get work, and consequently could not get wages, and consequently could not get bread – they were left to suffer on . . . the unemployed underwent their destiny – ate the bread, and drank the waters of affliction' (p. 37). Brontë uncompromisingly brings scriptural passages to bear on material social problems, refusing a separation of the material and the spiritual. The sensual greed, self-satisfied authority and lust for command of Malone are set against the powerlessness of the starving unemployed. As Gilbert and Gubar have pointed out, the plight of Caroline Helstone is also linked to that of the workers through the imagery of bread and starvation.[11] The relationship, I will suggest, is not simply analogical; Brontë's analysis draws on Victorian medical discourse to explore the interconnections between the circulatory economies of society, and the psychological and physiological system.

Malone's even more peremptory second command brings together issues of class and gender: '"Cut it, woman", . . . and the "woman" cut it accordingly. Had she followed her inclinations, she would have cut the parson also' (p. 11). The exchange, silent on one side, suggests how the imperious social power wielded by the mill-owners operates in the domestic scene. As lower-class figure, and 'woman', thus doubly abased in the social order, Mrs Gale acts as the median point in the shifting levels of the text. Her mute physical obedience, which masks a repressed need for violent retort, links her to her peers, the unemployed workers, whose violence finally achieves expression. It also links her to the middle-class figure of Caroline Helstone who, locked in struggle with the mill-owner Robert, and having fully internalized the social proscriptions on female physical or verbal response, takes refuge in the only permitted resort: self-repression. Whilst Mrs Gale finds in a loaf of bread a convenient object of displacement, Caroline channels her anger entirely inwards. The material destruction of the frames by the workers is paralleled by her internal psychic destruction.

MORAL EARTHQUAKES

Endurance, overgoaded, stretched the hand of fraternity to sedition; the throes of a moral earthquake were felt heaving under the hills of the northern counties. (p. 37)

The language of physical and moral assault which Brontë uses to describe the social situation of 1811–12 is that to be found in all the contemporary newspaper and periodical discussions of the upheavals of the 1840s. Brontë herself, for instance, refers to the continental revolutions in terms of 'the shock of moral earthquake' and earnestly prays that 'England may be spared the spasms, cramps and frenzy-fits now contorting the Continent' (31 March 1848).[12] Social, physiological and psychological health all melt into one in the discourse on social unrest. In 1831 one commentator expressed the fear that the 'moral conflagration' raging in Europe would be transferred to England for 'symptoms of this mania' were already discernible in the leaders of the populace.[13] Throughout the 30s and 40s the discussions of the social problems raised by industrialism and unemployment spoke interchangeably of a physical and moral menace, or disease. An article on infant labour depicted socialism and Chartism as 'symptoms of an universal disease spread throughout the vast masses of the people' and calls for social change for 'we know that our system begets the vast and inflammable mass which lies waiting, day by day, for the spark to explode it into mischief'.[14] Sympathy for the individual subjects of distress in no way moderates the tendency to view them as a seething mass whose eruptions are to be feared. Even with subjects such as infants or distressed needlewomen who in no way participate in overt social action, the processes of association seem nonetheless to lead inexorably back to the spectre of Europe. Thus an 1848 article on distressed needlewomen refers their plight to the 'human misery convulsing Europe' which has at last found tongues: 'Its wails melt us to pity, its ravings terrify us, its sores sicken us.'[15] The description aptly captures the peculiar mixture of concern, fear and revulsion which fuelled middle-class responses to the interwoven problems of social suffering and social unrest. Brontë's fiction shares this ambivalence, though unlike Elizabeth Gaskell she steers well clear of any detailed depiction of physical deprivation, choosing to enter solely the cottage of William Farren which is singled out, in line with ruling-class prescriptions for social improvement, as a model of cleanliness and order.[16]

Unifying all aspects of the industrial debate in the 40s was the consensus that the labour market was overstocked.[17] The plight of male weavers and industrial workers, 'distressed needlewomen' and governesses was linked to a single cause. Interestingly, however, it was invoked more readily with reference to the women. These 'vulnerable victims' were figures of greater public sympathy than the potentially seditious male workers and thus a more appropriate target for a form of market explanation which would exonerate them from personal blame for their plight.[18] Peculiar discursive contortions were thus produced as writers extolled the refining virtues of femininity whilst simultaneously discussing women as mere surplus commodities in a marketplace. As one writer put it 'the market is stocked with them to repletion'.[19] The whole unemployment debate was highly charged in gender terms. Men were blamed for brutally forcing women out of the sanctity of their own homes and thus creating unemployment for themselves and a life of domestic hell.[20] Conversely, however, the 'fallen' woman who had entered the factory was seen to lose her 'ordained' station, and to become a source of pollution to her daughters and an inciter of male violence. The rhetoric mirrors that of medical depictions of female insanity: once the frame of domestic respectability is breached, the flow of violence and sexuality is irrepressible: 'the women are the leaders and exciters of the young men to violence in every riot and outbreak of the manufacturing districts; and the language in which they indulge is of a horrid description; in fact, while they are themselves demoralized, they contaminate all which comes within their rank'.[21] The contamination carried by the female worker is inevitably linked with that other female source of contamination – prostitution – where moral infection is underscored by the threat of physical disease. A woman outside the home becomes the target for a unified discourse of moral and physical corruption. As I suggested earlier, even that object of social pity, the governess, was a source of sexual alarm. The Victorian discussion of the problem of female labour was indeed inseparable from that of prostitution.

Throughout the political spectrum, domestic ideology was upheld as the one way of rectifying political and economic instability. Thus one Chartist spokesman argued that the 'pale, haggard countenances' and 'diminutive and decrepid forms' of the factory workers were brought on not by the labour itself, but by the failure of working women to provide their men with the requisite domestic comforts. He concludes, apocalyptically, that 'if the females still continue to work in factories, the race of Englishmen will be extinct'.[22] The employment of women threatens not only the economic structure of English society but, more seriously, the virility, and hence the very existence, of its menfolk.

The whole social and ideological edifice grounded on the domestic ideal was shaken, however, by the problem of overstocked markets, both with respect to labour and matrimony. Willing participants in the given hierarchical structures of labour and gender were turned into machine wreckers, in the case of the male workers, and into questioning subjects, as in the case of Caroline. Brontë's own letters around this time record a strong preoccupation with the figure of the 'old maid'.[23] In an exchange of letters with W. S. Williams concerning the future of his daughters she dwells on the necessity of women finding employment in order to make them independent of the uncertainties of the marriage market, even though employment as a governess will necessarily entail suffering. Indeed its value seems precisely to lie in the 'discipline equally painful and priceless' that it ˙mposes.[24] In the perverted value structures of Victorian culture such suſįˑˑng becomes, for Brontë, the primary indicator of female worth. Engagement with the labour market for women is not envisaged as a freeing of the faculties, an extending outward of energies, but rather a reinforcement of the violence of self-repression which marks Caroline Helstone's life. Unlike men, women are not free to pursue external goals but, if permitted to enter the labour market, must use their work as a means of extending and intensifying the private domain of self-discipline. The one advantage, it seems, is that in gaining a measure of financial independence women become subjects for themselves, rather than the 'piteously degraded' objects of their parents' mercenary speculations in the matrimonial market.

Charlotte Brontë's reflections on this issue were clearly influenced by her independent-minded friend, Mary Taylor, who figures as Rose Yorke in *Shirley*. As early as 1841 Mary had declared her intention of emigrating to New Zealand. Charlotte wrote to Emily that 'Mary has made up her mind she can not and will not be a governess, a teacher, a milliner, a bonnet-maker nor housemaid. She sees no means of obtaining employment she would like in England, so she is leaving it'.[25] Interestingly, Mary's despised list of jobs extends far beyond the range of acceptability for a middle-class woman, but marriage is significantly absent from her calculations. Charlotte was at once excited and appalled by her friend's daring, but resolutely refused to follow her advice and do likewise. Mary finally sailed in 1845. Charlotte's reflections to Ellen reveal a real note of envy: 'Mary Taylor finds herself free – and on that path for adventure and exertion to which she has so long been seeking admission.' Contrary to her usual pattern of thought, Charlotte observes that tackling real material dangers should bring true satisfaction, 'whereas I doubt whether suffering purely mental [h]as any good result unless it be to make us by comparison less sensitive to physical suffering – I repeat then, that Mary Taylor has done well to go out to New Zealand'.[26]

Charlotte's self-defensiveness subsequently undermines her ability to maintain this open stance towards Mary's action. It is significant that, in *Shirley*, Rose is not given the life of energetic labour that Mary enjoyed in New Zealand, trading cattle and running a clothing store, but is rather depicted as a 'lonely emigrant' amidst 'virgin solitude' (p. 167). Mary's own response to *Shirley* was characteristically robust:

I have seen some extracts from 'Shirley' in which you talk of women working. And this first duty, this great necessity you seem to think that some women may indulge in – if they give up marriage and don't make themselves too disagreeable to the other sex. You are a coward and a traitor. A woman who works is by that alone better than one who does not and a woman who does not happen to be rich and who *still* earns no money and does not wish to do so, is guilty of a great fault – almost a crime – a dereliction of duty which leads rapidly and almost certainly to all manner of degradation. It is very wrong of you to *plead* for toleration for workers on the ground of their being in peculiar circumstances and few in number or singular in disposition. Work or degradation is the lot of all except the very small number born to wealth.[27]

Mary Taylor aptly pinpoints the timidities and evasions in the work of her less radical friend. *Shirley* is no radical socialist or feminist text, but in its explorations of the impossible demands and restrictions which encompass Caroline Helstone's life it offers a more subtle analysis of the problems impeding female progress than could ever be obtained from Mary Taylor's swingeing idealism.

The flaw in Mary Taylor's argument lies in her insistence on the necessity of female labour when she herself had to flee to another hemisphere to find an adequate outlet for her energies. Her actions were highly unusual for the time. By 1848, however, when Brontë was writing *Shirley*, the fears about the overstocked matrimonial and labour markets for women were reaching a crescendo. Mrs Caroline Chisholm set up her Family Colonization Loan Society in 1848 amidst a blaze of publicity, closely followed in 1849 by Sidney Herbert's Fund for Promoting Female Emigration and the British Ladies' Female Emigrant Society.[28] Officials of the Governesses' Benevolent Institution also drew up plans in 1849 for a scheme for the emigration of unemployed governesses.[29] As the post bag of the Brontës' favourite journal at this time, *Chambers*, testified, female emigration was one of the most engrossing concerns of the day.[30] Interest in all these schemes for exporting respectable women (who were thus to be sharply distinguished from the fallen women who had preceded them) was in direct ratio to the public concern voiced about the numbers of 'surplus' middle-class women. Demographics pointed to an imbalance of males and females in the country (roughly 106 females to 100 males); worries focused, however, on the large numbers of middle-class women who were believed to be unmarried and were thus deemed 'surplus' to requirements.[31] This figure of the spinster or 'old maid' received repeated attention in popular literature, periodicals and even scientific texts. She figured both as the butt of cruel ridicule and as an object of supreme pathos, being unable to attain the one ordained goal of female life. Throughout these discussions there was an extraordinary blending of sentimental and economic rhetoric: all held unquestioningly to the assumption that a middle-class woman who remained unmarried was superfluous, or as W. R. Greg later declaimed, 'redundant'.[32]

The schemes for female emigration in the late 40s and 50s were clothed in pious rhetoric about woman's civilizing mission but were primarily schemes for disposing of unwanted spinsters (unlike the more feminist, job-oriented schemes in the 1860s).[33] Amidst the general euphoric reception of these schemes there was a degree of concern voiced that 'wives should be exported like so many bales of printed cotton'.[34] Brontë's text draws attention, through its structure, to the implied commodification of women which governed discussions of the 'surplus-woman question'. She chooses, however, to end her novel with the exporting of bales rather than female bodies. Robert's goods are exported, thus allowing Caroline to enter the sanctified state of marriage in England's hallowed land, but, as I suggested earlier, the ironic structuring of this 'Winding-Up' calls attention to the unsatisfactory nature of the text's conclusion.

Caroline herself is earlier granted a scathingly accurate dissection of the problems of the young women in her neighbourhood:

The great wish – the sole aim of every one of them is to be married, but the majority will never marry: they will die as they now live. They scheme, they plot, they dress to ensnare husbands. The gentlemen turn them into ridicule: they don't want them; they hold them very cheap: they say – I have heard them say it with sneering laughs many a time – the matrimonial market is overstocked. Fathers say so likewise, and are angry with their daughters when they observe their manoeuvres: they order them to stay at home. (p. 442)

The statement that men hold unmarried women 'cheap' has a devastating accuracy: the dual sexual and economic meaning highlights the ways in which the social mores for women, exemplified by the high value placed on modesty and self-control, are a direct outcome of the social marketplace, where woman's sexuality is one of the principal objects of trade. The passage clearly articulates the double-bind in which women are placed: deemed of social value only if they succeed on the marriage market, but considered worthless if they are seen to be trying to achieve that end.

Shirley confirms this social value structure when she angrily responds to Robert's suggestion that she seemed to encourage his advances: 'you deny me the possession of all I value most. That is to say, that I am a traitor to all my sisters: that I have acted as no woman can act, without degrading herself and her sex: that I have sought where the incorrupt of my kind naturally scorn and abhor to seek'

(p. 610). To act so that one's feelings can openly be read is to align oneself with prostitutes, women who market their wares without disguise. As in the contemporary labour debates, the figure of prostitution forms a constant undertow of female thought, operating an effective mechanism for policing women's emotions and behaviour.

The imagery of treachery which Shirley invokes is one which ties together the class and gender dimensions of the text. The workers commit political treachery by openly enacting their grievances against the economic structures. The women, however, form their own court of law, convicting themselves of self-treachery for any movement into the public domain of expressivity. The workers, trapped within the stagnant cycles of the economy, vent their rage on the machines. Caroline, similarly trapped within the constraints of the marriage market, turns her anger against herself. In one of the bitterest passages in Victorian fiction, Brontë highlights the problems of passivity for the female lover who has no socially permitted mechanisms of response to a changeful lover:

A lover masculine so disappointed can speak and urge explanation; a lover feminine can say nothing: if she did the result would be shame and anguish, inward remorse for self-treachery. Nature would brand such demonstration as a rebellion against her instincts, and would vindictively repay it afterwards by the thunderbolt of self-contempt smiting suddenly in secret. Take the matter as you find it: ask no questions; utter no remonstrances: it is your best wisdom. You expected bread, and you have got a stone; break your teeth on it, and don't shriek because the nerves are martyrized: do not doubt that your mental stomach – if you have such a thing – is strong as an ostrich's – the stone will digest. You held out your hand for an egg, and fate put into it a scorpion. Show no consternation: close your fingers firmly upon the gift; let it sting through your palm. Never mind: in time, after your hand and arm have swelled and quivered long with torture, the squeezed scorpion will die, and you will have learned the great lesson how to endure without a sob. (pp. 117–8)

With its crucial invocation of the imagery of bread and stone, the passage links the psychological deprivation of Caroline with the physical starvation of the workers, indicting equally the class and gender norms which dictate that they should suffer in silence. Women, however, are doubly imprisoned, locked so securely within the ideological projections of female nature that any attempt at rebellion becomes a form of 'self-treachery'. Whilst rebelling against the necessity of grasping the proffered male scorpion (with all its implicit imagery of destructive male sexuality, as opposed to the desired symbol of female fertility, the egg), Caroline nonetheless endorses the belief that femininity, and thus identity itself, is sacrificed if the 'natural' instincts of modesty are transgressed. The analysis highlights the multivalent, contradictory role played by 'Nature' in the text: it describes the idealized space outside the social which Shirley and Caroline enter in Nunnwood, but it is also the site of the determinant male social encodings of the female body and psyche within Victorian social and scientific discourse. 'Nature', for Caroline, is a force which ensures her adherence to the social norms of femininity: self-suppression and non-expressivity.

In the violent physicality of its imagery the passage breaks down divisions between the physiological and psychological domains. The smitings of self-contempt are later echoed by Caroline's description of those 'sharp recollections that return, lacerating your self-respect like tiny penknives' (p. 258). Female self-definition is founded on a model of inexpressivity which effectually strangles the self: any attempt to articulate personal thought or feeling inevitably leads to self-hatred, to a wish to destroy the self which has thus struggled so painfully into being.

Class and gender treachery in *Shirley* are alike the focus of intense ambivalence. Sympathy is extended to the workers only for as long as they refrain from expressing their grievances. As Shirley observes, she would listen to Mercy only till it was 'drowned by the shout of ruffian defiance . . . If once the poor gather and rise in the form of the mob, I shall turn against them as an aristocrat' (p. 300). Just as the workers are demoted, by their actions, from full human status to become an animal mob, so women who violate the ideals of female nature are deemed to have forfeited their femininity. In its overt stance, the text seems to offer no easy resolution to these ideological knots. Like George Eliot, who recorded the fear that women might be unsexed by education, Brontë was bound by the ideologies of her time.[35] The seeds of radical social analysis are firmly planted, however, in Caroline's observation that 'to such grievances as society cannot readily cure, it usually forbids utterance, on pain of its scorn: this scorn being only a sort of tinselled cloak to its deformed weakness' (p. 441). The tone and language are those of the second preface to *Jane Eyre*; a similar anger and commitment to unveiling social hypocrisy fuel this text as Brontë explores the different ways in which the unemployed workers and Caroline attempt to defy or evade the paralysing effects of such social scorn.

OLD MAIDS

As the text progresses Caroline emerges, in flashes, from the self-lacerating, bitter stoicism of the scorpion passage to a form of defiance. Contemplating a probable future as an 'old maid', she challenges fiercely the socially prescriptive role model of duty and good works which is, she observes, 'a very convenient doctrine for the people who hold it'. The base currency of praise for virtuous behaviour is insufficient reward for such self-denial: 'Is there not a terrible hollowness, mockery, want, craving, in that existence which is given away to others, for want of something of your own to bestow it on? I suspect there is. Does virtue lie in abnegation of self? I do not believe it. Undue humility makes tyranny; weak concession creates selfishness' (p. 194).

Such an aggressive and cynical dissection of current ideology is remarkable for its time, though the reflections still remain bound within the framework of the Victorian domestic ideal. 'Something of one's own', it emerges, is a husband. The text is quite clear in its physiological analysis of the old maids' decline. The sustenance they lack is not bread but sex. The provocatively named Miss Mann is figured as harbouring a 'starved, ghostly longing for appreciation and affection'; she is an 'extenuated spectre' to whom 'a crumb is not thrown once a year' (p. 201). Similar terms are later employed to depict Caroline's 'famished heart', failing in life for want of 'a drop and crumb of nourishment' (p. 282) whilst she is forced to watch the 'banquet' being spread before another. The analogy with the workers' plight is not simply metaphorical; the deprivation of both groups is physiological. The narrator intervenes decisively to expose the worthlessness of the palliative philosophies offered to old maids. Caroline's devotion to good works is to little avail: 'Yet I must speak truth; these efforts brought her neither health of body nor continued peace of mind: with them all, she wasted . . . the heaviness of a broken spirit, and of pining and palsifying faculties, settled slow on her buoyant youth' (p. 206). The phrenological language highlights the inseparability of mind and body; decaying faculties cause attrition throughout the physiological system. The blocked circulation in the marriage market here leaves its physiological imprint in the blocked circulation of Caroline's internal energies.

Against the doctrine of self-control, so prevalent in contemporary economic, social, and psychological thought, Brontë asserts that powerful countervailing idea, which fuelled the almost manic Victorian insistence on control: the overwhelming dominance of the body. Behind all the pious assertions of the value of control, particularly for those unruly subjects, women and workers, lay palpitating fears that restrained forces, whether in the psyche or in the labour force, might break free. It is significant that the psychological theories of self-control which emerged in the nineteenth century were directly interwoven with a physiological theory of repression. Texts simultaneously defined madness as a 'deficiency in self-control', but argued that failure to give outward expression to disordered emotions or desires would only strengthen somatically the internal hold of the disease.[36] But what was to become of the poor female who was deemed to have the 'circulating fluid' in greater abundance than the male, and to be less capable than her male counterpart of controlling it? Spinsterhood, the failure to give the body's energies their natural mode of expression, was depicted as a form of physiological disaster.

Many Victorian medical writers on the position of women displayed a keen awareness of the contradictory nature of contemporary attitudes: women were expected, socially, to exhibit strong self-control, whilst, physiologically, they were deemed to have a lower capacity than men to achieve this end. Robert Carter, in his 1853 treatise on hysteria, argues that there is a literal truth to the idea of being 'worn down by grief and care'. If emotions are denied their normal channels of 'discharge' 'the imprisoned power is driven to seek another opening'. The problem is particularly acute with reference to sexual passion in women, for not only are women 'more prone to emotions' than men, but they are also 'more frequently under the necessity of endeavouring to conceal them'. Whilst man, has 'facilities' which permit him to express his sexual desires through 'the proper channel' (clearly a coded reference to the social 'facilities' provided by prostitutes) a woman, 'if unmarried and chaste, is compelled to restrain every manifestation of its sway'. Carter's image of the cumulative impact of repression is that of violent eruption: emotion, 'after being kept down . . . often breaks forth at last with increased violence, and through more dangerous channels'.[37] There were two models for the effects of repression, however, in contemporary medical works: eruption and implosion. In Caroline's case, the illness produced by sexual repression is clearly of the imploding form.

Caroline's analysis of the situation of old maids follows closely the models set up in contemporary psychological discussion. Her assumption that women like Miss Ainley turn to religion as the inevitable, and only viable substitute for sexual passion, is a commonplace of the era. Millingen, for example, observes that woman, because of her greater susceptibility to the body, is therefore,

> subject to all the aberrations of love and religion; ecstatic under the impression of both, the latter becomes a resource when the excitement of the former is exhausted by disappointment, infidelity, and age – when, no longer attractive, she is left by the ebb of fond emotions on the bleak shore of despondency.[38]

Millingen's eloquence does not disguise his contempt for the unattractive old maid; he shares with his contemporaries in this supposedly religious age a disbelief in the possibility, for women, of religious emotion *per se*. The text of *Shirley* suggests a similar value structure. Although the worth of the old maid is self-consciously asserted, the constant return to the issue of physical appearance suggests a different perspective. Good works performed by women (and here Shirley's activities are included) are regarded solely as displacement activities.

The representations of Miss Mann and Miss Ainley conform in large measure to the two possible scenarios offered in a contemporary medical discussion of the 'arid virginity' of the 'Old Maid' who fails to fulfil her 'duties' as a woman, and the 'great *physical* end of her existence'. Either, 'the love that should have found its natural outpouring on a husband or children, may be directed by religious feelings to suffering humanity' and she will develop the admirable traits of 'self-denial and humility'; or, she will become a *virago*. In this case, not only would she become 'strong-minded' and 'bold and unfeminine in her manners' and thus 'repulsive to man', she would also possibly develop male physical characteristics, such as a beard and a hoarse voice. The complete picture of 'the *typical* "Old Maid"' is thus someone who is overbearing in temper with 'quaint untidy dress, a shrivelled skin, a lean figure, a bearded lip, shattered teeth, harsh grating voice, and manly stride'.[39] This image, gross caricature though it is, suggests that something more is at stake for Caroline than a life of singleness and celibacy. With the Victorian emphasis on the ovarian determination of the female system, the 'punishment, or . . . penalty' for failure to reproduce was nothing less than a biological loss of feminine identity, figured externally in the physical appearance.[40] The emphasis placed on female beauty thus takes on a new charge.

Miss Mann and Miss Ainley, who offer the two contrasting faces of spinsterhood, sour and sweet, are alike distinguished by their ugliness, which is invoked each time they appear. The 'corpse-like' appearance of Miss Mann is explained in terms of a 'malady that now poisoned her own life' which owed its origin to her efforts to support a wretched male relative 'in the depths of self-earned degradation' (p. 196). Since Brontë was writing this section of *Shirley* shortly before Branwell died, when his 'self-earned degradation' was at its height, it is possible we are being offered here a despairing future self-portrait by Brontë.[41] Branwell's fecklessness not only forced Charlotte into the hated role of governess, but also, following this model, potentially robbed her of her sexual identity. Ugliness and spinsterhood become external signs of an inner 'malady'.

In later reflections on 'old maids' Caroline draws directly together the two themes of sexuality and religion, likening the life of Miss Ainley to that of nuns: 'with their close cell, their iron lamp, their robe strait as a shroud, their bed narrow as a coffin'. The imagery anticipates the ghostly haunting and the theme of live burial in *Villette*. Caroline clearly subscribes to contemporary medical theories of sexual repression, believing that nuns, 'having violated nature, their natural likings and antipathies are reversed: they grow altogether morbid' (pp. 440–1). Her model is that of a fixed force of sexual energy which, if diverted from 'natural' expression, is turned into morbid forms (the term 'morbid' carrying a medical precision in the nineteenth century which we have now lost).

From a consideration of sexual repression, Caroline passes directly to a cultural and economic analysis of the position of women. Her arguments here echo the terms of current debate; she complains that the stagnant system which offers women no form of profitable occupation makes them 'decline in health: they are never well; and their minds and views shrink to wondrous narrowness'. She calls the attention of the Men of Yorkshire and England to 'look at your poor girls, many of them fading around you, dropping off in consumption or decline; or, what is worse, degenerating to sour old maids, – envious, backbiting, wretched, because life is a desert to them' (pp. 442–3). Caroline's hierarchy here is a significant indicator of social attitudes: she esteems death by consumption (which was associated with sexual repression but at least had a poetic and 'feminine' value attached to it) as preferable to the horrors of celibacy. Her attack on enforced female idleness, and her belief that this actively caused a decline of health and even consumption, are both part of the medical discourse of the day.[42] Pre-eminent amongst these critics of the education and overbred idleness of middle and upper-class women were the phrenologists, George and Andrew Combe, who were unfailing in their efforts to promote female education and to transform upbringing.[43] As one commentator later claimed, George Combe's teachings had transformed the quality of women's lives: without his counsels, many women would have 'come to an untimely end, or vegetated in ill health and nonentity'.[44]

Brontë herself was clearly influenced by such work: Caroline's arguments draw on phrenological language and assumptions. Caroline not only shares the belief that female physical ailments may often be traced to psychological causes, but actively employs the phrenological vocabulary of faculty development to explain her position. In language which recalls Jane Eyre's strident assertion of women's and workers' rights she calls to men to give their daughters 'a field in which their faculties may be exercised and grow . . . Keep your girls' minds narrow and fettered – they will still be a plague and a care, sometimes a disgrace to you: cultivate them – give them scope and work – they will be your gayest companions in health; your tenderest nurses in sickness; your most faithful prop in age' (pp. 443–4). The radical note of the address is toned down at the end; the 'eccentric murmurs' and laughter of Bertha are here suppressed. Women are to be allowed to develop their faculties, but only so that they can better fulfil their traditional roles. It is possibly this passage that prompted Mary Taylor to accuse her friend of being 'a coward and a traitor'.[45] Caroline's arguments are ultimately conservative in import, mirroring the concerned Tory attitude to the labour force: education should be offered to the masses, so that the prevailing hierarchical social system will function more smoothly. Against these timid conclusions, however, we should set the scathingly accurate depiction of the operations of the marriage market, and Caroline's rhetorical demand whether men could submit themselves uncomplainingly to the stagnant, narrow routine of women's lives: 'And, when there came no relief to their weariness, but only reproaches at its slightest manifestation, would not their weariness ferment in time to phrenzy?' (p. 442).

Class and gender concerns again run together. The weariness fermented to frenzy is outwardly exhibited not by Caroline, or a displaced Bertha figure, but by the workers, in a parallel which underscores the political underpinnings of *Jane Eyre*. The workers' outward violence is mirrored, however, in Caroline's inward violence: her passive destruction of her own body. The workers express their resistance through acts of violence directed towards their own simulacrum, the machine. Their attack is aimed both at the threat to their own livelihood and at the expressive symbols of an economic system which reduces man to the status of an expendable, mechanical object. Caroline similarly embarks on a course of resistance aimed at what she sees as her own simulacrum – her body. Her physiological decline suggests a form of self-hatred focused on a desire to separate mind from body – to place her self outside the sexual marketplace with its commodification of the body. Caroline is repeatedly depicted as the object of Robert's gaze. He is a 'spectator of [her] liveliness', a wary purchaser who inspects the presented goods for flaws (p. 89). Caroline's decline reveals a determination to rid herself of that too expressive system, the body, even at the cost of life itself. The material and psychological economies are directly tied to an economy of signs which determines Caroline's value in the marketplace. In the first stages of her suffering, Caroline tries to keep 'her pale face and wasted figure as much out of sight as she could', wishing to avoid young ladies 'look[ing] at her in a way she understood . . . Their eyes said they knew she had been "disappointed," as custom phrases it' (p. 215). Later, when she encounters Robert again, she initially turns away, trying to keep 'out of view each traitorous symptom' (p. 278), and seeking then the protection of shadow until, inevitably, the light falls on her face and 'all its paleness, all its change, all its forlorn meaning were clearly revealed' (p. 283). Only by destruction of the body can Caroline withdraw from the semiotic economy and control the body's 'traitorous' function as legible indicator of her psychological state.

THE FEMALE ECONOMY

The course of Caroline's illness follows Victorian medical theories on the functioning of female sexuality. Her decline is traced as a physiological process which the arrival of Shirley and Mrs Pryor initially helps to arrest: 'a turn was thereby given to her thoughts; a new channel was opened for them, which, diverting a few of them at least from the one direction in which all had hitherto tended, abated the impetuosity of their rush, and lessened the force of their pressure on one worn-down point' (p. 229). Mind and body are envisaged as one indivisible system, in which the operation of thought is that of channels of force which are apt to wear down the system, if too narrowly directed. The arrival of the ebullient Shirley, which initially helps arrest Caroline's descent into paralysing, self-consuming inertia, subsequently becomes the cause of its exacerbation. As idealized other, 'Shirley' is a necessary construct for Caroline which allows her to negotiate her own sense of failure: 'I am poverty and incapacity; Shirley is wealth and power' (p. 282). While the mass anger of the mill workers overthrows the psychic structures of social hierarchy, Caroline over-invests in them. Brought up amidst insistent assertions of her feminine inferiority, Caroline actively needs to believe that the two superior beings she constructs in her imagination, Robert and Shirley, will marry. Only by their imagined union can she affirm her own, inferior, sense of self.

Through the self-torturing workings of Caroline's mind, Brontë explores the psychological consequences of the social structures of hierarchy. Catching sight of Robert and Shirley as she passes Fieldhead one night she casts herself in the role of Satan, consumed by envy as he watches Adam and Eve within their paradise: 'And what am I – standing here in shadow, shrinking into concealment, my mind darker than my hiding-place?' (p. 263). The image is emblematic of the psychic structures of Victorian femininity: excluded from the scene of happiness by an internalized belief in personal inferiority, projected sexual desires and envy become the grounds for an even more intense self-hatred. Shrinking from the 'darkness' of a mind which could conceive such visions, Caroline is reduced to asking 'in ignorance and hopelessness, wherefore she was born' (p. 263). Unlike the workers who define objective, external causes for their suffering, Caroline assumes a personal sense of guilt, locating the origins of her unhappiness firmly within her own psyche.

The day of Caroline's final collapse is marked by a three-fold assault on her sense of self. Venturing to visit Hortense, Caroline finds Mrs Yorke, Rose and Jessie ensconced. Rose launches into the form of criticism of Caroline's life that Mary Taylor had repeatedly made of Brontë's. Rose voices her determination to explore both hemispheres: 'I am resolved that my life shall be a life: not a black trance like the toad's, buried in marble; nor a long, slow death like yours in Briarfield Rectory' (p. 451).[46] The image is one which, as Boumelha has pointed out, draws on the symbolic resonances of Caroline's name: her life is 'the hell within the stone'.[47] Rose accuses Caroline of a form of treachery in failing to develop her talents, voicing her own determination not to imprison her talent 'in the linen-press to find shrouds among the sheets' (p. 452). From the hostile Mrs Yorke, who is predisposed to dislike 'a shrinking, sensitive character – a nervous temperament' (p. 456), Caroline is subject to another form of attack which draws its ammunition from current medical concern that the 'modern young lady – morbid, delicate, professing to like retirement' and given to 'romancing' and too much novel reading was guilty of placing an over-emphasis on the development of feeling (p. 457).[48] Reading the treacherous details of Caroline's worn, and too-expressive face, Mrs Yorke further accuses her of the ultimate sin – plotting to entrap a husband. Though Caroline rouses her spirits to defend herself, Mrs Yorke's accusations clearly have a germ of truth, albeit reflected by a coarse mirror. They function as the social embodiment of her own self-censorship.

The final assault on Caroline's precarious sense of self comes with her surrender to the world of dream as she encounters Louis: 'the enigma of the dream (a dream it seemed) was at its height: she saw a visage like and unlike, – Robert, and no Robert' (p. 465). By separating Robert into cold, watching spectator, before whose 'secret power' she bent as if under a 'spell', and warm interlocuter (Louis), she enters into the illusory promise of sexual fulfilment which is quickly shattered by the symbolic entry of Shirley's radiant flowers of 'carmine and snow and gold', imaging both her wealth and luxurious physical presence. Hortense's hints confirm Caroline's fears that it is Shirley, not herself, who forms the third person within this triangle of mediated desire. Following on from the earlier assaults on her self-confidence, this abrupt termination of her surrender to the tempting realm of illusion precipitates her final collapse.

Caroline's illness is introduced by the extraordinary image of Lazarus which picks up on Rose's references to graves and shrouds: 'At other times this Future bursts suddenly, as if a rock had rent, and in it a grave had opened, whence issues the body of one that slept. Ere you are aware, you stand face to face with a shrouded and unthought-of Calamity – a new Lazarus' (p. 473). The New Testament image of new life and hope, of miraculous redemption, is turned into its very opposite. The near-blasphemous conceit contains a deliberate negation of the Christian perspective: in place of Christian healing the modern sufferer can expect only the eruption of the imprisoned forces of the body, destroying all the carefully-constructed defences and controls by which the personality is kept socially in place. The preceding references to the cholera epidemic which swept through England at this time place disease in a sexual frame: English domesticity is undermined by the infection of Eastern sensuality, 'with the poisoned exhalations of the East, dimming the lattices of English homes' (p. 399). The explanation of Caroline's illness follows contemporary beliefs in the effects of 'poisoned' air, or miasma, and the susceptibility to physical disease of individuals whose internal emotions were ill-regulated.[49] Probably, 'some sweet, poisoned breeze, redolent of honey-dew and miasma, had passed into her lungs and veins, and finding there already a fever of mental excitement, and a languor of long conflict and habitual sadness, had fanned the spark to flame, and left a well-lit fire behind it' (p. 474). The description is both physiologically precise and metaphorically suggestive; the reference to 'honey-dew' carries associations with 'Kubla Khan' and 'La Belle Dame Sans Merci', recasting the poisoned breeze as a force of mental, and most probably sexual, illusion. Caroline too has indulged in forbidden fantasies, and must pay the price.

Brontë does not allow her heroine to fall into the form of insanity so often associated with her state in medical and popular literature. Newspapers and medical texts were full of accounts of how the most well-bred and chaste young women uttered fearful obscenities when collapsing into insanity from pressure of disappointment or jealousy in love (the Ophelia syndrome).[50] As Millingen records 'it is invariably observed that those females who have been educated with the greatest care and precaution, are the most obscene and disgusting in their language and conduct, when labouring under mental aberration'.[51] Caroline's 'brain-fever' saves her from that degradation. Unlike her successor, Lucy Snowe, she is allowed to preserve in tact her pleasant personality, becoming neither hard nor cold, but maintaining all the domesticated charm of a Victorian heroine. Even during the course of her illness she retains the essential veneer of modesty, refusing to part with her inner sexual secret. The necessary revelation is accomplished, however, firstly through her overheard soliloquy when, in Romantic vein, she envisages herself as a tortured aeolian harp, and secondly by the moon-lit wanderings of her mind when illusion holds sway and she imagines herself Robert's wife. Even here, under the symbol of female insanity, her fantasies remain rigorously chaste, although the images of honeysuckle, refreshing dew, and ripening peaches are redolent with a displaced sensuality. The narrator suggests that 'perhaps healthy self-possession and self-control were to be hers no more' (p. 479). Her waning health is in direct proportion, however, to her retention of self-control.

Caroline is saved from the inevitable outcome of her internal collapse – death, or permanent mental derangement – only by the discovery of a new identity. With the revelation of her long-lost mother she is rescued from the orphan status so frequently assigned to the Victorian protagonist. This acquisition of identity is shown to be regressive, however. Only by moving backwards to an earlier developmental stage, associated with an unproblematic bonding with the mother, can Caroline escape the crushing pressures of puberty and entry into the sexual market, to find a form of self-definition not based on self-denial. Yet the mother-daughter bond is itself subject to questioning in the text.[52] Mrs Pryor's claiming of her child is troubling; there are vampirish echoes as she exultantly stakes her claim, ousting those of her hated husband: 'God permitted me to be the parent of my child's mind: it belongs to me: it is my property – my *right*' (p. 486). The fierce possessiveness and assertion of a *right* to ownership suggest that Caroline is once more being treated as a commodity. She has been appropriated as an instrument in her mother's sexual struggles.

Caroline's induction into the role of daughter is accomplished through her mother's garish warnings of the concealed horrors of male sexuality, the 'transfiguration on the domestic hearth' when 'the white mask [is] lifted, the bright disguise put away' (p. 489). Praise of Caroline's soft voice immediately recalls her father: '"he spoke softly too, once, – like a flute breathing tenderness; and then, when the world was not by to listen, discords that split the nerves and curdled the blood – sounds to inspire insanity"' (p. 492). Rescued from the threat of insanity evoked by sexual repression, Caroline is now introduced to the notion of insanity inspired by sexual intimacy. It was her mother's experience of the inherently deceptive nature of male sexuality which forced her to be an 'unnatural parent', and abandon Caroline, seeing in her pretty features 'the stamp of perversity'. Whereas Caroline, in her innocence, had rejected for herself the nun-like existence of the old maids, 'their robe strait as a shroud, their bed narrow as a coffin', her mother had conversely chosen to accept 'rather a bier for a bed – the grave for a home' than return to sexual bondage (p. 493). The 'old maid's' life was to her one of blessed release: '"How safe seemed the darkness and chill of an

unkindled hearth, when no lurid reflection from terror crimsoned its
desolation! How serene was solitude, when I feared not the irruption
of violence and vice!"' The contemporary images of violent, eruptive
female sexuality, focused on Bertha in *Jane Eyre*, are here transposed
to the male sex, explicitly linking the inherent violence of patriarchal
control with sexual domination.

Although Caroline has imprisoned herself within romantic fantasies
about Robert, her mother's account of sexuality does not come
entirely unheralded to Caroline's mind. Mrs Pryor's words summon
to memory Caroline's earlier dream-like reverie on her father,
stimulated, significantly, by her uncle's refusal to listen to her request
to be allowed to earn her living.[53] Her dark recollections summon
images of being shut in a garret, her father returning 'like a madman,
furious, terrible; or – still more painful – like an idiot, imbecile,
senseless' (p. 115). At that time, too, she fell ill, and was rescued only
when her screams, evoked by his threats to murder her, brought aid.
Whilst she recovered then to see her father in his coffin, now, in
symmetrical parallel, she awakes to find herself claimed by her
long-lost mother. The past is not thereby annulled, however, but
rather reinstated in her mind. In accepting her role as daughter she
reaffirms these two images of man: furious madman, or senseless
imbecile, both, in their departure from the rational norm, equally
threatening. Memories of the past had already coloured her vision in
the present, causing her to see 'another figure standing beside her
uncle's – a strange shape; dim, sinister, scarcely earthly: the
half-remembered image of her own father, James Helstone, Matthewson
Helstone's brother' (pp. 114–5). The sinister shape enacts her fears of
the possible duplicity of men: behind the upright exterior there lurks
the hidden madman. The history of her uncle's wife, Mary Cave,
whose name suggests the mystery and essence of womanhood,
reinforces these fears: once married, Mary Cave literally faded from
life, enacting the kind of self-consumption Caroline endures outside of
marriage, turning into the purified, still-image her husband desired: a
'beautiful-featured mould of clay ... cold and white' (p. 62). Helstone
reveals his conjugal mastery by inverting the myth of Pygmalion,
reducing his wife to an external sign of beauty. Male power can take
many forms, the outward, crimsoned violence of Caroline's father, or
the 'respectable' freezing power of her uncle.

The name of Cave is also carried, significantly, by Shirley Cave
Keeldar, or Captain Keeldar, Brontë's fantasized experiment in male

empowerment. The text suggests, however, that gender is a stronger determinant than class. Shirley's decline in the text is in many ways even more dramatic than that of Caroline since she moves from a position of quasi-masculine empowerment to complete abjection by the conclusion of the novel. The turning point, which marks the beginning of her fall, is her illness which in many respects follows the pattern of Caroline's. Although different in origin, arising from her fear of contracting rabies from a dog bite she received, it is nonetheless a product of the workings of her mind, and similarly threatens both her bodily health and her sanity. As with Caroline's illness, it is inaugurated by self-laceration. In cauterizing the wound, Shirley consciously violates her own psychic and bodily integrity: '"I took an Italian iron from the fire, and applied the light scarlet glowing tip to my arm"' (p. 579). She closes her hand firmly on the scorpion and learns to endure without a sob. Shirley's apparent recovery is marked by her 'confession' to Louis: in relating the history of her 'little mark', Shirley completes the process of her violation. By exposing her inner secrets, Shirley destroys the last vestiges of her self-containment, turning now to Louis for 'the benefit of your self-possession' (p. 578). Her fears of her own behaviour, once she has lost self-control and is dominated by the forces of madness, mirror those of contemporary medical and popular accounts. She asks Louis, the only one, who will, she believes, be 'self-possessed', to keep away Mr Sympson and her favourite, Henry, 'lest I should hurt him' and to lock the door against those licensed intruders into the secrets of the female body and mind, the doctors (p. 582).[54] Shirley's vision of her 'madness' is of a highly contagious disease, that will affect all males around (apart from her chosen master).

The fear that her transgression of the bounds of social decorum will provoke the loss of male self-possession, arises from the same guilt expressed in the image she paints for Caroline of the mermaid luring men to their doom, 'Temptress-terror! monstrous likeness of ourselves' (p. 276). Like Jane Eyre, who was haunted by the image of Bertha, Shirley is troubled by images of female monstrosity, rampant sexual energy that turns to violence. The notion of contagion, furthermore, introduces once more associations with prostitution, the ever-present underworld of female sexuality, and the pollution carried by women in the marketplace. In the event that she can no longer retain decorum, Shirley makes Louis promise that he will kill her: 'if I give trouble, with your own hand administer to me a strong narcotic: such a sure dose of laudanum as shall leave no mistake' (p. 582). Louis is to ensure that she makes, in fine novelistic convention, the traditional exit of the fallen woman. Through her confession, however, which renders her, in Louis' eyes, the apotheosis of the feminine, 'nervous and womanish' and 'childish', she commits herself to the requisite control of one man, and thus avoids this end. The stifling she chooses belongs to that other strand of novelistic tradition: suffocation by marriage.

The disappointment of Shirley's fall is all the more intense since she has been given, effortlessly, the wealth and power the struggling workers crave. The bastion of patriarchy remains impervious to her assault, however. Like Caroline she is consistently placed in a child-like role, and excluded from the political sphere.[55] She may carry a brace of pistols, but her position on the night of the attack on the mill is, like that of Caroline, one of voiceless exclusion, on pain of masculine scorn. Their position on the hillside is emblematic of their purity and essential superiority. They are distinguished alike from the lewd women who participate in social unrest, spreading corruption around them, and from the men of both classes who succumb to their baser animal instincts: 'the fighting animal was roused in every one of those men there struggling together, and was for the time quite paramount above the rational human being' (p. 388). As women frequently discover, however, the ideological conferment of superiority usually carries with it effective social disempowerment. Caroline and Shirley retain their self-control, and even occupy a position associated with power, for they were able to 'see without being seen' (p. 389), but this has little impact on their political marginality. Shirley attempts to use this power of illegibility for all its worth, taunting Robert the following day with her knowledge: '"Ah! friend, you may search my countenance, but you cannot read it."' Caroline too, she insists, '"though gentle, tractable, and candid enough, is still perfectly capable of defying even Mr. Moore's penetration"' (p. 408). Compared with the gravity of the political struggle, the victory seems a very hollow one; achieving little more than the momentary puzzlement of Robert and in no way affecting the balance of power. Shirley, for all her wealth and land, is reduced to the level of spectator in the crucial class conflict, forced to scrabble for an illusion of power in the alternate arena of gender relations.

As in Brontë's previous works, gender struggles are focused on the terrain of bodily legibility, a realm where, as this text forcefully reveals, women are doubly disadvantaged. Caroline's humiliation at the hands of Mrs Yorke, who claims to be able to read the secret of her 'lackadaisical' features, is paralleled in a similar scene where Mr Yorke attempts to confound Shirley when she dares to enter into political debate with him. Yorke listens unmoved to language he would not have borne from a man, reading her opinions solely as expression of romantic attachment: 'if he wished to avenge himself for her severity, he knew the means lay in his power: a word, he believed, would suffice to tame and silence her, to cover her frank forehead with the rosy shadow of shame' (p. 415). Shirley, as woman, is to be doubly excluded: from the riots of the night before, and from political discussion of their consequences. Her words pass unheard as this defender of the workers' cause enters with zest into the project of her humiliation. Mr Yorke, prefiguring Louis' desires, wishes to master and 'tame' Shirley, turning her from political adversary into an object for his erotic pleasure. Whilst the workers can only be silenced by Moore's 'gift of tongues' – the soldiers rifles – women can be rendered mute and abject through their own internalized subjection to male norms of femininity. Yorke fails in his bid for power, yet only because he has not been able to identify the true object of her romantic concern. He has, nonetheless, effectively closed Shirley out of the realm of political debate, and locked her into a power battle where all her energies are to be dissipated in defending her inner 'secret' from the masterful male gaze.

Women, Brontë suggests, can have no such answering power of the gaze which can wield such public humiliation. The most they are permitted is a covert glance:

Men rarely like such of their fellows as read their inward nature too clearly and truly. It is good for women, especially, to be endowed with a soft blindness: to have mild, dim eyes, that never penetrate below the surface of things – that take all for what it seems: thousands, knowing this, keep their eyelids drooped, on system; but the most downcast glance has its loophole, through which it can, on occasion, take its sentinel-survey of life. (pp. 306–7)

The passage draws attention to a necessary, systematic, duplicity on the part of women. In order to survive, women must manipulate their surface appearance so as to suggest they are mere reflectors of male meanings. Connotations of imprisonment are carried by the loophole image, but also of warfare, where women, in their enclosed tower, looking out on their exposed enemy, are in a position of strength. Yet Brontë herself is also wary of this feminine power of concealment. She wishes to suggest, with Shirley, that men do not read women 'in a true light' (p. 395), and that male readings, for example, of the 'language' of Caroline's 'expressive' face and 'pliant' form are simply mirror images of their own desires (p. 86). She remains, however, caught up within the ideological confines of her day, unable to find a formula for expressing female illegibility and concealment which does not simultaneously evoke the dreaded image of the wily mermaid luring men to their doom, whose beautiful upper form conceals her fishy tail.

The male need to render woman transparent is revealed in Louis' insistent externalizing of Shirley's psyche. Women, it seems, must police not only the expressivity of their face and body, but even the disposal of their possessions. Shirley's desk provides Louis with a 'loophole of character', which will enable him, he believes, to make himself master of her inner secrets: 'a whole garment sometimes covers meagreness and malformation; through a rent sleeve, a fair round arm may be revealed' (p. 595). Voyeurism is here linked to violence in the sexually charged metaphor of the rent sleeve. His reading of Shirley from her possessions, 'the pure kid of this little glove . . . the fresh, unsullied satin of the bag' (p. 595), suggests a complete conflation of the female psyche and sexuality, and of masculine knowledge and sexual mastery. Brontë's representation of the male fantasy structure suggests an overwhelming fear of masculine dominance through surveillance: no matter how far the woman tries to escape her allotted role, to enter into male spheres of social activity and control, she will be reduced by the male gaze to an inner core of sexuality. The only course of defence open is to ensure that the desk is always kept clean, the satin bag 'unsullied'. Brontë's desire to empower her heroines is undercut by her need to confirm their expressive purity.

In the concluding sections of the novel, devoted to chronicling the 'taming' of Shirley, the women, like the workers, are restored to their rightful (lowly) place in the social hierarchy. For many modern readers the ending of *Shirley* is disappointing, even 'unbelievable'.[56] Such disappointment is a measure of the subversive potential conveyed earlier in the work. The neat conclusion, with its symmetrical pairing off of heterosexual couples belies previous troubling of these gender boundaries. Virtually each permutation of this foursome has presented itself at one stage as a possibility. Shirley shifts between female and masculine lover of Caroline. In her jealousy and anger at

Robert's greater hold on Caroline she invokes her masculine role: 'I have pistols, and can use them' (p. 294). For her, Robert is the 'black eclipse', the 'Troubler'. Caroline and Shirley weave a fantasy of female communion focused on the feminized landscape of Nunnwood, where, in a deep dell, lie the ruins of a nunnery. In this Edenic world of female love, the fall, initiation into heterosexual love, would constitute a *loss* of knowledge: Nature would then veil herself from their eyes (p. 239).

Brontë's most overt celebration of female potentiality and alternative knowledge comes in Shirley's rewriting of the triple authorities of the Bible, Milton and classical legend in her inspiring vision of Eve, mother of all men, whose breast 'yielded the daring which could contend with Omnipotence' (p. 360). Originating force is denied to masculinity and located in this symbolic figure of womanhood who becomes an icon of political struggle. Torture and deprivation, the sting of the scorpion or the ravages of the vulture, will be endured triumphantly, and womanhood will eventually bring forth the new millenium. Caroline too joins in this challenge to political and religious orthodoxy. Her deft retranscription turns St Paul's famous proscription on female speech into a proto-feminist text: woman is to be permitted to speak out and teach as much as she wishes whilst the male is enjoined to hold his peace (p. 371). The dream is quickly quashed, however: Brontë underscores the unattainability of the girls' visions by interrupting them with the alternate vision of 'martial scarlet', heralding the coming bloodshed, and the religious and political chauvinism of Joe Scott. The male community of the novel band together to enforce a unified interpretation of a single text: women's subordination.

Brontë persistently offers radical visions of female potentiality in this novel, only to then expose the illusory nature of such dreams. Caroline finds her long-lost mother, and is immediately entangled in her sexual traumas. Shirley and Caroline pledge sisterhood, outside of the sphere of male influence, but Shirley then concludes their conversation by glorifying man as 'the first of created things' and articulating her own bondage to the sexual power dialectic of domination and submission: 'the higher above me, so much the better: it degrades to stoop – it is glorious to look up' (p. 246). Far from existing outside the male order, Shirley and Caroline act towards each other as rigorous guardians of its edicts. Shirley polices Caroline during the riot, ensuring that she does not 'make a spectacle' of herself, and subjecting her to the 'jesting, gibing laugh' usually reserved for male ridicule (p. 384). Caroline for her part not only triumphs over Shirley in near sadistic fashion once she has grasped the secret of her sexual desire, but is also quick to express male doubt about female capacity. To Shirley's idea that she should write an article revealing the falsity of male views of women, Caroline responds with the damning comment 'you could not write cleverly enough; you don't know enough; you are not learned, Shirley' (p. 396). Shirley herself had responded to Caroline's thoughts on Cowper and Rousseau with the reiterated question 'Who told you this, I ask? Did Moore?' (p. 255). Both women are quick to imprison each other in the straitjacket of male expectation.

On each of these latter occasions the focus of their conversation is writing, a subject which remains for Brontë a peculiarly conflicted one. Caroline does not presume to write herself, but stands, nonetheless, in judgment on Cowper's character as unveiled in his work. To write out of autobiographical pain is to render oneself unloveable, revealing a character 'unnatural, unhealthy, repulsive' (p. 255). Such a violation of social decorum is 'unhealthy' in a man, but doubly proscribed for a woman. Whilst the crippled Henry is enjoined by Shirley to write, 'that you may give your soul its natural release' (p. 524), such a realm of 'natural release' is not open to women. Shirley possesses an 'inborn delight' in her veins, a 'free dower of Nature' 'not to be reached or ravished by human agency' (p. 437). Yet if this enclave of nature is impervious to male ravishment, it also remains outside Shirley's own grasp. The narrator suggests that if Shirley had 'a little more of the organ of Acquisitiveness in her head' she would write and 'thus possess what she was enabled to create' (p. 438). Self-possession is precisely, however, what the heroines of this novel are not allowed to attain. As in the medical models of the female economy, female energy or flow remains unthreatening to the degree that it remains uncontrolled. Shirley's purity is guaranteed by her inability to harness or possess her own energies. The fishy tail remains submerged. Unable to attain self-possession she seeks self-unity in the polar extreme: total self-submission.

Language and writing, the only weapons open to women socially to express their dissent, act finally as the vehicles of their own defeat. As in *The Professor*, the taming of the women is enacted through their acquisition of their master's language. Both Caroline and Shirley are reduced to the state of a 'docile child' as they recite their French lessons at their lover's command (p. 107). Shirley's eager recitation enacts her own annihilation of difference: 'she reproduced his manner, his pronunciation, his expression' (p. 558). Emptying herself of all content, Shirley not only mirrors, but, in her appropriation of tone and expression, actively embodies, the male stance. Louis' linguistic domination of Shirley is powerfully figured in the rewriting of her revolutionary Titan visions into the crawling subservience of the French text, 'La Première Femme Savante', which is appropriated and recited by Louis. In this French text, which Shirley now significantly terms 'that rubbish', Humanity, here figured as a woman, is no longer a powerful originating force but is haunted by a sense of insufficiency and waste until 'taken' by her bridegroom, Genius, who speaks in the voice of Louis: 'Unhumbled, I can take what is mine' (p. 547).

The decline of the women and the rise of male linguistic dominance is marked structurally in the text by a shift in narrative voice and genre. The impersonal narrative voice is repeatedly displaced by that of Louis Moore, whether in internal monologue or through the pages of his notebook. Although critics have had difficulty with this section of the novel, castigating Brontë for her apparent descent into celebrations of male mastery, it is important to bear in mind that what we are offered here are Louis' fantasies and interpretations of events. From the moment that Shirley gives up 'self-possession' and 'confesses' to Louis, she starts to fade even further from the text. The crucial proposal scene is recounted solely in Louis' words, graphically portraying the Victorian male's fear of female secrecy and self-containment. Louis bars Shirley's way, ordering her to speak the word he demands: '"what I *must* and *will* hear; what you dare not now suppress"' (p. 709). The fantasy of violent extortion, of humiliating the woman by forcing an avowal of hidden sexual desire, completes the necessary destruction of female opposition. Shirley is reduced to a pining captive whose only power lies in her feeble attempts to once more baffle Louis' penetration.

Set alongside the decline of Shirley is the illness of Robert Moore. In symmetrical parallel, all four protagonists have been threatened by illness. Louis' was of shortest duration. Arising from a brief loss of confidence when Shirley is courted by Sir Philip Nunnely, it is soon healed by the visit of Shirley proffering, suggestively, a 'rich cluster' of

grapes, and offering to bring him "'dreams of all you most desire'"
(p. 543). Louis' responding assertion of illegibility – "'my character is
not, perhaps, quite as legible to you as a page of the last new novel
might be'" – marks his reinstatement to a position of self-containment
and control (p. 543). Robert's illness, by contrast, is externally
inflicted. He is shot in retribution by the 'mad' Antinomian weaver,
Mike Hartley, whose visions of the symbolic red and white forces of
the army, silently heading for Briarfield, are introduced in the first
chapter as intimations of 'bloodshed and civil conflict' (p. 22). Whilst
Hartley's role as 'visionary' automatically associates him with the
female cause, the context of the murder makes abundantly clear the
connection between gender and labour exploitation. Robert has just
returned from running down the ringleaders of the attack on the mill,
and seeing them safely transported, shipped off to an exile which
parallels that held out to the 'surplus woman'. His conversation with
Yorke, however, focuses not on the workers, but on his relations with
Shirley. Robert's confession of his mercenary proposals to Shirley
draws from Mr Yorke the equivalent confession concerning his life's
idol, Mary Cave. If he had been "'secure of her affection, certain of
her constancy . . . the odds are, I should have left her!'" (p. 615). In
the marriage market, as in the labour market, value comes only from
scarcity, from unattainability. As a reflection on the relationship
between power and desire, whether personal or political, the anecdote
strikes a chilling note, offering an explanatory model which encompasses
only too well the ready laying off of workers and the fluctuations of
male sexual desire. Robert's confused response makes the connection
between political and sexual economy. His proposal, however, of
even greater paternalism, is met by the requisite response: attempted
murder.

Like Rochester, Robert is to be subject to a symbolic truncation of
power. Whilst Shirley fears the intrusion of male surgeons, Robert is
given in charge to the terror of the male imaginary, the tyrannical
Mrs Horsfall who beats him, and starves him, reducing him to a 'mere
ghost' (p. 663), a 'poor, pale, grim phantom . . . more pitiable than
formidable' (p. 688). In Martin Yorke's judgment, the triumvirate of
Mrs Horsfall, Hortense and Mrs Yorke mean 'to make either an idiot
or a maniac of him, and take out a commission of lunacy' (p. 674). Yet
all the insistent parallelism to Caroline's case seems little more than a
comic rerun. The tone of the narrative changes, indeed, at this point
as we enter into the structure of the adolescent Martin's fantasies. As

he casts around for ideas to add another chapter to the romance he has commenced, with Caroline and Robert as his principals, the narrator intervenes to add that 'he did not yet know how many commenced life-romances are doomed never to get beyond the first – or, at most, the second chapter' (p. 667). Martin is writing an impossible romance. From now on Brontë insistently draws attention to the constructed nature of her text, undercutting any claims to realism. What we are offered is a mere fairy tale of an adolescent male imagination, created by a boy whose investment in the project bears an unnerving resemblance to the adult male characters' will to dominance. Martin constructs his plots and stories with a sadistic skill, always wanting to see 'how far' Caroline will go (p. 675).

The voice of male fantasy dominates the concluding sections of the text as Brontë abdicates responsibility for its creation. Following the defeat of Shirley, the novel is brought to an end with almost unseemly haste. The final chapter, 'The Winding Up', ostentatiously draws attention to its own fictionality. The curates are paraded one by one on the stage and their fates pronounced, by an author who comments all the while on her own strategies and adherence to convention: 'There! I think the varnish has been put on very nicely' (p. 723). The disconsolate Shirley, 'vanquished and restricted' (p. 730) is given a brief glance, but the conclusion itself is reserved for the final chapter of male fantasy. Economically secure once more, with the repeal of the Orders in Council, Robert enlarges his stock of goods by lifting Caroline off her pedestal and claiming her as 'mine'. Bales rather than female bodies are to be exported; the return to free flow in the cloth markets has a direct impact on the marriage market. Caroline embraces with alacrity the newly-opened position offered to her, her happiness standing in symbolically for that of the workers for whom, 'work abounded, wages rose: the good time seemed come' (p. 729). We are warned, however, that these hopes 'might be delusive' (p. 729). Just as the prospect of future prosperity for the workers is destabilized by our knowledge of those male bodies who have been forcibly transported, and by our historical awareness of the coming of the 'hungry forties', so the question of whether the women will be happy in their future marriages is also put in doubt. The symmetrical pairings of the two couples are to be presided over, significantly, by that implacable opponent to marriage, and dire prophet of the dangers of masculine sexuality, Mrs. Pryor, improbably transformed into dear 'Mamma'.

Her very presence necessarily calls into question the possibility of marital contentment for a woman.

Robert offers for Caroline's delectation a vision of total economic and social dominance on the part of Louis and himself; they will 'divide Briarfield parish betwixt us' (p. 736). His picture of economic and domestic paternalism is complete, celebrating, as Eagleton has pointed out, the union of the rising industrial magnates, and the landed gentry.[57] Whilst the lower-class woman, Mrs Gill, is permitted to mete out portions 'till the first pay day', Caroline and Shirley are to be restricted to running a Sunday school. Robert's description of the destruction he will wreak on the countryside, rooting up the copse (scene of Shirley and Caroline's vision of an alternate female society) and destroying the wild ravine, strikes even Caroline's ears as an ominous note. His image of the 'firm, broad, black, sooty road, bedded with the cinders from my mill' (p. 737), which sounds for all the world like a description of the path to hell, is reinvoked in the final paragraphs, where the narrator once more takes control of the text:

I suppose Robert Moore's prophecies were, partially, at least, fulfilled. The other day I passed up the Hollow, which tradition says was once green, and lone, and wild; and there I saw the manufacturer's day-dreams embodied in substantial stone and brick and ashes – the cinder-black highway, the cottages, and the cottage-gardens; there I saw a mighty mill, and a chimney, ambitious as the tower of Babel.(p. 739)

The reference to the tower of Babel, which recalls the 'confusion of tongues' of those 'presumptuous Babylonish masons' (p. 46), the curates, in the opening chapter, confirms that this is indeed a fallen world. Attention is focused on the relationship between the structures of fantasy and the operation of social power. The embodiment in 'substantial stone', of the manufacturer's day-dreams ensures the vanquishment of the alternative visions of the women and workers. In place of bread they have been offered stone. The dominant feeling is one of loss: loss of the identities of Shirley and Caroline who are reduced to 'Mrs Louis' and 'Mrs Robert', loss of the natural spaces associated with femininity, and loss of the alternative reality signalled by the world of fairy. All are erased by the ruthless onslaught of phallic grime.

CHAPTER 10

Villette: 'The surveillance of a sleepless eye'

Brontë's final novel, *Villette*, represents her most explicit engagement with Victorian psychological theory and medical practice. The narrator, Lucy Snowe, is subject, seemingly, to hallucinations, undergoes a total nervous collapse, and discusses her symptoms at great length with her doctor. Whereas Brontë had distanced Jane Eyre from the mania of her 'darkest double',[1] Bertha, and preserved Caroline Helstone from the unbecoming display of 'weariness ferment[ing] . . . to phrenzy' she creates in Lucy Snowe a figure whose psychological stability is permanently in question. In probing the inner processes of mind of a subject who defines herself as 'constitutionally nervous' (p. 531), Brontë has chosen to focus not on the flamboyant extreme of 'mania', but on the more subtle area of neurosis. The reader, entering the world of *Villette*, is forced to relinquish cherished assumptions of rational order. Lucy as narrator teases and bewilders her audience, contradicting herself, withholding vital information, and confounding, as in the notorious open ending, biographical fact with readerly desire. Her commitment to evasion and displacement is articulated in the very title of her book, which gives precedence not to selfhood but to place. Through the autobiographical account of 'shadow-like' Lucy, Brontë both explores and interrogates contemporary theories of mental alienation.

In *Shirley*, Brontë had examined how social and political issues could impinge directly on the life of the body and mind. *Villette* takes further this exploration of the interaction between the social and psychological economies, focusing this time on the personal and institutional operations of surveillance. In this, her seemingly most inward text, Brontë brings to the fore the social framework which had remained implicit in her earlier dramas of psychological penetration.

The text of *Villette* is dominated by the practice of surveillance. The constant self-surveillance and concealment which marks Lucy's own narrative account, is figured socially in the institutional practices of those who surround her. All characters spy on others, attempting, covertly, to read and interpret the external signs of faces, minds and actions. Madame Beck runs her school according to the watchwords, '"Surveillance", "espionage"' (p. 99); M. Paul reads Lucy's countenance on her arrival in Villette, and later studies her through his 'magic lattice'; and Père Silas focuses on her 'the surveillance of a sleepless eye' – the Roman Catholic confessional (p. 592). Lucy is subjected to educational, professional and religious surveillance. Each observer tries to read her inner self through the interpretation of outer signs. This practice takes its most authoritative form in the narrative in the medical judgments of Dr John.

After Lucy's first encounter with the nun, as she is attempting to read Dr. John's letter, he in turn tries to 'read' her: '"I look on you now from a professional point of view, and I read, perhaps, all you would conceal – in your eye, which is curiously vivid and restless, in your cheek, which the blood has forsaken; in your hand, which you cannot steady"' (p. 355). Dr John directs onto Lucy the gaze of medical authority, calmly confident of his ability to define inner experience from outer signs. His verdict is distinguished by his insistence on his professional status, and by his unshakeable belief that, no matter how hard Lucy might try to hide from his gaze, he would penetrate through to her innermost secrets. The rhetoric of unveiling and penetrating the truth, so prevalent in nineteenth-century science, is here located as a discourse of gendered, social power: male science unveils female nature. All those who subject Lucy to surveillance present her with interpretations of her mind and character, but only Dr John claims the authority of science for his interpretation (though M. Paul, to a lesser extent also assumes this power when he offers a phrenological reading of her skull). Against the descriptive labels offered by Madame Beck and Père Silas, Dr John actually presents a whole language of analysis and a theory of psychological functioning. His diagnosis on this occasion is that it is 'a matter of the nerves', a 'case of spectral illusion . . . following on and resulting from long-continued mental conflict' (pp. 357, 358). The terms of his analysis are drawn directly from contemporary medical science where the subject of 'spectral illusion' proved a constant source of debate.[2] Against more visionary explanations of the nun, who functions as a site of crucial interpretative conflict in the text, he offers a materialist explanation based on the functioning of the nervous system. On one level, the text falsifies Dr John's materialist explanation by presenting an even more material cause – the physical presence of the Count de Hamal masquerading as a nun. The authority of science is not, however, thereby erased from the text. The very inadequacy of the 'literal' explanation, indeed, feeds further speculation into the question of the relationship between body and mind which functions as a sub-text in the novel. As readers, interpreting the signs of Lucy's discourse, we are constantly tempted by the text into re-enacting the role of Dr John, as we attempt to pierce through the external linguistic signs of the narrative to a concealed unity lying below. The text, however, frustrates all such quests for a hidden unitary meaning, deliberately undermining the social and psychological presuppositions which underlie such a quest.

In focusing interpretative attention in the novel on Lucy's 'sightings' of the nun, Brontë is deliberately raising the issue of Lucy's psychological stability. Hallucinations, as Brontë was clearly aware, were classically regarded as signs of madness. Lucy herself invokes this mode of explanation on her first glimpse of the nun, challenging the reader to say 'I was nervous, or mad' (p. 351). Despite Lucy's stated resistance to Dr John's system of analysis, she herself constantly employs contemporary scientific language to describe her own psychological functioning. The term 'nervous system', which she distances herself from as alien and technical when used by Dr John, has already figured largely in her narrative (p. 261). Other terms from contemporary scientific discourse, such as 'monomania', 'hypochondria' and 'hysteria' are also employed with precision in her analysis. Scientific language in the novel is not confined to Dr John's specific diagnoses – the imposition of 'male reason' on a largely Gothic text – it permeates Lucy's narrative construction of her self.

The nun who becomes subject to Dr John's medical gaze is of a very different species from that which had haunted the Gothic novel. The intervening years had witnessed the rise of psychiatric medicine: doctors from henceforth claimed exclusive right to define and treat aberrations of the mind. Under the principles of moral management, the insane were no longer to be sharply distinguished from the sane, but, correlatively, no one could now rest assured of their own sanity. All had to remain vigilant against the momentary slippage of the social mask. As in the economic philosophy of the period, self-control was the watchword of the moral managers. In the medical and popular press of the period, however, one can trace increasing numbers of articles and stories devoted to explorations of dreams, apparitions, and the operations of the unconscious mind, which seem to defy control. The emphasis on an individual's necessary responsibility for action was coupled with an overwhelming sense that control was at every moment liable to be overthrown.

Social fears of an unstoppable rise in nervous disease were at their height in the mid-century. The medical and popular press were full of alarmist reports of an exponential rise in cases of insanity, and the question of how to draw the subtle dividing line between sanity and insanity received frequent press attention.[3] Such social fears and anxieties were condensed in heightened form in the Brontë household where the Reverend Brontë anxiously annotated his medical Bible, Thomas John Graham's *Domestic Medicine*, with his fears regarding his family's nervous diseases and potential insanity. In naming Dr John Graham Bretton after her father's treasured medical tome, Brontë was giving embodiment to the system of medical surveillance which had governed her own life.

Although Bronte claimed that '*Villette* touches on no matter of public interest' her actions on completing the novel suggest another story.[4] She went down to London, resolved to see 'the *real* rather than the *decorative* side of Life'. In a letter to Ellen Nussey she records that 'I have been over two prisons ancient and modern – Newgate and Pentonville – also the Bank, the Exchange, the Foundling Hospital, – and today if all be well – I go with Dr Forbes to see Bethlehem Hospital.'[5] Her definition of the 'real' is highly significant. It encompasses the centres of financial control, together with the institutional structures designed to control the marginalized groups within society: the criminal, the poor and the insane. Such a visiting list reveals a marked preoccupation with the mechanisms and operation of institutional power. *Villette*, indeed, with its obsessional concern with surveillance, fits almost too perfectly into the paradigm of nineteenth-century social control outlined by Foucault in *Discipline and Punish*. The ideal of Bentham's Panopticon, where inmates are trapped, isolated in their cells, subject always to the gaze of authority, without themselves being able to see, might describe the underlying nightmare of *Villette* from which Lucy is for ever trying to escape. If Brontë did indeed visit Bethlehem hospital with her illustrious medical guide, she would have found a microcosm of Victorian society: social and psychological ordering was achieved through constant surveillance, and its psychological reflex, the internalization of social controls.

As Lucy constructs her narrative, it is she, in the initial stages of her history, who is the principle surveillant, subjecting the passionate excesses of her alter ego, Polly, to the scrutiny of what, she insists, is her calm, and hence decorous, gaze (although her claims to possess a 'cooler temperament' are immediately undermined by her vision of Polly 'haunting' a room, and by the pressure of her emotional identification: 'I wished she would utter some hysterical cry, so that *I* might get relief and be at ease' p. 18, my emphasis). On her entry into Villette, however, it is the inner passions of Lucy herself that become subject to the calm gaze of institutional authority. Her employment at the pensionnat is based on M. Paul's reading of her head. To Lucy, reading *his* brow, (a reading she is not allowed to articulate), it 'seemed to say that he meant to see through me, and that a veil would be no veil for him' (p. 90). Like Dr John, in his later medical diagnosis, M. Paul tries to look beyond the surface sign to all that Lucy would conceal below. His reading is significant in its indeterminacy: he leaves it as an open question whether good or evil predominate in her nature. This is not a physiognomical reading, but a phrenological diagnosis of latent potential which reinforces economic ideologies of self-help. M. Paul's reading inaugurates the system of surveillance into which Lucy has entered, and reinforces its underlying central code: if Lucy is to succeed, it must be by a process of *self*-control, subduing her 'evil' propensities, and encouraging the good.

The 'system of management' employed by Madame Beck in running her school is linked by Lucy to the practices of political and industrial control (and Madame Beck herself to masculine figures of authority). Lucy observes that Madame Beck, 'ought to have swayed a nation . . . In her own single person, she could have comprised the duties of a first minister and a superintendent of police' (p. 102). The industrial parallel is suggested by her reference to Madame Beck's 'system of managing and regulating this mass of machinery' (p. 99). Like Dr John in his 'materialist' diagnosis of Lucy's experience, Madame Beck reduces her pupils to material elements, cogs within a machine. Her motives, in Lucy's eyes, are in keeping with industrial practice: 'interest was the master-key of madame's nature – the mainspring of her motives – the alpha and omega of her life' (p. 101).

Throughout her surveillance, Madame Beck herself remains totally inscrutable and impervious; she constructs a machine which seems to function independently of any personal intervention, operating rather on the participants' internalization of the mechanisms of control. Lucy, inscribing in herself these institutional constraints, allows all her actions to be dictated by the sense that she might be overlooked. Thus at one stage she even invests inanimate nature with the qualities of a spy: 'the eyes of the flowers had gained vision, and the knots in the tree-boles listened like secret ears' (p. 161). The internalization of the principles of surveillance breeds a paranoia verging on neurosis. Lucy's relationship to surveillance is not only passive, however, she actively supports its operation. On coming across Madame Beck searching her clothes, she refuses to confront her. Having invested herself in a system based on concealment and disguise, she, like Madame Beck, can ill afford exposure.

The third form of surveillance to which Lucy is subject is that of the Roman Catholic church. Her impulse to confession – the voluntary revelation of the secrets of the inner self – represents for Lucy the nadir of her mental state. Worn out by suffering, product of her internalization of the social contradictions of the female role, she sacrifices the last vestiges of her autonomy, thus opening herself up to the continued intervention of both medical and religious authorities in her life (and precipitating her entry into the 'very safe asylum' offered by the Brettons) (p. 244). Père Silas proves even more assiduous in his 'treatment' than Dr John. From that moment on, as he later informs her, he had not 'for a day lost sight of you, nor for an hour failed to take in you a rooted interest' (p. 571). He envisages her 'passed under the discipline of Rome, moulded by her high training, inoculated with her salutary doctrines' (the manuscript originally read 'sane doctrines') (p. 571). With its aim of total dominion over the mind through the discipline of its sane or salutary doctrines, Lucy's Roman Catholic church replicates precisely the alienists' system of moral management of the insane.

The perceived threat of the church to Lucy does not end with her confession. As her relationship with Dr John is subject always to the scrutiny of Madame Beck 'glid[ing] ghost-like through the house, watching and spying everywhere' (p. 100), so her relationship with M. Paul is attended by that 'ghostly troubler' (p. 600), Père Silas, and the threat of the confessional: 'We were under the surveillance of a sleepless eye: Rome watched jealously her son through that mystic lattice at which I had knelt once, and to which M. Emmanuel drew nigh month by month – the sliding panel of the confessional' (p. 592). Lucy's use of the term 'magic lattice' echoes, significantly, M. Paul's description of his 'post of observation', his window overlooking the garden, where he sits and 'reads' 'female human nature': '"Ah, magic lattice! what miracles of discovery hast thou wrought!"'' (pp. 526, 528). The 'magic lattice' forms another medium for the male gaze to penetrate through to the recesses of the female psyche, furnishing information which is then appropriated to judge and censor, in accordance with male definitions of female decorum (M. Paul rejects Zelie St Pierre on the basis of his observations). Lucy herself, M. Paul observes, wants 'checking, regulating, and keeping down'. She needs 'watching, and watching over' (p. 526). Lucy vehemently repudiates M. Paul's methods: '"To study the human heart thus, is to banquet secretly and sacrilegiously on Eve's apples. I wish you were a Protestant"' (p. 530). The phrase 'Eve's apples', used in connection with the voyeuristic practice of spying on women, takes on a decisive sexual charge. The implicit connection, made throughout the book, between Roman Catholicism and the threatened exposure, and suppression, of female sexuality is here brought to the surface.

The anti-Catholicism of Brontë's earlier texts is explicitly fore-grounded in this novel which was written at the time of extreme anti-Catholic agitation.[6] The local newpapers in Leeds were full of tales of 'papal aggression', and fears that 'Romish encroachments are approaching stealthily' and will soon reimpose 'an intolerable civil and spiritual bondage upon us'.[7] The case of the heiress, Miss Augusta Talbot, who after being placed in a convent, then decided to leave all her money to the Roman Catholic Church, offered further cause for outcry against the intrigues of a Church whose aims, it was asserted, were to mould and subdue the soul into 'perpetual subjection'.[8] All this agitation had a peculiar force in Leeds where the 'Perverts of Saint Saviours' were reintroducing Catholic ritual and confession, under the guidance of John Newman. The *Leeds Intelligencer* went overboard on its reporting of the libel trial in which the Protestant turned Catholic, John Newman, was called upon to defend his accusation of gross immorality and debauchery against the ex-Catholic priest, turned Protestant, Dr Achilli. The paper, only too willing, normally, to trumpet any allegation of sexual misconduct in the Roman Catholic Church, reserves its horror this time for the activities of the Church in persuading women to confess to such 'ineffaceable infamy', and for pursuing Dr Achilli with 'the unsleeping eye of Romish jealousy and vengeance'. In Brontë's text, this 'unsleeping eye' is manifest both in the workings of the confessional, and also in the malign pursuit of Lucy and M. Paul by Père Silas and the aptly named Malevola. Just as in *The Professor*, where the move to Belgium helped Crimsworth resolve, by displacement, his problems of gender and class identity, so in *Villette* Lucy's worst fears can be projected outwards onto an alien culture, against which she can then assert her own fierce Protestantism. Her real enemy, however, remains not these extreme projections of Catholic surveillance and intrigue, which modulate into fairy tale form, but the equivalent forces of surveillance offered by the attractive, seemingly benign, Dr John.

The force of Anti-Catholic sentiment in *Villette* is clearly tied, as in the local newspaper agitation, to a nexus of sexual fear. The school legend of the nun 'buried alive, for some sin against her vow' (p. 148) establishes a chain of association between nuns, ghosts, and sexuality which reverberates throughout the novel. Lucy, burying her precious letters from Dr John above the nun's grave, is clearly associating the unspecified 'sin' with sexual transgression. Her 'sightings' of the nun occur, significantly, at moments of heightened sexual tension, whilst the ghostly pursuit to which she is subject seems to embody externally her own activities of self-suppression. Lucy's violent antagonism to Roman Catholicism, treated so often by critics as an intrusion of Bronte's personal prejudice, not germane to the narrative, stems from this associative sexual charge. The intensity of her response is signalled initially by her seemingly excessive reactions to the 'lecture pieuse': 'it made me so burning hot, and my temples and my heart and my wrist throbbed so fast, and my sleep afterwards was so broken with excitement, that I could sit no longer' (p. 163). The description of the content of the tales helps explain Lucy's extreme response: they contain 'the dread boasts of confessors, who had wickedly abused their office, trampling to deep degradation high-born ladies, making of countesses and princesses the most tormented slaves under the sun' (p. 163). It is this 'abuse of office' which Lucy most fears: the subjection of the self to a male authority consequent on the revelation of the inner self. The tales, 'nightmares of oppression, privation, and agony', offer an analogue of her own narrative, as she strives to keep herself hidden from the prying eyes of those who surround her.

The explicitly sexual nature of this revelation and subjection is suggested by the one tale specifically named, that of 'Conrad and Elizabeth of Hungary'. Brontë's source for this tale was Charles Kingsley's verse drama, *The Saint's Tragedy; or, The True Story of Elizabeth of Hungary* (1848). In a letter to Elizabeth Gaskell in 1851, Brontë records that her 'eyes rained' as she read this tale which offered, she believed, 'Deep truths . . . truths that stir a peculiar pity, a compassion hot with wrath and bitter with pain. This is no poet's dream: we know that such things *have* been done; that minds *have* been thus subjected, and lives thus laid waste'.[9] The process of subjection described arises directly from Elizabeth's internalization of the 'Manichean contempt' for sexuality embodied, for Kingsley, in Roman Catholicism. Elizabeth is found lying on the floor on her wedding night, covered with self-inflicted lacerations, unable to reconcile her sexual love for her husband with the teachings of the church. Burdened by these social contradictions, she later turns to the priest Conrad 'to save this little heart – The burden of self-rule', thus sacrificing the self-control prized by the Victorians as the index of sanity.[10] Conrad's reponses to her are shown to be an unsavoury mixture of sexual lust, worldly ambition, and crude love of power: 'She calls herself my slave, with such an air/ As speaks her queen, not slave: that shall be looked to – /She must be pinioned'.[11] The shadowy fears which lie behind Lucy's attempts to render herself illegible to male authoritative eyes are given explicit form in this work.

The parallels between *The Saint's Tragedy* and *Villette* are reinforced by comments in Bronte's letters in which she speaks of Elizabeth and Lucy in remarkably similar terms. Of Elizabeth she observes:

We see throughout (I *think*) that Elizabeth has not, and never had, a mind perfectly sane. From the time that she was what she herself, in the exaggeration of her humility, calls 'an idiot girl', to the hour when she lay moaning in visions on her dying bed, a slight craze runs through her whole existence. This is good: this is true. A sound mind, a healthy intellect, would have dashed the priest power to the wall . . . Only a mind weak with some fatal flaw *could* have been influenced as was this poor saint's. But what anguish – what struggles![12]

Her comments on Lucy, written whilst she was still in the midst of producing *Villette*, occur in response to observations made by W. S. Williams:

You say that she may be thought morbid and weak, unless the history of her life be more fully given. I consider that she *is* both morbid and weak at times; her character sets up no pretensions to unmixed strength, and anybody living her life would necessarily become morbid. It was no impetus of healthy feeling which urged her to the confessional, for instance; it was the semi-delirium of solitary grief and sickness.[13]

In both cases the weakness or morbidity (a term which in the nineteenth century designated specific mental disease) of the protagonist's mind is demonstrated by her subjection to the mind of a priest. There is a crucial difference, however: whereas Elizabeth's morbidity is assigned to an inherent mental flaw, Lucy's is attributed to the pressures of social circumstances. Insanity, Brontë here suggests, can be socially created.

The threat of confession for Lucy lay in the enforced articulation of that which should be kept hidden even from her own consciousness. In her excessive commitment to concealment, from her self, her readers and the external world, Lucy has fallen victim to the Victorian social code which stressed that women retained their necessary 'innocence' only if they remained ignorant of sexual desire. Thus, against all seeming evidence to the contrary, Lucy insists at one stage in her narrative that she never held 'warmer feelings' towards Dr John. Lucy has imbibed, and now admirably reproduces, the social code which decrees that women violate their femininity if they exhibit, or even experience, feelings which suggest a capacity to initiate desire. In keeping with this code, Lucy attempts to create for her readers a heroine who is calm and impervious, but as the narrative progresses, and the question of 'Who are you, Lucy Snowe?' becomes a focus of near-explicit attention, she acknowledges the constructed nature of this social persona.[14] After she has fled, pulse throbbing, from the 'lecture pieuse', only to discover Madame Beck searching her drawers for a love-letter which, to her sorrow and triumph, is non-existent, she undergoes a 'strange and contradictory . . . inward tumult . . . Complicated, disquieting thoughts broke up the whole of my nature. However, that turmoil subsided: next day I was again Lucy Snowe' (p. 166). This precarious division between the rigidly-defined social self, and the inner impulses which can never be articulated or even acknowledged, is to precipitate her breakdown.

In constructing Lucy's self-contradictory narrative, with its displacements, evasions and ghostly sightings which clearly signal to the modern reader the presence of sexual repression, Brontë was not thereby unconsciously articulating patterns in the human psyche which were to remain unrecognised, or even untheorized, until the advent of Freud. As I have argued, the belief that sexuality was a primary cause of nervous disorder and insanity in women was common currency in mid-Victorian England. Medical texts of the nineteenth century emphasized repeatedly that hysteria occurred mainly in young, unmarried women.[15] By mid-century one also finds the repeated suggestion that the social constrictions imposed on the unmarried, respectable female intensify the pressures of sexual repression until fire breaks out (a process which is literally embodied by Brontë in the burning of Thornfield by the demonic Mrs Rochester, and in the outbreak of fire in the theatre as the 'fallen angel' Vashti is acting).[16]

In Caroline's reflections in *Shirley*, the life of the old maid was linked to that of nuns who 'having violated nature ... grow altogether morbid' (pp. 440-1). Although Caroline might become 'nervous' and even look 'as one who had seen a ghost', after her veins have been kindled by the 'apparition' of her lover, she is saved from the extremes of morbidity by the textual device of brain fever. In *Villette*, by contrast, Brontë explores the mental effects of repression, exposing, through the twists and turns of her narrative, the morbid processes of mind of her designedly uncongenial 'Miss Frost', who, unlike pretty, sweet-natured Caroline Helstone, is permitted to retain none of the characteristics of a traditional heroine.[17]

The question of Lucy's actual instability must remain unanswered if we, as readers, are to avoid falling into the error of Dr John in assuming unproblematic access to a realm of hidden truth. It is possible, however, to trace the degree to which Lucy, in analysis of her own history, draws on the constructions of appropriate and 'insane' feminine behaviour to be found in mid-nineteenth-century psychological science. In her explicit use of contemporary scientific terms, Lucy draws attention to the explanatory complexes which underpin the often unconscious associations that direct her interpretation of behaviour. Her first noticeable use of scientific terminology occurs in her judgment on what she perceives to be the emotional excesses of Polly's behaviour with regard to her father: 'This, I perceived, was a one-idead nature; betraying that monomaniac tendency I have ever thought the most unfortunate with which man or woman can be cursed' (p. 16). The idea of monomania, displaced here onto Polly, is later appropriated by Lucy for herself to describe her distress at losing Dr John's letter: '"Oh! they have taken my letter!" cried the grovelling, groping, monomaniac' (p. 353).[18] Monomania, as first defined by Esquirol, and later popularized in England by James Prichard, was a form of partial insanity, unmarked by mania, which could possibly exist within the compass of normal daily life.

Esquirol's formulation of his categories of insanity was firmly founded on assumptions of 'female vulnerability'. Women, he believed, were more susceptible, both physiologically and psychologically to religious and erotic melancholy, and hence to the 'hallucinations the most strange and frequent' of religious and erotic monomania (a conjunction of religion and sexuality which clearly lies behind the figure of the nun).[19] The unleashing of religious or erotic passion, which for Esquirol marked incipient insanity, is figured in *Villette* in the young 'monomaniac', Polly, whom Lucy catches sight of 'praying like some Catholic or Methodist enthusiast – some precocious fanatic or untimely saint'. Lucy's thoughts on this occasion, she remarks, 'ran risk of being hardly more rational and healthy than that child's mind must have been' (p. 15). The correlation of 'rational' and 'healthy' suggests that Lucy endorses Esquirol's association of mental health with socially-prescribed forms of rationality. Whilst her own moderate Protestantism represents for her the requisite model of mental balance and control, Catholicism, and extreme Methodism, suggest a frightening addiction to passionate excess, and hence a sacrifice of the mind's autonomy and control.

Lucy's own monomania clearly follows the course of Esquirol's erotic monomania which he defines as a literal disease, a 'chronic cerebral affection ... characterized by an excessive passion'.[20] In a formulation which reflects cultural attitudes of the era, Esquirol divides sexual afflictions into chaste erotomania, whose origins lie in the imagination, and 'obscene', 'shameful and humiliating' nymphomania and satyriasis which originate in the organs of reproduction. Erotomaniacs differ from the latter class in that their affections are 'chaste and honourable', they 'never pass the limits of propriety'. Instead, these subjects tend to 'forget themselves; vow a pure, and often secret devotion to the object of their love; make themselves slaves to it; execute its orders with a fidelity often puerile; and obey also the caprices that are connected with it'.[21] The description offers an outline of Lucy's 'chaste', obsessional behaviour; her devotion to Dr John, like that of the erotomaniac, is secret: 'I liked entering his presence covered with a cloud he had not seen through, while he stood before me under a ray of special illumination, which shone all partial over his head, trembled about his feet, and cast light no farther' (p. 250). In this passage which describes Lucy's 'system of feeling', her determined refusal to reveal her identity to Dr John, knowledge and sexuality are clearly assimilated: whilst Lucy wishes not to be 'seen through', the projection of her ray of illumination, which trembles about Dr John's feet, clearly functions as a displaced enactment of her own sexual desire, her longed-for self-abasement. Lucy's first concern, like that of Esquirol's erotomaniacs, is to reduce self so as to glorify the chosen object of her passion.

Esquirol's formulation of erotomania, like his other categories of insanity, dresses recognized social stereotypes in the authority of science. In his hands, the disease becomes socially respectable. Erotomaniacs, he insists, do not, even in fantasy, seek fulfilment of their desires: 'The erotomaniac neither desires, nor dreams even, of the favors to which he might aspire from the object of his insane tenderness.'[22] The social repression, so evident in Lucy's narrative, which forbad women the articulation, or even conscious acknowledgement, of their desires, is encoded in his very definition of the disease. Esquirol's theory of erotomania, however, does not merely reinforce accepted social wisdom: chaste, hopeless passion is transformed into a cerebral disease, and must henceforth be treated as a possible symptom of insanity. The fear of mental illness signalled by Lucy's references to monomania underpins all her narrative: insanity is no longer limited to the recognizably disruptive forces of sexual desire, which may be locked away in the attic, but lurks as an incipient threat even in the 'chaste' repressed imaginings of the 'respectable' woman.

Lucy's imposition of the label 'monomaniac' on her 'double', Polly, is clearly expressive of a self-revelatory fear.[23] Polly's function as Lucy's alter ego is made explicit in Lucy's later confession that:

'As a child I feared for you; nothing that has life was ever more susceptible than your nature in infancy: under harshness, or neglect, neither your outward nor your inward self would have ripened to what they now are. Much pain, much fear, much struggle would have troubled the very lines of your features, broken their regularity, would have harassed your nerves into the fever of habitual irritation: you would have lost in health and cheerfulness, in grace and sweetness.'(p. 545)

Beneath the anguish of self-portrait that directs these lines, there lies the disturbing suggestion that mental health is not a norm, from which only an unfortunate, physiologically determined, minority deviate, but rather an ideal which few are lucky enough to attain. To encounter pain or struggle is to develop nerves 'harassed' into 'habitual irritation'. Mental disease, Lucy suggests, is incipient in us all.

Polly's successful capture of that golden prize, Graham Bretton (a figure distinct from the Dr John of Lucy's acquaintance) is attended both by material conditions denied to Lucy, and superior psychological powers of self-control. The child who had demonstrated a 'sensibility which bends of its own will, a giant slave under the sway of good sense', (p. 17) which proved so 'burdensome' to Lucy, displays in adolescence a perfect mastery of the socially requisite powers of repression. Lucy writes two letters to Dr John, one dictated by Feeling and the other by Reason, but Polly writes 'three times – chastening and subduing the phrases at every rescript' until her letter resembled 'a morsel of ice' (p. 544). Despite her attempts to live up to her name, Lucy fails to attain this icy level of control. Yet, not withstanding Lucy's envy of her ideal counterpart, *Villette* does not fundamentally endorse the doctrine of control which had been so central to *Jane Eyre*. Jane's history had seemed to vindicate the mid-Victorian belief that successful regulation of the mental economy would lead to material social success. Bertha is sent to her death so that Jane can achieve the bourgeois dream. *Villette*, a more radical work, politically, than *Jane Eyre*, refuses this compromise. The limited form of success allotted to Lucy, who dwells outside the realm of the ideal inhabited by Graham and Polly, actually stems from her allowing her passion to break bounds as she finally defies Madame Beck. Although Lucy achieves economic competency at the end, the dominant final note in the novel is not one of triumph or content, but rather overwhelming loss (though marriage to M. Paul might, as Brontë hints in a letter, have been an even worse fate).[24]

In calling into question in *Villette* the doctrine of control, Brontë is thereby implicitly challenging the economic model of healthy regulation which underpinned mid-Victorian theories of social, psychological and physiological functioning. The mind, like the body, or the social economy, was to be treated as a system to be guided, regulated and controlled. As John Elliotson observed, 'the laws of the mind are precisely those of the functions of all other organs, – a certain degree of excitement strengthens it; too much exhausts it'.[25] In the mental, as in the social economy, the aim must be to obtain maximum efficiency, neither over-stretching, nor under-deploying the natural resources. Theories of insanity drew on this model. Whether the cause were seen to be physical or moral, menstrual irregularities or the exclusive direction of the efforts of the mind into one channel, the net effect was seen to be the unbalancing of the body's natural economy which was founded on the free flow of 'secretions' and a hierarchical regulation of the mental forces.[26] Such theories of the bodily economy were based, however, on normative, gender-specific, codes of social behaviour. The social construction of insanity went hand in hand with that of femininity.

Lucy, in her vocabulary, seems initially to endorse enthusiastically the phrenological world view, believing that cultivation of the correct faculties and suppression of the troublesome lower propensities would lead directly to social advancement. In London she feels a surge of confident energy: 'Who but a coward would pass his whole life in hamlets, and for ever abandon his faculties to the eating rust of obscurity?' (p. 64). Later, once launched in her teaching career, she feels satisfied 'I was getting on; not lying the stagnant prey of mould and rust, but polishing my faculties and whetting them to a keen edge with constant use' (p. 113).[27] Such confidence soon dissolves, however, to be replaced by a rather different theory of social and psychological life. Brontë still uses the vocabulary of regulation and control, but to rather different effect. Lucy's efforts at regulation are no longer seen to be healthful. She strives for a literal form of live burial, recapitulating the experience of the nun: 'in catalepsy and a dead trance, I studiously held the quick of my nature' (p. 152). In a world where inner energies, when duly regulated, can find no external outlet, it is better, Lucy argues, that they be suppressed, if they are not to become self-consuming. Alternatively, they should be allowed to range in the world of fantasy. In this, her last novel, Brontë finally, tentatively, asserts the claims of the realm of imagination, in opposition to the reason and control of the masculine world, with all its spurious offers of healing aid. Lucy deliberately rejects her envenomed stepmother, Hag Reason, for the saving spirit of the imagination (pp. 327–9), while the 'Real' – that realm to which the moral managers sought so assiduously to return their patients – is figured for her in the iconography of the fallen woman: 'Presently the rude Real burst coarsely in – all evil, grovelling, and repellent as she too often is' (p. 153). The description, which prefigures the emergence of that 'grovelling, groping, monomaniac', Lucy, suggests the consequences for women of living according to male-defined reality (the 'Real' here is the casket containing the love letter which simultaneously dismisses Lucy as a sexual possibility and condemns her as a monster). Lucy's narrative, which dissolves the real into the imaginary, challenges male constructions of the social and psychological world.

This is not to suggest, however, that Lucy thereby steps entirely outside the formulations of psychological experience to be found in contemporary science. Her descriptions of her sufferings during the Long Vacation follow medical wisdom in assigning both physical and moral causes for this 'strange fever of the nerves and blood' (p. 222). Her fantasies concerning Ginevra (who functions as rival, alter ego and object of desire) and Dr John, and her nightmares of rejection, are underpinned by the responsiveness of her physical frame to the winds and storms outside, held by contemporary alienists to occasion and exacerbate insanity (pp. 219–20).[28] In projecting herself as a physical system, at the mercy of external physical changes, Lucy is able to deny her responsibility for her mental disorder: it is her 'nervous system' which cannot stand the strain; the controlling rational ego is dissolved into the body. The figure of the cretin, however, with its 'propensity . . . to evil' (p. 220), stands as a warning projection of a model of mind where the physical is dominant, and the passions and propensities are not subject to any mental restraint.

Lucy seems to shift in and out of physiological explanation of the self as it suits her convenience. In opposition to Dr John, who clearly regards her in the same professional light as the 'singularly interesting' disease whose symptoms had detained him in the old town, she denies understanding of his diagnosis: '"I am not quite sure what my nervous system is, but I was dreadfully low-spirited"' (p. 261). Her attempt to define why she went to confession is marked by a similar resistance: '"I suppose you will think me mad for taking such a step, but I could not help it: I suppose it was all the fault of what you call my 'nervous system'"' (p. 264). Rejecting this materialist mode of interpretation, she admits to the difficulty of finding language to describe her state, concluding that '"a cruel sense of desolation pained my mind: a feeling that would make its way, rush out, or kill me – like (and this you will understand, Dr John) the current which passes through the heart, and which, if aneurism or any other morbid cause obstructs its natural channels, impetuously seeks abnormal outlet"' (p. 264). Although Lucy distances herself from Dr John's technical explanation, her description of her own mental state actually draws even more decisively on current theories of physiological psychology. Her interpretation is founded on a metaphorical transposition of the medical explanation of insanity as a morbid obstruction of the channels of the mind.

Lucy's resistance to Dr John stems less from the actual content of his medical verdicts, than from his reduction of her to a bundle of symptoms, open to his professional definition and control. Her first preoccupation after her collapse, occasion of her double exposure to the eyes of religious and medical authority, was to re-establish her private domain, subduing feeling so as to be 'better regulated, more equable, quieter on the surface' where the 'common gaze' will fall.

The turbulent realm below was to be left to God: 'Man, your equal, weak as you, and not fit to be your judge, may be shut out thence' (p. 255). Dr John, however, attempts just that act of judgment, but in diagnosing her case as one of hypochondria, he is forced to acknowledge limitations in his medical art which 'looks in and sees a chamber of torture, but can neither say nor do much' (p. 261). He is restricted to recommending the cheerful society and exercise listed by Graham as the means by which 'moral management' should attempt to cure hypochondriasis.[29] Even Dr John's more limited claim to an authoritative power of diagnosis is undermined, however, by his failure to remark, as Lucy does, that the King of Labassecour is a sufferer from 'constitutional melancholy' (p. 304). Medical knowledge is matched against experiential understanding and found wanting.

Lucy claims for herself the sole power of deciphering the 'hierogylphics' of the king's countenance which suggest to her that, 'Those eyes had looked on the visits of a certain ghost – had long waited the comings and goings of that strangest spectre, Hypochondria' (p. 303). The conflation of medical and Gothic terminology in this passage echoes Brontë's description of her own experience of hypochondria in a letter written several years earlier. Brontë speaks initially of the suffering of a friend who 'has felt the tyranny of Hypochondria – a most dreadful doom, far worse than that of a man of healthy nerves buried for the same length of time in a subterranean dungeon'. Of her own experience she remarks that she had endured 'preternatural horror which seemed to clothe existence and Nature – and which made life a continual waking Nightmare – Under such circumstances the morbid nerves can know neither peace nor enjoyment – whatever touches – pierces them – sensation for them is all suffering'. Considering her effect upon Margaret Wooler, she concludes she must have been 'no better company for you than a stalking ghost'.[30] The letter, like the novel, suggests a sense of powerlessness in the face of physiological tyranny. The terms of the description offer a similar mixture of metaphorical and physiological language: the idea of being buried alive, literally embodied in *Villette*, is linked to the notion of 'morbid nerves', which are themselves then personified, endowed with the capacity to suffer and experience. The ghostly qualities, attributed to hypochondria in the novel, are here appropriated by Brontë for herself, in a transposition which mirrors the novel's dissolution of the boundaries of the self. Lucy not only dwells in a realm where furniture becomes 'spectral', but also attributes that quality to herself in others' eyes: she feels, at one stage, she must look to Dr John 'like some ghost' (p. 157). Perception, in Lucy's spectral world, is integrally related to the social construction of identity.

Lucy's final discussion of hypochondria returns once more to the question of the relationship between physiology and mental suffering. She contrasts the world's ready acceptance of the idea of physical illness with its reluctant understanding of an equivalent mental disease:

The world can understand well enough the process of perishing for want of food: perhaps few persons can enter into or follow out that of going mad from solitary confinement. They see the long-buried prisoner disinterred, a maniac or an idiot! – how his sense left him – how his nerves first inflamed, underwent nameless agony, and then sunk to palsy – is a subject too intricate for examination, too abstract for popular comprehension. Speak of it! you might almost as well stand up in an European market-place, and propound dark sayings in that language and mood wherein Nebuchadnezzar, the imperial hypochondriac, communed with his baffled Chaldeans. (p. 392)

The idea of psychological deprivation, dramatized throughout the novel in the motif of live burial, is here grounded in the physiological experience of the nerves which undergo inflammation and then 'nameless agony'. As soon as Lucy moves away from available technical vocabulary she reaches the limits of the expressible: the agony must remain 'nameless'. Unlike her Biblical counterpart, Lucy knows better than to try and describe to others a form of experience that has never received social recognition or articulation. The passage represents an implicit rebuke to the medical establishment who believe that in naming the 'symptoms' of hypochondria, they have somehow mastered the experience. Lucy is both asserting her own belief in the material basis of psychological suffering, and denying Dr John's claim to authoritative knowledge.

Lucy's battle for control over self-definition and interpretation of the processes of her own mind is not conducted solely with Dr John; the fiery M. Paul also enters the lists. On encountering Lucy in the art gallery after her illness, M. Paul berates her for her unfeminine behaviour in not being able to look after the cretin: '"Women who are worthy the name,"' he proclaims, '"ought infinitely to surpass our coarse, fallible, self-indulgent sex, in the power to perform such duties"' (p. 290). The covert subject of this conversation is clearly the model of the female mind which suggested that women are more 'naturally' able than men to suppress their 'evil propensities'. Lucy, in self-defence, resorts to another male model of the female mind, asserting a physical illness: '"I had a nervous fever: my mind was ill"' (p. 290). Diminished responsibility, which figured so largely in mid-Victorian trials of female criminals, becomes the basis of her excuse for 'unwomanly' conduct. Unlike Dr John, M. Paul refuses to accept this model of the mind and so draws attention back again to his own image of the constitution of the feminine. Dismissing the idea of nervous fever, he points instead to Lucy's 'temerity' in gazing at the picture of Cleopatra. The portrait of the fleshy Cleopatra, and the four pictures of 'La vie d'une femme', 'cold and vapid as ghosts', which M. Paul prefers for Lucy's instruction in the arts of femininity, take on iconographic significance in the narrative, representing the two alternative models for womanhood created by men.[31] Lucy's challenge to these models, implicit throughout her narrative, takes decisive form in the Vashti section.

The narrative sequence which culminates in the performance of Vashti actually starts, not in the theatre, but on Lucy's apparent sighting, that evening, of the nun. Dr John, refusing to respect her reticence, invokes once more his professional authority to diagnose the symptoms of her 'raised look', thus provoking Lucy's angry dismissal of his explanation: 'Of course with him, it was held to be another effect of the same cause: it was all optical illusion – nervous malady, and so on. Not one bit did I believe him; but I dared not contradict: doctors are so self-opinionated, so immovable in their dry, materialist views' (p. 368). Lucy rejects the 'doctor's' opinion on principle, although his physiological explanation appears perhaps surprisingly close to views she herself has expressed elsewhere. The grounds of her objection to Dr John's 'dry' materialism are made explicit, however, in her analysis of their mutual responses to the performance of Vashti.

For Lucy, Vashti on stage transcends socially imposed sex-roles; she is neither woman nor man, but a devil, a literal embodiment of inner passion: 'Hate and Murder and Madness incarnate, she stood' (p. 369). Lucy's response is to invoke the male author of a rather different image of womanhood: 'Where was the artist of the Cleopatra? Let him come and sit down and study this different vision. Let him seek here the mighty brawn, the muscle, the abounding blood, the full-fed flesh he worshipped: let all materialists draw nigh and look on' (p. 370). In a significant elision, Lucy has drawn together the materialism of doctors who seek to explain the processes of the mind with reference only to the physiological behaviour of the nerves, and the materialism of men who construct their images of women with reference only to the physical attributes of the flesh. The creation of the feminine in male-executed art is directly allied to the medical construction of women.

Lucy perceives, in Vashti, a force which could re-enact the miracle of the Red Sea, drowning Paul Peter Rubens [sic] and 'all the army of his fat women', but Dr John remains unresponsive to her challenge. He replicates, in the 'intense curiosity' with which he watches her performance, the professional gaze he has recently imposed on Lucy. His verdict underscores, for Lucy, his indifference to the inner movements of female experience: 'he judged her as a woman, not an artist: it was a branding judgment' (p. 373). Dr John's response is determined entirely by predefined categories of suitable female behaviour. As in his medical practice, he is insulated from any attempt to understand the causes or experiential detail of the cases he is examining through his possession of a socially validated system of classification which allows him to speak with unreflecting authority. Like his counterparts in the Book of Esther (from where the name Vashti is drawn) he trusts to the codification of male power to protect him from the 'demonic' challenge of female energy. (Queen Vashti's refusal to show her beauty at the king's command had provoked, from a worried male oligarchy, a proclamation 'to every people after their language, that every man should bear rule in his own house'.)[32]

In choosing to equate medical and artistic constructions of the female identity through the notion of 'materialism,' Brontë was drawing on the terms of contemporary debate. As an artistic term, implying the 'tendency to lay stress on the material aspects of the objects represented' the first use of materialism seems to date only from the 1850s (OED). Although the philosophical usage of materialism dates back to the eighteenth century, it had, at the time of Brontë's writing, become the focus of a virulent social and theological debate concerning the development of psychological theories which stressed that the brain was the organ of mind. Phrenology and mesmerism were located, in the popular press, at the centre of this controversy, as evidenced by the 1851 *Blackwood's* article which inveighed against the phreno-mesmerism of authors who believed that 'upon the materialism of life rest the great phenomena of what we were wont to call mind'.[33] Clearly, as Brontë's use of phrenological terms and concepts reveals, she was not stirred into opposition by this controversy. Lucy's objections to materialism are not based on the religious grounds of contemporary debate; nor, as her own use of physiological vocabulary demonstrates, are they founded on an opposition to the use of a physiological explanation of the mind *per se*. Her rejection of medical and artistic materialism stems rather from the rigid and incomplete nature of their conception; she objects less to the idea of an interrelationship between body and mind, than to their rather partial vision of this union. Under the medical and artistic gaze, woman is *reduced* to flesh and the material functioning of nerves.

In describing the impact of Vashti, Lucy herself employs the vocabulary of contemporary physiological psychology; Vashti's acting,

instead of merely irritating imagination with the thought of what *might* be done, at the same time fevering the nerves because it was *not* done, disclosed power like a deep, swollen, winter river, thundering in cataract, and bearing the soul, like a leaf, on the steep and steely sweep of its descent.(p. 371)

The term 'irritating' here is a technical one as used, for example, in Graham's observation that 'The nervous headache generally occurs in persons with a peculiar irritability of the nervous system.'[34] Coupled with the idea of 'fevering the nerves' it suggests two different levels of response within the nervous system, whilst the concluding imagery of the thundering river draws on physiological ideas of channelled energy within the brain. The power disclosed is both internal and external: it describes the force of Vashti's own inner energy, and the impact on the observer Lucy. What Brontë has done, in this metaphorical usage of contemporary physiological theory, is to dramatize an even closer integration of body and mind than physiology envisaged, while simultaneously breaking down the traditional boundaries of the self. Mind is not reduced to body, it becomes literally 'embodied', as Lucy earlier observed: 'To her, what hurts becomes immediately embodied: she looks on it as a thing that can be attacked, worried down, torn in shreds. Scarcely a substance herself, she grapples to conflict with abstractions. Before calamity she is a tigress; she rends her woes, shivers them in convulsed abhorrence' (p. 370). Whilst the artist reduces woman to a material expanse of flesh, and the doctor to a mere encasement of nerves, Vashti reveals a true union between the worlds of mind and body: abstractions, the experiential details of mental life which physiology cannot describe, are given material form. In her treatment of Vashti, as throughout the novel, Brontë actually employs contemporary physiological theory to break through the narrow definition of the self it proposes.

The description of Vashti tearing hurt into shreds anticipates Lucy's later destruction of the figure of the nun:

All the movement was mine, so was all the life, the reality, the substance, the force; as my instinct felt. I tore her up – the incubus! I held her on high – the goblin! I shook her loose – the mystery! And down she fell – down all round me – down in shreds and fragments – and I trode upon her.(p. 681)

Like Vashti, Lucy undertakes a material destruction of an inner hurt: the force and *substance* are Lucy's own.[35] The term 'incubus', with its associations of sexuality and mental disturbance, draws together the arenas of physical and mental life. In nineteenth-century psychological usage, incubus had become synonymous with nightmare. In a passage noted by Patrick Brontë, Robert Macnish observed in *The Philosophy of Sleep* that it was possible to suffer nightmare whilst awake and in 'perfect possession of [the] faculties'. Macnish records that he had 'undergone the greatest tortures, being haunted by spectres, hags, and every sort of phantom – having, at the same time, a full consciousness that I was labouring under incubus, and that all the terrifying objects around me were the creations of my own brain'.[36] Brontë takes this idea of waking nightmare or incubus one stage further, giving it a literal embodiment in her fiction which defies attempts to demarcate the boundaries between 'creations of the brain' and external forms.

Brontë offers, in *Villette*, a thorough materialization of the self. The construct 'Lucy' is not a unified mental entity, located within a physiological frame, but rather a continuous process which extends beyond the confines of the flesh. Lucy's entire mode of self-articulation breaks down the hierarchy of outer and inner life upon which definitions of the 'Real' (and sanity) depend. Her description of the death of Hope, for instance, parallels that of the literal burial of the letters: 'In the end I closed the eyes of my dead, covered its face, and composed its limbs with great calm' (p. 421). The burial itself is the wrapping of grief in a 'winding-sheet'. Later, as Lucy pauses beside the grave, she recalls 'the passage of feeling therein buried' (p. 524). Metaphor has become inoperable: it functions, as Lucy's text makes clear, only if the speaker endorses normative social demarcations between different states. Thus the classrooms which initially only 'seem' to Lucy to be like jails quickly become 'filled with spectral and intolerable memories, laid miserable amongst their straw and their manacles' (p. 652). The controlling distance of 'seems' is collapsed, as 'memories', normally restricted to the realm of the mind, take on vivid physical form.

Lucy's intricate dramatizations of her feelings undermine traditional divisions between external social process and inner mental life, revealing their fictional status.[37] Her tale of Jael, Sisera and Heber, for example, simultaneously portrays physiological pain, psychological conflict, and the social drama of repression. Speaking of her desire to be drawn out of her present existence, Lucy observes:

> This longing, and all of a similar kind, it was necessary to knock on the head; which I did, figuratively, after the manner of Jael to Sisera, driving a nail through their temples. Unlike Sisera, they did not die: they were but transiently stunned, and at intervals would turn on the nail with a rebellious wrench; then did the temples bleed, and the brain thrill to its core. (p. 152)

The distinction between figural and literal quickly fades, as the inner psychic drama develops, and the rebellious desires themselves perpetuate their torture, in a description which captures the physiological and psychological experience of socially inflicted repression (the term 'thrill' carried the medically precise meaning, in the mid-nineteenth century, of 'vibratory movement, resonance, or murmur'). The narrative evocation of inner life does not, however, end there. Lucy develops the story, envisaging, with a precision of detail unmatched in the descriptions of the external scenes of her life, the physical landscape of the action under the soothing light of imagination. Jael, the controlling self responsible for maiming the desires to whom she had promised shelter, begins to relent, but such thoughts are soon outweighed by the expectation of her husband, Heber's, commendation of her deed: female self-repression is accorded patriarchal endorsement. This drama of internal pain and division, with its precise enactment of the social processes of control, reveals the falsity of normative divisions between inner and outer experience.

The famous account of Lucy's opiate-induced wanderings into the night landscape of Villette also dissolves the divisions between inner and outer realms, as social experience now takes on the qualities of mental life, defying the normal boundaries of time and space. Amidst the physical forms of Cleopatra's Egypt, Lucy witnesses all the figures of her inner thoughts parade before her eyes (only Ginevra and De Hamal are excluded, but, as Lucy later insists, it was her own excursion which released them into sexual freedom).[38] Even here, however, where she seems most free from external social controls, she is still subject to fears of surveillance: she feels Dr John's gaze 'oppressing' her, seeming ready to grasp 'my identity ... between his never tyrannous, but always powerful hands' (p. 661). As dominant male, and doctor, empowered by society to diagnose the inner movements of mind, and legislate on mental disease, Dr John threatens Lucy's carefully-nurtured sense of self. Identity, as Brontë has shown throughout *Villette*, is not a given, but rather a tenuous process of negotiation between the subject and surrounding social forces.

The opposition to male materialism, voiced by Lucy in her confrontation with medical authority, gives dramatic expression to the interrogation of male constructions of the female psyche which underpins the narrative form of *Villette*. In seeking to avoid the surveillance of religious, educational and medical figures, trying to render herself illegible, Lucy attempts to assume control over the processes of her own self-definition. Yet her narrative, as I have argued, reveals a clear internalization of the categories and terms of contemporary medical psychology. Lucy employs physiological explanations of mental life and appropriates to herself theories of a female predisposition to neurosis and monomania. In creating the autobiography of her troubled heroine, Brontë explores both the social implications of contemporary psychological theory, and its inner consequences. The form of her account, with its dissolution of divisions between inner psychological life, and the material social world suggests an alternative vision – one that challenges the normative psychological vision implicit in male definitions of the 'Real'.

Conclusion

Villette marks the culmination of Brontë's struggle against the authority of the 'real.' As in the 1834 story, 'The Spell,' the reader is tempted into offering diagnoses of the protagonist, whilst simultaneously being shown how arbitrary, and inadequate any such readings would be. We form, as readers, one more layer of social surveillance which Lucy, our narrator, is determined to frustrate. Her autobiography operates not as a form of confession, which would then transfer power to the reader, but rather as a form of creative evasion which leads finally to a new vision of embodied selfhood. No longer do the real and the imagination, the outer world and inner feeling, stand in painful conflict; Brontë's text opens up a space where the metaphoric world of desire is actively embodied. In place of the reductive materialism of medical science, with its claims to authoritative interpretation of the symptoms of selfhood, we are offered a materialism which embraces the realm of imagination.

In foregrounding the interpretative conflict between the man of medical science, Dr John, and Lucy, Brontë makes explicit the concerns which had underpinned the narrative methodology of all her writing. Medical science, Rothfield has suggested, offers a paradigm for the realist novel in its 'immanent power to penetrate and know the embodied self it treats'.[1] Brontë's distrust of such claims to authority is encoded in the narrative form of all her writings, from the teasing, unreliable narrators of her earliest stories, to the conflictual, autobiographical forms of her major novels. Where she does adopt third-person narration, in *Shirley*, the text is so interwoven with alternate forms of discourse and other voices that no single one can be accorded precedence. The medical claim to knowledge is shown in *Villette* to be not so much a discourse of truth as one of power. Brontë's Lydgate is judged and found wanting, not because of spots of commonness which drag him down into the mire of sexual relations, setting science and the life of the emotions at odds, but rather because his exercise of scientific authority itself is shown to be part of a gendered struggle for power. Medical surveillance, Brontë reveals, is but one type of the many forms of surveillance which structure the social confines of individual life. Whereas in Brontë's earlier fiction protagonists had always sought to avoid the penetrating glance of other individuals, surveillance in *Villette* operates at an institutional level: medical science vies with the Roman Catholic Church, and educational and employment practices in its attempts to know, and hence control, the private self. Brontë, despite her much vaunted social 'isolation,' offers a brilliant anatomy of the structures of power within the industrial culture of Victorian England.[2]

Although in formal terms Brontë's fiction sets out to challenge and subvert the culture of surveillance, one of the greatest strengths of her writing lies in her ability to depict the ways in which external social practices and struggles become inscribed within the self. Brontë has been hailed as the high priestess of the truth of the soul; far from revealing the inner mysteries of a secret, interior realm of essential selfhood, however, she reveals how a sense of selfhood is only constructed for her protagonists in the experience of social conflict. The private self is thus a social creation, brought into being by the experience of the power to withhold, and to baffle penetration. What Brontë has achieved here is to cut through the ideologies of her time, with their insistent demarcation of the realms of public and private, and to show, in terms that anticipate current theoretical debate, the ways in which the very experience of selfhood is socially defined. The Romantic belief in inner authenticity is translated into a figure of beleaguered selfhood, beset on all sides, but whose sense of authenticity is only constructed through the experience of pursuit and conflict. Gothic mechanisms are here brought into play to define, not the workings of plot, in outlandish and extreme guise, but rather the domain of ordinary selfhood.[3] As Alexander Welsh has shown, the rise of information culture in the nineteenth century brings with it in the fiction of the period an obsession with the workings of blackmail, the fear of revelation of hidden secrets from the past. One finds this structure not only in the sensation fiction of the 1860s, but also in the work of such figures as Eliot and Dickens. Dickens' *Bleak House* (1852–3) possesses strong similarities with *Villette* in its depiction of social networks of surveillance, but it differs in one crucial detail: there is an actual secret from the past waiting to be unveiled. Crimsworth, Jane and Lucy, however, have no dark secrets to be unearthed, and unlike Lady Dedlock, they are not merely passive victims of others' surveillance, but enter with zest into the project of interpretative penetration. Brontë's fiction differs in this respect from all her contemporaries in that she bestows on her protagonists frank enjoyment in their activities of baffling decipherment and unveiling their opponents, activities which then become ends in themselves. Far from depicting romance as a great union of souls, Brontë cuts through such ideological camouflage to show the competitive ethos of capitalism at work in the private domain.

Brontë's protagonists possess all the striving aspirations of the Romantic hero, but their forms of expression are firmly Victorian. In the paradigmatic Victorian discourse of phrenology to which Bronte subscribed, social surveillance was linked to ideas of social mobility and self-improvement, and selfhood defined by the experience of conflict and struggle, both internally, between competing faculties, and externally, between self and other. All these elements are to be found in other contemporary writers, but no one else brings them together with such clarity, nor explores their consequences so remorselessly. Competition and conflict, for Brontë, define not just the realms of economics and labour, but the interior domain of selfhood. The yearning towards romance which runs through all her fiction is decisively undercut by her dissection of its workings. Sentimental, reductionist readings have established Brontë as a great writer of romance; I would suggest she should be celebrated rather for her ability to trace through the internal psychological dynamics of Victorian competitive individualism.

Other works of the period, most notably *Wuthering Heights* and Dickens' novels, also register a world of struggling, conflicting energies, but these are not defined with the psychological detail to be found in Charlotte Brontë's work. The physiological precision with which she traces the rise and fall of her protagonists' energies anticipates the fiction of George Eliot who, with the benefit of subsequent developments in physiological psychology, explored the relationship between the inner life of the emotions and organic structure. In *Shirley*, with its projection of a direct relationship between the life of the individual body and that of the social organism, the constricted flow of Caroline's energies paralleling that within the surrounding social economy, we have a precursor of *Middlemarch*, where the contorted labyrinths within which Dorothea's energies are forced to flow mirror the structures of both Middlemarch and her marital life. Brontë's text, however, while it might lack the scope of Eliot's novel, is more precisely targeted in economic, political and sexual terms.

One crucial distinction between the work of Charlotte and Emily Brontë and that of their contemporaries lies in the absence of an overarching moral frame to their work. Dickens' individualists are wrapped around by a constraining discourse of mutual kindliness, while Eliot's heroines are permitted, like the Brontës', to aspire beyond the confines of their lot, but are forced always to ask how individual desire can be reconciled with social duty. Charlotte and Emily's creations ask only how they can achieve their desires. These desires, as I have suggested, are given unmistakable sexual form. We should not, however, therefore see the Brontës as transcending the limits set by the discourse of their time. On the contrary, as I have argued, Charlotte's depictions of the workings of the female body and desires give articulation to the contradictory formulations of femininity in Victorian culture. In tracing through the ways in which general cultural and medical theories of personal agency, selfhood and femininity would have percolated through into local Haworth culture, I have sought not only to break down notions of Brontë's cultural isolation, but also to show how such in-depth research can give us a clearer understanding of the ways in which complex and contradictory ideologies interact within a given culture. Brontë negotiates in her work not only the conflict between ideas of female spirituality, and bodily subjection, but also that between the ideologies of self-development to be found in her local culture and alternate notions of respectable feminine containment, conflicts exacerbated for Brontë by her marginal social position and sense of allegiance to her Tory father.

Analysis of the linguistic texture of Brontë's depiction of the psyche reveals a more political figure than criticism has hitherto acknowledged: subtle forms of linguistic association which operate across different forms of discourse allow her to project the turbulence of the body in political terms. Her work is distinguished finally, however, not by the clarity with which she articulates an achieved position, but rather by the intensity with which she wrestles with contradictions. The 'preternatural power' of her work lies in its ability to lay bare the inner, psychological consequences of social ideology.[4] Like Vashti, she 'grapples to conflict with abstractions'.

Brontë's texts pose huge interpretative problems for the critic: there is no overall moral vision against which to set the novels' achievements; no omniscient narrative voice in which we can place our trust. The only overall frame seems to be that of romance, but this is persistently undercut, not only in the depiction of the perpetual conflict it seems to entail, but also in the framing of the novels' conclusions: Crimsworth's violent shooting of the dog, Rochester's maiming and the dank atmosphere of Ferndean, the facetious 'winding up' of *Shirley*, and the invocation of readerly fantasy in the dual ending of *Villette*. A teleology is proposed only to be almost ostentatiously revoked. Brontë's novels are in themselves maddening, tormenting, offering us illusions of order which are then destroyed. In place of the dispassionate voice of literary or medical authority which leaves the readerly self intact we are rather drawn into the turmoil, forced, in the experience of reading, to question our cherished assumptions of subjective integrity and literary unity. As readers we, like the protagonists, undergo a fundamental destabilization of selfhood.

Notes

INTRODUCTION

1 This model of interpretation also lies behind John Maynard's work, *Charlotte Brontë and Sexuality* (Cambridge: Cambridge University Press, 1984): 'I do not think it too much to claim that Brontë realizes, in her artistic vision, most of the major assumptions of the sexual revolution of Havelock Ellis, Freud, and their successors' (p. viii). Although Maynard's work overlaps in some areas with my own, our methodologies are quite distinct.

2 Sandra Gilbert and Susan Gubar, *The Madwoman in the Attic: The Woman Writer and the Nineteenth-Century Literary Imagination* (New Haven: Yale University Press, 1979). The work of Elaine Showalter, particularly in *The Female Malady: Women, Madness and English Culture, 1830–1980* (New York: Pantheon, 1985), is a very honourable exception to this ahistoricism.

3 Terry Eagleton's work, *Myths of Power: a Marxist Study of the Brontës* (London: Routledge and Kegan Paul, 1974) forms an obvious exception to this apolitical trend in Brontë criticism, though he tends to ignore the gender politics and, in concentrating on the sub-text of the narrative, often misses the politics encoded in the linguistic texture of the work. John Kucich's excellent discussion of Brontë in *Repression in Victorian Fiction* (Berkeley: University of California Press, 1987) highlights the psychological dynamics of power struggles in the text but suggests that 'the novels refuse to examine how the kind of personal power in repression that they glorify is related to either class struggle or sexism' (p. 112).

4 Michel Foucault, *Discipline and Punish: The Birth of the Prison*, trans. A. Sheridan (Harmondsworth: Penguin, 1979) and *The History of Sexuality*, vol. 1, trans. R. Hurley (Harmondsworth: Penguin, 1981). See also Richard Sennett, *The Fall of Public Man* (New York: Knopf, 1977) for similar arguments from a rather different theoretical perspective.

5 In focusing on the role of phrenology, I am departing from Foucault who suggests that concern is no longer focused on 'the signifying elements of behaviour or the language of the body' (*Discipline and Punish*, p. 137).

6 See Ian Jack, 'Physiognomy, Phrenology and Characterisation in the Novels of Charlotte Brontë', *Brontë Society Transactions*, 15 (1970), pp.

337–91 and Wilfrid M. Senseman, 'Charlotte Brontë's Use of Physiognomy and Phrenology', *Papers of the Michigan Academy of Sciences, Arts and Letters*, 37 (1952), pp. 475–86. Karen Chase in *Eros and Psyche: The Representation of Personality in Charlotte Brontë, Charles Dickens, and George Eliot* (London: Methuen, 1984) does look at the social context of phrenology, but does not then sustain this social dimension in her wider analysis of Brontë's psychological thought.

1 THE ART OF SURVEILLANCE

1 Charlotte Brontë, *Villette*, ed. H. Rosengarten and M. Smith (Oxford: Oxford University Press, 1984), p. 355.

2 See Ludmilla Jordanova, *Sexual Visions: Images of Gender in Science and Medicine between the Eighteenth and Twentieth Centuries* (London: Harvester Press, 1989) and Evelyn Fox Keller, *Reflections on Gender and Science* (New Haven: Yale University Press, 1985).

3 Charlotte Brontë, *The Professor*, ed. Margaret Smith and Herbert Rosengarten (Oxford: Oxford University Press, 1987), p. 21.

4 Charlotte Brontë, *Jane Eyre*, ed. Jane Jack and Margaret Smith (Oxford: Oxford University Press, 1969), pp. 452, 511.

5 See, for example, Mrs Henry Wood, *St Martin's Eve* (1866) and Mary E. Braddon, *Lady Audley's Secret* (1862). For a discussion of the doctor's role in the earlier decades of Victorian fiction see F. R. Leavis and Q. D. Leavis, *Dickens the Novelist* (London: Chatto and Windus, 1970), p. 180.

6 'The origin of the Islanders', p. 6 in Christine Alexander, ed. *An Edition of the Early Writings of Charlotte Brontë*, vol. I: *The Glass Town Saga 1826–1832* (Oxford: Basil Blackwell, 1987).

7 'Characters of the Celebrated Men of the Present Time, by Captain Tree', in *Early Writings*, I, p. 126.

8 Thomas John Graham, *Modern Domestic Medicine* (London: Simpkin and Marshall et al, 1826). This work is in the Brontë Parsonage Museum, together with several other of the Reverend Brontë's medical books.

9 Foucault, *The History of Sexuality*, vol. I, trans. R. Hurley (Harmondsworth: Penguin, 1981).

10 For a discussion of Eliot's indebtedness to science see S. Shuttleworth, *George Eliot and Nineteenth-Century Science: The Make-Believe of a Beginning* (Cambridge: Cambridge University Press, 1984) and for Collins, Jenny Bourne Taylor, *In the Secret Theatre of Home: Wilkie Collins, Sensation Narrative, and Nineteenth-Century Psychology* (London: Routledge, 1988).

11 Christine Alexander, ed., *An Edition of the Early Writings of Charlotte Brontë*, vol. II: *The Rise of Angria 1833–1835. Part 2: 1834–1835* (Oxford: Basil Blackwell, 1991), p. 237.

12 See Elaine Showalter, *The Female Malady: Women, Madness and English Culture, 1830–1980* (New York: Pantheon, 1985), p. 68.

13 For an excellent discussion of this issue with reference to physiology see

Georges Canguilhem, *Essai sur quelques problèmes concernant le normal et le pathologique* (Paris: Publication de la Faculté des Lettres de l'Université de Strasbourg, 1950).

14 See, for example, John Barlow, *On Man's Power Over Himself to Prevent or Control Insanity* (London: William Pickering, 1843), p. 10 and John Conolly, *An Inquiry Concerning the Indications of Insanity* (1830; repr. London: Dawsons, 1964), p. 109.

15 John Charles Bucknill and Daniel H. Tuke, *A Manual of Psychological Medicine* (Philadelphia: Blanchard and Lea, 1858; repr. New York: Hafner, 1968), p. 184.

16 See Cynthia Eagle Russett, *Sexual Science: the Victorian Construction of Womanhood* (Cambridge, MA: Harvard University Press, 1989).

17 T. J. Wise and J. A. Symington, *The Brontës: their Lives, Friendships and Correspondence*, 4 vols. (Oxford: Basil Blackwell, 1933), II, p. 173. Letter to W. S. Williams, 4 January 1848. (Cited in future as *Letters*.)

18 James Cowle Prichard, *A Treatise on Insanity and other Disorders Affecting the Mind* (London: Sherwood, Gilbert and Piper, 1835). For a brief discussion of this point see, Elaine Showalter, *A Literature of their Own: British Women Novelists from Brontë to Lessing* (Princeton: Princeton University Press, 1977), pp. 119–20.

19 For a book-length demonstration of this tendency see John Charles Bucknill, *The Mad Folk of Shakespeare: Psychological Essays*, 2nd edn. (London: Macmillan, 1867). As Helen Small has argued, the use of literary texts also helped medical writers to consolidate their professional and social position by confirming their cultural credentials ('Representing Madness: the Politics of Insanity in Nineteenth-Century English Novels and Medical Texts, c. 1800 – c. 1865', University of Cambridge PhD, 1992, ch. 1).

20 Conolly, *An Inquiry*, p. 348.

21 *Letters*, III, p. 314. To George Smith, 14 February 1852. For her complaints about the behaviour of her doctor, see her letter to Ellen Nussey, 16 February 1852, *Letters* III, pp. 315–16.

22 *Letters*, III, p. 172. To G. H. Lewes, 17 October 1850.

23 In this regard, Richardson's work is far closer to the paradigms of the nineteenth-century novel.

24 See G. Canguilhem, *Etudes d'histoire et de philosophie des sciences* (Paris, 1968), pp. 148–50.

25 Michel Foucault, *The Birth of the Clinic: An Archaeology of Medical Perception*, trans. A. M. Sheridan (London: Tavistock, 1973), p. 120.

26 Lawrence Rothfield, in *Vital Signs: Medical Realism in Nineteenth-Century Fiction* (Princeton: Princeton University Press, 1992), argues that the rise and decline of realism as an 'authoritative literary praxis' can be directly tied to the cultural position of clinical medicine in the nineteenth century. While endorsing the obvious relationship between the two fields, I would argue for more of a dynamic, interactive exchange within a wider cultural field.

27 Charles Dickens, *Dombey and Son*, ed. Peter Fairclough (Harmondsworth: Penguin, 1970), p. 738.

28 George Eliot, *Middlemarch*, ed. W. J. Harvey (Harmondsworth: Penguin, 1965), p. 194.

29 For a subtle discussion of this idea with reference to *Middlemarch* see Gillian Beer, 'Circulatory Systems: Money, Gossip and Blood in *Middlemarch*', in *Arguing with the Past: Essays in Narrative from Woolf to Sidney* (London: Routledge and Kegan Paul, 1989), pp. 99–116.

30 Rothfield, *Vital Signs*, p. 85.

2 THE HAWORTH CONTEXT

1 Richard Offor, 'The Brontës – their Relation to the History and Politics of their Time', *Brontë Society Transactions*, 10 (1946), p. 160.

2 Such investment in notions of intuitive genius can be found in early feminist readings, and also in John Maynard, *Charlotte Brontë and Sexuality* (Cambridge: Cambridge University Press, 1984).

3 Elizabeth Gaskell, *The Life of Charlotte Brontë* (London: Dent, 1958), p. 58.

4 Harriet Martineau, 'Death of Currer Bell', *Daily News*, April 1855.

5 Charlotte writes to Branwell, for example, on 17 May 1831 of her 'extreme pleasure' at the news of 'the Reform Bill's being thrown out by the House of Lords' which has thoroughly revived her 'penchant for politics' (T. J. Wise and J. A. Symington, The Brontës: their Lives, Friendships and Correspondence, 4 vols. (Oxford: Basil Blackwell, 1933), I, p. 88. Cited in Future as *Letters*). References to the political arena continue to pepper her letters, particularly at times of crisis as in 1848. The picture we have is only partial, however, and it is clear from the spread of the extant letters that she tended to confine herself more to domestic matters when corresponding with Ellen Nussey who is the recipient of the main bulk of surviving letters. It is unfortunate, in this regard, that we do not have her letters to the fiercely political Mary Taylor.

6 See John Lock and Canon W. T. Dixon, *A Man of Sorrow: The Life, Letters and Times of the Reverend Patrick Brontë, 1777–1861* (London: Nelson, 1965), pp. 352, 345.

7 See Lock and Dixon, *Man of Sorrow*, pp. 330–3.

8 See Maxine Berg, *The Machinery Question and the Making of Political Economy, 1815–48* (Cambridge: Cambridge University Press, 1980), pp. 102, 165.

9 See E. P. Thompson, *The Making of the English Working Class* (Harmondsworth: Penguin, 1980), p. 319.

10 See J. Horsfall Turner, *Haworth – Past and Present: A History of Haworth, Stanbury and Oxenhope* (Brighouse: J. S. Jowett, 1879), p. 128, and William White, *Directory and Topography of Leeds, Bradford ... and the whole of the Clothing Districts of the West Riding of Yorkshire* (Sheffield: R. Leader, 1847), p. 328.

11 Benjamin Herschel Babbage, *Report to the General Board of Health on a*

Preliminary Inquiry into the Sewerage, Drainage, and Supply of Water, and Sanitary Condition of the Inhabitants of the Hamlet of Haworth, in the West Riding of the County of York (London: Her Majesty's Stationery Office, 1850), p. 6.

12 Lock and Dixon, *Man of Sorrow*, pp. 100–13.

13 Gaskell, *Life*, p. 32.

14 Lock and Dixon, *Man of Sorrow*, pp. 316, 332.

15 Babbage, *Report*, pp. 12–13.

16 'Influence of Free Trade upon the Conditions of the Labouring Classes', *Blackwood's Edinburgh Magazine* (1830), quoted in Berg, *Machinery Question*, p. 257.

17 Edward Baines, 'The Social, Educational, and Religious State of the Manufacturing Districts', in *The Factory Education Bill of 1843. British Labour Struggles: Contemporary Pamphlets 1727–1850* (New York: Arno Press, 1972), pp. 54–5. The quotations are taken from the second open letter to Sir Robert Peel, dated 24 June 1843.

18 *Letters* II, p. 220. To W. S. Williams, 15 June 1848.

19 See letters to Ellen Nussey and her father, 24 and 26 June 1851, *Letters*, III, pp. 251–2. The national excitement generated by the exhibition is suggested in some small measure by the two local newspapers, the *Leeds Intelligencer* and the *Leeds Mercury*. For a full year before the exhibition opened they ran articles on the subject nearly every issue, whilst the Keighley Mechanics' Institute held lectures in February 1851 on how to organize clubs and parties to attend the Exhibition.

20 *Report of the West-Riding Union of Mechanics' Institutes, 1851* (Leeds: Edward Baines, 1852), p. 54. The existence of the Haworth Mechanics' Institute has generally been overlooked by Brontë critics. Although founded a lot later than the Keighley branch, its emergence points to the groundswell of interest in self-cultivation and the sciences in the local area in the 1840s. The exact date of the founding is unclear; when it petitioned to join the Yorkshire Union of Mechanics' Institutes in 1850 it had 106 members and ten women listed, and a library of 385 volumes (with 2682 annual issues).

21 The Reverend Brontë is officially registered as a member from 1833, but it is clear that he had connections with the Institute, which was founded in 1825, before this time. The report for 1831 lists a book bill in his name.

22 Editorial in the first edition of *The Monthly Teacher*, January 1829. Dury was a friend of Faraday and an enthusiastic member of the Society for the Diffusion of Useful Knowledge which brought him into contact with some of the foremost scientists of the day. For further information on Theodore Dury see the memoir included in Robert Holmes, *Keighley Past and Present* (London: Arthur Hall, 1858).

23 See *Report of the West-Riding Union of Mechanics' Institutes Yorkshire Union* (Leeds: Edward Baines, 1847).

24 Editorial, *Leeds Mercury*, 4 January 1851.

25 Keighley Mechanics' Institute, Annual Report, 1825, p. 5.

26 *Ibid.*, 1831, p. 4.
27 *Ibid.*, 1840, p. 4.
28 *Ibid.*, 1832, p. 5.
29 *Letters*, ii, p. 115. To Ellen Nussey, 14 October 1846.
30 This was very much the model for other local libraries such as the Bradford Mechanics' Institute, set up in 1832, which had 800 books by 1833, but not one work of fiction (Miles E. Hartley, 'The Literary Institutions of Bradford: With Notes on Early Printers and Booksellers', *Book Auction Record*, 14, part 2 (1917), p. 2). The Bradford Library and Literary Society, which listed the Reverend Brontë as a subscriber during his years at Thornton, had a similar array of books.
31 Barbara Munson Goff, 'Between Natural Theology and Natural Selection: Breeding the Human Animal in *Wuthering Heights*', *Victorian Studies* 27 (1984), pp. 477–508. What Goff does not note in this article is that the discourse on breeding she traces with reference to the animal world was also present in the medical writing of the time, and was available to Emily in her father's copy of William Buchan's *Domestic Medicine*, an eighteenth-century work constantly reprinted in the nineteenth century. His observations here on the failure of men to follow, with respect to their own breeding, the laws they follow with respect to their dogs and horses are extended further in his *Advice to Mothers* which concludes with a 'Sketch for a Plan for the Preservation and Improvement of the Human Species' (*Domestic Medicine* 6th edn, London: W. Strahan, 1779), p. 9 and *Advice to Mothers* (Boston: J. Bumstead, 1809), p. 103.
32 For a list of the library holdings in 1841, see Clifford Whone, 'Where the Brontës Borrowed Books', *Brontë Society Transactions*, 11 (1950), pp. 44–58.
33 Keighley Mechanics' Institute Annual Report, 1849.
34 *Report of the West-Riding Union of Mechanics' Institutes*, 1851.
35 *Letters*, i, p. 89. To Ellen Nussey.
36 *Letters*, i, p. 168. To John Milligan, 9 October 1838.
37 Other published authorities to which the Reverend Brontë refers include Buchan, presumably William Buchan's *Domestic Medicine*, which he notes in 1831 that he will retain together with the Graham, and John Elliotson. He notes opposite the title page in 1848: 'I have read many works, of Dr. Elliotson, and the ablest medical writers, and found this Book, as far as it goes, perfectly to accord with them, both in its descriptions of the symptoms of diseases, and their causes and remedies.'
38 Popular understanding of tic douloureux is suggested by references to it in advertisements for medical remedies where it is associated with hysteria and insanity. An advert for sasparilla in the *Leeds Intelligencer* 23 February 1852, speaks of its capacities to cure 'tic doloreux, or Neuralgia, palsy, epilepsy, insanity, idiocy, and many other distressing ailments, both of body and mind'. On a more elevated plane, Thomas Laycock in *A Treatise on the Nervous Diseases of Women* (London: Longman, 1840), argues that tic douloureux is one of the symptoms of hysteria, pp. 334–45.

39 Thomas John Graham, *Modern Domestic Medicine* (London: Simpkin and Marshall et al., 1826), pp. 197 and 368 (under the headings of 'apoplexy' and 'Indigestion or Dyspepsia').

40 Graham, *Modern Domestic Medicine*, entry on Night-mare. Robert Macnish's *Philosophy of Sleep* (Glasgow: W. R. M'Phun, 1830) was in the Keighley Mechanics' Institute library.

41 Charlotte first made contact with Dr John Forbes in 1849 with reference to Anne's illness. He was then physician to the Queen's Household. In 1853 he was to conduct her round Bethlehem hospital during her visit to London (see *Letters*, IV, p. 35. To Ellen Nussey, 19 January 1853.)

42 Mary Poovey, '"Scenes of an Indelicate Character": The Medical Treatment of Victorian Women', *Representations*, 14 (1986), pp. 137–68.

43 *Letters*, II, pp. 157–58. To Ellen Nussey, 29 November 1847.

44 'Electro-Biology', *Westminster Review* 55 (1851), p. 312. The article directly follows Harriet Taylor's article 'The Enfranchisement of Women' which Charlotte Brontë mentions in her letter to Elizabeth Gaskell, 20 September, 1851 (*Letters*, III, pp. 277–8).

45 John Eagles with postscript by J. F. Ferrier, 'What is Mesmerism?' *Blackwood's Edinburgh Magazine*, 70 (1851), p. 80.

46 *Ibid.*, postscript, p. 85.

47 'Electro-Biology', p. 312.

48 Even Eagles in 'What is Mesmerism?' grants 'a physical power to their science', p. 76.

49 Laycock, *A Treatise* p. 3. Such eminent figures as Dugald Stewart and David Brewster were also interested in mesmerism, as was the prominent physician, Dr Elliotson, whose work on *Human Physiology* the Reverend Brontë possessed.

50 This entry is placed opposite the title page in Graham: 'In 1850, I read a Treatise on *Mesmerism* – from which I learned that in order to mesmerize a subject he must be placed in a sitting posture, and the mesmerizer must stand before him, moving his hand, with the fingers pointed towards him, from the back of the crown, and at about an inch distance, slowly downwards for half an hour or nearly so, and when the mesmeric sleep takes place, in order to *demesmerize* the patient, the backs of the hands must be brought into contact, before him – and quickly separated in a horizontal line – for half an hour. To effect the sleep, steady looks are required, and both the operator, and the patient must have their minds absorbed in the undertaking.
    There is no danger. P. B.'

51 *Letters*, III, p. 200. To James Taylor, 15 January 1851.

52 William Grove, 'Mesmerism,' *Blackwood's Edinburgh Magazine*, 57 (1845), p. 222.

53 Eagles, 'What is Mesmerism?', p. 83.

54 T. M. Parssinen, 'Popular Science and Society: The Phrenological Movement in Early Victorian Britain', *Journal of Social History*, 7 (1974), pp. 1–20, p. 13.

55 See William Grove, 'Mesmerism', p. 239.
56 'Biographical notice of Ellis and Acton Bell', *Wuthering Heights*, ed. Hilda Marsden and Ian Jack (Oxford: Clarendon Press, 1976), p. 360.
57 *Letters*, III, p. 316. Letter to Ellen Nussey, 16 February 1852.
58 *Letters*, II, p. 292. Letter to W. S. Williams, 9 December 1848.
59 See, for example, her letter to Laetitia Wheelwright, 15 March 1849 (*Letters* II, pp. 315–16), and her letter to George Smith, 31 March 1851 (*Letters* III, p. 216).
60 *Letters*, III, p. 8. To Ellen Nussey, 14 July 1849.
61 *Letters*, III, p. 312. To Mrs Gaskell, 6 February 1852.
62 *Letters*, III, p. 286. To Mrs Gaskell, 6 November 1851.
63 *Letters*, II, p. 77. To Miss Wooler, 30 January 1846.
64 Graham, *Modern Domestic Medicine*, annotation p. 393.
65 *Ibid.*, p. 422. The Reverend Brontë also records that the recommended 'strengthening tincture for the weak and nervous' had been injurious to him, p. 111.
66 *Ibid.*, pp. 422–3.

3 INSANITY AND SELFHOOD

1 Quoted in V. Skultans, *Madness and Morals: Ideas on Insanity in the Nineteenth Century* (London: Routledge and Kegan Paul, 1975), p. 172.
2 For an account of this transition and the development of 'moral management' in England see: Andrew Scull, *The Most Solitary of Afflictions: Madness and Society in Britain 1700–1900* (New Haven and London: Yale University Press, 1993); M. Foucault, *Madness and Civilization: A History of Insanity in the Age of Reason*, trans. R. Howard (London: Tavistock, 1971); and R. Smith, *Trial by Medicine: Insanity and Responsibility in Victorian Trials* (Edinburgh: Edinburgh University Press, 1981).
3 John Conolly, *An Inquiry Concerning the Indications of Insanity* (1830; repr. London: Dawsons, 1964), p. 8.
4 *Ibid.*, p. 227.
5 See Scull, *The Most Solitary of Afflictions*, p. 110.
6 Barlow, *On Man's Power over Himself to Prevent or Control Insanity* (London: William Pickering, 1843), p. 45.
7 As Roy Porter has pointed out, however, we should be wary of following Foucault in speaking of an epistemological rupture at the end of the eighteenth century. In England 'moral' forms of therapy were being tried out long before the end of the eighteenth century: Roy Porter, *Mind-Forg'd Manacles: A History of Madness in England from the Restoration to the Regency* (Cambridge, MA: Harvard University Press, 1987), p. 277.
8 J. E. D. Esquirol, *Mental Maladies: A Treatise on Insanity* trans. E. K. Hunt (1845: repr., New York: Hafner, 1965), p. 19. Esquirol was the successor of Pinel, the pioneer of moral management techniques in France. Although *Des mentales maladies* (1838) was not translated until 1845, his

work had been very influential in England long before then. John Conolly, for example, had made great use of Esquirol's *De la folie* (1816) in his 1821 dissertation, and he like many other physicians, such as the phrenology supporter Andrew Combe, went to observe Esquirol's work in France. A measure of Esquirol's popularity is the fact that the Keighley Mechanics' Institute added 'Esquirol, On Insanity' to their library in 1834. This was probably the collection of two short works, *Observations on the Illusions of the Insane, and On the Medico-Legal Question of their Confinement*, ed. William Liddell (London: Renshaw and Rush, 1833).

9 Esquirol, *Mental Maladies*, p. 20.
10 For a more extensive discussion of this point see Shuttleworth, *George Eliot and Nineteenth-Century Science* (Cambridge, Cambridge University Press, 1984), ch. 1.
11 Esquirol, *Mental Maladies*, p. 21.
12 In 'The Figure of the Hypocrite: Some Contours of an Historical Problem', *Studies in the History of Psychology and Social Sciences*, 4 (1987), pp. 256–74 and 'The Body In Question. Some Perceptions, Problems and Perspectives of the Body in Relation to Character, 1750–1850' (PhD, University of Leeds, 1985), Michael Shortland draws attention to the growing concern with the figure of the hypocrite in the eighteenth century. I would suggest that in the nineteenth century a form of masking starts to be seen as an essential attribute of the social being.
13 Charlotte Brontë, Juvenilia Fragment: 'But it is not in Society', transcribed by Hatfield, Brontë Parsonage Museum, HT67. The content suggests that this is an earlier or alternate version of the story 'Henry Hastings'.
14 Quoted in Michel Foucault, *The Birth of the Clinic: An Archaeology of Medical Perception*, trans. A. M. Sheridan (London: Tavistock, 1973), p. 166.
15 *Ibid.*, pp. 119–20.
16 Graeme Tytler, *Physiognomy in the European Novel: Faces and Fortunes* (Princeton: Princeton University Press, 1982), p. 135. For further studies in the impact of physiognomy on literature see Jeanne Fahnestock, 'The Heroine of Irregular Features: Physiognomy and Conventions of Heroine Description', *Victorian Studies*, 24 (1981), pp. 325–50, and F. Price, 'Imagining Faces: the Later Eighteenth-Century Sentimental Heroine and the Legible, Universal Language of Physiognomy', *British Journal for Eighteenth-Century Studies*, 6 (1983), pp. 1–16.
17 *The Italian* is invoked in *Shirley* in the scene where Caroline is subjected to Mrs Yorke's malign reading of her features.
18 The anti-Catholicism of *The Professor* and *Villette* is central to the nationalistic politics of those texts. Anti-Catholicism can be found, however, throughout Brontë's corpus. In *Shirley*, for example, Caroline, in rejecting the ideology of self-abnegation, singles out Catholicism as a pernicious threat to selfhood: 'Does virtue lie in abnegation of self? I do not believe it. Undue humility makes tyranny; weak concession creates selfishness. The Romish religion especially teaches renunciation of self, submission to others, and nowhere are found so many grasping tyrants as

in the ranks of the Romish priesthood'. Charlotte Brontë, *Shirley*, eds. Herbert Rosengarten and Margaret Smith (Oxford: Clarendon Press, 1979), p. 195.

19 *Leeds Intelligencer*, 26 January 1826.

20 Patrick Brontë, 'Popish Securities', *Leeds Intelligencer* 15 January 1829.

21 Quoted in Tytler, *Physiognomy*, p. 115.

22 Thomas Woolnoth, *Facts and Faces: or the Mutual Connexion between Linear and Mental Portraiture Morally Considered* (London: pub. by the author, 1852), p. 5.

23 *Ibid.*, p. 8.

24 John Reid, *Essays on Hypochondriasis and other Nervous Afflictions*, 2nd edn (London: Longman, 1821), p. 11.

25 'Moral Physiology; or, the Priest and the Physician', *The Journal of Psychological Medicine and Mental Pathology*, 1 (1848), p. 557.

26 Smith, *Trial by Medicine*, p. 35.

27 Reid, *Essays*, p. 314.

28 *Ibid.*, p. 316.

29 For example, the *Leeds Intelligencer*, 15 June 1850 advertisement for the Revd D. Willis' potion to cure 'Thoughts of self-destruction, Fear of Insanity, and other Nervous Sufferings, and Insanity itself'.

30 For a discussion of this case see S. Shuttleworth, '"Preaching to the Nerves": Psychological Disorder in Sensation Fiction', in M. Benjamin, ed., *A Question of Identity: Women, Sceince and Literature* (New Brunswick, NJ: Rutgers University Press, 1993).

31 John Haslam, *Considerations on the Moral Management of Insane Persons* (London: R. Hunter, 1817), p. 4.

32 *Ibid.*, p. 5.

33 The concern that physicians are taking on the rather disturbing powers of the Roman Catholic priesthood continues through the century. Frances Power Cobbe, for example, observes in 1878 that the medical profession occupies 'with a strangely close analogy, the position of the priesthood of former times, assumes the same airs of authority ... and enters every family with a latch key of private information', 'The Little Health of Ladies' *Contemporary Review* (1878) quoted in Jeffrey Weeks, *Sex, Politics, and Society: The Regulation of Sexuality since 1800* (Harlow: Longman, 1981), p. 42.

34 See Richard Hunter and Ida Macalpine, *Three Hundred Years of Psychiatry, 1535–1860* (London: Oxford University Press, 1963), p. 538, and Porter, *Mind-Forg'd Manacles*, pp. 209–13.

35 John Conolly, *The Treatment of the Insane without Mechanical Restraints* (1856; repr. London: Dawsons, 1973), p. 282.

36 Jeremy Bentham, *Panopticon; or, The Inspection-House* (1791) in *Works* (Edinburgh: William Tait, and London: Simpkin Marshall, 1843), IV, p. 39.

37 J. C. Bucknill and D. H. Tuke, *A Manual of Psychological Medicine* 3rd edn. (London: J. and A. Churchill, 1874), pp. 671–72.

38 John Haslam, in 1809, had similarly referred to 'this fascinating power'

which the mad doctor possessed over the lunatic in *Observations on Madness and Melancholy*, quoted in Porter, *Mind-Forg'd Manacles*, p. 275.

39 See Shuttleworth, 'Preaching to the Nerves'.

40 Alexander Welsh, *George Eliot and the Art of Blackmail* (Cambridge, MA: Harvard University Press, 1985). The opening sections of this work offer an excellent introduction to the rise of the new information culture in the mid-Victorian era.

41 Charlotte Brontë *The Professor*, ed. Margaret Smith and Herbert Rosengarten (Oxford: Oxford University Press, 1987) p. 21.

42 Bentham, *Panopticon*, p. 44.

43 Conolly, *An Inquiry Concerning the Indications of Insanity*, p. 496.

44 Barlow, *On Man's Power*, p. 49.

45 See Scull, *The Most Solitary of Afflictions*, ch. 7.

46 See Roy Porter, 'The Rage of Party: A Glorious Revolution in English Psychiatry?' *Medical History*, 27 (1983), p. 43.

47 Charles Turner Thackrah, *The Effects of Arts, Trades, and Professions, and of Civic States and Habits of Living, on Health and Longevity*, 2nd edn 1832; repr. with intro. by A. Meiklejohn (London: E. and S. Livingstone, 1957), p. 164. A copy of Thackrah's work was purchased by the Keighley Mechanics' Institute.

48 *Ibid.*, p. 164.

49 Thomas Trotter, *A View of the Nervous Temperament; being a Practical Enquiry into the Increasing Prevalence, Prevention, and Treatment of those Diseases* (London, 1807; repr. New York: Arno Press, 1976), p. xi.

50 For a study of this area see George Rosen, *From Medical Police to Social Medicine: Essays on the History of Health Care* (New York: Science History Publications, 1974).

51 Barlow, *On Man's Power*, p. 40.

52 T. J. Wise and T. A. Symington, *The Brontës: their Lives, Friendships and Correspondence*, 4 vols, (Oxford: Basil Blackwell, 1933), II, pp. 202–3.

53 Esquirol, *Mental Maladies*, p. 200.

54 J. C. Prichard, *A Treatise on Insanity and Other Disorders Affecting the Mind* (Philadelphia, 1837; repr. New York: Arno Press, 1973), p. 16.

55 J. C. Prichard, 'Insanity', in J. Forbes, A. Tweedie and J. Conolly (eds.), *The Cyclopaedia of Practical Medicine*, 4 vols. (London: Sherwood et al, 1833), II, p. 350.

56 *Ibid.*, II, p. 330.

57 John Conolly, *The Croonian Lectures. On Some of the Forms of Insanity* (London, 1849; repr. York: Ebor Press, 1960), pp. 68–69.

58 Prichard, *Treatise on Insanity*, p. 60.

59 Bucknill and Tuke, *Psychological Medicine*, pp. 188–9.

60 Emily Brontë, *Wuthering Heights,* ed. Hilda Marsden and Ian Jack (Oxford: Clarendon Press, 1976), p. 394.

61 In his *Treatise on Insanity* Prichard suggests that moral insanity usually precedes monomania (p. 31), while Esquirol, in turn, draws distinctions

between intellectual, affective, and instinctive monomania. The latter, he suggests, is equivalent to Prichard's moral insanity (*Mental Maladies*, p. 321).

62 Prichard, *Treatise on Insanity*, p. 17.
63 John Wilson, review of R. H. Horne, *The False Medium, Blackwood's Edinburgh Magazine*, 34 (1833), p. 440.
64 Roger Cooter, 'Phrenology and British Alienists, 1825–1845', in ed. A. Scull, *Madhouses, Mad-doctors, and Madmen: The Social History of Psychiatry in the Victorian Era* (London: Athlone Press, 1981), pp. 58–104.
65 George Combe, *Letter from George Combe to Francis Jeffrey, Esq., in Answer to his Criticism on Phrenology*, 2nd edn (Edinburgh: John Anderson, 1826). See also Andrew Combe, *Observations on Mental Derangement* (Edinburgh: John Anderson, 1831).
66 Esquirol, *Observations on the Illusions of the Insane*, p. 82.
67 A. Brierre de Boismont, *On Hallucinations: A History and Explanation of Apparitions, Visions, Dreams, Ecstasy, Magnetism, and Somnambulism*, trans. Robert T. Hulme (London: Henry Renshaw, 1859), p. 191.
68 Prichard, 'Insanity' in Forbes, Tweedie and Conolly, *The Cyclopaedia*, p. 327.
69 Esquirol, *Observations on the Illusions of the Insane*, p. 35.
70 For a detailed study of this area see Sander Gilman, *Seeing the Insane* (New York: John Wiley, 1982).
71 Conolly, *The Indications of Insanity*, p. 379.
72 Roger Smith, *Trial by Medicine*, p. 3.
73 *Ibid.*, p. 39.
74 *Ibid.*, p. 11.
75 *Fraser's*, for example, carried an article in 1849 on 'The Lord Chief Baron's Law of Lunacy', 40, pp. 363–73.
76 'The Plea of Monomania in Criminal Cases', *Journal of Psychological Medicine and Mental Pathology*, 1 (1848), p. 484.
77 'On Monomania', *Journal of Psychological Medicine and Mental Pathology*, 9 (1856), p. 504.
78 *Ibid.*, p. 520.
79 *Ibid.*, p. 519.
80 *Ibid.*, p. 505.

4 READING THE MIND: PHYSIOGNOMY AND PHRENOLOGY

1 Philip Collins, review of David Giustino, *Conquest of Mind: Phrenology and Victorian Social Thought*, *TLS*, 25 April 1975, p. 455.
2 Brontë and Smith visited the phrenologist, Dr J. C. Browne, in June 1851. His analysis identifies Brontë as having remarkable intellectual development, a 'fine organ of language' and 'originality and power' in 'analysing the motives of human conduct'. This phrenological estimate is reprinted, rather inaccurately, in T. J. Wise and J. A. Symington, *The Brontës: their Lives, Friendships and Correspondence*, 4 vols. (Oxfors: Basil

Blackwell, 1933), vol. III, pp. 256–8. Hereafter cited as *Letters*. ('Gale's doctrine', for example, should read 'Gall's doctrine'.)

3 'The Duke of Zamorna', in T. J. Wise and J. A. Symington eds., *The Miscellaneous and Unpublished Writings of Charlotte and Patrick Branwell Brontë*, 2 vols. (Oxford: Basil Blackwell, 1936), II, p. 379. The piece is dated 21 July 1838.

4 *Letters*, III, p. 341. To Ellen Nussey, 1 July 1852; III, 178. To James Taylor, 6 November 1850.

5 *Letters*, III, p. 315. To George Smith, 14 February 1852.

6 *Letters* I, p. 212. This forms part of a draft of a letter of reply to Wordsworth when he returned a story she had sent him in 1840.

7 *Letters*, III, p. 24. To W. S. Williams, 21 September 1849.

8 *Letters*, III, p. 183. To G. H. Lewes, 23 November 1850.

9 *Letters*, III, p. 282. To W. S. Williams, 26 September 1851.

10 See Wilfrid M. Senseman, 'Charlotte Brontë's Use of Physiognomy and Phrenology', *Papers of the Michigan Academy of Sciences, Arts and Letters*, 37 (1952), pp. 475–86 and Ian Jack, 'Physiognomy, Phrenology and Characterisation in the Novels of Charlotte Brontë', *Brontë Society Transactions*, 13 (1970), pp. 337–91. Karen Chase, in *Eros and Psyche: The Representation of Personality in Charlotte Brontë, Charles Dickens, and George Eliot* (London: Methuen, 1984), looks briefly at Brontë's use of phrenology, highlighting some of the conflictual aspects of the phrenological system which will figure in my own analysis. A good general discussion of physiognomy in the novel is to be found in Graeme Tytler, *Physiognomy in the European Novel: Faces and Fortunes* (Princeton: Princeton University Press, 1982).

11 For an in-depth analysis of the importance of phrenology in the development of psychology as a biological science see Robert M. Young, *Mind, Brain and Adaptation in the Nineteenth Century: Cerebral Localization and its Biological Context from Gall to Ferrier* (Oxford: Oxford University Press, 1970).

12 For an analysis of other eighteenth-century theorists of physiognomy see Ludmilla Jordanova, 'The Art and Science of Seeing in Medicine: Physiognomy, 1780–1820' in W. F. Bynum and R. S. Porter eds., *Medicine and the Five Senses* (Cambridge: Cambridge University Press, 1989).

13 John Graham records in his article, 'Lavater's *Physiognomy* in England', *Journal of the History of Ideas*, 22 (1961), pp. 561–72, that by 1810 there were twenty English versions, p. 562. There was a copy of Lavater's *Aphorisms on Man* in the Ponden House Library which the Brontës are known to have used.

14 John Caspar Lavater, *Essays on Physiognomy*, trans. Thomas Holcroft, 9th edn (London: William Tegg, 1855), p. 11.

15 *Ibid.*, p. 14.

16 For an analysis of the relationship between Lavater and contemporary theories of semiotics see Michael Shortland, 'Skin deep: Barthes, Lavater

and the Legible Body', *Economy and Society*, 14 (1985), pp. 273–312.

17 Lavater, *Essays*, p. 55.

18 *Ibid.*, p. 55.

19 *Ibid.*, p. 7.

20 Francois Joseph Gall, *On the Functions of the Brain*, trans. W. Lewis, 6 vols. (Boston: Marsh, Capen and Lyon, 1835), v, p. 262.

21 Lavater, *Essays*, p. 180.

22 Oswei Temkin, 'Gall and the Phrenological Movement', *Bulletin of the History of Medicine*, 21 (1947), pp. 275–321, see pp. 277–8.

23 Gall, *On the Functions*, v, p. 265.

24 Robert M. Young, *Mind, Brain and Adaptation*, p. 56; and Temkin, *Gall and the Phrenological Movement*, p. 278.

25 Gall *On the Functions*, vi, p. 308.

26 G. H. Lewes, *The Biographical History of Philosophy* (London: John W. Parker, 1857), p. 632. See also Young, *Mind, Brain and Adaptation*, p. 250.

27 Gall, *On the Functions*, vi, p. 308.

28 George Combe, *Elements of Phrenology*, 3rd edn (Edinburgh: John Anderson, 1828), p. 60.

29 Gall, *On the Functions*, ii, p. 43, quoted in J. Y. Hall, 'Gall's Phrenology: A Romantic Psychology', *Studies in Romanticism*, 16 (1977), pp. 305–17, p. 315.

30 For an excellent study of the social aspects of the phrenological movement see Roger Cooter, *The Cultural Meaning of Popular Science: Phrenology and the Organization of Consent in Nineteenth-Century Britain* (Cambridge: Cambridge University Press, 1984). See also De Giustino, *Conquest of Mind: Phrenology and Victorian Social Thought* (London: Croom Helm, 1975), and T. M. Parssinen, 'Popular Science and Society: The Phrenological Movement in Early Victorian Britain', *Journal of Social History*, 7 (1974), pp. 1–20.

31 Gall had maintained that, as the forms of crystals and plants had not changed since the creation, so man's moral and intellectual character could experience no essential change (Gall, *On the Functions*, vi, p. 278).

32 Parsinnen, 'Popular Science', p. 9.

33 See *Leeds Intelligencer*, 7 February 1829.

34 Keighley Mechanics' Institute Annual Report, 1836. For an analysis of the role of Mechanics' Institutes in popularizing phrenology see Cooter, *Cultural Meaning* and Parssinen, 'Popular Science' p. 9.

35 For a detailed list of the lectures at the Leeds Philosophical and Literary Society see E. Kitson Clark, *The History of One Hundred Years of the Leeds Philosophical and Literary Society* (Leeds: Jowett and Sowry, 1924).

36 See Richard W. Hamilton, *An Essay on Craniology* (London: Hurst Robinson; Edinburgh: Constable; and Leeds: Robinson and Hernaman, 1826); and William Wildsmith, *An Inquiry Concerning the Relative Connexion which subsists between the Mind and the Brain: with remarks on Phrenology and Materialism* (London: Effingham Wilson; John Baines: Leeds, 1828).

37 For brief details on the relationship between the work of Combe and

Smiles see Angus McLaren, 'Phrenology: Medium and Message', *Journal of Modern History*, 46 (1974), p. 96 and Cooter, *Cultural Meaning* p. 178. The lectures which went to form *Self-Help* were delivered originally to the Leeds Mutual Improvement Society in 1845. For further details of Smiles' activities in Leeds, see A. Tyrrell, 'Class Consciousness in Early Victorian Britain: Samuel Smiles, Leeds Politics, and the Self-Help Creed', *Journal of British Studies*, 9 (1970), pp. 102–25.

38 For an important debate on responses to phrenology in Edinburgh see G. N. Cantor, 'The Edinburgh Phrenology Debate: 1803–28', and 'A Critique of Shapin's Local Interpretation of the Edinburgh Phrenology Debate', *Annals of Science*, 32 (1975), pp. 196–219, and pp. 245–56; and S. Shapin, 'Phrenological Knowledge and the Social Structure of Early Nineteenth-Century Edinburgh', *Annals of Science*, 32 (1975), pp. 219–43. See also S. Shapin, 'The Politics of Observation: Cerebral Anatomy and Social Interests in the Edinburgh Phrenology Disputes', in R. Wallis ed., *On the Margins of Science: The Social Construction of Rejected Knowledge*, Sociological Review Monographs, 27 (University of Keele, 1979), pp. 139–78, and 'Homo Phrenologicus: Anthropological Perspectives on a Historical Problem', in B. Barnes and S. Shapin eds., *Natural Order: Historical Studies of Scientific Culture* (London: Sage, 1979), pp. 41–71. A local study of responses in Sheffield is offered by I. Inkster, 'A Phase in Middle-Class Culture: Phrenology in Sheffield, 1824–1850', *Transactions of the Hunter Archaeological Society*, 10 (1978), pp. 273–9. The most extensive work on popular reception of phrenology is Roger Cooter's excellent study, *Cultural Meaning*. See also De Giustino, *Conquest of Mind*, and John D. Davies, *Phrenology, Fad and Science: A Nineteenth-Century Crusade* (New Haven: Yale University Press, 1955).

39 Quoted in Shapin, 'Phrenological Knowledge', p. 228.

40 'Mares'-Nests found by the Materialists, the Owenites, and the Craniologists', *Fraser's Magazine*, 9 (1834), pp. 424–34.

41 Temkin, *Gall and the Phrenological Movement* and Cooter, *Cultural Meaning*.

42 *Letters*, III, 75. To Margaret Wooler, 14 February 1850.

43 Quoted in Cooter, *Cultural Meaning*, p. 157. This was by no means the only reading of phrenology's position on sexual equality; phrenological theory could equally be used to sustain women's natural inequality as it was later used to sustain views of racial inequality. See, for example, 'On the Female Character', *The Phrenological Journal and Miscellany*, 2 (1824–5), p. 276.

44 For an analysis of women's relations to phrenology and mesmerism see Alison Winter, 'The Island of Mesmeria: the Politics of Mesmerism in Early Victorian Britain', (unpublished dissertation, Cambridge University, 1993).

45 *Letters*, I, p. 155. From Robert Southey, March 1837.

46 *Letters*, I, p. 240. To Ellen Nussey, 7 August 1841.

47 She thus advises Ellen Nussey to undertake the wearisome duties of

preparing for her brother's marriage since 'it is still exercise of the faculties which is always beneficial'. *Letters*, II, p. 37, 13 June 1845.

48 *Letters*, II, pp. 61–2. To Ellen Nussey, 18 September 1845.

49 *Letters*, II, p. 153. To G. H. Lewes, 6 November 1847.

50 *Letters*, II, p. 22. To M. Heger, 8 January 1845.

51 *Letters*, III p. 258. To George Smith, 2 July 1851.

52 *Letters*, III, p. 260. To George Smith, 8 July 1851.

53 Anne Brontë, *The Tenant of Wildfell Hall*, ed. Herbert Rosengarten (Oxford: Clarendon Press, 1992), p. 262. In a letter to Margaret Wooler, 30 January 1846, Charlotte observes of Branwell, 'the faculty of self-government is, I fear almost destroyed in him' (*Letters*, II, pp. 76–7).

54 Anne Brontë, *Tenant*, p. 206.

55 *Ibid.*, pp. 206–7.

56 From the *Encyclopaedia Britannica*, 8th edn, 1853–60, quoted in J. Graham, 'Lavter's *Physiognomy*', p. 562.

57 Richard Chevenix, *Phrenology Article of the Foreign Quarterly Review: with Notes by G. Spurzheim M.D.* (London: Treuttel et al, 1830), p. 38.

58 John Eagles, 'What is Mesmerism?' *Blackwood's Edinburgh Magazine*, 70 (*1851*), *p. 82.*

59 John Elliotson, *Human Physiology*, 5th edn (London: Longmans, 1840), pp. 388–9. This was one of the medical books which the Reverend Brontë owned and frequently referred to.

5 THE FEMALE BODILY ECONOMY

1 Charlotte Brontë, *Shirley*, eds. Herbert Rosengarten and Margaret Smith (Oxford: Clarendon Press, 1979) p. 128, and *Jane Eyre*, eds. Jane Jack and Margaret Smith (Oxford: Clarendon Press, 1969), p. 246.

2 'A Peep into a Picture Book', in T. J. Wise and J. A. Symington eds., *The Miscellaneous and Unpublished Writings of Charlotte and Patrick Branwell Brontë*, 2 vols. (Oxford: Basil Blackwell, 1936) I, p. 358. This piece has been republished in Christine Alexander, *An Edition of The Early Writings of Charlotte Brontë*, vol. II: *The Rise of Angria 1833–1835*. Part 2: 1834–1835 (Oxford: Basil Blackwell, 1991). The transcription of the early writings is a notoriously difficult task. Wherever possible I will be using the recent Alexander edition. On this occasion, however, the earlier Wise and Symington seems to be closer to the general sense of the piece. Alexander reads 'through' for 'though' and 'a vein [of] gold' for 'virgin gold' (pp. 88–89). 'Though' is clearly more appropriate, and 'virgin' avoids the awkward insertion of an additional 'of'.

3 For analysis of the associations between prostitutes and sewers see Alain Corbin, 'Commercial Sexuality in Nineteenth-Century France: A System of Images and Regulations', *Representations*, 14 (1986), pp. 209–19, and Peter Stallybrass and Allon White, *The Politics and Poetics of Transgression* (Ithaca, NY: Cornell University Press, 1986), ch. 3.

4 Quoted in Mary Putnam Jacobi, *The Question of Rest for Women During Menstruation* (New York: G. P. Putnam, 1877), p. 8.

5 'On the Hygenic Condition of Towns. Street Sweeping', *The Lancet*, 1 (1844), p. 104.

6 Herbert Spencer, *Social Statics: or The Conditions Essential to Human Happiness Specified, and the First of them Developed* (London: John Chapman, 1851), pp. 323–4.

7 John Hawkes, 'On the Increase of Insanity', *Journal of Psychological Medicine and Mental Pathology*, 10 (1857), p. 520. Although the emphasis in this article falls on the 'mental sanitary reform' of the working classes, women, that other troublesome class, were also ideological and practical targets.

8 For a detailed account of the Victorian practice of clitoridectomy, see Elaine Showalter, *The Female Malady: Women, Madness and English Culture, 1830–1980* (New York: Pantheon, 1985), pp. 75–78.

9 John Power, *Essays on the Female Economy* (London: Burgess and Hill, 1821), p. 4.

10 T. J. Wise and J. A. Symington, *The Brontës: their Lives, Friendships and Correspondence*, 4 vols. (Oxford, Basil Blackwell, 1933). Hereafter cited as *Letters*. III, p. 207. To George Smith, 5 February 1851.

11 'The Manufacturing Poor: the Means of Elevating their Moral Condition: Education', *Fraser's Magazine*, 39 (1849), pp. 127–8.

12 *Letters*, II, pp. 126–7. To Ellen Nussey, 14 February 1847.

13 See, for example, Louis Moore's inspection of Shirley's desk, *Shirley*, p. 595.

14 'Cholera Gossip', *Fraser's Magazine*, 39 (1849) p. 705; 'The Asiatic Cholera', *Fraser's Magazine*, 4 (1831), p. 625.

15 W. R. Greg, 'Prostitution', *Westminster Review*, 53 (1850), p. 477.

16 Charles Dickens, *Bleak House*, ed. Norman Page with an introduction by J. Hillis Miller, 1st edn. 1853 (Harmondsworth: Penguin, 1971), p. 364.

17 J. G. Millingen, *The Passions; or Mind and Matter. Illustrated by Considerations on Hereditary Insanity* (London: J. and D. Darling, 1848), p. 157. Millingen had been a resident at the famous Middlesex Lunatic Asylum at Hanwell, and wrote novels as well as medical texts. This work was designed for a general audience.

18 For an account of the development of theories of menstruation in the nineteenth century see Thomas Laqueur, *Making Sex: Body and Gender from the Greeks to Freud* (Cambridge, MA: Harvard University Press, 1990), ch. 5.

19 George Man Burrows, *Commentaries on the Causes, Forms, Symptoms, and Treatment, Moral and Medical, of Insanity* (London: 1828; repr. New York: Arno Press, 1976), p. 146.

20 For a discussion of earlier uses of the imagery of a thermometer and barometer, and its often overt sexual implications see Terry Castle, 'The Female Thermometer', *Representations*, 17 (1987), pp. 1–27.

21 Burrows, *Commentaries*, pp. 12–13. The case cited is drawn from the work of Esquirol.

22 *Ibid.*, p. 278.

23 The most influential text in this regard was Henry Maudsley's 'Sex in Mind and Education', *Fortnightly Review*, 15 (1874), pp. 466–83.

24 Thomas Laycock, *An Essay on Hysteria* (Philadelphia: Haswell, Barrington and Haswell, 1840), p. 69.

25 See Elaine Showalter, *A Literature of their Own: British Women Novelists from Brontë to Lessing* (Princeton: Princeton University Press, 1977), pp. 113–15.

26 Burrows, *Commentaries*, pp. 20–1.

27 Thomas Pidgin Teale, *A Treatise on Neuralgic Diseases, dependent upon irritation of the Spinal Marrow and Ganglia of the Sympathetic Nerve* (London: S. Highley, 1829).

28 Thomas John Graham, *Modern Domestic Medicine* (London: Simpkin and Marshall et al., 1826), p. 413.

29 William Buchan, *Domestic Medicine*, 6th edn. (London: W. Strahan, 1779), p. 270.

30 See, for example, 'Strange Disclosure on a Death Bed', *Leeds Intelligencer*, 22 June 1850.

31 The September 1829 edition of 'Blackwood's Young Men's Magazine', for example, carries the following advertisement: 'Sir Alexander Badey has discovered a medicine, the property of which is to cure people of all diseases' (ed. Christine Alexander, *An Edition of vol. 1: The Glass Town Saga 1826–1882, the Early Writings of Charlotte Brontë*, (Oxford: Basil Blackwell, 1987), p. 68.

32 *Leeds Intelligencer*, 25 February 1837.

33 *Ibid.*

34 A writer in *The Lancet*, which waged a wrathful campaign against these 'quack' remedies (on territorial rather than on medical grounds), calculated that five well-known advertisements appeared throughout the country newspapers and magazines a total of 626 times a week, which would make the expenditure on advertising alone, £16,000 per year. *The Lancet*, 2 (1845), p. 564.

35 *Leeds Mercury*, 11 January 1845.

36 It is possible, as was the case in some later American advertising, that the condition of obstruction which some of these pills claimed to cure was also that of pregnancy. This association, however, does not feature in the rhetoric of medical opposition to these remedies in the 1840s and 50s, an omission which suggests that abortion was not perceived to be the dominant message of these particular advertisements. Their ambiguous wording, nonetheless, often left this interpretation open to women who were seeking such a remedy.

37 *Leeds Intelligencer*, 2 February 1850. (This advertisement appeared the week prior to an extensive review of *Shirley*.)

38 See, for example, the advertisement for Dr Grandison's Charity Pills (*Leeds Mercury*, 18 January 1845).

39 John Elliotson, *Human Physiology*, 5th edn. (London: Longmans, 1840), p. 699. Patrick Brontë refers to this text frequently in his annotations in Graham's *Domestic Medicine*.

40 *Ibid.*, pp. 700–1.

41 William Acton, *The Functions and Disorders of the Reproductive Organs in Childhood, Youth, Adult Age, and Advanced Life Considered in their Physiological, Social and Moral Relations* (Philadelphia: Lindsay and Blakiston, 1865), p. 106.

42 'Woman in her Psychological Relations', *Journal of Psychological Medicine and Mental Pathology*, 4 (1851), p. 20.

43 *Ibid.*, p. 41.

44 My argument here differs substantially from that of Helena Michie in *The Flesh Made Word: Female Figures and Women's Bodies* (Oxford: Oxford University Press, 1987), who argues that the Victorian norm of femininity was that of the thin and delicate body, and that Gaskell, the Brontës and George Eliot use plumpness as a sign of fallen nature (pp. 21–2).

45 *Jane Eyre*, p. 181.

46 It is significant, however, that we are not informed at the end of the novel whether Caroline, or Shirley, do reproduce. In Brontë's final novel, *Villette*, Lucy Snowe, physically the slightest of her heroines, is left resolutely childless.

47 For details of these professional struggles see: Jean Donnison, *Midwives and Medical Men: a History of Inter-Professional Rivalries and Women's Rights* (London: Heinemann, 1977).

48 W. Tyler Smith, 'Introductory Lecture to a Course of Lectures on Obstetricy, Delivered at the Hunterian School of Medicine, 1847–48', *The Lancet*, 2 (1847), p. 371.

49 Laycock, for example, prefaces his analysis of female sexuality with a detailed account of the functions of 'ovaries' in plants. Laycock, *Hysteria*, p. 64.

50 See, however, the excellent study by Leonore Davidoff and Catherine Hall, *Family Fortunes: Men and Women of the English Middle Class, 1750–1850* (London: Hutchinson, 1987), which goes some way towards placing the increasing gender polarization at this period within the requisite economic frame.

51 Andrew Ure, *The Philosophy of Manufactures*, quoted in Maxine Berg, *The Machinery Question and the Making of Political Economy 1815–1848* (Cambridge: Cambridge University Press, 1980), p. 199.

52 Peter Gaskell, *Artisans and Machinery*, quoted in Berg, *Machinery Question*, p. 265. I am indebted to this latter work for much of the material in this section.

53 John Reid, *Essays on Hypochondriasis and other Nervous Affections*, 2nd edn. (London: Longman, 1821), p. 2.

54 Thomas Laycock, *A Treatise on the Nervous Diseases of Women; Comprising*

an Inquiry into the Nature, Causes, and Treatment of Spinal and Hysterical Disorders (London: Longman, 1840), p. ix.

55 *Jane Eyre*, p. 318.

56 The 'disease' became popular in England in the 1840s. See Michael Mason, *The Making of Victorian Sexuality* (Oxford: Oxford University Press, 1994), pp. 295–8.

57 For an elaboration of the economic argument see, B. Barker-Benfield, 'The Spermatic Economy: a Nineteenth-Century View of Sexuality', *Feminist Studies*, 1 (1972), pp. 45–74.

58 Samuel Hibbert, *Sketches of the Philosophy of Apparitions; or, An Attempt to Trace such Illusions to their Physical Causes*, 2nd. edn. (Edinburgh: Oliver and Boyd, 1825), p. 81.

59 Robert Brudenell Carter, *On the Pathology and Treatment of Hysteria* (London: John Churchill, 1853), p. 15.

60 *Ibid.*, p. 34.

61 See the discussion of Carter in Ilza Veith, *Hysteria: the History of a Disease* (Chicago: University of Chicago Press, 1965), ch. 9.

62 Herbert Spencer, 'The Social Organism', in *Essays: Scientific, Political, and Speculative*, 3 vols. (London: Williams and Norgate, 1891) I, p. 290.

63 *Ibid.*, p. 294.

64 Spencer, 'State-Tamperings with Money and Banks', in *Essays*, III, 350–2.

65 W. Tyler Smith, *The Lancet*, 2 (1847), p. 544.

66 William Buchan, *Domestic Medicine*, p. 591.

67 *Ibid.*, pp. 273–4.

68 Although the basic connection with ovulation was more or less understood by the 1860s, it was not until well into the twentieth century that the precise relationship was articulated. Well into the 1920s contraceptive advice literature offered woefully mistaken definitions of the 'safe' period.

69 Elliotson, *Human Physiology*, p. 768.

70 *Ibid.*, p. 770.

71 C. Locock, 'Menstruation, Pathology of', in *The Cyclopaedia of Practical Medicine*, ed. J. Forbes, A. Tweedie, and J. Conolly, 4 vols. (London: Sherwood et al., 1833), III, p. 110. Even in the 1854 revised reprint there is still no reference to any ovarian function: revised edn. by R. Dunglison (Philadelphia: Blanchard and Lea, 1854), III, p. 308.

72 See also Mason, *Making of Victorian Sexuality*, ch. 4, for a similar emphasis on Victorian perceptions of female sexuality.

73 'Woman in her Psychological Relations', p. 25.

74 'A Plea for Physicians', *Fraser's Magazine*, 37 (1848), pp. 293, 294.

75 J. C. Bucknill and D. H. Tuke, *A Manual of Psychological Medicine*, 3rd edn. (London: J. and A. Churchill, 1874), p. 47.

76 On fears of the effects of 'lesbian pleasures' see 'Woman in her Psychological Relations', p. 38.

77 M. Baillarger, 'A course of lectures on Diseases of the Brain, Lecture II', *The Lancet*, 1 (1845), p. 109.

78 Bucknill and Tuke, *Manual*, p. 104.

79 J. E. D. Esquirol, *Mental Maladies: A Treatise on Insanity*, trans. E. K. Hunt (1845: repr. New York: Hafner, 1965) p. 62.

80 See for example, 'Woman in her Psychological Relations', p. 19; and Burrows, *Commentaries*, p. 148.

81 Laycock, *Hysteria*, p. 76.

82 Buchan, *Domestic Medicine*, p. 577.

83 C. Locock, 'Menstruation', in Forbes ed., *Cyclopaedia* (1833), III, p. 111.

84 For Clifford Allbutt's wonderfully dismissive response to the gynaeocologists' obsession with the uterine diesase, see *On Visceral Neuroses* (Philadelphia: P. Blakiston, 1884), p. 17. The lectures were originally delivered at the Royal College of Physicians, 1884. Allbutt was a nephew of Brontë's teacher, Margaret Wooler, and was known to Brontë during his childhood in Dewsbury, see *Letters*, IV, p. 83. To Margaret Wooler, 30 August 1853.

85 Forbes ed., *Cyclopaedia* (1833), I, pp. 67–9.

86 E. Kennedy, 'On Uterine Diseases', *The Retrospect of Practical Medicine and Surgery*, 15 (1847), p. 350.

87 Robert Lee, 'On the Uses of the Speculum', *The Retrospect of Practical Medicine and Surgery*, 22 (1850), p. 357.

88 Carter, *Hysteria*, pp. 66–7.

89 *Ibid.*, p. 69.

90 Protheroe Smith, 'Proposals for the Improvement of the Diagnosis in the Investigation of Diseases of the Uterus, etc with an account of a newly-Invented Speculum Uteri', *The Lancet*, 1 (1845), p. 210.

91 See, for example, Thomas H. Burgess, *The Physiology or Mechanism of Blushing: Illustrative of the Influence of the Mental Emotions on the Capilliary Circulation* (London: John Churchill, 1835), p. 196.

92 Acton, for example, suggests that the reabsorption of semen into the body creates strength and vigour, *Functions and Disorders*, p. 197.

6   THE EARLY WRITINGS: PENETRATING POWER

1 'Silence, by the Marquis of Douro', in Christine Alexander, ed., *An Edition of the Early Writings of Charlotte Brontë*, vol. I: *The Glass Town Saga 1826–1832*, (Oxford: Basil Blackwell, 1987), p. 246. Hereafter cited as *Early Writings*, I.

2 T. J. Wise and J. A. Symington eds., *The Miscellaneous and Unpublished Writings of Charlotte and Patrick Branwell Brontë*, 2 vols. (Oxford: Basil Blackwell, 1936) II, p. 404. Hereafter cited as *Miscellaneous and Unpublished Writings*.

3 I do not wish to suggest that all realist texts actually follow this model, but rather that it exists as a regulatory ideal, from which texts then diverge, to a greater or lesser degree.

4 *Early Writings*, I, p. 343.

5 *Ibid.*, p. 344.

6 *Ibid.*, p. 345.

7 *Ibid.*, p. 346.

8 *Miscellaneous and Unpublished Writings*, II, p. 139. This tale is reprinted by Winifred Gerin under the title, 'Passing Events': Charlotte Brontë, *Five Novelettes* (London: Folio Press, 1971).

9 *Ibid.*, p. 139.

10 Christine Alexander, ed., *An Edition of the Early Writings of Charlotte Brontë* vol. II: *The Rise of Angria, 1833–1834*. Part 1: 1833–1834 (Oxford: Basil Blackwell, 1911), p. 13. Hereafter cited as *Early writings*, III.

11 *Ibid.*, p. 24.

12 *Ibid.*, p. 29. The quotation is from *Paradise Lost*, I, l. 742–3.

13 *Ibid.*, p. 38.

14 See, for example, Christine Alexander, *The Early Writings of Charlotte Brontë* (Oxford: Basil Blackwell, 1983), ch. 30.

15 Gerin ed., *Five Novelettes*, p. 177.

16 Brontë's source for her depiction of Zenobia was probably Edward Gibbon's *The History of the Decline and Fall of the Roman Empire*. The heroic ruler of Palmyra is praised for her formidable 'manly' intellect and learning. Like Brontë's heroine she was a Greek scholar who had studied under Longinus (notes by Rev H. H. Milman, 2nd edn, 6 vols. (London: John Murray, 1846), I, p. 314.

17 'Visits in Verreopolis', in *Early Writings*, I, p. 313.

18 *Ibid.*, pp. 313–4.

19 See T. J. Wise and J. A. Symington, *The Brontës: their Lives, Friendships and Correspondence*, 4 vols. (Oxford: Basil Blackwell, 1933), I, pp. 154–7. Hereafter cited as *Letters*. From Robert Southey, March 1837. Irene Tayler has pointed out in *Holy Ghosts: The Male Muses of Emily and Charlotte Brontë* (New York: Columbia University Press, 1990) that in 'Albion and Marina' Brontë was responding to Patrick's statement in 'The Maid of Killarney; or Albion and Flora' (1818) that an intellectual woman could never be loved. The echoes seem even more explicit in 'Visits to Verreopolis'.

20 *Early Writings*, I, pp. 300–1.

21 Gerin ed., *Five Novelettes*, 'Julia', p. 118 and 'Caroline Vernon', p. 307.

22 *Ibid.*, 'Captain Henry Hastings', p. 254.

23 'Four Years Ago', Hatfield Transcription 10, Brontë Parsonage Museum, p. 58.

24 'The Return of Zamorna', *Miscellaneous and Unpublished Writings*, II, pp. 286–93.

25 'The Green Dwarf. A Tale of the Perfect Tense by Lord Charles Albert Florian Wellesley', *Early Writings, II*, I, pp. 174–8.

26 *Ibid.*, p. 178.

27 There are also strong parallels between the figure of Quashia and Heathcliff in *Wuthering Heights* who is also probably of ethnic origin and rebels against the white family who have taken him in.

28 In addition to the examples given in the text, see also, for example, 'A Scene in my Inn', *Early Writings*, I, p. 82.

29 'The Adventures of Mon Edouard de Crack', (22 February 1830), *Early Writings*, I, p. 136.

30 'An Interesting Passage in the Lives of Some Eminent Men of the Present Time by Lord Charles Wellesley, June the 18 1830, by Charlotte Brontë', *Early Writings*, I, p. 175.

31 'Visits in Verreopolis', *Early Writings*, I, p. 315. Christine Alexander suggests that this might be one of Brontë's own texts that we have now lost.

32 'Four Years Ago', Hatfield Transcription 10, Brontë Parsonage Museum, p. 22.

33 *Ibid.*, pp. 25–6.

34 In one tale, Brontë suggests that writing is an act of self-instantiation. See 'Strange Events by Lord Charles Wellesley', *Early Writings*, I, pp. 257–8.

35 'The Spell, An Extravaganza. By Lord Charles Albert Florian Wellesley', in Christine Alexander, ed., *And Edition of the Early Writings of Charlotte Brontë, vol. II: The Rise of Angria 1833–1835. Part 2: 1834–1835*, p. 149. Hereafter cited as *Early Writings*, II, 2.

36 *Ibid.*, p. 150.

37 *Ibid.*, p. 151.

38 *Ibid.*, p. 150.

39 *Ibid.*, p. 159.

40 *Ibid.*, p. 186.

41 *Ibid.*, p. 211.

42 *Ibid.*, p. 211.

43 In a later reworking of this material in *The Professor*, Brontë was to draw on the language of this passage for the depiction of her most openly sexually ambivalent character, Yorke Hunsden. See *The Professor*, eds. Margaret Smith and Herbert Rosengarten (Oxford: Clarendon Press, 1987), p. 35.

44 In 'A Leaf from an Unopened Volume' *Early Writings* III, we learn that Arthur, Marquis of Douro, seduced and abandoned Sofala, and on her deathbed 'she prayed that her child might be a shame and a dishonour to its false father'. The fair infant then became hideous and deformed and subsequently had been brought up to hate its father (p. 376). For a description of the hideous deformity of Finic, see 'The Foundling', *Early Writings*, II, 1, p. 60.

45 *Early Writings*, II, 2, p. 187.

46 For a detailed theoretical exploration of the role of homoerotic and homosocial desire in English literature see Eve Kosofsky Sedgwick, *Between Men: English Literature and Male Homosocial Desire* (New York: Columbia University Press, 1985), and *Epistemology of the Closet* (Berkeley: University of California Press, 1990).

47 *Early Writings*, II, 2, p. 235.

48 *Ibid.*

49 *Ibid.*, p. 237.

50 *Ibid.*

51 *Ibid.*, pp. 237–78.
52 *Ibid.*, p. 238.
53 *Ibid.*, p. 234.
54 The text of 'John Henry' is reprinted in Charlotte Brontë, *Shirley*, eds. Herbert Rosengarten and Margaret Smith (Oxford: Clarendon Press, 1979), pp. 803–35. The editors suggest that it is probably a reworking of the material of *The Professor*, written some time before *Shirley*. 'The Story of Willie Ellin', a fragment of an unfinished novel, was written in the summer of 1853, illustrating the fact that Brontë's fascination with the theme of rivalry between two brothers continued to the very end of her writing career. The text was reprinted in *Brontë Society Transactions*, 9 (1936), pp. 3–22.
55 The letter itself, written by Branwell, is not given in the tale, but can be found in *Miscellaneous and Unpublished Writings*, 1, p. 460. This complex textual interrelationship illustrates both the closeness and rivalry between Branwell and Charlotte in their literary endeavours.
56 'My Angria and the Angrians, by Lord Charles Albert Florian Wellesley. October 14th 1834', *Early Writings*, 11, 2, p. 271.
57 'And When You Left Me', *Miscellaneous and Unpublished Writings*, 11, p. 241.
58 *Ibid.*, 11, p. 241, 243
59 'Four Years Ago', Hatfield Transcription 10, p. 17.
60 Gerin ed., *Five Novelettes*, p. 331.
61 *Ibid.*, p. 358.
62 'The Spell', *Early Writings*, 11, p. 200.
63 For a discussion of the negative social and sexual connotations attached to the figure of the governess in Victorian culture see, Mary Poovey, *Uneven Developments: The Ideological Work of Gender in Mid-Victorian England* (London: Virago, 1989), ch. 5. Miss Foxley is made to reside in a street known for prostitution. On attempting to find Harley Street, where Miss Foxley lives, Marian is informed that it is also called 'Paradise Street, my lady, 'cause there's a house in it that you wouldn't like to pass by yourself at this time of night', *Early Writings*, 11, 1, p. 281.
64 *Ibid.*, p. 285.
65 *Ibid.*, p. 289.
66 *Ibid.*, p. 299.

7 THE PROFESSOR: 'THE ART OF SELF-CONTROL'

1 Although *The Professor* was the first novel of Charlotte Brontë to be written, it was the last to be published, not seeing the light of day until after her death, in 1857. She made several attempts to revive it during her lifetime, but still encountered rejection from her publisher, George Smith. The Clarendon edition, eds. Margaret Smith and Herbert Rosengarten (Oxford: Clarendon Press, 1987) has gone back to the original manuscript, and gives a detailed textual history of the novel. The working title 'The

Master', was pasted over with the subsequent title, 'The Professor'. All future references to this edition will be given in the text.

2 Michel Foucault, *Discipline and Punish: The Birth of the Prison*, trans. A. Sheridan (Harmondsworth: Penguin, 1979).

3 Aeschylus, *The Orestian Trilogy*, trans. Philip Vellacott, (Harmondsworth: Penguin, 1959), p. 140.

4 For the story of Rebecca, being brought to Isaac as his bride, see Genesis 24.

5 See Robert Brudenell Carter, *On the Pathology and Treatment of Hysteria* (London: John Churchill, 1853), p. 34.

6 Janet Oppenheim, *'Shattered Nerves': Doctors, Patients, and Depression in Victorian England* (Oxford: Oxford University Press, 1991), p. 178.

7 See, for example, 'Woman in her Psychological Relations', *Journal of Psychological Medicine and Mental Pathology*, 4 (1851), p. 45.

8 Anne Brontë, *The Tenant of Wildfell Hall*, ed. Herbert Rosengarten (Oxford: Clarendon Press, 1992), ch. 3. Mrs Graham is advised by the Markham family that if she continues in her system of rearing her son she will make him into a 'milksop', and a 'Miss Nancy' (pp. 28–9).

9 See, for example, Elizabeth Fee, 'Nineteenth-Century Craniology: The Study of the Female Skull', *Bulletin of the History of Medicine*, 53 (1979), pp. 415–33.

10 George Combe, *The Constitution of Man Considered in Relation to External Objects*, 9th edn (Edinburgh: Maclachlan and Stewart, 1866), p. 132. This example was endlessly reproduced in popular phrenological manuals. The example was originally given in J. G. Spurzheim, *Phrenology in Connection with the Study of Physiognomy* (1826).

11 George Combe, *Elements of Phrenology*, 3rd edn (Edinburgh: John Anderson, 1828), pp. 35–6.

12 See Evelyn Fox Keller, *Reflections on Gender and Science* (New Haven: Yale University Press, 1985), ch. 2.

13 For an interesting analysis of the men and women's different relations to secrecy, see Evelyn Fox Keller, 'From Secrets of Life to Secrets of Death', in eds. Mary Jacobus Evelyn Fox Keller and Sally Shuttleworth, *Body/Politics: Women and the Discourses of Science* (New York and London: Routledge, 1990) *Body/Politics*, pp. 177–91.

14 For an excellent analysis of the dynamics of repression and repulsion which govern Crimsworth's narrative, see Heather Glen, ed., *The Professor* (Harmondsworth: Penguin, 1989), pp. 7–31.

15 For a discussion of the empowering nature of bi-lingualism in Brontë's fiction see Patricia Yaeger, *Honey-Mad Women: Emancipatory Strategies in Women's Writing* (New York: Columbia University Press, 1988), ch. 2. See also Penny Boumelha, *Charlotte Brontë* (Hemel Hempstead: Harvester Wheatsheaf, 1990), p. 10.

16 Similarly, in *Shirley*, Louis tames Shirley by making her recite in French.

17 George Combe, *The Constitution of Man considered in Relation to External Objects*, 7th American edn (New York: Appleton, 1836), pp. 46–7.

18 T. J. Wise and J. A. Symington, *The Brontës: their Lives, Friendships and*

Correspondence, 4 vols. (Oxford: Basil Blackwell, 1933), I, p. 158. Letter to Robert Southey, 16 March 1837. Hereafter cited as *Letters*.

19 For an interesting analysis of this 'menstrual image', see Boumelha, *Charlotte Brontë*, p. 55.

20 See Ludmilla Jordanova, *Sexual Visions: Images of Gender in Science and Medicine between the Eighteenth and Twentieth Centuries* (London: Harvester Press, 1989), ch. 5.

21 Despite the emphasis on the ovarian determination of femininity in the nineteenth century, this Aristotelian viewpoint still held considerable sway.

22 For a description of Brontë's own suffering from 'the tyranny of Hypochondria' whilst at Roe Head see *Letters*, II, pp. 116–7. In *Villette*, Lucy Snowe diagnoses the King as suffering from hypochondria (ch. 10).

23 See J. C. Bucknill and D. H. Tuke, *A Manual of Psychological Medicine* 3rd edn. (London: J. and A. Church, II, 1874), p. 234. The fact that hypochondria was very much part of the general public's understanding of mental disorder, and its relations to sexuality, is shown by the popular work, frequently advertised in Brontë's local newspapers, of J. R. Brodie, *The Secret Companion, a Medical Essay on the Treatment of Hypochondriacal Affections, Nervous and Mental Debility . . . (Leeds Intelligencer*, 1 January 1848).

24 Bucknill and Tuke, *Psychological Medicine*, p. 233.

25 L. Deslandes, *Manhood; the Causes of its Premature Decline* (Boston: Otis, Broaders and Company, 1843). This text was one of the regulars in the advertising columns of the Leeds newspapers, along with Charles Lucas' *The Controul of the Passions*.

26 Deslandes, *Manhood*, p. 30.

27 Acton, p. 133. Michael Mason, in his recent work, *The Making of Victorian Sexuality* (Oxford: Oxford University Press, 1994) offers a similar revision of our views of Acton, and offers a well-argued case for the continuance in the Victorian period of the belief that female orgasm was necessary for conception (ch. 4).

28 W. R. Greg, 'Why are Women Redundant?' (*National Review*, 1862) repr. in *Literary and Social Judgments* 4th edn (London: Trubner, 1877).

29 William Acton, *The Functions and Disorders of the Reproductive Organs in Childhood, Youth, Adult Age, and Advanced Life Considered in their Psychological, Social and Moral Relations* (Philadelphia: Lindsay and Blakiston, 1865), pp. 103, 134.

30 For an exploration of some of these contradictory views, see Michael Mason, *The Making of Victorian Sexuality*, 1994), ch. 4.

31 Deslandes, *Manhood*, p. 30.

32 See R. and L. Perry, *The Silent Friend; A Practical Work, Treating on the Anatomy and Physiology of the Organs of Generation, and their Diseases* (London, 1854), a regular in the local Leeds papers; and on a more elevated plain, 'A Case of Monomania, with Remarks', *Journal of Psychological Medicine and Mental Pathology*, 1 (1848), p. 647.

33 See p. 242. Although the insult is directed against Hunsden, he immediately reinforces the structural parallel between himself and

Crimsworth by suggesting that it will be the latter who will be Desdemona's victim.

34 The Clarendon edition actually reads, 'of mental'; this would appear to be a misprint and I have corrected it to 'or'.

8 JANE EYRE: 'LURID HIEROGLYPHICS'

1 See Sandra Gilbert and Susan Gubar, *The Madwoman in the Attic: The Woman Writer and the Nineteenth-Century Literary Imagination* (New Haven: Yale University Press, 1979), and Barbara Hill Rigney, *Madness and Sexual Politics in the Feminist Novel* (Madison: University of Wisconsin Press, 1978).

2 It is on this point that I would like to differentiate my work from Elaine Showalter's excellent study, *The Female Malady: Women, Madness, and English Culture, 1830–1980* (New York: Pantheon, 1985), which considers the notion of female madness within a narrower framework of social explanation.

3 Charlotte Brontë, *Jane Eyre*, eds. Jane Jack and Margaret Smith (Oxford: Clarendon Press, 1969), p. xxxi. All references to this edition will be given in future in the text.

4 See Matthew 23: 27.

5 T. J. Wise and J. A. Symington, *The Brontës: their Lives, Friendships and Correspondence*, 4 vols. (Oxford: Basil Blackwell, 1933), II, p. 198. Hereafter cited as *Letters*. To W. S. Williams, 11 March 1848.

6 *Letters*, II, p. 201. To W. S. Williams, 29 March 1848.

7 See Georges Canguilhem, *Essai sur quelques problèmes concernant le normal et le pathologique*, (Publications de la Faculté des Lettres de l'Université de Strasbourg) (Paris: 1950), p. 18.

8 Margot Peters, *Charlotte Brontë: Style in the Novel* (Madison: University of Wisconsin Press, 1973), p. 57.

9 See Mary Poovey, *Uneven Developments: The Ideological Work of Gender in Mid-Victorian England* (London: Virago, 1989), ch. 5, and M. Jeanne Peterson, 'The Victorian Governess: Status Incongruence in Family and Society' in Martha Vicinus, ed., *Suffer and Be Still: Women in the Victorian Age* (Bloomington: Indiana University Press, 1972), pp. 3–19.

10 See Peter Stallybrass and Allon White, *The Politics and Poetics of Transgression* (Ithaca, NY: Cornell University Press, 1986), ch. 3.

11 For a further reading of this interiority see Elaine Showalter, *A Literature of their Own: British Women Novelists from Brontë to Lessing* (Princeton: Princeton University Press, 1977) and Karen Chase, *Eros and Psyche: The Representation of Personality in Charlotte Brontë, Charles Dickens, and George Eliot* (London: Methuen, 1984), chs. 3 and 4.

12 Brontë's text points to the inadequacies of forms of Lacanian analysis which do not take full acount of the contradictory subject positions offered within a given culture.

13 George Combe, *Elements of Phrenology*, 3rd edn (Edinburgh: John Anderson, 1828), p. 60.

14 George Combe, *The Constitution of Man Considered in Relation to External Objects*, 7th edn (Boston: Marsh, Capen and Lyon, 1836), p. 104.

15 As Susan Meyer has pointed out in her excellent article, 'Colonialism and the Figurative Strategy of *Jane Eyre*', *Victorian Studies*, 33 (1990), the language of fire was also employed in representations of the revolt of that other oppressed group whose presence informs the text of *Jane Eyre*, the West Indian Slaves (p. 254).

16 James Kay Shuttleworth, *The Moral and Physical Condition of the Working Classes employed in the Cotton Manufacture in Manchester* (London, 1832; repr. Shannon: Irish University Press, 1971), p. 47.

17 Quoted by John Conolly in 'Hysteria', in J. Forbes, A. Tweedie and J. Conolly (eds.), *The Cyclopaedia of Practical Medicine*, 4 vols., (London: Sherwood et al., 1833), II, p. 572.

18 'Woman in her Psychological Relations', *Journal of Psychological Medicine and Mental Pathology*, 4 (1851), p. 33. The writer here is echoing the work of Thomas Laycock. See for example, the section on 'Insane Cunning' in *A Treatise on the Nervous Diseases of Women; Comprising an Inquiry into the Nature, Causes, and Treatment of Spinal and Hysterical Disorders* (London: Longman, 1840), p. 353.

19 John Reid, *Essays on Hypochondriasis and other Nervous Afflictions*, 2nd edn (London: Longman, 1821). p. 314

20 See Laycock, *An Essay on Hysteria* (Philadelphia: Haswell, Barrington and Haswell, 1840), p. 107.

21 See Nancy Stepan, 'Race and Gender: the Role of Analogy in Science', *Isis*, 77 (1986), p. 264.

22 Combe, *Constitution of Man*, p. 72.

23 Combe, *A System of Phrenology*, 3rd edn (Edinburgh: John Anderson, 1830), p. 540.

24 *Ibid.*

25 For an examination of the fears aroused by the passionate child, see Michel Foucault, *The History of Sexuality, vol I*, trans. R. Hurley (Harmondsworth: Penguin, 1981).

26 See Penny Boumelha, 'George Eliot and the End of Realism', in Sue Roe, ed., *Women Reading Women's Writing* (Brighton: Harvester Press, 1987), pp. 15–35; George Eliot, *The Mill on the Floss*, ed. S. Shuttleworth (London: Routledge, 1991), p. 495; and Susan Fraiman, *Unbecoming Women: British Women Writers and the Novel of Development* (New York: Columbia University Press, 1993), chs. 4 and 5.

27 For a discussion of the economic side of this debate see Maxine Berg, *The Machinery Question and the Making of Political Economy, 1815–48* (Cambridge: Cambridge University Press, 1980).

28 Elizabeth Rigby, Review of *Jane Eyre*, *Quarterly Review*, 15 (April 1848); repr. in Miriam Allott, *The Brontës: The Critical Heritage* (London: Routledge and Kegan Paul, 1974), pp. 109–10.

29 *Letters*, II, 203. To W. S. Williams, 20 April 1848.

30 *Letters*, II, 216. To W. S. Williams, 12 May 1848.

31 Kay Shuttleworth, *The Moral and Physical Condition*, p. 38.

32 Susan Fraiman in chapter 4 of *Unbecoming Women* offers a very insightful reading of the centrality of Grace, the servant figure, in the text, highlighting the importance of Jane's concern with her relations to the working class.

33 See, for example, Rigney, *Madness*, ch. 1, and Gilbert and Gubar, *Madwoman*.

34 Julia Kristeva, *Revolution in Poetic Language* (New York: Columbia University Press, 1984).

35 Bertha's racial designation has been the subject of debate in recent criticism. In 'Three Women's Texts and a Critique of Imperialism', *Critical Inquiry*, 12 (1985) Gayatri Spivak identified Bertha as a 'native female' (p. 245). Susan Meyer, however, in 'Colonialism and the Figurative Strategy of *Jane Eyre*' has highlighted the complex associations surrounding the term Creole, and the slippages in Spivak's own designations. Meyer argues very convincingly for the centrality of race in Brontë's works, showing clearly how awareness of shared oppression does not preclude racism.

36 Spivak, 'Three Women's Texts' p. 255. My reading of *Jane Eyre* differs from that of Spivak in that the challenge to imperialism which she locates solely in Jean Rhys' rewriting of the novel in *Wide Sargasso Sea* I find also, to a lesser degree, in the original. Philip Martin in *Mad Women in Romantic Writing* (Brighton: Harvester Press, 1987) offers an interesting reading of the text in the light of the development of the figure of the madwoman in Romantic psychiatry and literature. Like Spivak, however, he emphasises the divide between Jane and Bertha, and sees in *Wide Sargasso Sea* a novel which splits apart the double standards of *Jane Eyre* (ch. 5).

37 See, for example, Showalter, *A Literature of their Own* and *The Female Malady*; Rigney, *Madness* and Gilbert and Gubar, *Madwoman*.

38 Hermione Lee has pointed out in 'Emblems and Enigmas in *Jane Eyre*', *English*, 29–30 (1981), pp. 235–55, the ways in which Brontë is drawing on a theological, pre-novelistic tradition of emblematic display which is in conflict with her sense of the enigmas of psychological states.

39 John Reid, *Essays on Hypochondriasis and other Nervous Afflictions*, 2nd edn (London: Longman, 1821). This passage was added in the second eition, in line with the emergence of a new emphasis on self-control as the defining characteristic of sanity.

40 J. E. D. Esquirol, *Mental Maladies: A Treatise on Insanity*, trans. E. K. Hunt (1845: repr., New York: Hafner, 1965). 'In general those who have black hair, who are strong, robust, and of a sanguine temperament, are maniacs, and furious. The course of their insanity is more acute, its crises more marked, than among those composing the other classes' (p. 38).

41 Prichard outlines the stages of an often cited case of raving madness,

starting with the 'impetuous, audacious, shameless habits, a bold menacing aspect' which are soon followed by 'shrieking, roaring, raging, abusive expressions and conduct towards the dearest friends and relatives who are now looked upon as the bitterest enemies. The patient tears his clothes to tatters, destroys, breaks in pieces whatever comes in his way.' As the violence increases, so does the physical strength of the patient, and in the final stage when the paroxysms subside, that patient 'sings or laughs in a strange manner, or chatters with incessant volubility'. James Cowle Prichard, *A Treatise on Insanity and other Disorders Affecting the Mind* (London: Sherwood, Gilbert and Piper, 1835), pp. 64–5.

42 Showalter, *The Female Malady*, pp. 66–9.

43 *Ibid.*, p. 67.

44 Esquirol, *Mental Maladies*, p. 392.

45 Laycock, *Nervous Diseases*, p. 353.

46 'Woman in her Psychological Relations', p. 31.

47 My reading clearly differs from that of Nancy Armstrong in *Desire and Domestic Fiction: A Political History of the Novel* (New York and Oxford: Oxford University Press, 1987), who sees Bertha as part of the ahistorical 'Gothic claptrap' of the Brontës' fictions (p. 197).

48 Laycock, *Nervous Diseases*, p. 141.

49 Goss and Company, *Hygeniana; a Non-Medical analysis of the Complaints Incidental to Females*, 20th edn (London: Sherwood, 1829), p. 66. See also 'Woman in her Psychological Relations', on the 'vicious habit' of lesbian pleasures' (p. 38).

50 See Sander L. Gilman, *Difference and Pathology: Stereotypes of Sexuality, Race, and Madness* (Ithaca: Cornell University Press, 1985), p. 58.

51 *Ibid.*, p. 213.

52 My argument here diverges from that of Fraiman in *Unbecoming Women* who, in highlighting the associations between Jane and Grace, tends to overplay Jane's sense of community with the working class.

53 A similar opinion had earlier been voiced by Brontë in a letter to Ellen Nussey in 1840. See *Letters*, I, p. 206.

54 See Joshua, 7: 11.

55 J. G. Spurzheim, *Phrenology in Connexion with the Study of Physiognomy* (Boston: Marsh, Capen and Lyon, 1836), p. 182.

56 Kucich has also drawn attention to this oppositional structure in Brontë's fiction: 'Reciprocal combat defines passion as an aggressive opposition to others, rather than as an unguarded relaxing of personal boundaries.' *Repression in Victorian Fiction* (Berkeley: University of California Press, 1987), p. 47.

57 Foucault, *History of Sexuality*, p. 45.

58 Although Foucault's *History of Sexuality* illuminates the sexual dynamics in play, he does not explore the complex inter-relationship with the economic sphere.

59 Jason Y. Hall in 'Gall's Phrenology: A Romantic Psychology', *Studies in*

Romanticism, 16 (1977), draws attention to the emphasis on internal and external conflict in the writings of Gall, and to Gall's links, in this respect, with German Romantic psychology, p. 316.

60 J. F. Ferrier, 'An Introduction to the Philosophy of Consciousness'. Part vii, *Blackwood's Edinburgh Magazine*, 48 (1839), p. 429.

61 *Ibid.*, part v, 44 (1838), p. 550.

62 *Ibid.*, part vii, 48 (1839), p. 423.

63 *Ibid.*, part v, 44 (1838), p. 547.

64 *Ibid.*, part vi, 48 (1839), p. 207 and part vii, 48 (1839), p. 419.

65 *Ibid.*, part vii, 48 (1839), pp. 420–4.

66 See George Eliot, *Middlemarch*, Cabinet edition, 3 vols. (Edinburgh: William Blackwood, 1878–80), i, p. 337.

67 For similar sentiments expressed in the medical literature of the day, see Conolly's article on 'Hysteria' in J. Forbes, A. Tweedie and J. Conolly, *The Cyclopaedia of Practical Medicine*, 4 vols., (London: Sherwood et al., 1833), ii, p. 572.

68 Jane has thus reversed her position in relationship to Rochester. In a cancelled passage in ii, ch. 9 she had observed, 'The name Edward Fairfax Rochester was then my Alpha and Omega of existence' (p. 346).

69 For a discussion of the male need to identify selfhood through the reflecting female gaze see Shoshana Felman, 'Women and Madness: the Critical Phallacy', *Diacritics*, 5 (1975), p. 8.

9 SHIRLEY: BODIES AND MARKETS

1 Charlotte Brontë, *Shirley*, ed. H. Rosengarten and M. Smith (Oxford: Oxford University Press, 1979), p. 442. All further references to this edition will be given in the text.

2 There are of course honourable exceptions to this rule: see A. Briggs, 'Private and Social Themes in *Shirley*', *Brontë Society Transactions*, 13 (1958), pp. 203–20; and T. Eagleton, *Myths of Power: a Marxist Study of the Brontës* (London: Macmillan, 1975). Both, however, merely invert the biases of earlier criticism. Briggs holds that the governess theme is 'not related at all ... to the Luddite background' (p. 217), whilst Eagleton asserts that 'Chartism is the unspoken subject of *Shirley*' (p. 45). For one of the first attempts truly to link the two sides see Helen Taylor's excellent article, 'Class and Gender in Charlotte Brontë's *Shirley*', *Feminist Review*, 1 (1979).

3 Catherine Gallagher, *The Industrial Reformation of English Fiction: Social Discourse and Narrative Form, 1832–1867* (Chicago: University of Chicago Press, 1985), p. xi, fn. 1.

4 T. J. Wise and J. A. Symington, *The Brontës: their Lives, Friendships and Correspondence*, 4 vols. (Oxford: Basil Blackwell, 1933), ii, pp. 215–16. Hereafter cited as *Letters*. To W. S. Williams, 12 May 1848.

5 Disraeli's *Sybil* (1845) where the love plot appears to cut across the class

divide is an example of the former mode. Elizabeth Gaskell's *Mary Barton* (1848) provides a more threatening image of sexual relations across the classes with Harry Carson's attempted seduction of Mary. Gaskell's subsequent *North and South* (1855) offers a perfect model of the latter mode, where marriage is used as a mechanism for resolving the class divide.

6 *Letters*, II, p. 221. To W. S. Williams, 15 June 1848. The letter, written whilst Brontë was working on the first volume of *Shirley*, is one of a series to Williams in which she discusses the position of women in the labour market, and the advantages and disadvantages of taking a position as a governess.

7 See p. 465: 'the enigma of the dream (a dream it seemed) was at its height: she saw a visage like and unlike, – Robert, and no Robert'.

8 We rely, for example, on Robert's account to Mr. Yorke of her reactions to his proposal, Louis' intimate diary descriptions of their courtship, and Caroline's unveiling to Robert of Shirley's unspoken secret. Even Shirley's written word does not remain unmediated: her essay 'La Première Femme Savante' is recited from memory by Louis.

9 See *Letters*, II, pp. 312–14. To James Taylor, 1 March 1849, and W. S. Williams, 2 March 1849.

10 *Shirley* was repeatedly attacked for its irreligiosity. See Miriam Allott, *The Brontës: The Critical Heritage* (London: Routledge and Kegan Paul, 1974): *Atlas*, 3 November 1849, p. 121; *Church of England Quarterly Review*, January 1850, p. 156.

11 Gilbert and Gubar, *The Madwoman in the Attic: The Woman Writer and the Nineteenth-Century Literary Imagination* (New Haven: Yale University Press, 1979), p. 390.

12 *Letters*, II, p. 202–3. To Margaret Wooler.

13 'Political State of Europe', *Fraser's Magazine*, 4 (1831), pp. 25–6.

14 'Infant Labour', *Quarterly Review*, 67 (1840), repr. in John Saville, *Working Conditions in the Victorian Age: Debates on the issue from nineteenth-century critical journals* (Greg International: Farnborough, 1973), p. 180.

15 'The Distressed Needlewomen and Cheap Prison Labour', *Westminster Review*, 50 (1848), repr. in Saville, *Working Conditions*, p. 374.

16 For the alignment of working-class social advancement with the adoption of domestic cleanliness see, for example, 'Work and Wages', *Fraser's Magazine*, 38 (1849), p. 526.

17 An article on 'Juvenile and Female Labour', for example, concludes: 'The melancholy truth is forced upon us from every side, that all occupations are overstocked; that the labour market is not sufficiently extensive for the numbers of labourers who crowd into it'. *Edinburgh Review*, 79 (1844), repr. in Saville, *Working Conditions*, p. 152.

18 Thomas Carlyle is a major exception to this rule. In 'The Nigger Question' (1849) he claimed that 'Distressed Needlewomen' are 'in fact Mutinous Serving-maids, who instead of learning to work and obey,

learned to give warning.' *Carlyle: Selected Essays*, ed. Ian Campbell (London: Dent, 1972), p. 318.

19 'Work and Wages', p. 524.

20 *Ibid.*, pp. 524–5.

21 *Manufacturing districts. Replies of Sir Charles Shaw to Lord Ashley, M.P. Regarding the Education and Moral and Physical Condition of the Labouring Classes.* 1843, repr. in *The Factory Education Bill of 1843. British Labour Struggles: Contemporary Pamphlets 1727–1850* (Arno Press: New York, 1972), p. 28.

22 *Ibid.*, p. 35.

23 Brontë repeatedly refers in her letters to the social perception of herself as an 'old maid'. See, for example, *Letters* II, p. 101. To Ellen Nussey, 10 July 1846.

24 *Letters*, II, p. 220. To W. S. Williams, 15 June 1848. See also 12 May 1848, II, pp. 214–6 and 3 July 1849, III, pp. 4–6.

25 *Letters*, I, p. 230. To Emily Brontë, 2 April 1841.

26 *Letters*, II, p. 30. To Ellen Nussey, 2 April 1845.

27 *Letters*, III, pp. 104–5. From Mary Taylor, 25 April 1850.

28 For details of these various schemes see A. James Hammerton, *Emigrant Gentlewomen: Genteel Poverty and Female Emigration, 1830–1914* (London: Croom Helm, 1979), ch. 4.

29 *Ibid.*, p. 94.

30 *Ibid.*, p. 119.

31 Before the 1851 census included reference to marital status, it had been calculated that of the four million women aged between fifteen and forty-five, more than two million were unmarried. See Mason, *The Making of Victorian Sexuality* (Oxford: Oxford University Press, 1994), p. 238. The 1851 census showed the actual proportion to be 29 per cent, but this did little to allay social anxieties.

32 W. R. Greg's frequently reprinted article, 'Why are Women Redundant?' (1862), *Literary and Social Judgments*, 4th edn (London: Trubner and Co., 1877), was not original in its arguments, but drew on the social commonplaces of the era.

33 Maria Rye's Female Middle-Class Emigration Society, founded in 1862, for example, was pre-eminently concerned with finding jobs for the respectable, unemployed female. See Hammerton, *Emigrant Gentlewomen*, ch. 5.

34 'The Iron Seamstress' in *Household Words*, 8, 11 February 1854, p. 575, cited in Hammerton, *ibid.*, p. 106. Dickens' journal was one of the prime supporters of Caroline Chisholm and Sidney Herbert's schemes.

35 See Gordon Haight, ed., *The George Eliot Letters*, 9 vols. (New Haven: Yale University Press, 1954–78), IV, 467–8.

36 See, for example, an early expression of these beliefs in J. Reid, *Essays on Hypochondriasis and other Nervous Afflictions*, 2nd edn (London: Longman et al, 1821), p. 10.

37 R. B. Carter, *On the Pathology and Treatment of Hysteria* (London: John Churchill, 1853) pp. 13–33.
38 J. G. Millingen, *The Passions: or Mind and Matter* (London: J. and D. Darling, 1848), p. 157.
39 'Woman in her Psychological Relations', *Journal of Psychological Medicine and Mental Pathology*, 4 (1851), p. 35.
40 *Ibid.*
41 On Branwell's death, Brontë did not rescind her strong belief that his life had been wasted by 'self-earned degradation'. Her letter to W. S. Williams on 2 October 1848 emphasizes the suffering he has caused his family; there is also an evident undertone of jealousy in her observation that 'My poor father naturally thought more of his *only* son than of his daughters'. *Letters*, ii, p. 261.
42 See, for example, J. Conolly, 'Hysteria', in J. Forbes, A. Tweedie and J. Conolly (eds.) *The Cyclopaedia of Practical Medicine*, 4 vols. (London: Sherwood et al, 1833), ii, p. 572.
43 Andrew Combe highlights the plight of middle and upper-class women who do not work, and who have 'no objects of interest on which to expend and exercise their mental faculties, and who consequently sink into a state of mental sloth and nervous weakness'. *Observations on Mental Derangement: Being an Application of the Principles of Phrenology to the Elucidation of the Causes, Symptoms, Nature, and Treatment of Insanity* (Edinburgh: John Anderson, 1831), p. 117.
44 Anon, 'George Combe', *The English Woman's Journal*, 2 (1858–9), pp. 53–56.
45 The internal conflicts in Brontë's own position are clearly revealed in her comments to Elizabeth Gaskell on Harriet Taylor's article on the Emancipation of Women (which Brontë mistakenly attributed to J. S. Mill). Although many of the arguments echo Caroline's fierce rejection of doctrines of self-abnegation her verdict is damning: 'J. S. Mill's head is, I dare say, very good, but I feel disposed to scorn his heart'. In her eyes 'the writer forgets there is such a thing, as self-sacrificing love and disinterested devotion'. The writing is such as one might attribute to an 'old maid': 'a woman who longed for power, and had never felt affection'. Fear of the loss of femininity here binds Brontë into accepting the current sexual division of labour. *Letters*, iii, p. 278. To Elizabeth Gaskell, 20 September 1851.
46 The image of the toad buried in marble is one which Brontë was to use, significantly, about her own life in a letter to W. S. Williams (*Letters*, iii, p. 9. 26 July 1849).
47 Penny Boumelha, *Charlotte Brontë* (Hemel Hempstead: Harvester Wheatsheaf, 1990), p. 80.
48 For an exposition of this medical position see Kate Flint, *The Woman Reader, 1837–1914* (Oxford: Oxford University Press, 1993), ch. 4.

49 The miasma theory of contagion through poisoned winds or air was central to contemporary debates on disease and cholera. See 'Cholera Gossip', *Fraser's Magazine*, 40 (1849), pp. 702–11.

50 For a discussion of the popularity of the figure of Ophelia in the Victorian period, see Elaine Showalter, 'Representing Ophelia: Women, Madness and the Responsibilities of Feminist Criticism', in P. Parker, and G. Hartman (eds.), *Shakespeare and the Question of Theory* (London: Methuen, 1985), pp. 77–94.

51 Millingen, *The Passions*, p. 158.

52 My reading differs here from that of Miriam Bailin in '"Varieties of Pain": The Victorian Sickroom and Brontë's *Shirley*', *Modern Language Quarterly*, 48 (1987), who sees the sickroom as 'immune to the disruptive aspects of male desire and dominion' (p. 267). Her subtle argument that the sickroom scenes feminize and transform the threatening father figure does not, finally, take sufficient account of the violent emotional effects of Mrs Pryor's outbursts.

53 For an interesting psychoanalytic account of this earlier scene see Dianne Sadoff, *Monsters of Affection: Dickens, Eliot, and Brontë on Fatherhood* (Baltimore: Johns Hopkins University Press, 1982), p. 133.

54 Dr MacTurk, to whom she alludes, was one of the doctors who attended the Brontës. There are obviously strong similarities here to the life of Emily, who also cauterized herself after a dog bite, and who refused to allow the doctors access during her final illness.

55 On hearing that Shirley has radical ideas, for example, Mr Helstone makes her recite the creed, which she meekly does, 'like a child' (p. 221).

56 Dianne Sadoff, *Monsters of Affection*: 'Brontë's decline into a dualistic libidinal economy of master and servant makes the end of *Shirley* entirely unbelievable', p. 155.

57 Eagleton, *Myths of Power*, p. 59.

10 VILLETTE: 'THE SURVEILLANCE'

1 Sandra Gilbert and Susan Gubar, *The Madwoman in the Attic: the Woman Writer and the Nineteenth-Century Literary Imagination* (New Haven: Yale University Press, 1979), p. 360.

2 The Leeds Philosophical and Literary society, for example, had a public lecture on 'The Philosophy of Apparitions' in 1850–1. (E. K. Clark, *The History of 100 Years of Life of the Leeds Philosophical and Literary Society*, Leeds: Jowett and Sowry, 1924). Two works held in the Keighley Mechanics' Institute library offer extensive discussions of the relationship between 'spectral illusion' and insanity: John Abercrombie, *Inquiries Concerning the Intellectual Powers* (Edinburgh: Waugh and Innes, 1832) and Robert Macnish, *The Philosophy of Sleep* (Glasgow: W. R. M'Phun, 1830), a work the Reverend Brontë quotes in his medical annotations.

3 See, for example, the article in the *Times*, July 1853, quoted ch. 3, n. 1.

4 T. J. Wise and J. A. Symington, *The Brontës: their Lives, Friendships and Correspondence*, 4 vols. (Oxford: Basil Blackwell, 1933), IV, p. 14. Hereafter cited as *Letters*. Letter to George Smith, 30 October 1852.

5 *Ibid.*, IV, p. 35. 19 January 1853.

6 For a helpful account of the ways in which *Villette* relates to contemporary anti-Catholic literature see Rosemary Clark-Beattie, 'Fables of Rebellion: Anti-Catholicism and the Structure of *Villette*', *English Literary History*, 53 (1986), pp. 821–47.

7 *Leeds Intelligencer*, 5 April 1851. The concern about 'papal aggression' had arisen in 1850 when the Pope had proclaimed a Catholic hierarchy in England, which was seen to exert territorial claims. Combined with all the fears about the influence of the Tractarians, this papal move resulted in the passing, in July 1851, of the Ecclesiastical Titles Act, the last measure of discrimination against religious denominations to be passed by a British Government. See G. I. T. Machin, *Politics and the Churches in Great Britain, 1832–1868* (Oxford: Clarendon Press, 1977), pp. 218–28. Leeds was a particularly vociferous centre of anti-Catholic feeling at this time, holding public meetings and setting up petitions on 'papal aggression' (see reports in the *Leeds Intelligencer* for March and April, 1851).

8 *Leeds Intelligencer*, 22 March 1851. The paper not only ran extensive reports on the case, but also devoted several editorials to what it revealed about Catholic ambitions for subjecting the British soul.

9 *Letters*, III, p. 269. To Mrs Gaskell, 6 August 1851.

10 Charles Kingsley, *Poems* (London: Macmillan, 1884), p. 46.

11 *Ibid.*, p. 51.

12 *Letters*, III, p. 268–9. To Mrs Gaskell, 6 August 1851.

13 *Letters*, IV, p. 18. To W. S. Williams, 6 November 1852.

14 Lucy's question of the nun, 'Who are you?' (p. 426) is echoed by Ginevra 'Who *are* you, Miss Snowe?' (p. 440).

15 See George Man Burrows, *Commentaries on the Causes, Forms, Symptoms, and Treatment, Moral and Medical, of Insanity* (London: 1828; repr. New York: Arno Press, 1976), p. 191, and for unmarried women's susceptibility to nightmare see Macnish, *Philosophy of Sleep*, pp. 139, 143.

16 See J. G. Millingen, *The Passions; or Mind and Matter* (London: J. and D. Darling, 1848), p. 158, and Robert Brudenell Carter, *On the Pathology and Treatment of Hysteria* (London: John Churchill, 1853), p. 34.

17 Brontë's original name for Lucy was 'Frost'. As she observes in a letter to W. S. Williams, 'A *cold* name she must have ... for she has about her an external coldness'. *Letters*, IV, p. 18. 6 November 1852.

18 The edition here actually reads 'monamaniac'. I assume, however, that this is a printing error.

19 J. E. D. Esquirol, *Mental Maladies: A Treatise on Insanity* trans. E. K. Hunt (1845: repr., New York: Hafner, 1965), p. 109. In a passage which reveals all the nineteenth-century preconceptions about 'female vulnerability', Esquirol observes: 'Are not women under the control of

influences to which men are strangers; such as menstruation, pregnancy, confinement, and nursing? The amorous passions, which among them are so active; religion which is a veritable passion with many, when love does not exclusively occupy their heart and mind, jealousy, fear, do not these act more energetically upon the minds of women than men?' (p. 211).

20 *Ibid.*, p. 335.

21 *Ibid.*, p. 336.

22 *Ibid.*

23 Lucy, meeting Polly again in Villette, views her as her own 'double' (p. 398).

24 See *Letters*, iv, p. 55–6. To George Smith, 26 March 1853.

25 Elliotson, *Human Philosophy*, 5th edn (London: Longmans, 1840), p. 37.

26 These were two of the causes of insanity cited by Thomas John Graham in *Modern Domestic Medicine*, (London: Simpkin and Marshall et al, 1826) p. 392.

27 Her vocabulary is preceisely that employed in the Annual Report of the Keighley Mechanics' Institute in 1832: 'The faculties of the mind can only be preserved in a sound and healthful state by constant exercise...as the metallic instrument corrodes and wastes with indolence and sloth, so with continued use, an edge is produced capable of cutting down every obstacle'.

28 See T. J. Graham, *Modern Domestic Medicine*, p. 392, Esquirol, *Mental Maladies*, p. 31, and *Villette*, p. 388.

29 *Ibid.*, p. 346.

30 *Letters*, ii, 116–7. To Margaret Wooler, approx. November–December 1846.

31 For an analysis of the functions of these paintings, see Gilbert and Gubar, *Madwoman*, p. 420.

32 Esther, i, 22.

33 'What is Mesmerism?' *Blackwood's Edinburgh Magazine*, 70 (1851), p. 84.

34 Graham, *Modern Domestic Medicine*, p. 332.

35 Mary Jacobus, in her excellent article on *Villette*, offers a slightly different reading of this passage: 'The Buried Letter: Feminism and Romanticism in *Villette*', in *Women Writing and Writing about Women*, ed. M. Jacobus (London: Croom Helm, 1979), p. 54.

36 Macnish, *Philosophy of Sleep*, p. 136. The Reverend Brontë records under 'nightmare' in his copy of Graham, 'Dr McNish, who has written very ably on the philosophy of sleep – has justly described, the sensations of Night mare, under some modifications – as being amongst the most horrible that oppress human nature – an inability to move, during the paroxysm – dreadful visions of ghosts etc ... He was, himself – often distressed by this calamity, and justly said, that it was worst, towards the morning. 1838 B.' (Graham, *Modern Domestic Medicine*, pp. 425–6).

37 As Inga-Stina Ewbank has observed in *Their Proper Sphere: A Study of the Brontë Sisters as Early Victorian Female Novelists* (London: Edward Arnold, 1966), the personifications, lengthened into allegories of Lucy's emotional

crises 'do not arrest the action of *Villette*, for in a sense they *are* the action: even more than in *Jane Eyre* the imagery of *Villette* tends to act out an inner drama which superimposes itself on, or even substitutes for, external action' (p. 189).

38 The sequence of events is rather unclear since Lucy herself walks easily out of the pensionnat, but in the ensuing debate as to how Ginevra could have escaped, Lucy cannot forget how she, 'to facilitate a certain enterprise' had neither bolted nor secured the door (pp. 684–5).

CONCLUSION

1 Rothfield, *Vital Signs: Medical Realism in Nineteenth-Century Fiction* (Princeton: Princeton University Press, 1992), p. 85.

2 Obviously Roman Catholicism was not in itself a strong organizing force in England, but the fears with which it is invested in the press and fiction of the period, point to its role as a symbolic condensation of contemporary anxieties concerning the social structures of regulation and surveillance. The displacement of the action of *Villette* to Belgium actually intensifies the engagement with the problems of English culture.

3 While the sense of beleaguerment is clearly there in all of Ann Radcliffe's novels, perhaps the closest precursor of Brontë's work in this respect is William Godwin's *Caleb Williams* (1794), where the pursuit and conflict becomes, for both Falkland and Caleb, the defining structure of selfhood.

4 George Eliot, on first reading *Villette*, which she found to be 'a still more wonderful book than *Jane Eyre*' observed that 'there is something almost preternatural in its power' (Letter to Caroline Bray, 15 February 1853), *The Letters of George Eliot*, ed. Gordon Haight, 9 vols. (New Haven: Yale University Press, 1954–78), II, p. 87.

Index

CAMBRIDGE STUDIES IN NINETEENTH-CENTURY
LITERATURE AND CULTURE

Titles published

The Sickroom in Victorian Fiction: The Art of Being Ill
by Miriam Bailin, *Washington University*

Muscular Christianity: Embodying the Victorian Age
edited by Donald E. Hall, *California State University, Northridge*

Victorian Masculinities: Manhood and Masculine Poetics in Early
Victorian Literature and Art
by Herbert Sussman, *Northeastern University*

Byron and the Victorians
by Andrew Elfenbein, *University of Minnesota*

Literature in the Marketplace: Nineteenth-Century British Publishing and
the Circulation of Books
edited by John O. Jordan, *University of California at Santa Cruz*
and Robert L. Patten, *Rice University*

Victorian Photography, Painting and Poetry
The Enigma of Visibility in Ruskin, Morris and the Pre-Raphaelites
by Lindsay Smith, *University of Sussex*

Charlotte Brontë and Victorian Psychology
by Sally Shuttleworth, *University of Sheffield*